More Praise for *A Heart Poured Out*

"Sister Gargi . . . has outdone herself with this magnificent tribute to her guru, Swami Ashokananda."
                                                                                    —*Prabuddha Bharata*

"An engaging biography that takes the reader on a powerful journey into the story of Swami Ashokananda . . . it is through her vivid insider's account that we learn about the relationship of this extraordinary teacher to his students in their day-to-day spiritual training."
                                                                                    —*AZ Net News*

"Sister Gargi conveys Swami Ashokananda's spiritual fervor as she discusses how he presented Vedanta as a philosophy and religion of infinite hope with its powerful messages about universality, harmony, and infinite affirmation."
                                                                                    —*Spirituality & Health*

"Swami Ashokananda . . . saw in his students their potential perfection. He brought courage and strength to hundreds of lives."
                                                                                    —*The Beacon*

"Sister Gargi has written a remarkable book . . . the story of a powerful and very human man who remained 'unsinkable to the very end' for the sake of his mission to the New World."
                                                                                    —*Vedanta Kesari*

"Eminently moving . . . fortunate indeed was the author in having been inducted into spirituality by such an extraordinary personality, and in having known and worked at close quarters with him."
                                                                                    —*Samvit*

"The teachings of Swami Ashokananda are a welcome addition to the literature of the Vedanta movement, and further illuminate the history of the spread of Vedanta in the West."
                                                                                    —*Common Ground*

"This book allows us the opportunity to use the teachings of this spiritual teacher to strengthen our lives with purpose, courage, and wisdom."
                                                                                    —*One!*

Also by

Sister Gargi (Marie Louise Burke)

Swami Vivekananda in the West: New Discoveries

  His Prophetic Mission (vols. 1 and 2)

  The World Teacher (vols. 3 and 4)

  A New Gospel (vols. 5 and 6)

Swami Trigunatita: His Life and Work

Vedantic Tales

Hari the Lion

A Disciple's Journal:

  In the Company of Swami Ashokananda

A HEART POURED OUT

A Story of Swami Ashokananda

A HEART POURED OUT

A Story of
SWAMI ASHOKANANDA

SISTER GARGI
(Marie Louise Burke)

Kalpa Tree Press
New York

The original hardcover edition of this book was published in 2003
by Kalpa Tree Press

Library of Congress Catalog Card Number: 2004100143

Publisher's Cataloging-in-Publication Data

Burke, Marie Louise, 1912-
    A heart poured out : a story of Swami Ashokananda /
Sister Gargi (Mary Louise Burke). — 1st pbk. ed.
    p. cm.
    Includes bibliographical references and index.
    LCCN 2004100143
    ISBN 0-9706368-4-9
    ISBN 0-9706368-1-4 (hardcover)

    1. Ashokananda, Swami. 2. Ramakrishna Mission—
Biography. 3. Vedanta Society—Biography. 4. Hindus—
India—Biography. 5. Hindus—California—San Francisco
—Biography. I. Title

BL1175.A74B87 2004   294.5'55'092
                                          QBI04-200041

10 9 8 7 6 5 4 3 2 1

FIRST PAPERBACK EDITION

Designed by Fearn Cutler de Vicq
Set in Monotype Fournier
Printed in the United States of America

This book is a gift to my revered teacher, Swami Ashokananda,

with my prayer that in his boundless, unconditional,

and unaccountable grace he will accept it—

even as, long ago, he accepted its author.

CONTENTS

PART 3

SHEETS OF CLEAR GLASS
SAN FRANCISCO, 1959–69

PREFACE

Anyone who has ever known a truly spiritual person knows that there is a quality about him or her that defies all description. Yes, it is goodness and charity and selflessness; it is compassion and heroism and universality; it is love, purity, and fearlessness—it is all of these, but it is also something much more that lifts such persons far above the sea level of ordinary human life into the Himalayas of sainthood. At that altitude, all human excellence shines with a divine and ineffable light. Down here, we cannot imagine the quality of that light; we have to see it, and even then we cannot grasp it, let alone write about it. Hagiography must always fail in this respect.

Why, then, have I tried to write about Swami Ashokananda, who habitually dwelt in high altitudes of the Spirit where we cannot, or think we cannot, follow? I write about him because in whatever height he had his moorings, his heart beat in tune with that of every human being who aspires upward, and he led us with a firm and unerring hand into his own realm, where, he was convinced, we all belong. In short, I have written about him because he was an authentic spiritual teacher whom each of us can benefit by knowing.

Such men and women are not found on every street corner in the Western world—or, for that matter, in the Eastern one. And when we happen to meet such a person, it behooves us to let others know that, yes, such people do exist, and not only do they exist, but their essential glory—the thing we love and revere—is as integral to our own humanity as it is to theirs; moreover, they can show us how to uncover that divine essence and claim it as our own.

With his dying breath Buddha said to a grieving disciple, "Be a lamp unto yourself!" In the Vedantic tradition Swami Ashokananda, convinced that every human being is a light unto herself or himself, would say the same thing. We are all thrashing about in a dark and hurtful world, and all the while we can light our own inextinguishable lamp of strength and wisdom by which we can see our way. This was Swami Ashokananda's faith, indeed, his knowledge, and so sure was that knowledge that he gave his life to showing us how to light our own lamps. That is the principal reason I have tried to write his story.

Another reason is that Swami Ashokananda himself told me to write it, and his mandate is, for me, justification enough. He also said to me, "Don't collect the memories of other people. Just write your own account." Largely, I have followed that instruction, although here and there I have included the reminiscences of others, for I believe they enhance, rather than confuse, the story, and I am grateful for them all.

Part i of this book narrates the tale of the Swami's life in India before any of his future friends or disciples knew him. Later in his life he himself told the tale of his early years in bits and pieces, both to groups of students (of whom I was one) who gathered around him in the evenings and during public lectures and classes. In the latter case, he almost always said that the experiences he related were those of a "friend" of his.

"A friend of mine once told me," he would say, and then would tell some extraordinary experience of that remarkable "friend"—an experience pertinent to and illustrating the subject he was discussing. Very seldom did he use the pronoun "I" in his public discourses. But in his intimate talks to his disciples, when the friend-of-mine device would have deceived no one, he spoke openly of his spiritual experiences by way of teaching or sometimes simply to communicate the treasures of his heart to those close to him.

What reason is there for now revealing those treasures? To my mind, and also in the opinion of some of his other disciples, there is good reason. The story that emerges from his confidences and from glimpses of his "friend" is one that cannot but be inspiring to spiritual aspirants everywhere. It is a story that provides a record of spiritual struggle and attainment such as enrich all great religious traditions, indeed such as bring religion to life for travelers along the sometimes barren and lonely road to God.

Further, those premonastic years were an immensely fruitful time for Swami Ashokananda. He lived habitually in a realm of consciousness where spiritual experience was the norm, and where his realizations came fast and thick. The certainty they carried was to form the basis of his later teachings; indeed, that God-absorbed boy was the authority behind the man.

Part 2, which chronicles the Swami's life and work in the Western world before I knew him, relies primarily upon his own memories told in the author's presence, as well as upon the eyewitness accounts of others. In addition I have made liberal use of material from the archives of the Vedanta Society of Northern California, such as the Society's minutes and other documents that ensure this book's historical accuracy. While accuracy is always important, history is not an object of the book; it is not a history of the Vedanta movement in the West. Some of that history will become apparent as the story unfolds, but the primary purpose of this book is to tell of a remarkable man and to reveal something of his personality that was always a source of delight, and sometimes of awe, to those who knew him.

The narrative continues in Part 3—but now I enter the picture as one of Swami Ashokananda's disciples, and my own eyewitness accounts and memories serve as an additional source of information.

I should perhaps remind the reader that Swami Ashokananda lived before the feminist movement changed the English language. He saw no harm in using the words *man* and *he* to refer to human beings in general. I have kept his idiom intact, hoping the modern reader will, like his contemporary listeners, not take offense. Had he lived a little longer, I feel sure he would have tried to change his language, for he held women in the highest esteem and would never have chosen to offend them. Indeed, with the Divine Mother firmly championing their cause, he would very likely have avoided doing so.

For kindly giving me access to the Vedanta Society's archival material, I am deeply indebted to Swami Prabuddhananda, as well as to the Society's secretary, Marian Harrington, and its archivist, Pravrajika Dharmaprana. I am grateful also to Pravrajikas Vedaprana and Dharmaprana for going carefully over the manuscript and giving me their valuable suggestions for its improvement and their even more valuable encouragement—a gift of the heart that few writers can do without. My thanks are also due to Pravrajika Vijnanaprana, who helped compile the glossary. Many of the glossary entries have been taken from other books, to whose publishers—notably Kalpa Tree Press and Advaita Ashrama—I am much indebted.

My thanks are due particularly to the editor and publisher Dr. Shelley Brown, without whose dedicated and tireless attention to all its aspects this book could never have taken shape. Her thorough, sympathetic, and expert editing beggars gratitude. Above all, and casting delight over our work together, were her unwavering friendship and unbroken good humor. I want also to express my thanks to Ms. Patricia Farr for her precise and elegant copyediting.

For this book to express its debt to its subject, Swami Ashokananda, would be like a small ripple saying thank you to the ocean to which it owes its very existence. The book can only hope, as a ripple might hope, that its effort to catch the light has not altogether failed.

Gargi

San Francisco
September 23, 2002

PROLOGUE

I came to my first lecture at the Vedanta Society in San Francisco in October of 1948. It was a Wednesday evening, and Swami Shantaswarupananda, who had come from India in February of that year, was the lecturer. His title was "How to Perceive the Infinite." Although the lecture was undoubtedly full of arresting thoughts, I do not remember anything of it. The Swami, only seven or eight months in America, was not yet a good lecturer, nor had he acquired anything close to an American way of speaking. But even though the lecture had not gripped me, the experience of having been in the Temple had struck a chord deep within. I knew I had found something of profound significance to my life, to my very being. Looking at the two large colored photographs of orange-robed and turbaned swamis that hung on the curtained wall behind the platform, I had known—not because of the photographs themselves, but because of something that came through them—I had known that I was home. I did not yet know what Vedanta was; I had no idea. But I knew that whatever it was, I would follow it to the end. I knew for an absolute certainty in the depths of my being that this was *it*.

Like most stories of how people discovered Vedanta in its early pioneering days in the Western world, my story is one of miracle and epiphany. But though all-important to my own life, that story has almost no place in this present account. The bare fact was that in those days my mind was extremely turbulent; my life was not as I wanted it to be in any respect. Above all, I felt that I had lost God; somehow, I had lost an inner joy and an awareness, however dim, of divinity. That loss was the basic problem, although there were other problems large and small. The hub was gone, and the wheel was flying to pieces—or was it the other way around? In any case, I was searching for some spiritual truth, if there was such a thing, and in the course of that search, I stumbled upon a mention of the Vedanta Society of Northern California and found my way to the fabulous, newly painted, and somehow inwardly glowing building on the corner of Webster and Filbert Streets. Inquiring at the door, I learned that a lecture would be held there that evening and that anyone could attend it.

After that first lecture, I came again as soon as possible—which was, it so happened, the following Wednesday evening. Swami Ashokananda was lecturing; the auditorium was full; there was total silence, a sort of tension, a slight wait, and then the green velveteen drapes that covered the wall behind the platform parted and the Swami stepped out. His presence, as it struck me, was indescribable. It was not dynamic; it was not, at that moment, powerful. But it was, somehow, total; it filled the auditorium. He was of medium height, a little stocky in build, his hair was iron gray, and his robe, tailored and sashed, coming below the knee over black trousers, was a deep terra-cotta color. His demeanor was anything but assertive. And yet, when he stepped onto the platform the atmosphere in the Temple, already hushed and reverent, became, it seemed to me, sanctified. There is no other word for it. He seemed to have come upon that platform reverently, as though coming into the presence of a living deity. Or, rather, a living deity seemed to be evoked by his coming. His own person was effaced; there was nothing that said "I," nothing that said, "Here I am." He turned to the large oil painting of what I came later to know was Sri Ramakrishna and with folded hands bowed his head. He then sat in a high-backed chair, upholstered in silvery green Fortuny cloth, and closed his eyes. There was music—singing accompanied by a small organ. When it was over, he rose and stepped to the lectern and with the utmost gentleness said "Good evening" to the audience. Those words themselves seemed an act of worship. And then, still with humility and quietness, he said, looking at a paper on the lectern, "My subject this evening is the power of words." After a few measured sentences, in which he explained something of what he intended to say, he launched himself, or eased himself, into his topic—and was off. It was as though a fire within him had burst into flame; his whole demeanor changed, his voice became charged with energy, his skin began to glow and redden a little, until it seemed to match the color of his robe. His words poured out at a mile a minute, as though propelled. I remember thinking or, rather, somehow knowing, for I was not thinking much, that there was an inexhaustible reservoir of truth behind him, pouring through him. The force of it seemed to thrust him across the platform and back; he did not stand still at the lectern (there was no microphone in those days, or recording apparatus). Totally absorbed in what he was saying, he moved about, coming to the lectern only now and then to thump on it in emphasis. The whole auditorium became vibrant, without anyone knowing it, because everyone had themselves been lifted up into that dynamic, rarefied atmosphere.

I remember that once, a few years later, I entered the auditorium when the Sunday morning lecture was in full swing. It was like entering a charged field. Swami Ashokananda was shimmering on the platform, a living flame. The power in the hall was almost unbearable to me, coming as I had from an ordinary, everyday street. I realized then that this was the way it always was. During his lectures Swami lifted the atmosphere to another pitch; he lifted all of us, until we did not know that we had entered another world. And after the lecture was over, there was no face that was not radiantly transformed, beaming. Of course, as Swami himself would point out, "As soon as you get outside, you begin talking worldly things and dissipate everything you have gained." Still, something surely remained; nor was it ever possible for him not to give everything to the audience before him—the living deity of his worship.

I hope I am not giving an impression that his lectures were bombastic. They were never so. Although his ideas seemed to pour out in torrents, they were always restrained by rational thought, always precisely worded, never ambiguous or vague. As a whole, they were wonderfully organized—and not in an ABC way; their organization was more like that of a tree with many intertwining branches and sometimes branches of branches, which, however proliferating, never broke away from their main unifying trunk. There were digressions and illustrative stories, immensely entertaining in themselves, and excursions seemingly far afield into discussions of other ideas. But invariably he would return to precisely where he had left off and continue with his main theme, having deliberately enriched it. And when things became too taut, when our minds were being stretched to a breaking point, he would inject an exceedingly funny remark that would send his listeners into gales of tension-breaking laughter. Above all—at least, this is what always struck me—his brilliance of thought was never cold, never dry or pedantic. It was somehow suffused with sweetness. He was speaking to his listeners, wanting with his whole heart for them to understand what he was saying, wanting to give to them his own joy. He never talked down to them; on the other hand, he never talked so far above their heads that they were left bewildered. And yet his lectures, there is no doubt, required intense concentration from his audience. They were not meant to entertain, to console, or to reassure. He made his listeners lift their minds, and this without their knowing that they were doing so; he awakened in them their own immortal fire.

But to return to the first time I ever heard him speak, my mind, as I said, was in a highly upset state; I could not concentrate on what he was saying, let alone understand it. His subject—the power of words—seemed to me extremely abstruse. I remember that I cried out in my mind, "Help! Help! Help me!" And the Swami said almost at once in the natural course of his talk, "If someone cries out 'Help!' you will understand what he is saying whatever language he is speaking." "He is reading my mind," I thought, "but that is not possible." And a sentence or two later he said, again in the course of his lecture, "You think it is not possible to read someone's mind? It is very possible." There was another instance during that same lecture in which he seemed to echo or to reply directly to my thought, but I cannot now remember what it was. In any case, those strange instances are all I remember of the lecture. But the tangible holiness of the Swami's presence changed my life forever.

Drawn by that holiness, I came to more lectures and became familiar with the thought of Vedanta; I became more and more certain, intellectually, that this was the philosophy that had always been mine. Cloudy and confused though my idea of God and the world and myself had been, it was nevertheless Vedantic through and through. To learn for the first time that these thoughts were a part of an age-old philosophy, known to millions of people, was an enormous relief to me. I had believed for years that no one in the world thought as I did and that that was because what I thought was entirely wrong—in which case, life was not worth living. But here, spoken by someone who clearly spoke from the very heart of truth was my philosophy; everything he said was my own, clarified and immensely, infinitely enriched. I needed only to change my life in accordance with it, and that, I knew, was not going to be easy. I also knew that Swami Ashokananda, through whom truth flowed unhindered, straight, was the only person on earth who could help me.

Even so, it was many months before I asked him for an appointment. I was afraid he would say, as I had heard he had recently said to an unready newcomer, "Come back in five years and ask me again." I could not have stood that answer, and to avoid it, I simply didn't ask. Besides, he seemed too awesome, too exalted, for the likes of me to approach.

But I had two older and sympathetic sisters, who kept urging me to see the Swami. Finally, sometime in January of 1949, I decided to speak to him. So after a Friday evening class or Wednesday evening lecture, which my sisters had also attended, I fell in the line that was making its way to the foot of the platform to shake his hand. Midway, I became terrified and turned back. But my sisters were there in the line behind me. "Another time," I said to them. Without saying a word, one of them took me by the shoulders and turned me around; the other gave me a push. I think they never, in all the years of their love, did me a greater service. I kept on going toward Swami until I found myself face to face with him and overcome with diffidence. I could barely make myself heard. "I would like to make an appointment to see you," I whispered. He looked at me kindly. "What do you want to see me about?" he asked, and I was tongue-tied. What about? I am dying! I am falling into an abyss! Help! And then finally I said, perhaps in a very high and squeaky voice, "I have to find something." At that, he reached in the pocket of his robe and drew out a small and thick black-bound appointment book. He is going to give me an appointment! He is actually going to give me an appointment! He did not say, "Come back in five years." Consulting his book, he very seriously made an appointment to see me in two weeks. Two weeks! How could I possibly wait that long? And indeed, those two weeks seemed forever.

I do not remember the exact date, but it must have been in late January that I sat in the library of the Temple, which had been lovingly redecorated two or three years earlier, waiting to see him. The walls were papered with woven grass; the woodwork was creamy; there were tall mahogany bookcases with glass doors on three sides of the room, and two or three small wooden tables where students could read or type. A Persian carpet gave the room a warmth and elegance. On the wall facing the windows that looked out onto Webster Street was a large photograph of a stern-looking man in a Prince Albert coat, a white shirt and vest, and a white bow tie, who I later learned was Swami Trigunatita. He looked directly at me with penetrating, unsmiling eyes that seemed to disapprove of what they saw. I sat under that gaze for what seemed a long time. Then at last Swami Ashokananda came to the door and very courteously, kindly, not at all the awesome lecturer, asked me to come into his office.

I wish I had taken notes of that life-changing, lifesaving appointment, and of those that followed regularly, every two weeks. But at the time I did not think I would ever forget a word of what was said. Now those appointments have run together in my mind; I remember only highlights of them. And since the talk was intensely personal—all about me, my life and my thoughts, my despairs and my aspirations—it has no place here.

His office was small, but it, too, had been recently renovated. On the left, a tall-backed light brown leather swivel chair stood behind his desk, and behind that and also on its far side were built-in bookcases. On the other side of the desk was an armchair upholstered in dark green leather with bronze bosses. There were other green leather chairs in the room, and another bookcase against the right wall. Books were piled on the chairs and on his desk. A three-foil arched window took up most of the far wall. On the floor, almost wall to wall, was another rich Persian carpet, a corner of which, I later learned, had to be turned back to accommodate the door. The Swami asked me to sit down in the chair opposite his own, and then he took his seat. I remember only that I was too shy to speak and could answer his questions only very faintly. I told him that I had lost God; he asked exactly how and when. But I couldn't answer. He had kind, very luminous eyes, a dark line down the middle of his forehead, smooth, unlined skin, and the broadest face I had ever seen. Later, I recognized that same breadth of jaw in the photographs of Swami Vivekananda and of Swami Trigunatita—the "Bengali jaw." His hair was thick and iron gray; it rose in a small pompadour above his forehead. He wore rimless glasses and, to my dismay, a clerical collar, which led me to think, for a moment, that perhaps he would see the world as I thought a Christian minister would see it, through a conventional, run-of-the-mill mindset. I could not have been more wrong. He asked questions. Now and then I would say something that showed some glimmering of thought, and he would beam at me, his eyes becoming very large and more luminous than ever. It was a look full of joy, and behind that joy was inexpressible love and delight, the love and delight of a parent who had encountered some spark of intelligence in a backward child. And this was long before I became his disciple. I would see that luminous look often again. It was more than joy, more than love, though it was these to overflowing. I came to call it "Swami-light"—a light that I have not seen in any other eyes but his. I suppose every disciple, or prospective disciple, sees that light in his or her guru's eyes. Perhaps it should be called "guru-light," the light of *guru shakti*. In any case, it is a very special kind of light, and I will never forget it. I felt bathed in it, baptized by it, and it made me stop feeling altogether unworthy.

When the interview was over, he opened his door for me, turning back the carpet, and as I walked down the hall to the entrance door, he called after me, "Courage!" It was not meant for any specific situation that had to be faced just then; it was more general—at least I took it that way and have remembered it that way throughout my life.

Who was this man that one word of his could bore its way to the very heart of my being and resound there for years like a rousing gong? This is his story as I know it.

PART I

THE WORLD OF THE SPIRIT

INDIA, 1893–1931

I

BOYHOOD AWAKENING

If we had to rely solely on Swami Ashokananda's own accounts, a great deal of his personal life would be vague, for he either purposefully made it so or truly did not know the facts. He did not, for instance, know the exact date of his birth. "September 23, 24, or maybe 25, 1893," he said.[1] He was as elliptical about his birthplace and his family. He was born "somewhere in Sylhet," he would say. And about his family, he spoke not at all.

Much later a brother monk of his divulged that Swami Ashokananda's premonastic name was Yogesh Chandra Datta and that he had been born and raised in Durgapur, a village seven or eight miles west of the town of Habiganj in, to be sure, the Sylhet district of Assam (now part of Bangladesh). To be even more accurate, he was born in his mother's village of Bekitaka, for it was customary that a Hindu woman repair to her native village to bear a child. But he grew up in Durgapur.

The Datta family was of the Kayastha caste. They were Vaishnavas, as were most people in East Bengal, although Shaktas (devotees of the Divine Mother) were also abundant, and people even of the same family could be one or the other without friction. The Dattas' family deity, for instance, was Kanailal (Sri Krishna), but Yogesh

Durgapur fields

worshiped Kali. Swami Ashokananda's father, Nabin Chandra Datta, was the postmaster in the district and could well support his wife and family of three girls and two boys. The eldest daughter was Sunita, then came Yogesh, then his younger brother, Nagesh, then the second daughter, Sarojini, and finally the youngest daughter, Monohorini— all facts hard to come by, for he never told us a single one of them.[2]

Durgapur was a small village of about seventy families. A road led to it off the main road coming from Habiganj. The Dattas' house, made of bamboo and mud, like most of the houses in the village, was the first house on the left of the road. It was, actually, a compound of several buildings. The other houses in the village clustered north, east, and west of the Datta compound. A small pond (or tank) for the women, elegant with stone turrets and ghats on its four sides, lay to the north, and to the south, directly in front of the Dattas' house, was a very large pond for general use. Fields extended beyond the pond to the horizon, and the whole expanse was inundated in the rainy season, when the water came down in steady torrents and only clumps of trees here and there made islands in an endless, unrippled sea. At such times, to go anywhere—to one's neighbors, to nearby villages, or to the town of Habiganj—one went by boat. Sometimes the boat was made of clay and shaped like a pot, in which one person with an oar could paddle wherever he or she pleased, or, if fancy willed, spin round and round.

In his early years Yogesh did not have to go far to attend school. The elementary school for the village children was in his own backyard, so to speak. It was one of the buildings of the Datta family compound and was run by his paternal uncle, Bharat Chandra Datta, who, after the untimely death of Yogesh's father in 1905, would become head of the family. Every now and then the inspector of schools, a stalwart Muslim with a long beard parted in the middle and swept back on either side, would pay a visit in the course of his rounds. He rode a small horse, for which he seemed too big. The little boys were in awe of this imposing personage, but he made them laugh with his jokes. When a boy stood in his light, he would say, to their vast amusement, "You are not made of transparent glass, you know!"

When he was an infant, and later as a child, Yogesh never cried. Nor did he often confide his inner feelings to his family. Once when he was very young, he inadvertently swallowed some pumpkin seeds. With impeccable logic he reasoned that the seeds would sprout within him and a vine would eventually come out of his mouth and ears and probably through the top of his head. For weeks he kept this dreadful knowledge to himself, stoically waiting for the inevitable to happen, until, when no sprouts appeared, he assumed the danger had somehow passed. No one, not even his mother, knew the peril he had been in. He was full of affection and generally joyful, but he was not, on the other hand, much interested in the things the other boys of the village did, such as climbing trees or teasing frogs or playing games. "I just watched them playing," he once said, "and I wondered what they saw in it. I felt very sedate and serene within. Outwardly I may have seemed like a little boy, but within I was never a little boy. I always felt that I didn't belong to this world. Everything seemed strange. It was a very strong feeling."

But some things peculiar to little boys Yogesh did. He would, for instance, spend hours in the deep pools of the river, with friends or alone, swimming, diving, floating, or simply going up and down—touching bottom, springing up into the sun, and down again, up again into the sky, the wonderful blue of which he loved to look at, thinking, when he was very young, that if he could run up a hill to the summit he could touch that blueness. And he went with other boys to a nearby temple dedicated to Jagannath, where the priests offered *payash* to the Lord. The boys would ask the priest in charge for this sweet, delicious rice pudding. Yogesh also, by the hour and with fascination, watched his mother cook—a favorite occupation of many a village child—taking it all in and remembering it in detail. "The cows would look in the window," he told us, illustrating the devotee's long, patient wait for God. Sometimes one cow, sometimes two would put their heads in the window, waiting for the rice husks soaked in water and the vegetable peelings that would, without fail, be theirs. When he told it, his face would take on the look of an infinitely patient cow, waiting, just waiting, with large unfretful eyes. He adored his mother, Sushila Devi. Once when he was very little, she went for a week or so to another village, perhaps the village of her parents, leaving him behind. He was overwhelmed with grief, as though the sun had been eclipsed. And whenever she fell ill, he was overcome by a terrible fear that she would die. Again, the whole universe would appear dark, all light and joy gone out of it.

Much as Yogesh liked to watch his mother cook, he did not like to eat, considering it a sort of indignity. There was, however, a concoction of hot rice and small, sweet bananas that he, along with the other children of the village, liked very much. And of course there was the *payash* at the Jagannath temple.

He played at worship with his friends. They would make clay images and pretend to worship them. "It was an absorbing game," he recalled. And sometimes he walked along the bank of a nearby river where creepers grew. On the creepers were small golden beetles that the children liked to collect; the little girls would put them on their foreheads between the eyes. "They looked very nice," the Swami recalled. One day he went to a place where the creepers grew to collect some bugs for his sisters, and there on a bank fairly high above the water level, he saw a big fish lying on the ground. "When the fish saw me," he said, "it squealed with great annoyance and irritation, as though angry to be disturbed. It then jumped into the water. How it had got there and what it was doing, I have never understood."

In that peaceful village, where pumpkin vines grew over the thatched roofs of mud houses, where fish could bask undisturbed on a riverbank, where the mustard-oil presses creaked in the early morning, where women winnowed paddy, and cows looked through the windows—in that village Yogesh grew. And one could not grow up in an Indian village without becoming saturated with God. "Everything in India reminds one of God," the Swami told us. "Nature itself is permeated through and through with spirituality; for thousands of years people have thought of God, sung of Him, meditated on Him." In Durgapur, as in all other Indian villages, men and women sang of God as they went about their daily tasks; Vaishnava monks came to the house for alms and sang of God or talked of Him; travelers passing through the village sang of Him; boatmen and cowherds sang of Him; and the rural mailman walking all day long from house to house might sing that he was knocking at every door for the Lord to open it and appear before him. There were enactments of the *Ramayana* and the *Mahabharata*, and throughout the year there were festivals in celebration of one deity or another. And then there was the man who had taken a vow to repeat aloud the name of God continuously for twelve years. The practice had transformed him from an ordinary householder to a God-intoxicated saint. The Dattas had heard of him and had asked him to come to visit them. Now and then he would come and stay for a week or so. There would not be much conversation with him, but the name of God would ring through the Datta compound and charge the air. Or, rather, charge it further, for the air was already charged and vibrant in the village: God was everywhere, as close and as natural as life itself.

And, of course, there was the family guru, an elderly Vaishnava brahmin, who, it so happened, was a truly spiritual man—not just a guru following in the wake of his family tradition. Generally he was away on pilgrimage all over India, and on the occasions when he came to the Dattas' house he told stories of what he had seen and of the many different customs throughout the land. "I don't believe in caste anymore," he once said. "It is all just custom and tradition—no more than that. I don't want to upset people, but I, myself, don't believe in it." The small Yogesh was drawn to this wise and gentle man, and long remembered his beautiful smile.

Those who knew Yogesh as a child and a youth remembered him as being mainly serious, studious, reading endlessly. He was deeply thoughtful, sometimes coming up with ideas that he was too young to handle. Once when he was around eleven, the thought struck him that all human relationships were based only upon food. Heartbroken at the emptiness this made of all life and all love, he cried uncontrollably. His aunt, trying to comfort the sobbing boy and assuming that he was crying because he did not want to go to school, assured him that he did not have to go. He could not tell her the real reason for his tears; he felt she would not have understood, and most likely he was right. But he himself did not yet understand, as he would in a few years, that there was another basis for love that lay far beyond self-gratification, and his not knowing that other truth was a terrible grief for the little boy, beyond all consolation. This was perhaps the real beginning of his spiritual life, the first abysmal hunger.

A year or so later, a different kind of grief came to Yogesh when his father died. He then found consolation in reading an unabridged Bengali edition of the *Mahabharata* from beginning to end. He became lost in that world of *rishis* (Vedic sages) and heroes, rejoicing in their victories, suffering for their sorrows. The stories of the *Mahabharata* became burned into his mind. Even many years later he felt heartbroken over Drona's having to pacify his little son with white rice powder and water, assuring him it was milk such as gladdened and nourished the Pandava princes. "One of the hardest things to rise above," he sometimes said, "is the pathos of human existence," and he would give that episode as an example.

Yogesh's early schooling was sporadic. Early on, he contracted malaria and had severe attacks periodically, which kept him at home. For years, countless remedies were tried, but none availed. During his enforced days in bed, he developed a habit of reading, which never left him. Another, temporary side effect of his malarial fever was a fear of fire, phobic in its proportions. At the very sight of flames, he would tremble. One day he saw a village burning fiercely across the river, and his hands shook so uncontrollably that, abashed, the little boy said sternly to himself, "This won't do!" And while that terrible fire raged, he forced himself, with a great effort of will, to stop shaking. After that, his fear of fire left him.

After attending his uncle's elementary school, which covered the first five grades, he entered junior high school at Shaistaganj, two or three miles from Durgapur. Serious though Yogesh was at this age, he could be as convulsed with laughter as any of his friends. Once when he was around thirteen or fourteen, a Christian revival meeting took place in the government high school building in Habiganj. A group of eight or nine Protestant missionaries from America and England was allowed to hold this "revival" for several afternoons, in order (it was clear) to convert the high school teachers and students. Five or six interested Hindus attended the meetings, among them the young Yogesh and a friend. Since this was a religious meeting, the boys came with respect, but almost at once their mood broke. "I don't know what they meant by *revival*," the Swami recalled in his later life, "but first of all, one of the women would sing an English song. To our ears it was exactly like the crying of wild jackals." Naturally, this sent the boys into uncontrollable laughter, muffled, because the song, after all, was addressed to God. Later during the course of these same missionary

The junior high school at Shaistaganj

meetings, Yogesh's sense of respect evaporated entirely: "The chairman of the meeting asked one of their group to say the prayer. So the chosen man flung up his hands into the air and gave out a stream of language with the rapidity of an express train. We were learning English in junior high school, but we could not make head or tail of it. That disgusted us thoroughly." This was Yogesh's first brush with Western music and with Western religion. But that is by the way.

YOGESH'S HABIT OF READING voluminously became of paramount importance in his life in middle school. This was due to the friendship of a brahmin who had been a highly respected teacher of Bengali literature. One night, some three years before Yogesh enrolled in the school, this cultured and gentle teacher had been attacked and unmercifully beaten by a gang of thugs. They had mistaken him for the principal of the school, whom, because of some feud or other, they had been paid to attack. The teacher was so deeply mortified by this affront that he lost his sanity. He could no longer teach, and thus he no longer had any means of livelihood. His family had perforce to live else-where. He remained in his house alone in dire poverty, without the money even to rethatch his roof. During the rainy season, when the water came in torrents through his tattered roof, he slept in the only dry corner. By the time Yogesh entered junior high school this unfor-tunate man was slowly recovering. One day Yogesh and two or three of his friends went to call on him to pay their respects and try to restore his self-confidence. Yogesh was evidently taken by him, for after that he went often to visit him and would spend hours with him, discussing philosophy and religion. The brahmin never talked down to the boy, who was then in his early teens; he talked man to man with him, and slowly his self-esteem was restored.

Yogesh read endlessly in this brahmin's extensive library, of which he was given free run. It was during this time that he read the book that opened up a new world to him—the world that he would live in on deeper and deeper levels for the rest of his life—the realm of the Supreme Self, the world of the Spirit. The book was *Bhakti Yoga*, by Aswini Kumar Datta.[3]

In the Swami's own words, "It was as though a great storm passed through my mind. Many old thoughts were swept away, new thoughts came. I was shaken to the depth of my being." Or again, "It was like being caught up in a raging flood, carried and turned over and over. I could not say what was happening, but the experience lasted for sev-eral days. Afterwards I felt an absolute serenity and for weeks was in a state of joy." "The effect of reading that book never left me," he said at yet another time, "although the sense of extreme exaltation wore off."

Yogesh continued to visit the brahmin after school, spending long hours talking with him. He was, of course, always late getting home. One day as he passed by the side of his house, he overheard his mother and uncle discussing him. His mother was saying crossly, "Why does he always have to come home so late!" His uncle was also annoyed, and they went on to discuss some plan for Yogesh's future. This conversation came upon him as a great shock. How could others have control over his life! So strong was his sense of independence and of freedom from all relationship that the idea seemed incredible to him, unreal. And to be sure, Yogesh's life would always be his own—until it became Sri Ramakrishna's, which, in the deepest sense, was the same thing.

On one of his daily visits to the brahmin's house, Yogesh announced, "Well, sir, the only thing is to renounce the world. Let us renounce!" The brahmin took this very seriously; he did not laugh it off as the romantic idea of an adolescent. "I will think it over," he said. And a day or two later, "I have thought about it. Yes, it would be right to renounce. There is only one thing that I cannot bear to leave. I cannot bear to think that the fire would go out on the family hearth; there would be no one to tend it." Yogesh did not press him, but his desire to renounce the world remained and, despite its ups and downs, steadily grew.

When Yogesh entered junior high school, he and other boys of his class found that the teacher who had taken the brahmin's place was woefully incompetent. This was not unknown to the authorities of the school, but the boys brought the matter to a head. The inept teacher was discharged, and the boys urged that the recovering brahmin be reinstated in the now-vacant post. This was done: the brahmin again taught Bengali literature in the school, and again he made enough money to support his family, who again lived with him under a rethatched roof, his son now tending the family fire. Thus the brahmin's story had a happy ending—but the moment for his walking off to the Himalayas with an exalted boy had passed.

As far as is known, the remainder of Yogesh's schooling at the junior high school proceeded uneventfully. As for his studies, he did moderately, unnoticeably well—except in arithmetic, in which he distinguished himself in an examination by getting one-half of one question correct out of 125. The math teacher "gave me a good dressing down to his heart's content," he related, "telling me I must do better." So Yogesh decided to do better. In no time, all the problems in arithmetic, geometry, and algebra, which before had seemed totally incomprehensible, suddenly became very simple. The answers flashed into his mind, and in the next examination he passed highest. In fact, he began to teach the math class when the teacher was absent, which was often. This mathematical proficiency, the Swami later said, lasted only a year or two. The same thing happened in regard to chemistry. The students took the chemistry course because it was easy, but Yogesh did nothing in it at all; he neither read the texts nor listened to the teacher, and quite naturally he got a very low grade. It was the principal of the school, this time, who berated him. So Yogesh decided that since he was taking the class, he should do it well—and the next year he got the highest mark.

He continued to read voluminously and to arrive home late. At some point probably around this time one sees him walking along the road toward Durgapur carrying in his arms an infant child. The mother of the baby, Yogesh's eldest sister, had recently died of cholera, and to Yogesh the infant seemed to know he had suffered a great and irreparable loss. There was a sense about him of desolation, and, perhaps remembering his own inconsolable grief when his mother had left home for barely a few days, Yogesh felt a great tenderness toward the motherless infant. Why he was carrying him to Durgapur he never explained, but one guesses that the Datta family took over the baby's care. It may have been this same child that Yogesh used to baby-sit, rocking its cradle and repeating to it, "Tvamasi niranjana, tvamasi niranjana" (Thou art the Pure One, thou art the Pure One), as Queen Madalasa in the *Mahabharata* had chanted to her infant sons, one after the other, to ensure that in adulthood they would realize their true spiritual identity and renounce the world. For a long time the baby did not respond to Yogesh's chanting, but one day when he said, "Tvamasi niranjana," the baby looked up all alert, with keen intelligence in his eyes. He had heard; perhaps he had understood. In any case, Yogesh was elated—certain that the words had struck a responsive chord somewhere deep in the soul of that infant. He would tell the story years later to illustrate the response of the soul to the call of truth.

The time came for Yogesh to enter the government high school in Habiganj—the same building in which the missionaries had held their revivals. But only a few weeks into the school term, his malaria came on with a vengeance. He became very ill and was bedridden from February through October. Those months, though, were far from wasted. During them, free from routine study, he read every book he could get his hands on—some came from the Bengali library of his brahmin friend, some from the school library, brought to him by friends, and some belonged to one or another of his uncles. He was so ill, so cold from the chills of malaria, even during the stifling summer months, that he could not put his hands outside the bedcovers, so he read with a blanket held over his hands and book.

He read Indian history thoroughly, reading in different books about each period of that fabulous, millennia-old drama; he read many English books, including most of Dickens, Thackeray, and Scott. All this reading of both fiction and nonfiction awakened in him a sense of the beauty, the wonder, the humor, the heartbreak, and the joy of human life. And because he never forgot anything he read, he was accumulating a huge fund of knowledge—varied and sometimes odd.

At last, all other remedies failing, an Ayurvedic doctor was called in. This tall, dark-skinned *kaviraj* said that for fifteen *takas* (rupees) he would cure the boy (medicine included), and, the family agreeing, he at once set about brewing a bagful of herbs. For hours the herbs were simmered until the brew became dark and thick and exceedingly bitter. Day after day, Yogesh's mother brewed herbs according to the Ayurvedic prescription, and every day Yogesh dutifully drank the black and bitter brew. Within a week or two he was cured, and the cure was permanent: the malaria that had plagued him for years never returned. It was then decided among his aunts, uncles, and mother that he should go back to school and try somehow to make up for the months he had missed. He would, it was determined, live with an uncle whose house stood near the government high school. So Yogesh, though convalescent and still extremely weak, walked the eight or so miles to Habiganj, and somehow got there, exhausted.

Although he had missed some nine months of school, he wanted to take the examinations that were being held for his class, and the authorities, after due deliberation, decided to let him try on the chance that he would get a passing grade. The chance was remote, and if he failed, he would have to take the whole year over again. Of course, if he did not take the examinations, he would have to take the whole year over again anyhow, so there was nothing to lose. Yogesh not only passed in every subject but passed highest in his class. "This caused a commotion," he related many years later. "Some of the bright boys glared at me; some of them left the school for good in chagrin." "What did your uncle think of you?" a disciple asked. Without answering the question, the Swami said, "He was an irascible man. One's blood turned cold in fear of him. He wanted to impose his will on us; to live in his house was virtual imprisonment. I did not stay there for long, but moved to the house of a doctor whose son I used to tutor. I think this hurt my uncle very much, but he was too difficult a man to live with."

If Yogesh felt a sense of satisfaction at passing his examinations, he also felt that to have excelled had its drawbacks: he now had an intellectual reputation to uphold. Never again could he be mediocre and unnoticed. "It was an uncomfortable position," he later said. "I felt that the middle road was better. I did not want to study."

During the brief school holiday in December and January, he returned to his village and again plunged into the brahmin's library. There he came upon a volume of Rabindranath Tagore's collected works published by a householder disciple of Sri Ramakrishna. Tagore's poems hit him like a lightning flash. Suddenly, as never before, the inner beauty of everything was opened to him—the beauty of nature and the beauty of people. Tagore's subtle psychological portrayals were a revelation. Day and night during that vacation he read Tagore endlessly; nothing else existed.

In later years he once said to a small group, "Tagore opened a new world before me. I used to feel that there were some bars and I had to just push against them and push against them, and there would be that world of light. Oh, how much I used to love poetry. I used to just get absorbed in it!"

In 1909 one of Habiganj's leading citizens had organized the town's first celebration of Sri Ramakrishna's birthday. Out of this had been started a sort of Ramakrishna-Vivekananda society. Although Yogesh was then still a junior high school student and had not yet read Swami Vivekananda, he influenced his friends to join this group, which held its meetings in the home of a prominent townsman named Jashada Nandan Modak. At Durga Puja time in the autumn of what was probably 1911, the year of Tagore's fiftieth birth anniversary, Yogesh conceived the idea of installing a portrait of Tagore in Jashada Babu's house. As it happened, Indradayal Bhattacharya of Sylhet was in Habiganj, and the boys invited him to officiate at the ceremony. Indradayal, later to become Swami Premeshananda of the Ramakrishna Order, was also a great lover of Tagore. He was around nine years older than Yogesh and already a leader of spiritual culture in Sylhet. He and the boys went eagerly to Jashada Modak's place, but when they arrived they discovered that Jashada Babu had gone to his village home in order to offer worship there to Durga and had locked up his house. What to do? Jokingly someone suggested breaking into the adjacent house, also owned by Jashada, and installing the portrait there. The motion was jokingly seconded, and then suddenly it was no longer a joke. The next day, the lock of the adjacent house was broken by Yogesh and the portrait was duly installed by Indradayal.

One might think that Jashada Nandan Modak would have felt some annoyance at finding his property broken into by a bunch of schoolboys. Not at all. He was, on the contrary, delighted to find a shrine set up to Tagore in a house of his, and he gave ten *takas* to the boys to purchase sweets for offering to Tagore and distributed *prasad* to them. Everyone was happy. Later on, Indradayal set up a shrine in this house to Ramakrishna and Swamiji (Swami Vivekananda), and later still Jashada Nandan gave the house by a deed of gift to the Ramakrishna Mission to be the first home of the Ramakrishna Ashrama and Ramakrishna Mission Seva Sambaed in Habiganj. It is said by some that because of his having broken the lock of Jashada Nandan's house, Yogesh was instrumental in starting this center; however that may be, he remained closely associated with it.

ALONG WITH HIS APPRECIATION of Tagore, his reading of Aswini Kumar Datta's *Bhakti Yoga* had awakened within Yogesh an intense yearning for God.[4] His mood alternated between ecstatic joy when God seemed close and deep depression when He seemed to turn away. The latter mood was exacerbated by a sense of his spiritual unworthiness, which was possibly also induced by *Bhakti Yoga*, for while the book had opened up the world of the Spirit for Yogesh, more than half of it is given to a discussion of the obstacles to devotion—the mental states such as lust, anger, greed, vanity, envy, and so on that can stand between the soul and God. The author advises unblinking and continual self-examination. "Any moment you search into your heart," he wrote, "you will find how innumerable are the sins that are eating into your very vitals." And, "Keep your defects constantly present before the mind by means of self-examination, for vanity will then vanish." Again, "We can fully realize the seriousness of our position if only we examine ourselves every day, and see . . . what progress we are making in the battle with sin." It was all good counsel, but to a schoolboy intensely yearning for God it could have been deeply disturbing. Still, it was no doubt this book that started Yogesh assiduously examining and perfecting his character. No flaw escaped him.

There were, for instance, the times he felt devastating envy for a classmate who proudly wore the Theosophical Society's Star of the

East, a badge of spiritual merit. Yogesh felt sure that that boy must be far advanced in spiritual life. During such episodes, the thought of his own spiritual inferiority struck him so forcibly that within a few hours his whole appearance changed. Normally healthy, he would look so thin and sick that people asked what had happened to him. Those dark moods would last for weeks at a time. Eventually, Yogesh's natural independence of spirit took over. It occurred to him during one of those bleak spells that what others did or what virtues others had made not the slightest difference to what he did or had: his approach to God was his own, unique. He was who he was. Never again did he envy others or compare himself with them.

Those bouts of depression and struggle, intense though they were, were just that—bouts. The greater part of the time Yogesh was, to all appearances, normally cheerful and active. For one thing, he used to write poetry in Bengali and was considered a good poet. In high school, he was once chosen to write a marriage poem for a friend of his, it being the custom to present the groom with a poem. Yogesh's poem, printed on dark pink paper sprinkled with gold dust, was read at the wedding festival. "We were very literary," the Swami later said. "We brought out a magazine in manuscript form. I would write the whole thing—editorials, poems, articles—everything. We also had a debating society." Of this last, Yogesh was the chief debater. But none of this had meaning for him. "Everything seemed hollow to me," he said, "like a game."

It was probably in his college years, when the fire of renunciation was burning within him, that he set all his poems ablaze, reducing them to ashes. Many years later one of his professors, then an old man, remembered this holocaust. "I begged him not to do it," he recalled. "The poems were very beautiful, worthy of Tagore himself. But he thought nothing of them, nor did he want the fame they would bring him. It was a terrible loss."

IT WAS DURING Yogesh's early high school days that the world he cared about—the world of the Spirit—suddenly expanded far more wonderfully than all his reading had so far promised, even his reading of *Bhakti Yoga*. One day he and a group of other boys were earnestly discussing immortality during a period between classes. They were so absorbed they did not notice that a teacher had entered the room and that it was time for the next class to start. The teacher listened to their discussion for a while, and then he drew the boys' attention to the time. "So you are interested in these things," he said. "Very good. But let us have class now. Talk to me about it afterwards."

This teacher, whose name was Nalini Ghosh, was the second person who would have a strong influence on Yogesh's life, turning the direction of it for good. He had his own story: One day in the middle of a college examination, he had thought, "What am I doing?" and then and there he laid down his pen, left the college, and set out for the Himalayas, specifically for Mayavati, where the monks of the Ramakrishna Order had previously asked him to come someday. But he never got there. On the way he began to wonder whether he had enough money for the trip and whether he would have the proper food at the ashrama. In the midst of these worries, he suddenly realized how his mind was working, and he felt he was not fit to become a monk. So he turned back. He finished college and then took a job as a teacher in the Habiganj high school. "He was a fine young man," the Swami remembered; "his face shone with an inner peace."

After the class, the group of boys talked with this teacher, and seeing their interest in religious subjects, he arranged to hold a class every Sunday morning for them on the Upanishads. But the class, as it happened, was somewhat over the boys' heads. As Swami Ashokananda later recalled, "The Upanishads just state things as true. We wanted arguments to prove these things, yet we were not trained in philosophical thinking. We did not even know how to ask the right questions." There were about eight boys to start with; all but two dropped out. So on the third Sunday the teacher switched from the Upanishads to Swami Vivekananda's *A Study of Religion.*[5] "I read that book, and it was as if a whole new world opened up," the Swami later said. "I felt that my soul was beating against my ribs like a bird beating against the bars of a cage, trying to get free." In that book were many such passages as

> Blessedness, eternal peace arising from perfect freedom, is the highest concept of religion, underlying all the ideas of God in Vedanta—absolutely free Existence, not bound by anything, no change, no nature, nothing that can produce a change in Him. This same freedom is in you and in me and is the only real freedom. . . . Wherever anything shines, whether it is the light in the sun or in our own consciousness, it is He. "He shining, all shines after Him."[6]

and

> The sum total of this whole universe is God Himself. Is God then matter? No, certainly not, for matter is that God perceived by the five senses; that God as perceived through the intellect is mind; and when the Spirit sees, He is seen as Spirit. . . . That which existed eternally, independent of the senses and of the intellect, was the Lord Himself. Upon Him the senses are painting chairs and tables and rooms and houses and worlds and moons and suns and stars, and everything else.[7]

"It was autumn." Swami Ashokananda continued, "I remember walking in the countryside at dawn. The sky was all golden; I felt that infinity was just there—if only I could touch it. Then one day something happened, which I won't tell you."

But later, when there were just four devotees sitting with him in a forest retreat in California, he told at least something of that experience. "A great restlessness came over me," he said. "I was all right when I was talking with people. But as soon as I was alone I would be

seized with this terrible restlessness, a tremendous longing for the realization of the Infinite. The teacher [Nalini Ghosh] noticed it, and one
day he talked with me for a long time. It did not help—but there was
some effect. One morning—a Sunday morning—when I woke up it
seemed as though the whole sky was filled with the gladdest laughter.
After that God just enveloped me—poured over me and surrounded
me. I was absorbed in that awareness day and night. I was not aware of
anything that was going on around me. One day while walking slowly
to school, I felt that I had cornered my ego in one part of my body. I
tried to get hold of it and throw it out. It was like a living thing. It went
with lightning speed from one part of my body to the other, and with
lightning speed I pursued it. I couldn't catch it. And then suddenly it
became dispersed again through my whole body; it was no longer a
separate thing that I could put my finger on. I have never read in the
books of an experience like that, but it was very definite, very real."

"That was a very illuminating experience," Swami Ashokananda
once said years later, attributing the experience to a friend of his, "and
one which accords with our whole system of Vedantic thought. It not
only gave him the sense that the ego was something different from
himself; it also gave him a sense of what he really was—not the ego,
but the Self. . . . Once you have grasped this truth, once you have
brought about a little of the severance between the 'I am' and the pred-
icate, the rest will come easily. It is as though you had made a breach in
a tremendous dam; it is just a matter of time before the waters themselves will sweep the whole dam away."

The intensity of Yogesh's spiritual mood went on continuously for
about one week. Then the teacher, again noticing, asked him whether
he would like to visit Belur Math. He would. And so they went for Sri
Ramakrishna's birthday.

It was a long trip. They took a train from a station some ten miles
from Habiganj and traveled all night to the Brahmaputra River, then
by boat all day down the wide river, then on another train all the following night to Calcutta. From Calcutta, Yogesh and the teacher went

by a country boat about seven miles up the Ganges and arrived at the bank of the Math at dawn. It was still dark, and the mist was heavy on the water. The year was 1912.

At that early date very few monks were staying at Belur Math, but a few of the direct disciples of Sri Ramakrishna—Swami Brahmananda, Swami Premananda, Swami Shivananda, and Swami Turiyananda—had come there for the birthday celebration. As daylight came, Yogesh could see these great disciples walking along the riverbank, which then sloped down to the water. He was awestruck by the sight of them. "I had not known such beings could exist," he later recalled. "They were not at all like ordinary men. They were serene, majestic, fearless, and joyful. One could see that no one stood or could ever stand over their heads. Their bearing bespoke a sense of freedom that defied all fear from anything in the universe." Of Swami Turiyananda he said, "He was beautiful, tall and erect. He looked younger than the other swamis, though actually he was about the same age. His face was glowing. I did not think there could be such a human being! And when I came to know those great swamis more and more as years went on, I found that my first impression was only a small measure of their true greatness."

Later that morning there was a long *puja* in the shrine room, and in the afternoon another, shorter worship, after which the monks sang the evening *arati*, written by Swami Vivekananda. Yogesh was deeply moved by this sonorous singing. It seemed to him that the song, or hymn, was simultaneously all heroic and all devotional. He felt it was like Swamiji—*jnana* in its fullness, *bhakti* in its fullness. "Swami Premananda stood on the outskirts of the group that was singing. He stood quietly, clapping his hands and nodding his head from side to side. He was not very impressive at that time, but his gentleness was evident. Later, the following year, a great change came in him. His self-effacement went; in its place was a manifestation of strength—gentle strength."

During the week or so that Yogesh remained in Calcutta, he visited the Ramakrishna Math at Mukherjee Lane. There he saw Swami

Saradananda seated, very steady and calm. Before him a youngish-looking monk was standing. This again was Swami Turiyananda. "A most extraordinary sight he was! At this time he was in good health. Such a spiritual beauty in his face! His whole face was just lighted. His smile cannot be compared with anything on this earth. Later, even when he was ill, there was always an aura around his head."

Yogesh's first reaction to all this was surprising. On the long way back to Habiganj by train and boat and again train, he felt singularly unmoved. He decided that a spiritual life was not for him. The tremendous intensity of the feeling that he had had all the previous winter and that had reached a crest only a week or so earlier had left him. Although he had been very much struck by the swamis, he had not felt anything special at Belur Math. So he thought he would go his own way, meditating and thinking things out for himself. But on the ten-mile walk from the train station to Habiganj, the whole exalted feeling came back. "You know how a heavy fog descends from the sky, enveloping everything?" he said in later years. "It was like that. All the devotion came over me, engulfing me. Everything came back stronger than ever."

FROM THEN ON, Yogesh became deeply absorbed in the study of the *Sri Sri Ramakrishna Kathamrita* (the original Bengali version of *The Gospel of Sri Ramakrishna*)[8] and whatever works of Swami Vivekananda he could get his hands on. Over every page of Swamiji's *Jnana Yoga*[9] he shed tears. "Hours were spent in this study," he related. "I also set up a shrine to Sri Ramakrishna and Swamiji in the house where I was living. I would get up when it was still dark and go to a neighboring garden, and in the darkness I would pluck fragrant flowers. There was great joy in that part of it. Very soon I would bathe and then sit in worship and meditation." At first Yogesh found no joy in meditating, so he would look at the photograph of Sri Ramakrishna in which the Master is standing in *samadhi*, his right hand raised.

"There was that beautiful face!" he later said. "Those were the beginning days for me. I used to try to meditate, but meditation would not mean very much; my mind would not be concentrated, nor would I find any joy in it. But again and again I used to look at that smiling face of Sri Ramakrishna. What a beautiful smile! . . . I think that was the first photograph taken of the Master. No doubt many of you have seen it. He was younger in those days, and his face was just blooming with that smile, which you can see is coming from within." Gazing at Sri Ramakrishna's photograph was in itself a sort of meditation, and soon Yogesh's meditation proper became very deep and long.

After many hours of worship and meditation, he would go to school, which did not start until eleven o'clock. Actually, he did not go directly to school. Every morning he visited a lawyer, who liked the young boy—or one should say young man, for he was now eighteen. This lawyer knew Belur Math and many of the disciples of Sri Ramakrishna. Yogesh did not plague him with questions; he just sat quietly while the lawyer worked at his desk. He waited, alert and expectant, for some pearl of wisdom to fall from the man's lips. Telling of these morning expeditions, the Swami would show how he sat on the edge of his chair—a young, eager, and beaming boy, waiting for a pearl to fall. And now and then it did. The lawyer would take a minute from his work and, gazing upon the boy and stroking his beard, would tell some little thing about the Math or about the swamis, and Yogesh's heart would be satisfied for that day. This lawyer also gave Yogesh issues of the *Udbodhan*, to which he subscribed. Serialized in the magazine just then was Swami Saradananda's masterpiece, entitled *Sri Sri Ramakrishna Lilaprasanga* (the original Bengali version of *Sri Ramakrishna: The Great Master*).[10] And then a serialization of the diary of Sarat Chandra Chakravarti started, and he became absorbed.

Around this time, Yogesh learned that a friend of the lawyer's had a copy of *Inspired Talks*.[11] He begged the man to lend the book to him, but thinking the boy wouldn't understand so spiritual a work, the lawyer's friend refused. Yogesh persisted and finally had the book in his hands. He took it home and that night read it by his little lamp. He had read only a sentence or two when he saw a flash of light. He thought it was from some natural source and tested every possible cause. But there was nothing. That was his first experience of spiritual light. Later on, the experience came often, at any time and any place, whether it was day or night, whether his eyes were open or closed, whether he was alone or with people. He would have a slight intimation of it immediately before it came: his mind would become noticeably quiet. And afterward, as a result of this vision, his mind would be particularly serene.

"If others were present," he said, "they didn't see anything. And it was so bright a light that even the brightest sunlight didn't mean anything to it! Generally when in one light you see another light, the second light, if not bright enough, appears very dim, as the moon appears very dim in the daytime. But the brightness of that light, though of a different quality, was more than equal to the sun. Yet no one else would see it." He knew then that the cause was not from outside.

Those were wonderful days, the beginning of several years in which Yogesh's mind was almost always in an exalted state. If there were times of depression, it was only because God seemed to turn His face away for a while. "I used to feel great joy welling within me for no reason," he recalled. "Joy would flood my chest and the upper part would itch a little; I would stroke it." At another time, speaking of those high school years after his visit to Belur Math, he said, "I used to feel continuously a deep silence, although people would be talking all around me. The whole universe seemed to be disappearing and a vast round Being would be rising up. God, Brahman, is spoken of in the Upanishads as round or spherical. I understood the meaning of that. One cannot explain it; one can only say, 'a vast round Being.'"

And it may have been at this time that he felt a barrier between himself and the outside world. "Things, sights and sounds, couldn't reach me," he said. "I could see and hear, but it was as though there were a moat between me and the objects of the senses. They could not pass beyond that; they could not touch me. It is impossible to explain how it was. At such times, when one is undergoing such an experience of detachment, one responds to everything in just the right way. One's judgment is very clear; one does instinctively what is just right." In those days, as he read, or reread, *Inspired Talks,* he was struck by the sentence "Do not seek for Him, just see Him."[12] "It came upon me with a delightful shock," he said. "It seemed to go to the very heart of the matter. When I read that sentence I felt I was surrounded by God."

Of course there was the school day to be got through, but after that interruption, Yogesh spent any remaining hours of the late afternoon or evening studying the *Kathamrita* and reading whatever he could find of Swami Vivekananda, and in this way there came to him a gradual deepening of spirit.

In the autumn of 1912 Yogesh dismantled (for reasons unknown) his shrine to Sri Ramakrishna and stopped his morning worship; he began instead the worship of the Divine Mother in the afternoons. In his meditation, as he tried to reach toward that which he wanted, there seemed to be a barrier between himself and his Ishta (Chosen Ideal), which at that time was Kali. How to break through that barrier? He was then reading some articles by Swami Saradananda that were being published in the *Udbodhan,* and there he found some hints on meditation. He practiced in accordance with them. And one day he broke through the barrier! "The fish," he said, "came to the bait." The next day it didn't happen, but a day or two later it happened again, and after that, it happened more and more frequently, until it happened every day.

Speaking of this period, illustrating a state of spiritual growth, he once said, "A friend of mine had an experience in the beginning of his spiritual life. Suddenly his mind would become a little still and he would feel as if a screen had been rolled up from the face of the whole earth, the whole universe, and for a moment would be disclosed to him a most extraordinary Being, beautiful and sweet, pulling his heart out by His attraction; and then again the screen would fall and hide Him completely. And then my friend would not be able to reach this Being at all, as if He had completely disappeared. The whole universe, as it were, stood in front of Him, hiding Him. It was as though you saw a door in the wall and went to enter into it and suddenly there was no door, not even any sign that there had been a door there. Just a perfect, unmarked wall. You see, whether it comes suddenly or whether it lasts for some time, this is a state which is exceedingly frustrating. The thing is how to go systematically about removing this obstruction. If we know how to do that, then the rest becomes easier. Of course, there is still a lot of struggle, but you at least know that you are on the right path."

He began walking. In his early boyhood, exercise had always brought on a fever, but now he walked for miles and miles at a stretch, just wandering. In the rainy season, when the warm rain came straight down in heavy sheets without a breeze to slant it or disturb it, he would become drenched. His clothes would dry off when the rain stopped for a while, and again they would become soaked; it did not matter. His sense of time and space had become different: he could walk for long distances and for hours and think he had walked only a short distance, for a short time. "There comes a state," he said of this experience, "when time is not punctuated by day or night, light or darkness. One has another sense of time altogether. The patterns of ordinary existence are broken."

To study regularly and in accordance with the school curriculum seemed outlandish to Yogesh, as it would for the rest of his scholastic life. But because he had a reputation now for brilliance, his teachers expected him to pass highest in the class. Once in a while, seeing how he was living, that he was not studying, and knowing his potential, they admonished him. He would squirm, he later said, but that was all. He would go on in the same way. But in order not to let his teachers down, he would study the prescribed texts just before the examinations and, satisfying everyone's expectations, would pass highest.

Yogesh had a direct and also an indirect influence over some of the other boys in his school. There was, for instance, a boy in the class above him who was matriculating when Yogesh and some of his friends were discovering Swami Vivekananda and becoming absorbed in him. This boy was of a good Habiganj family but was known for associating with the shady boys of the town. His elders despaired. But the boy admired Yogesh, and because of this, he too became interested in Swamiji—and his way of life became thereby transformed. Two or three years later Yogesh came to know him in Calcutta, where they were both going to the university. The boy was living in a hostel with other young boys whom Yogesh knew. They were all devotees of Sri Ramakrishna and used to visit Belur Math. The boy had completely changed. He had become a serious student. He read Swamiji with fervor. One night he dreamt that Swamiji was most gracious to him, and he was overjoyed. Needless to say, his parents were delighted at the way their son was turning out. And then suddenly he caught cholera and died. Brokenhearted, his parents came to Calcutta from Habiganj for the cremation. Their son had often spoken to them of Yogesh, and they felt exceedingly grateful to him. "I had done nothing for the boy," the Swami later said, "yet his parents were so kind and gracious to me when they came."

2

FINDING HIS WAY

It was during his high school years, probably in the latter part of 1912, that Yogesh had an experience that would profoundly influence every part of his life from then on—that would, indeed, transform him. It happened one afternoon when he was still living at the doctor's house and, as was his custom, was meditating on Kali. "Suddenly," to put it in his own words as he spoke them in the last year of his life, "I felt that the presence of the Mother was replaced by the vivid presence of Swamiji. The change was very distinct, and immediately I began to feel that Swamiji was pouring his power and spirit into me. It was a definite and unmistakable experience. Just as you would put the mouth of a full jar against the mouth of an empty one, one above the other, and just as the contents of the first would pour into the second without reservation or obstruction, so his power poured into me. Swamiji's mind and mine became as though merged. I was astonished, and that brought me out of that state. But the thing had been accomplished, fully."[13]

"It all happened within," he said at another time. "You see, it was a meditative state. I had been meditating on the Divine Mother; then suddenly the Divine Mother was replaced by Swamiji, infusing his spirit into me. It was a very strange experience—very strange and very sudden and unexpected. I had not even been meditating on Swamiji. A little while later I looked at myself in a mirror, and I found that the whites of my eyes were deep red. I did not know what to make of any of it."

This had not been a dream, but a very definite waking experience. A few days later, however, Yogesh did have a dream in which Swamiji came to his family's house. Again in his own words: "I was so full of joy. I ran to tell my family to come quickly; my guru was there. They all came into the room where he was seated, and stood around him in a semicircle. But I sat close to his feet and was playing with his shoes. He paid no attention to anyone but me. He talked and talked to me. I had to tell him, 'Sir, please talk to the others also.' He poured his love over me. I could not believe it; I was his own, his very darling. I knew he was my teacher."

"That dream was very vivid," the Swami later said, "and it made me think a little: How much truth was there in it? Was Swamiji really my guru, and if so, was the experience I had had during my meditation initiation from him? How could I be sure?"[14]

"The mantra came to me of itself," he said at yet another time. "One day as I was walking along a road, a mantra started going through my head. I started repeating it and felt a deep sense of joy. Tears were streaming down my face." "How did you know it was the right mantra?" a disciple asked. "It was the right one," he replied with finality.

During the last year of high school (and also later in college) Yogesh spent his mornings in his usual way, gathering flowers for worship, performing worship and meditation (one blending into the other), and finally entering into deep meditation for hours. The last state often came upon him within a few seconds of his sitting down and closing his eyes. Then, his meditation finished, he would go to his lawyer friend for a morsel about Belur Math. He remembered standing in the lawyer's doorway, his mind pulled forcibly within, his eyes closing of themselves, as though on the verge of sleep. Often during the day this state of withdrawal would overcome him, or another state, less apparent to others, would come, in which he saw light—brilliant light—several times a day, every day, at any time. After leaving the lawyer, he would go to school, unable to listen to a thing the teachers said, not even trying to listen, scarcely aware that he was in a classroom. Fortunately, his teachers (most of them) had an understanding of what was going on within this God-engulfed boy.

Most of his fellow students were absorbed at this time in the freedom movement. Like the others, Yogesh was a firebrand, hating the English, wanting India to be independent. Yet this was by no means his consuming interest. Two of his intensely idealistic friends once approached him and asked him to join their movement. He told them that his mind had taken another turn, that he felt he must realize God and could not deny that longing. "Perhaps I was wrong," he later said. "Their lives were ones of very great sacrifice and heroism." Right or wrong, it was as impossible for Yogesh to give his mind to politics and violence as it was for him to give it to study. His mind was caught in a powerful current; there was no way he could attend to cultivating the banks of that swift-flowing river; he had simply to flow with it. "I was in full sympathy with the freedom movement. It was just that the other thing was an obsession with me," he said.

Indeed, ever since Yogesh had read Swami Vivekananda's words in *Inspired Talks* "Do not seek for Him, just see Him," he had been forcing his mind to see everything and everyone as divine. "If everything was Brahman," he said later, "then I *must* see Him. I felt that I *must* see rightly, hear rightly, understand rightly. I made a continuous, unremitting effort. Mind, nerves, senses *must* change. I told myself that I was not looking at sense objects, but at Brahman. At first it was a tremendous mental strain." After a time, that effort became spontaneous. Sometimes when people talked their voices seemed to him to be actually the voice of God. His mind spontaneously saw God everywhere. "If one makes a persistent effort for two or three years," he once said, "things begin to yield; one begins to break through the crust."

After school, Yogesh continued to walk in and around Habiganj for hours and hours. It was said that he walked like a king, his eyes always above the horizon. He walked sometimes late into the night, mostly alone, sometimes with a friend, sometimes in the town along dark empty streets, a lamp making a pool of light in the darkness here and there; sometimes in brilliant moonlight when the shadows were so sharp they seemed like solid objects—as real and as unreal; sometimes on the country roads, through the fields. That is how he spent his leisure time—walking, immersed in God, pushing his mind to actually perceive that all was He. Study? The thought never occurred to him. But study or no study, in the final examination of high school Yogesh passed second highest in the province and received a scholarship. He was awarded a silver medal, which he gave to his youngest sister, Monohorini, who was also a brilliant, medal-winning student. She kept her beloved brother's medal all her life.

DURING THE NEXT TWO YEARS Yogesh attended Murarichand College in the town of Sylhet, about forty-five miles northwest of Habiganj. Sylhet was not a large town. A wide river with many trees along its banks ran through it—a river that came from high in the mountains, down through the foothills and into the plains, where Sylhet lay, just below the hills. The town was full of mango trees, which in the spring were frosted with small white blossoms, delicately fragrant.

At first Yogesh stayed at a hostel connected with the college. A little later a boy who was a devotee of Sri Ramakrishna and Swamiji asked him to stay at his home. He thought he and Yogesh could have wonderful talks together; he did not know that there would be almost no talks at all, indeed, that he would rarely see his guest. As had been his custom for two years, Yogesh would get up very early, bathe, meditate, and then set out to walk. As usual, he would roam for hours, sometimes outside the town and into the hills, where tigers also roamed. At times he would be afraid, but at other times his mind would have gone too deep to think of tigers or of anything else. In the late morning, he would return to his friend's house, eat some rice and a bowl of, say, to-mato soup, and then go to the college, which he always dutifully at-tended. In the afternoon, after the classes were over, he would not go home. He could not stand to have a roof over his head. Again, he would walk and walk around the streets of the town, or, sometimes, out of the town, walking until late at night, looking up at the sky. He would not eat again, and yet he had abundant energy and robust health. Again, he never studied. He spent almost the whole day, when he was not in a classroom, and much of the night, walking, walking in God. After a time it seemed best that he live independently, so he left his friend's house and moved to rented quarters with another boy, who later became a disciple of Holy Mother (Sri Sarada Devi). He now felt totally free to come and go as he pleased.

Once as he was walking through the town late at night, he saw in a lamp-lit window a boy his own age who was a brilliant student, sitting at a desk, studying. Yogesh was stunned. The sight brought his mind suddenly to the world where studying was a valid thing to do, a good thing; he almost envied the boy. And then his mind turned again to the realm where study had no relevance or meaning, and he walked on.

It was perhaps the sight of this boy that inspired Yogesh to buy a textbook. It was a book on philosophy. But it was never opened. Fortu-nately, the professors at Murarichand College, like the teachers at the Habiganj high school, understood his state of mind. One of them, when he was about to explain an important point, would call to him: "Yogesh! Listen now," he would say. "This is important." And Yogesh would try his best to be attentive. The head of the college once called him in and begged him to study. "With just a *little* work you will pass highest," he said. But while Yogesh listened with respect to this coun-sel, he couldn't follow it. In later years he once said with genuine re-gret, "If I had studied, I would have been a scholar." His disciples demurred, "But then you would not have grown so much spiritually." "I could have studied without hurting anything," he replied. "One can study and think of God both."

Study or not, Yogesh was well liked at Murarichand College and was known for his wit and brilliance. Once, in his first year, the students in cooperation with the teachers decided to launch an antidowry drive in the community. They convened a meeting, at which they invited the elusive but popular Yogesh Chandra Datta to speak. "His very face was indicative of his brilliant intellect, his eyes glowing with a kind of divine lustre," a biographer wrote. "He was a jewel of the college and was popular with the students and teachers alike." Only one sentence of Yogesh's speech has been recorded, but that sentence was memorable: "We should not accept any dowry from our would-be fathers-in-law," he said; "nay, not even their daughters."[15] There was loud applause and roars of laughter. But Yogesh was only half joking. Whenever in those days he saw a marriage procession going by, with all its splendor and fanfare, he saw it as a funeral cortege on its way to a cremation pyre, and sorrow gripped him.

Yogesh continued to read voluminously—philosophy, English literature, essays of great thinkers, Sanskrit scriptures, and, of course, whatever he could find about Sri Ramakrishna and Swami Vivekananda. Novels were thrown in. Once when he was ill with a high fever brought about by a fish bone that had abraded his throat, he read Victor Hugo's mammoth *Les Misérables*, finishing it in two days. He was much moved by the story and remembered it vividly throughout his life. He also read many novels of Dickens, which he remembered equally well. Whether or not this reading helped Yogesh pass his examinations is a moot point—but it certainly increased his intellectual knowledge as well as his knowledge of and compassion for human nature. But the book that moved him most was the fourth and last volume of the *Life of Swami Vivekananda*, which was published while he was in Sylhet.[16] He read it avidly, absorbed, and when he came to the part that told of Swamiji's death, he felt that a terrible blow had been struck him and that a part of his head was gone. The feeling lasted for two or three weeks.

As for examinations, he had even less need to study for them than he had had in high school. Although every word of the extensive reading he had done throughout the years was stored in his memory, that was not his main source of knowledge. "Just a word," he said, recalling those days, "and like a flash of light the whole field of the subject in question, with all its interrelationships and ramifications, would open up. Ideas used to come into my mind with the impact of bullets. As in high school, we had a debating society, and during debates the answer to opposing statements would just flash in my mind.[17] I would give the answer, but it wasn't always clear what I meant, so I would have to trace the reasoning step by step to the conclusion. And then they would say, 'Yes, that is right.'"

Throughout his college life, Yogesh had no pride in his intellectual ability; he hardly gave it any thought. During the first and second years in Sylhet his whole being was reaching toward God day and night. Nothing else had any attraction or meaning for him. Around the close of his second year of college, though, there would come a near-catastrophic climax to his absorption and longing—but of that, more later.

Yogesh's meditation in those days was natural to him. He had had no spiritual instruction or guidance and seemed to need none. It was as though a mighty river were sweeping him forward, and his mind made headway of itself. Telling of his mental state in those days, he said in later years, "After just one or two minutes when sitting for meditation, my mind would plunge deep deep down, as though it were just sucked down; it became perfectly still. I would find myself looking into a far-reaching tunnel of light, at the end of which was Brahman. When one's mind becomes dislodged from its usual ruts, those things happen." With something of an understatement, he added, "Those were intense days!"

Without a living guru, he undertook spiritual practices on his own. In his second year of college he once determined to practice detachment in regard to food. "There are various ways you practice this," he later said. "[One way is,] you say, 'I am not eating this at all, it is the body that is eating, it is the mind that is eating.'. . . In the meanwhile, the food is passing through the mouth. There are a tremendous amount of nerves all around the mouth which come in contact with food and they set up a sensation. You have to watch it and you have to counteract it. Well, I practiced this and I remember that for some days all sense of taste just disappeared. I had no taste of food at all. Of course, my mind registered that it was not enjoying food. Afterwards that practice brought about a sense of freedom which made up for that loss of taste in an exceeding degree."[18]

But it was never enough. He was beset with longing for God. One evening as he was lying in bed, feeling disconsolate, a man passed by on the street singing. One line of the song came to his ears: "Have patience in your heart; surely you will find Him!" Those words brought to Yogesh a great sense of relief and peace, as though his cry had, in a way, been answered.

He began to see the world differently, as though from a different perspective or with a different level of perception. Once, for instance, during a morning walk he came to the outskirts of the town where the foothills started. There were many knolls on the line of hills, close together. Suddenly Yogesh saw those knolls as "emblems of Shiva immersed in deep meditation." "I hadn't been thinking of mountains looking like Shiva; I never thought of that, nor had I been thinking of Shiva. Actually, I had been thinking of the world being *nama-rupa* [name and form]. But I vividly saw every knoll as Shiva. I couldn't see them as other than that."

Again, one late spring day Yogesh walked the eighteen miles to the railway station in Sylhet, and as he walked along that road he was thinking of the compassion of Buddha and of how great was his sacrifice. The road passed between two rows of big hardwood trees that were covered with thick masses of pink rhododendron-like flowers. They had passed their zenith, and some had fallen, but the trees were still covered with blooms. As he approached those trees on either side of the road, thinking of Buddha, his mind in a kind of ecstasy, he heard every flower say, "Take me, take me!" as though they were offering themselves in complete self-sacrifice. "I had not been thinking of the flowers," the Swami said in later years, when telling of this incident. "I was not imagining that the flowers were offering themselves to the Lord. I was not thinking anything like that. I had been thinking only of Buddha. It occurred to me, of course, that my thought of Buddha's great sacrifice was objectified. But when one has such an experience, one cannot really think it is an illusion. It was not exactly in words that the flowers spoke, but the communication was so clear, it was the same as words. The flowers seemed to be the very embodiment of self-sacrifice. It is hard to explain how that is."

Another time, while walking in the afternoon, Yogesh came upon a chariot in which Rama and Lakshmana were seated. "It was quite a shock," he related. "There they were before me!" The next moment he realized that these divine personages were only members of a troupe of actors that was putting on the *Ramayana* in the village. "But later still, I thought that I had, after all, really seen Rama and Lakshmana, for it is the appearance only that makes the difference. Everything *is* God. The appearance was that of Rama and Lakshmana, and the substance also was God."

It was during this same period that Yogesh was able to see a thought rising in his mind, as though seeing a cart approaching along a road from far off. With a slight effort of will, he could squash that emerging thought, and as he did so, he would feel an access of great power in his mind. This did not happen only during meditation, but at other times, ordinary times.

As he walked, his mind going deeper and deeper into God, he would feel his consciousness withdrawing from his body, pulling from his hands. His fingers would look shriveled, then again they would become normal, full. His mouth and chin would feel numb, and there would be a sharp pain first in his eyes, then around his mouth, then in his hands, as though someone were tugging at the nerves. This would happen not only in meditation or while he was walking, but while he was sitting in a classroom—or any other time throughout the day as his mind went deep within. What wonder that at least one of his professors would say from time to time, "Yogesh! Listen now!"

If he heard a woman singing during this intense period, he at once had a strong feeling that the worship of the Divine Mother was taking place. His mind felt great joy and serenity in that worship, and all nature seemed to participate in it. Once, when he was walking through the streets of the town at night, he heard some women singing behind a wall of a courtyard. The sound plunged him into a deep mood. He stood transfixed, feeling that he had been a worshiper of Kali through all eternity. Perhaps he would reel a little at such moments, for there were times during these years of college that he would feel intoxicated, would feel a sort of ecstasy sweep over him—for any reason, or none. Not only did a woman's sweet voice give him the joy of worship, but at the voice of a crow his mind would leap up. The sound was not raucous to him, but thrilling. He did not know why at first, but then he remembered that a crow is associated with the Divine Mother: in depictions of the Divine Mother, there is a jackal on one side and a crow on the other. He wrote a long poem on the crow—which was among those he would later burn.

Fortunately, living nearby was a young man some nine years older than he who was also full of God. Yogesh and the boy with whom he lived used to go almost every day to see him and talk with him. "I greatly benefited from my contact with him," Yogesh would later write in a letter to a friend. "His wonderful conversation and beautiful singing, and the many things he told us about Sri Ramakrishna, Holy Mother, and Sri Ramakrishna's disciples were a great spiritual stimulus to me. He is a very sweet person and a person of very deep perceptions." This young man's name was Indradayal Bhattacharya. Yogesh had known him earlier, having met him when Indradayal had come to Habiganj and they had broken into the house of Jashada Nandan Modak in order to set up a shrine to Rabindranath Tagore. They now became good friends, both devoted to Swami Vivekananda. Indradayal had had a dream, he told Yogesh, in which he saw Swamiji. He had prostrated before him and had said that he wanted to become a monk. Swamiji had said, "Not yet." And actually Indradayal did not take *sannyas* (becoming Swami Premeshananda) until some time later, not wanting to leave the ashrama he had started in Sylhet.

DURING HIS FIRST YEAR at Murarichand College, Yogesh became certain that spiritual life was what he wanted above everything else, but in what way he should live that life was not clear to him. He felt that he needed help in deciding what he should do with his future. And so, seeking that help, he went again to Belur Math. It was the time of the autumn worship of Durga. He stayed at the home of friends in Calcutta, and from there went to the Math. "Only about fifteen monks were living there," he said, recalling that time. "Swami Premananda was in charge of the Math and, as it happened, was the only great swami there. I went with two friends, and we found him sitting on the upper veranda of the main building, talking to some monks and devotees. After paying our respects to him, my friends and I stood to one side. He was in a sort of ecstasy; he was sitting very erect; his face was an orange color—gold red; his eyes were blinking very fast. A boy was fanning him, and I thought, 'How fortunate that boy is! If only I could fan him!' As I was thinking that, he turned and looked at me and then asked the boy to give me the fan and let me fan him! He asked one of my friends, 'Have you put on shackles yet?' My friend did not know what he meant. So the Swami asked me if I knew. I said, 'I think, sir, you are asking if he is married.' 'He is smart,' the Swami said. After some time he went to his room, and we followed him. He lay down and talked with us a little while."

On another day of that same autumnal visit, Yogesh went from Calcutta to the Math very early in the morning, this time alone. He found Swami Premananda sitting near the kitchen, under the shrine room, surrounded by piles of vegetables, which he and a number of younger monks were preparing for the midday meal. Yogesh sat near the

monks, and the Swami lovingly asked him questions about himself—
where he came from, and so on. He also kept a keen eye on the way the
vegetables were being peeled: it must be done carefully, not wastefully,
but with control and attention. Yogesh would always remember that he
said, "Every work here is sacred. Whether you cut vegetables, whether
you prepare cow-dung balls, whether you go out to give a lecture or
worship in the chapel—everything is service unto the Lord. You have
to learn to do everything with an equal sense of reverence and sanctity
in your heart."[19]

Later in the day, the monks worshiped in the shrine. "I didn't participate in the worship. I was in an adjoining room, and I listened to them
singing. In a hymn to Sri Ramakrishna by Swamiji, the words were,
'Vice is transformed into virtue when one takes Your name.'—*Krtyam
karoti kalusam kuhakantakari / snantam sivam suvimalam tava nama
natha*. I thought, 'What a wonderful song!' It went through my mind
over and over."

Swami Premananda talked with him again that day and, to his overwhelming joy and surprise, for he had not imagined that he would be
so readily and quickly accepted, gave him the assurance that he would
become a member of the Order. Later that night, after the evening
worship was over, Swami Premananda called him to his room and in
that still night talked to him privately. "He told me many wonderful
things," Swami Ashokananda recalled. "Over and over he called me
their own, and he clasped me in his arms and said, 'My Yogen!' [an affectionate diminutive of Yogesh]. It was a very great blessing. He
asked me what I wanted. I said, 'Sir, I want purity.' He replied, 'You
have purity! If you didn't have purity, do you think I could embrace
you? Purity! You have it!' He made me promise I would join the Order
after graduating from college." Yogesh now knew that he belonged to
Sri Ramakrishna, that he had become a part of that divine existence.
But it would be almost seven years before his promise could be kept.

During the month that Yogesh remained in Calcutta, he visited
Belur Math several more times. On one of those visits he had an expe-

rience that one learns about only through his close friend Atul Chandra Chaudhuri, who was with him that day and who many years later
told of it. The two boys had attended the evening *arati* in the shrine.
After the worship was over, Atul and many others left, but Yogesh remained. Some time later Atul saw him come down the stairs from the
shrine room, visibly moved. He told Atul then, and many times later,
that he had seen Sri Ramakrishna; he had clearly seen him, as though
he were physically standing there. "Of course, this experience impressed him deeply," Atul Chandra Chaudhuri said to me. "He never
told us," I said. And Sri Chaudhuri replied that he would not speak
of such a deep and sacred experience.[20] I remembered how Swami
Ashokananda had once said to me, laughing, "Do you think I tell you
everything?" This was one of the things he never told. How many
others there must have been!

Nevertheless, Yogesh was still plagued by doubt about the meaning
of his high school experience of Swamiji—was it initiation? For that
matter, was it real? Yogesh told Swami Premananda of his experience
of Swamiji during another of his visits to Belur Math. "I didn't tell him
about it in all its details," he later recalled, "because I was very nervous, and I was very shy with him. I knew him quite well, it is true, but
in his presence I was awfully shy. I told him the experience I had had,
but I did not make myself clear, and the rather cold answer he gave was
'What we [the direct disciples] say is also from Swamiji.' I was in great
despair; I thought he meant that I did not believe what he had said to
me and that therefore I was telling him this.

"So afterwards, I wrote to him from Sylhet, telling him the whole
story, asking if it was a true experience. He replied promptly with a
long letter, in which he wrote, 'You have been born to do Swamiji's
work. You have been blessed indeed that you have been initiated by
him.' "[21] (Later Yogesh would burn this letter in his renunciatory holocaust.) Hearing this story, a disciple said, "That letter should have satisfied you, Swami." "Yes," he replied, "it should have. But doubt is a
peculiar thing." And, indeed, it would take the confirmations of three

more great swamis and another confirming dream of Swamiji himself before Yogesh would be fully convinced that he had been truly initiated by Swami Vivekananda. He even thought of taking initiation from Holy Mother, but his plans in this connection encountered some difficulty, which he took to be an unfavorable sign, and thus he did not go to her.

When Yogesh returned to Sylhet after a month in Calcutta, the fever of longing beset him; the whole world seemed to him to be truly unreal. Shining through it was the reality of God. He wanted to join the Order at once and wrote again to Swami Premananda asking to be admitted. But in a long and affectionate letter the Swami firmly replied no. "It is a misery," he wrote, "to be an ignorant monk!" He told Yogesh that he *must* complete his education and that he should, moreover, attend the University of Calcutta during the last two years of college. "The teachings of Sri Ramakrishna and Swamiji are so profound that one must be well educated in order to understand them," he wrote. "Moreover, there will be many Western devotees; how will you talk to them intelligently if you have no education?" At another time Swami Premananda told Yogesh that Swamiji had been very fond of philosophy, history, and Sanskrit, and that he should study those subjects. So Yogesh did not just then renounce the world.

Several times again during his college days in Sylhet, he visited Belur Math. Once he went because of a problem that had arisen in his life—or that he thought had arisen—and that was tormenting him. Through the schoolteacher who had first introduced him to Swamiji's writings, he had become involved with a group of people who were doing very good work in the name of Sri Ramakrishna. Their leader, Gauri-Ma, a direct disciple of Sri Ramakrishna, had come to Habiganj in order to recruit some able young men to help her cause. There was great excitement in the town, and Yogesh had no way of knowing that this group was not a part of the Ramakrishna Order; indeed, he assumed that it was, and thus as time went on he became more and more deeply involved with it. He even donated to it ten dollars a month, some of which he had collected from other boys who were interested. One day, however, the schoolteacher said something disparaging about Belur Math, and at once Yogesh, shocked, knew that the group and the Ramakrishna Order were not connected. But what to do? He felt he had to decide to which group he should belong. Both stemmed directly from Sri Ramakrishna, both were doing Sri Ramakrishna's work, and to both he had, he felt, pledged his allegiance; but it was not possible to belong to both.

With this gnawing problem he went once again to Belur Math. This time, he found Swami Premananda was not there. He had left word for Yogesh to wait, but the rainy season had begun and Yogesh was feeling feverish, so he left and went back to his village, where he remained for two or three weeks. Then again he set out. Before he left, he discovered in the courtyard of his home two large and perfect pineapples, miraculously unpecked by birds and ready to be picked. To the annoyance of his family, Yogesh took off with them. He carefully carried them throughout the long train ride, boat ride, second train ride, and then country-boat ride up the Ganges to the Math. He found Swami Premananda, who was recovering from an attack of cholera, sitting on one of the wooden benches of the ground-floor veranda of the main building, as though waiting for him. Yogesh could not put down the pineapples to make *pranam*, as they were to be offered to Sri Ramakrishna. "So I rushed by and took them to the room where offerings were prepared, and then I hurried back to him.

"I found him in a state of ecstasy. His face was suffused with a fiery red color, and his eyes were blinking rapidly. I saluted him, touching his feet, and at once something entered into me. Then, before I spoke, he said one short sentence that immediately solved my problem: 'I hear you have become mixed up with that crowd.' It was as though he had poured a bucket of cold water over me—I who had been almost scorched by the heat—and I felt that my whole being cooled down. Such was his grace."[22]

During that blessed day at the Math, Swami Premananda also

pointed out to Yogesh that his problem was not actually a problem at all. He had not committed himself anywhere and was entirely free to choose his future. And the Swami assured him again and again that everything would be all right.

Swami Premananda gave two gifts to Yogesh that day—one, the dismissal of the problem, and the other, the bestowal of spiritual exaltation. "I learned that spiritual fervor can truly be communicated by one person to another," Swami Ashokananda related. "When I touched his feet, I unmistakably received something from him, and when I returned to Calcutta, I remained in an exalted mood for three days; I felt like talking about God, singing about God. It was a most wonderful state. But at the end of the third day, I went out to buy some curd. Calcutta is famous for its sweet curd. I bought some and ate it, and at once my mind came down with a thud. That experience, too, proved something to me: I learned that the Hindu dictum that one should not eat food touched by impure people [as street food can be] has some truth in it, at least in relation to spiritual development."[23]

It was during this stay in Calcutta that Yogesh visited Holy Mother for the first time. "I had not believed that Holy Mother was as great as she was said to be," he told us. "I thought the disciples of Sri Ramakrishna made much of her because she had been his wife. Then one day when I was walking with a friend, he told me that he had read where Swami Vivekananda had said she was the Divine Mother. I was at once convinced of it; there was no doubt left in my mind at all. It was as though my mind had really become certain of her divinity without my knowing it; it needed only Swamiji's word for the fact to become fully, consciously accepted." So Yogesh became very eager to take the dust of Holy Mother's feet, and on the last day of his stay in Calcutta he went to her house in Bosepara Lane. The terrifying Swami Saradananda was Mother's attendant and stern doorkeeper at that time. He told this eager boy that Mother could not see anyone just then. He was a big man and spoke severely. But Yogesh pushed him aside and ran up the stairs. Holy Mother was sitting veiled on her bed. He did not see her face, but he touched her feet in awe and made a fervent prayer—silently, because he thought it would not be nice to say it out loud. "If I had had sense enough," he later said, "I would have shouted it!" When he went downstairs, he apologized to Swami Saradananda with embarrassment. But the great Swami just laughed and said, "That is how one should go to Mother. One should not let anyone stand in the way."[24]

On the way back to Sylhet that night, the train missed its connection with the morning boat that crossed the broad and often treacherous Brahmaputra River. The next boat would not leave until evening, so Yogesh had to wait all day in the town by the river. "All day long," he said, "I felt and saw a tremendous living power working through the universe, turning it topsy-turvy, kneading and molding and giving a different shape to the world. There was a terrible fear in it. If you were to find the Pacific Ocean lashed into waves fifty to a hundred feet high over the city, you would feel a sense of terror. I felt as if there were a tremendous wave of cosmic power moving over this universe. It was fearful, and at the same time there was a sense of great attraction and love and a sense of unity and nearness. Here was a little indication, a little perception of the *aishvarya* aspect, the power aspect, of God. I had touched Mother's feet, and she made me feel she was that power. It was like Swamiji's poem about the Divine Mother—just like that. When you have even a little of those experiences, you can no longer believe that the world of our present experience is real. It no longer has any reality. The way we see it is only a figment of our present state."

That night in the train, after crossing the Brahmaputra, Yogesh dreamed that Holy Mother herself was there in another form. "She gave me a blessing," he later said. "It was so vivid and so significant that from that time on I began to feel it more and more, and I knew it had been Mother's own words and her own blessing. It could not have been otherwise."

Back in Sylhet it seemed to Yogesh that there was always a worship going on. Day and night he felt keenly aware of a great cosmic festival of joy taking place just behind the relative universe. "When there is a carnival in town, one is aware of a sense of festivity; it was like that.

"If you catch a glimpse of its inner nature, this surface universe is completely wiped from your eyes; you are not able even to perceive it. Yes, there is this extraordinary world behind the one we know, and it is said that when a person begins to enter into this world, he feels that all over the universe a continuous festival is going on. And that is just the beginning!"

At the same time, he was in a state in which there seemed to be no difference between day and night. Neither time nor space had any meaning for him. Again, the hours that he walked seemed like only a few minutes; the long distances hardly far at all. Once, around noon, in front of the house where he was then living, the whole universe suddenly began to crumble before his eyes. "If you took a very dry leaf in your hand and crushed it," he later said, "it would crumble in thousands of pieces. It was just like that. The whole universe began to fall apart into thousands of small pieces. But the process stopped before it was complete." "What would have happened if it hadn't stopped?" a disciple asked. "Would you have had *samadhi*?" He smiled. "I don't know. Perhaps I would just have fallen unconscious."

Now and then Yogesh had dreams of Swamiji, in which Swamiji talked with him. Of one such dream, he said, "There was a young man in college who was a rather dissolute character. But he had a good side and he used to come and talk with me. He was in that dream, and I wanted Swamiji to talk with him. Of his own accord, Swamiji spoke a sentence to him—that is one of the things that made the dream seem so real. Then he [Swamiji] again talked and talked with me." And then Swami Ashokananda went on to say, "You have no idea of what Swamiji's affection was like in those dreams in which I talked with him. You can form no idea of his love and affection. It was beyond description and imagination."

He continued to have many small and big experiences during those two college years in Sylhet. Once, for instance, he stood looking at a cow and could not convince himself, could not imagine, that what he was seeing was just a cow with a cow mind. To him that cow was clearly a form of the Divine Mother. Another time, he came upon a cat who a few days before had given birth. "The cat's face," he later said, "was literally shining, luminous. Divine Motherhood was shining there in that form."

There was another cat whose predicament was the occasion of a very different kind of experience. It happened in Durgapur, where Yogesh had returned for a holiday or a vacation. An unwanted, troublesome cat had been put into a gunnysack to be taken to some distant place and there let loose. Seeing the thrashing of the cat within the bag, Yogesh found he could not breathe; he was suffocating. He told his mother, with signs, to release the cat. Only when the cat ran free could he again breathe. "Of course," he once said of this experience, "it was a loosely woven bag, and the cat could no doubt breathe a little. That I could not was a kind of sympathetic imagination."

There came a time in Yogesh's second year at Sylhet when, during meditation, the spiritual state in which he had been living reached an extreme depth, or extreme height—in any case, a sort of climax. The nature of this experience he never told. He only said that it had been a very deep experience and that afterward his headache began—an excruciating headache that lasted continuously for almost three years and that made even the thought of God, even the belief that God existed, impossible, "let alone meditation!"

It could well have been of this period that Swami Ashokananda once said in a lecture, "A friend of mine once told me that through earnest meditation he attained a wonderful spiritual state. But suddenly this condition left him. My friend said that in the following months it was as though rain were falling on the clear ground of his mind and everywhere weeds were springing up. In the *Mundaka Upanishad* there is a description of creation as coming spontaneously from Brahman, 'as on earth all kinds of grasses and plants spring up.' My friend told me it was just like that. The calmness of mind in which there had been nothing but the consciousness of God was disrupted, and there began to spring up thoughts of the multifarious things the senses pursue. It took him several years to recover his lost condition."

But college went on and, perforce, he took the final examinations. Earlier, he had decided to go to a college in a small town in Bengal for the last two years, because its principal was a world-famous scholar. But when he told his decision to Swami Premananda, the Swami had objected. "Don't be a rustic," he had said; "live in the city." (Swami Premananda's mother had told *him* the same thing when he was a youth.) So Yogesh enrolled in the inexpensive City College of the University of Calcutta, thinking he could not afford better. Sure that he had not done well in the Murarichand examinations, he did not bother to look at the bulletin board where the results were posted. Only when a friend pointed it out to him some time later did he learn that he had won a scholarship and could have gone to the most expensive college of the university, the Presidency College, run by the government, as Swami Premananda had wanted him to do. It was now too late.

About to leave Sylhet for Durgapur, Yogesh went around to the various professors, as was the custom, to pay his respects. When he came to the English professor, a proud man, the professor said, "Now I can tell you: Often your answers and the things you said were so deep that we did not always know what you meant. We had to think about it and discuss it together before we could grasp your meaning." Yogesh felt that it was very nice of the professor, usually so imperious, to tell him this. He thanked him, and then he walked the eighteen miles to the railway station and went home to his village.

The time came for him to take the entrance examinations for the University of Calcutta. This was a huge affair: thousands of students came to take the examinations from all over Bengal, Bihar, Orissa, and other states. The exams were given in a government building, where many rooms had been opened into one. As usual, Yogesh had not studied—but as was not usual, he felt nervous: this strange place, all these strange people, and him a country bumpkin from a small village. But he had been reading Swami Vivekananda around that time, and he suddenly thought, "All this is Brahman; all the boys are Brahman; I am surrounded by Brahman; what is there to fear?" At that, his mind was lifted and his nervousness left him, and for all the days of the test he was in a high mood. For half an hour every day he read all the questions carefully and then started to write. He wrote steadily, making up the answers out of his head. He finished before anyone else, turned in his blue book, and left. He was sure he had not passed. But, it so happened, he had passed.

YOGESH ENTERED the City College of the University of Calcutta in the third year. Because of his persistent headache, the next two years were comparatively dark, marked more by intense longing for God than by immersion in Him. He could rarely meditate; the absorbing joy of walking in solitude was gone. As for college itself, it had little attraction for him. At the very start, however, he made his presence felt among his contemporaries, almost by accident.

At the beginning of the term, the boys who came from various high schools and junior colleges were forming competitive groups and patterns of dominance. Yogesh had no interest in such matters, but one day, when he entered a community room, a husky would-be leader of one of the groups, who was standing in the doorway, blew smoke in his face. Yogesh felt a flame of anger rise in him. But, outwardly calm, he took the cigarette from the boy's mouth, crumpled it in his fingers, and dropped it on the floor. Then he just looked the boy, who was much bigger and stronger than he, steadily in the eye. There was nothing the boy could do. After that neither he nor his friends bothered Yogesh; they (as well as other bullyboy groups) showed him respect. The next day, a friend of Yogesh's who had "a great sense of honor" told him that he should apologize to that bully. To satisfy his friend, Yogesh apologized. "I am sorry," he said, "that I threw your cigarette away." But this by no means canceled out the deed.

During those two years, Yogesh stayed with some wealthy people who lived in a suburb of Calcutta and who had asked him if he would live in their home and act as tutor to their young son. Swami Premananda approved. "Oh yes!" he had said, "I would live with them myself." These people lived sumptuously and wanted to feed Yogesh well. Sometimes, by way of illustrating the inevitableness of karma, Swami Ashokananda would tell the story of the poor man who decided to pretend he was blind just at the time Shiva put a big lump of gold in his path. In this same connection he would relate how the people he stayed with in Calcutta wanted to feed him well. They served rich and nourishing food, exactly the kind of food he badly needed in those days and could get nowhere else. But just then, perhaps thinking that if he could not meditate he would at least practice austerity and renunciation, he took it into his head to see how little he could live on, so he never benefited from the bounty of those kind people—at least not as far as food went. The only other story that we know about his stay in this house is that outside his second-floor room was a bel tree. He kept track of a cocoon on this tree and finally watched, fascinated and moved, as a butterfly emerged, its wings slowly unfolding. It was a renascence that perhaps gave him hope.

Another sight that stirred him around this time was not an event in nature but a very fine reproduction of a painting of Buddha about to renounce the world. He came across it in a book about the paintings and sculpture of India in the Imperial Library. The painting shows Buddha taking leave of his horse, who is in agonies of grief. (A little later, the horse would drop dead of a broken heart.) In the painting, there is a red jewel on the horse's forehead, and his eyes and nostrils are fiery red. "When I saw that red jewel and the red in the eyes and nostrils of that horse, I was seized with a tremendous longing for God. The fiery red seemed to bring out the fire of Buddha's renunciation. I felt that I would burst, my desire for *vairagya* [renunciation] was so great. Little things—sights and sounds—used to pierce me like that." Yogesh was also deeply moved by a painting of the death of Shah

Jahan. When it was reproduced in a magazine, he walked three miles to buy a copy.

Such joys sustained him. His college classes not only did not attract him, in at least one instance they repelled him. There was a professor of philosophy, a Hegelian, whose lectures he could not endure. "He would often speak of how the Absolute has become the relative," he would recall. "He would just flip his hand over. It was so glib! It was a torture to listen to." So Yogesh used to cut that class and go to the movies—black and white in those days, and silent. *The Perils of Pauline,* a cliff-hanging serial, was then playing, starring Pearl White. At the end of each episode Pauline was left in a highly precarious position in which her survival did not seem to be an option. Once a week the past six episodes were shown at one sitting, Pauline somehow surviving each peril and going on to another. Yogesh enjoyed it all immensely. During this period of his headache he not only went to see *The Perils of Pauline* but read the works of Dumas *père* with great pleasure.

He did not find fault with all his professors. There was at least one—a professor of logic—whom he very much respected and liked. This professor once invited Yogesh to his home, and, knowing of the young man's spiritual interest, earnestly told him that it was important that he become established in logic, for otherwise how would he know what was truth? This seemed reasonable enough, but just then, the professor's little son entered the room, and to Yogesh's amusement all logic, discussion, everything flew out the window, and the professor became absorbed in his little boy, the darling of his heart, a reality that he knew to be true without the sanction of logic.

While he had friends (or at least acquaintances) among both professors and students, there seems to have been only one event at the University of Calcutta that Yogesh actually enjoyed. The occasion was the celebration of Swami Vivekananda's birthday. A lecture was given in the university auditorium, which Yogesh attended, not knowing that one of the direct disciples of Sri Ramakrishna would be present—

Swami Saradananda, then general secretary of the Order. Telling of this occasion in later years, Swami Ashokananda said, "A most extraordinary man he was—a great scholar, a giant of spirituality, a great administrator, and just calm as calmness itself, very thoughtful—and very frightening. When you first met him, you would think he was an iceberg. He would look at you with a penetrating glare, and as soon as you could, you would want to retire. And yet, the most softhearted of men he was. Those who came to know him knew his big heart, and those who didn't know him were just frightened away. Well, on that occasion he was asked to recite the prayer at the beginning of the meeting. So he stood up and chanted the prayer 'Lead us from the unreal to the Real. . . .' And when he did so, something in his voice, something in the way he pronounced the Sanskrit words made it seem as though the unreality was literally going away and Reality was being revealed." That was, of course, a deep, unforgettable joy for Yogesh.

His greatest delight, though, was going to Belur Math, which was easy now to get to. "When I entered the gate, I would feel as though I had stepped into a realm of joy," he later said. Still, his depression was persistent and would soon settle back over him. Even Swami Premananda did not understand Yogesh's dejection. "When I would come to the Math and salute him," Swami Ashokananda related, "he would look at my gloomy face and say, 'Why are you looking so? I have told you everything will be all right.'" Another day Swami Premananda said to him, "Now look! Sin in the mind is no sin at all! That is what Sri Ramakrishna taught us." "It came to me as a great surprise," Swami Ashokananda recalled in later years, "but of course also as a great message of hope." Swami Premananda often used to scold Yogesh for his gloom and then would avoid him. And this of course increased Yogesh's despair manyfold. It seemed to him that his headache and his unwanted thoughts, sprouting like weeds, would never go and that his spiritual life (which had become his only life) was doomed.

One afternoon at Belur Math he had an extraordinary encounter with Swami Brahmananda. The Swami had been seated on a large, wide bench on the lower veranda of the Math, facing the Ganges. Yogesh and several other young men were seated at his feet. "We used to be awed by his presence," Swami Ashokananda related. "He was so grave, and we sat silent a while. He expressed displeasure at our not asking him any questions. After some time, I saluted him and started towards the main gate on my way back to Calcutta. The pathway to the gate led across a field dotted here and there with trees. Near the eastern side of the gate was a small, unkempt plot of grass, and there was Swami Brahmananda pacing back and forth on that grass! How he had passed me and reached the gate ahead of me is still a matter of wonder, for I had not stopped on the way and had walked with normal speed. But there he was! When he saw me, he said anxiously, 'Do you want to ask me something?' We had a short conversation, and then he left. It seemed he had been waiting for me at the gate, and it was not at all unlikely that he had come there to intercept me. He could quite easily understand the minds of others, and I had gone that day to Belur Math with a very urgent question in my heart that I had not asked (and did not ask even then). But how he arrived at the gate before me, I shall never know."

Another day when Yogesh visited Belur Math, he encountered Swami Shivananda for the first time and, not knowing who he was, had a slight run-in with him. Yogesh had been standing in a corner of the Math's veranda watching the great swamis, unnoticed by them. Swami Shivananda came from the courtyard and, seeing the young man, said very sternly, "Why are you standing there?" Yogesh replied, "This is a good place." "How can that be a good place?" Swami Shivananda demanded. Yogesh, undaunted, replied, "I am not hurting anyone!" The other swamis looked askance at the brash young man, but Swami Shivananda said no more. Only later did Yogesh realize to whom he had spoken so boldly.

"He was so full of love," Swami Ashokananda once reminisced. "He never remembered anyone's faults. Twice I gave him cause to blame me, but he never did. Once was at Belur Math. That time it wasn't altogether my fault. He had asked me to get him some soap. Now, one could not get soap simply because the Swami had asked for it. The soap was kept under lock and key in a storeroom. I had to find the swami who had charge of those things. I ran here and there, but by the time I found that swami and got the soap, Swami Shivananda had gone." Perhaps the only person who remembered that misfortune was Swami Ashokananda himself. The other occasion took place at Madras, but that comes later in our story.

One summer (the summer of 1916) Yogesh went to Puri, hoping that being there would give him relief from his headache. He stayed about a month and every day visited the temple of Jagannath. Telling of those days, he said, "In the dark of early morning while dawn is just breaking, hundreds of worshipers go to the temple of Jagannath, the Lord of the Universe. I still remember vividly the inspiration of seeing their white-clad figures gleaming in the darkness as they waited calmly for the temple door to open. Countless were the hours such devotees spent in the temple in meditation." Again, "It is said that those who visit this temple have spiritual experiences, seeing their Ishta in place of the image of Jagannath, or seeing what is closest to their heart. One woman, making a pilgrimage there, saw the gourds on the roof of her house, about which she was worried, thinking someone would steal them in her absence. But devotees do sometimes see the living form of God in the aspect they like best. I saw no such thing, but when there I felt the vivid spiritual Presence, and always felt overwhelmed with great devotion, as if I were His eternal servant. The image of Jagannath is crudely formed—round eyes and stumps for arms. The idea is that the Formless God is trying to take a form and is not able to become clearly defined. There is a tremendous spiritual atmosphere there.

"Every day I would go to the beach to meditate on the Formless Brahman. Generally in the summer there is a breeze coming off the Bay of Bengal, which keeps the whole place pleasantly cool. But for four or five days during my stay there, that breeze suddenly stopped. Of course, the days became sultry and most unpleasant, but the bay

was a fascinating and inspiring sight. The sky and the water were absolutely calm. Except very close to the shore, where the waves still
lapped on the sand, not the slightest movement could you see. The
water was just like the proverbial sheet of glass and merged into the
sky at the horizon. I would think of the verse in *Vivekachudamani*
where Shankara describes Brahman: 'He is the nameless one; He is also
without any description, and He is absolutely quiet like the quiet, quiet
waters.' It was most wonderful to sit on the sand at that time and meditate. You open your eyes and you see Brahman; you close your eyes,
and you feel 'Here is Brahman.'" ("Yes," Swami Ashokananda said
years later when telling of this experience, "in nature there are many
opportunities given to the soul to perceive God. The Lord has thrown
an infinite number of clues everywhere for Himself. Everywhere!")

Near where he sat to meditate, there was a village of black-skinned
fishermen, who belonged to the same caste as the fishermen who in the
sixteenth century had found Sri Chaitanya floating in the ocean and
had rescued him. They made boats out of logs and on breezy days
would push them through the breakers—once, twice, three times, and
then through and out to the calm waters. Watching them, Yogesh was
reminded of his early efforts at meditation, trying to break through the
barrier between himself and God. Trying again and again—and then
suddenly through and away!

While in Puri, he twice had occasion to emulate his hero Swami
Vivekananda. In a courtyard behind the hotel where he was staying, a
big and fierce monkey once jumped down from a tree and stood in
front of him, puffing itself up so that it looked bigger than ever and
making threatening gestures. Yogesh, remembering that Swamiji had
just stood and looked at the face of a ferocious monkey, did the same.
The monkey shrank down to size and walked off. Another time, just
before dawn when Yogesh was walking to the beach, he was suddenly
accosted by another big and threatening monkey. He realized that a
whole troop of monkeys was crossing the road and that this was their
leader protecting them. Again Yogesh knew that the only thing to do

was to "face the brute." So calmly he stared him down, and the monkey deflated himself and walked off.

Being in Puri did indeed lift Yogesh's headache and dark state of mind, but when he returned to Calcutta, both headache and despair fell back, as devastating as before, and he studied as little as ever. At one time during these two university years in Calcutta he went to visit Mahendranath Gupta, the author of *Sri Sri Ramakrishna Kathamrita* (his recorded conversations of Sri Ramakrishna), which he had written in five parts in Bengali.[25] Yogesh had been reading the *Gospel* with deep absorption since his first visit to Belur Math in 1912, and he had a natural desire to meet its author. He found M's house in a narrow lane in Calcutta and entered with diffidence. He was in a depressed mood but had not gone to seek solace or cheer; he had gone simply to see M. But as he stood in the large entrance hall, M, as it happened, came down the narrow stairs from the floor above. He was singing a devotional song, the words of which precisely responded to Yogesh's mood and assuaged it.

This was not his first sight of M. Sometimes he had seen him walking along the street in the early morning. M would be absorbed in God and would walk like a drunken man, staggering and zigzagging. He had a beard and very beautiful eyes and looked much younger than he was. He always got up at four o'clock in the morning to meditate, worship, and so on. When he walked in the mornings, his mind was still in God, and his face had a serene beauty that left a deep impression on Yogesh. Whether or not M talked with Yogesh that day after he came down the stairs we do not know. But there was a time several years later when M was impressed by something Swami Ashokananda had said. In the Swami's own words: "Once I came to Calcutta after I had taken *sannyas*, and there I met a young man with whom I was acquainted. I asked him what he was doing. And he said, 'I am studying law in the University of Calcutta, but I have to earn money, so I also practice as a private tutor. I have a father whom I have to help.' Well, I was not very gracious. I said, 'Do you know, I am quite convinced that you cannot realize God and also look after your father. The two cannot be done at the same time.' Of course, that was a very cruel thing to tell a casual acquaintance.

"Anyhow, the young man told M about it, and M was very much pleased. He knew this youth's situation, and he said, 'That is just right! He said just the right thing!' And for several days M would say to everyone who came to see him, 'Do you know what a swami from the Belur Math told him?' And he would tell about it. Yes, you cannot give your heart to God and to someone else both. Even if you give your whole heart and whole mind to God, you will still have to struggle years and years and years before you come close to Him, He is such a stubborn person." And another time, even later, M spoke of Swami Ashokananda as "a very highly educated *sannyasin*" and quoted him on some subject.

Yogesh's education seemed all to come from within. Once in his college years he dreamt that a number of the disciples of Sri Ramakrishna, including Swami Vivekananda, were standing around his bed, discussing his future. "Let him be a scholar," one said. "No," Swamiji answered. "Not a scholar, but like a scholar." And that was the way it was: he was like a scholar, with an abundance of knowledge, but none of the plodding labor. Nonetheless, somewhere along the line at the University of Calcutta, he won a gold medal in English literature. Still, when the time came for him to take the graduation examinations, it was the same story: he had studied not at all.

"For days," he recalled of those exams, "we would have to write long, full answers morning and afternoon. I had made up my mind that I would fail because I had not studied a thing. I had gathered some books together at the last minute, but I was just not prepared. Well, as in the entrance examinations, I took a long time reading the questions, deciding what I would say. Then I would write furiously and turn in the paper an hour before the test was over. Every session I did that. About the philosophical questions, I had no idea what the philosophers had said, but I had my own ideas, so I wrote them down. Well, I knew

I would not pass and that Swami Premananda would not allow me to enter the monastery. We had to wait three months for the results. When they finally came, I found that I not only had passed, but had passed 'with distinction'—cum laude. The dread of failure had made such an impression on me that for years afterwards I used to dream that I could not answer *any* of the questions and that *this* time I would surely fail."

But he had not failed, and now he could join the Ramakrishna Order. Yogesh's headache was so bad, his health so poor, and his mind so depressed, though, that he did not think he should join just then. He wrote to Swami Premananda, whom he had promised he would join the Order on finishing college. He explained the situation and asked his advice. But Swami Premananda was traveling in East Bengal at that time and replied that Yogesh should go to Swami Turiyananda, who was then at the Math, and ask *his* advice. Yogesh went to see Swami Turiyananda but did not ask his advice, for he hoped to see Swami Premananda soon. As it turned out, he would never again see him.

Meanwhile, the world pressed in and robbed him of choice. It became necessary that Yogesh earn money, for since his father's death in 1905 his family had been poor. During Yogesh's college years, his paternal uncle had helped them, but now his mother's support fell upon her oldest son alone. Yogesh's elder cousin, Dinesh Chandra Datta, was headmaster at Beani Bazar High School in the town of Panchakhanda in the district of Sylhet. Through his influence Yogesh obtained the post of assistant headmaster. The job, though, did not serve to cure his headache or restore his spirits. And Swami Premananda, unbelievably, had passed away. So finally Yogesh wrote to Swami Turiyananda, who was in Benares at the time, telling him everything of his spiritual experience, his doubt, and his despair.

In the course of Swami Turiyananda's long reply, he wrote to Yogesh that his initiation from Swamiji had been real and explained that there are three kinds of initiation. One kind comes directly from Shiva and is called *shambhava;* another is called *shakti* and is made up of knowledge that enters into the disciple's body; and the third is the usual kind, in which the guru gives a mantra and other instruction. He said that Yogesh had received the second kind of initiation, in which no mantra or instruction is given. "You don't have to do anything," he added. "What you have received is enough. It will go on working and you will reach the goal. Swamiji will himself make you do what is necessary. You don't have to think about it." Those words gave Yogesh a great boost, at least for a time. Then again, his mind would, as he said, sag down.

Finally he went to an Ayurvedic doctor, the kind of doctor that had cured his fever when he was a child. Ayurvedic medicine now cured his headache. The physical relief was of course immense, but more than that, he found that spiritually he was far ahead of where he had been almost three years earlier when the headache started. His state of mind was now clear and full of joy. His desire to meditate came with double strength, and the moment he sat in meditation his mind, as before, plunged very deep and grew perfectly still. It was then that he began to have many deep spiritual experiences. These were among the ones he did not tell us.

We know of only one profound experience that very probably occurred during this period. It was the season when the paddy fields were flooded and the sky was a deep blue. One day Yogesh saw a man and woman walking hand in hand along a dike. There was nothing extraordinary in the sight, but suddenly his mind rose high up (or plunged deep down) into another kind of awareness, and he saw the whole process of creation from the causal state through the subtle to the material universe (or, in other words, from Ishvara to Virat). He saw the entire process evolving before his eyes. He said so little about this experience that one cannot now say more. But such was the timbre of his mind in those days that the least suggestive sight or sound could lift his consciousness into realms of a higher reality, revealing its mysteries.

———————

AMONG THE SUBJECTS that Yogesh taught in the Panchakhanda school were English, Sanskrit, and history—subjects that Swami Premananda had told him to study in college. (Although, strictly speaking, Yogesh hadn't studied these courses, he was well qualified to teach them. Sanskrit and English had always come easily to him, and on his own he had read history and English literature voluminously.) But his main teaching, though he would not have called it so, was done outside of classrooms in the woods and meadows that surrounded the town. Here, with a group of six or seven schoolboys he would take long walks, talking of God and of spiritual things. Almost all of these boys later joined the Ramakrishna Order. Among them were Swami Vimuktananda, Swami Sadhanananda, Swami Shantaswarupananda, and Brahmachari Akshaya Chaitanya, the last of whom did not join the Order but wrote now well known biographies in verse of Sri Ramakrishna, of Holy Mother, and of many of the Master's direct disciples. Of those days Swami Shantaswarupananda used to speak—when asked. Here are some of the things he recalled in 1970:

> Daily a group of us would go after school to Swami Ashokananda's place. Swami Ashokananda, then Yogesh Chandra Datta, was living with his cousin. One year we celebrated Christmas Eve. They (the two cousins and another teacher) put up a big red cross, and halva was prepared. We had studied how the Jewish people used to have their dinner, so we sat in the Jewish manner. There was some reading from the Bible and talking. Oh, that was a memorable occasion! It left a deep impression on me. It was this group—these three teachers and about five or six students— that became very close. Swami Ashokananda was about twenty-five years old; I was about fourteen. He exerted a tremendous influence over the whole school. There were other boys who were not spiritually inclined, some of whom were living a very low life. Even their lives were changed. Everyone felt uplifted by him.

The school was in the village of Panchakhanda, and there were forests on its outskirts. Swami Ashokananda and the group of spiritually minded boys and another teacher would spend the whole of Sunday mornings wandering around in these forests and meadows and talking of spiritual things. Those were the times we used to enjoy like anything! One day we went by country boat to a lotus lake—the lake was covered with hundreds of lotuses. We spent the whole day gathering lotuses. Swami Ashokananda became just like one of us. The other teachers in the school did not look on these outings with much favor. They wanted to observe dignity and all that.

He used to teach us English. Outside, he was so friendly, but when it was class time, my, he was a different person; we were just terrified of him!

In later years, Swami Ashokananda himself would laughingly tell of his teaching manner. "You there!" he would say, without pointing, to some boy in the class, and the boy thus addressed would know exactly who was meant by "you" and would at once come to galvanized attention. Sometimes he drew wisdom from the youngsters. Once, for instance, when he entered the classroom, bedlam was going on, as it does among boys. When he came in, the noise quieted, and then he asked, "How does one get silence?" The boys gave various answers, none of which satisfied him, and then finally a boy said, "If one can withdraw one's mind from all this noise, then one can have silence." "You've got it!" the teacher exclaimed. That boy later became a monk of the Ramakrishna Order.

In Panchakhanda, Yogesh again came in close contact with his friend Indradayal Bhattacharya (later Swami Premeshananda), who lived only a little way down the street from him. He used to visit him almost daily, taking a group of students with him, and again, he would listen to his inspiring talk and beautiful singing. In their monastic lives Swami Ashokananda and Swami Premeshananda would not come in contact with one another, so Swami Ashokananda was always grateful to have known the older boy in Sylhet, particularly during these still-formative years.

During Yogesh's teaching year in Sylhet a giant earthquake struck the district. He was sitting that afternoon in the library building of the school. Ordinarily it was his habit to sit in a certain chair by a wall, but for no reason he sat this day in another place. Suddenly he heard a loud rumbling, and with lightning speed two thoughts passed through his mind: I am in a railway station and a train is coming; no, I am in college—it is the sound of many feet at the close of a class. Then the truth dawned: earthquake! He shouted to the other teachers and students to get out of the building, and he himself ran out as walls collapsed. If he had been sitting in his accustomed chair, he would have been trapped. On the street he watched with amazement as the earth rolled in waves, the horizon tilting up and down. A little boy standing next to him fell and rolled on the ground; Yogesh lifted him and held his hand. The building he had been in, a brick and steel structure, was swaying far over to the right, far over to the left, and then it collapsed. Ordinarily at that hour children would have been playing in the yard of that building, but today, for some reason, they had been kept in school later than usual. Otherwise, they would have certainly been killed. Yogesh felt no fear. Later, speaking in San Francisco of earthquakes in general, he said, "When one loses body-consciousness, one feels no fear of these things. Even if two hundred hydrogen bombs were to explode over one's head, it would make no difference."

But the fate of others mattered to him—even the fate of fish. Later he sometimes told the story of a particular fish. A close friend of his in Sylhet, who was a disciple of Holy Mother's and with whom he had lived in his college days, became very ill. When he was recuperating, Yogesh used to cook for him. He would make a rice dish, and, later, he cooked a fish for him to build his strength. This fish had first to be killed. Every time Yogesh brought the knife near it, the fish squealed (yes, squealed) in fear, as though it knew exactly what was happening. Several times Yogesh grasped the fish and brought down the knife—

each time the fish squealed and tried to wriggle away. Then finally Yogesh determined that he must kill it, as his friend had to eat. So with one stroke he quickly did the deed. It bothered him for the rest of his life.

He empathized not only with fish, but with trees as well, and this in a far more intimate and complete way. One day, looking at a huge banyan tree, he was suddenly thunderstruck by the tremendous life force manifested there. It was such an enormous living being, bigger than any animal on earth! Later this sense of wonder grew. When he was near trees, his mind would sometimes grow very quiet, and his ordinary consciousness, human consciousness, would be obliterated, as it were, and tree consciousness would take its place, a consciousness entirely unlike our own—a different time sense, a different way of knowing and feeling, indescribable in terms of human consciousness. He felt at one with trees, just as we feel at one with human beings. He knew trees to be very happy, peaceful beings. He could almost hear their laughter. It was, he said, like the laughter of young girls around sixteen or seventeen years old, and yet restrained. Later, returning to ordinary human consciousness, he couldn't remember what tree consciousness was like. "Human consciousness is so very different," he said; "it blocks out the memory." "Don't tell anyone these things," he added when he told of this experience. "People will wonder what kind of man I am. Is that how he teaches Vedanta! Talking about tree consciousness!" Just the same, there will be occasion to speak of this again.

At the close of the school year Yogesh and his cousin were asked to leave. This was not so much because of Yogesh's popularity with the boys as because of his youthfully intolerant scorn of the school's secretary. This man was actually a very good man, though worldly. He had founded the school for the local boys using his own money. But Yogesh (and also his elder, though still young, cousin) felt that his philanthropy was only for name and fame and would have none of him. "In those days," Swami Shantaswarupananda recalled, "he was like a sword out of its scabbard. Whenever he found anybody not living up to the highest ideal, he just ignored him completely. We boys also became like this, because he was our model in those days." The secretary was naturally disconcerted by this young uncompromising idealist who would not speak to him, so he told Yogesh and his cousin to go. "But when Yogesh left, all the boys of the school followed him, walking after him for a long way. I, too, walked along with him," Swami Shantaswarupananda related. "But he said to me, 'Why have you come? You should not join these movements. You are to live a quiet life!'" Thus it was that after a year, Yogesh left Panchakhanda and went back to Habiganj, where he became a teacher in the Shaistaganj junior high school that he had attended in earlier years.

THE MOST MEMORABLE episode of this next period of Yogesh's life had to do with his relationship with a village of hide tanners that lay on the northern bank of the river Khowai, across from Habiganj. The name of the village was Gosainagar. Dealing as they did in the hides of animals, the villagers were outcastes, untouchables. "No one paid much attention to them or seemed much concerned about their welfare," Swami Ashokananda said. "They were pleasant, amiable people, making a very poor living by plying their trade."

One day Yogesh and others in Habiganj were celebrating Swami Vivekananda's birthday on the bank of the river opposite the hide tanners' village. A number of outcaste boys saw the festivities and swam across, and the devotees gave them food, as is customary during religious festivals. While this was going on, and as Yogesh looked at the village boys, the thought suddenly struck him that here was a wonderful opportunity to put Swamiji's teachings into action and to give education to these illiterate people. The very next day he and a few of his friends walked across the shallow river to the village and approached its chief. Yogesh told him that they wanted to teach the children. The man was astonished and not a little suspicious: Who would want to become friendly with outcastes, let alone serve them? "Why?" he asked.

Rather than explain to him Swami Vivekananda's doctrine of service and desire to uplift the masses, Yogesh simply said, "Our guru told us to find those in need and to serve them." This the chief understood: whatever anyone's guru said was law. So he agreed to let a school be started, and then and there it began.

Another, more dramatic story of Yogesh's first approach to that village has become a sort of legend in Habiganj. It happened, it is said, during the rainy season when the river was swollen and swift. Feeling concern over the plight of the hide tanners, Yogesh, risking his life, swam across to their flooded village and there discovered their miserable condition.

However that may be, since his high school days Yogesh had been pushing his mind through the form of things, particularly through the form of human beings, to their divine essence. The practice had become second nature to him. Here was a wonderful chance to worship that divinity. Thenceforth he used to walk across the river in the evenings, carrying books and supplies to the village. Surely he inspired his friends to join him, but how many came along, and how regularly they did so, we do not know. The outcaste boys, and perhaps also grown-ups, came happily to Yogesh's school, and he taught them. After a while he began to notice that these people had virtually nothing to eat. They never spoke of their hunger, nor showed it. The children always looked cheerful and strong enough, but Yogesh learned that on many days they had literally no food. He asked them what they did, and they replied, "We drink water and lie down." So Yogesh begged through Habiganj for food and clothes. Of course, he had to tell of his work with the outcastes, to the horror of the orthodox Hindus, one of whom suggested that he be dropped from society—to which another said, "Do you think he will care?" Slowly the scandal faded, and Yogesh, paying no attention, went on his way, begging for food, which he carried across the river.

As the days grew hot, the hide tanners developed a contagious skin disease. Small boils formed all over their bodies. Yogesh would take the children who were infected to the river and wash them with a solution he had made of neem leaves boiled in water. Then he would take a knifelike piece of split bamboo and scrape the sores, breaking the boils. His patients screamed in pain, but Yogesh simply held them down and continued the treatment. Then he again washed each patient in the clear river and applied another dose of medicine. This procedure cured the villagers.

"Doing this, I felt literally as though I were rubbing the body of God," Swami Ashokananda later said when telling of those days. "When I had finished, it was as though I had come out of deep meditation. The sense of the presence of God was vivid. Once I washed one boy with a particularly bad case of boils for three hours, becoming absorbed in the thought that the boy was God Himself. I proved to myself that Swamiji was right when he said that to serve man as God was a very effective form of spiritual practice." Not surprisingly, the people of the village, young and old, grew to love Yogesh and to have deep respect for him.[26]

In July and August of 1919, during the rainy season, the river became swollen and difficult to cross. Yogesh crossed it on foot for as long as possible. The water was so deep that it came up to his mouth. Holding books and supplies over his head, he moved step by step, touching bottom just with his toes. The current was so swift that he had to walk very slowly, and sometimes when the water was about to carry him away, he stood still, getting his footing and balance, and then took another cautious step. (Sometimes in later years he would tell this story of his crossing the flooded river to illustrate how to deal in life with adversities that seemed about to sweep one away.) It is said that when the river became too swift and deep to walk across, the wife of Yogesh's maternal uncle, a noble and devout woman, sold her jewelry in order to purchase a rowboat for Yogesh and his friends. And thus, for as long as Yogesh stayed in Habiganj, there was no break in the hide tanners' schooling.

One day while he was in the village caring for the people, a friend of his came there to see him. As they talked, Yogesh told him how much spiritual satisfaction he was getting from this work. The friend said, "Yes. But when are you going to renounce the world? I thought you were going to become a monk." Those words startled Yogesh, and he acted on them then and there.

3

FEARLESS YOUNG SWAMI

W hen you see Maharaj, ask him if he will accept me into the Order," Yogesh said to a friend who was about to see Swami Brahmananda in Calcutta. Telling of this, Swami Ashokananda would exclaim, "Can you imagine the audacity of it! People begged for years to be accepted, and here I was, a virtual stranger sending a message through another stranger!" Faithfully, Yogesh's friend gave Swami Brahmananda the message and also told him something about the candidate. Incredibly, Swami Brahmananda said, "Yes! Tell him to come at once! No. Tell him to wait; it is the malarial season at Belur now. No. Tell him to come at once. I can send him to another center." Just then another swami came into the room and, knowing Swami Brahmananda's frequent changes of mind, said wryly, "Tell him to come, but tell him not to give up his job."

When his friend wrote to him about all this, Yogesh was flabbergasted and of course overjoyed at the thought of joining the Order. The school term was over; there was nothing to stop him. Or was there nothing? Yogesh realized that there was indeed something he must do before he could renounce the world. This had been in the back of his mind all along, and now, when a decision had to be made, it loomed like a wall. His youngest sister, Monohorini, was yet to be married and required a dowry. "My father had died long before," Swami Ashoka-nanda once recounted, "and it is the eldest son who is responsible for such things. If I did not earn the money, my mother would have been forced to get it somehow. She had no money, and from whom would she get it? If I renounced the world, my uncles and cousins would not have lifted a finger. But a bride has to have a minimum amount of gold ornaments and silk clothes and such things. Her family has to give a minimum at least, and I thought I had better do that; otherwise I would always think about it, and probably some spiteful letters would come to my mother. It would be just heartbreaking. Then just at that time, a friend of mine who was working in Poona applied there for a job for me. While I was worrying about my sister's dowry, his letter came, and I decided to go directly to Poona and earn the money."

The job was as an accountant in a British cantonment—a good job with a six-month contract, a bonus of two months' pay, and passage to and fro. Outside the city of Poona, the English had a big barracks, which was an outcome of World War I. There they had established the financial office of the British Expeditionary Force. After the war, the English slowly and warily—so as not to overwhelm the home labor force—sent their clerical workers back to England, gradually replacing them with Hindus; thus from time to time there were clerical jobs open in Poona, a continent away from East Bengal.

Before he left for Poona, Yogesh asked a sympathetic friend to look after the hide tanners, and he himself obtained jobs for some of them in Habiganj as *punkah* (fan) pullers. (Later, another friend arranged for some of the outcastes to learn cobbling in Calcutta. They learned to make shoes and sold them in the city itself and thus became relatively prosperous and respected in the Hindu community.)

"The social status of those so-called untouchables underwent a complete change," Swami Ashokananda once related when speaking of the caste system in India. "High-class brahmins visited their village and presided over their religious functions. Their very appearance changed; their minds changed and they learned to meditate. Some became disciples of our great swamis. And not only that small village benefited, but many other villages inhabited by the same untouchable caste achieved social upliftment. Here was a clear case of a whole community being lifted to a higher social status."

With a heavy heart, Yogesh made the trip from Habiganj to Calcutta and thence to a railway station across the city, away from Belur Math, the only place in the world to which he wanted to go. Some of his friends—those who knew he had decided to renounce the world— were heartbroken at this turn of events. And in Poona, other friends who met him at the station were equally distressed, one of them saying with dark humor, "Et tu!" But most of Yogesh's friends knew that he had not given up the idea of renouncing the world. Indeed, during his stay in Poona that idea burned in his mind and heart with greater force than ever, "like a fire within," he later said. That fire reflected itself in his body: he had frequent high fevers, followed by severe nosebleeds, which somewhat relieved the fever. But then again the fever would come, and these symptoms grew worse as time went on.

When he was not too ill, he would get up at three or four in the morning, take a shower, and meditate. Then he would walk to a stone bridge that crossed the river and wait for the sun to rise. "I saw all different kinds of sunrise," he said. "There was a time when I used to realize the sun as the center of everything—the center of the universe. It is not astronomically true, but it is true in another sense."

At Poona the tree consciousness that had started during his teaching days in Sylhet came upon him often. Finding trees to be not at all inferior to human beings, he came to the conclusion that there are different types of consciousness in the scheme of things—not higher or lower in the scale of evolution, but different *types*—of equal value and equal potential. But this, he always added, was his own peculiar idea, which one may or may not accept.

As far as his job went, it was dull but not difficult. One remembers that in junior high school his grades in mathematics had been monumentally poor, but when he had applied himself, they had skyrocketed;

he had even enjoyed the subject. Then, with his discovery of Swami Vivekananda, he had again lost all interest in math and, with it, his sudden knack for figures. Still, his erstwhile aptitude would have stood him well in an accounting job. Indeed, at the end of his six months' contract he was asked to stay on, so to increase his sister's dowry, he stayed one more month.

And then, at last, he went straight to Bhubaneswar, where Swami Brahmananda, president of the Ramakrishna Order, was then living. Having heard that the Swami liked fruit, particularly figs, he carried a large basket of fruit, for which Poona was famous. It was late April and the train was stifling. Along the way Yogesh had to change trains, and here he bought a canteen, which was promptly stolen. The procedure in those days was to hold a cup or a canteen out the window wherever the train stopped; it would be filled by a water carrier. One did not dare get off the train to find water, for more likely than not the train would leave one behind. But Yogesh now had nothing to hold out the window. Finally, passing through Hyderabad, he asked two Hindu families if they would give him some of their water. Not knowing what caste he was, they said no. So he asked a Muslim, "Would you give me some water to drink?" Surprised, the Muslim said, "Yes, surely I will! But will you drink water from me?" Yogesh, perhaps remembering Swamiji, who had once smoked from a Muslim's hookah, and perhaps remembering, too, his own *advaitic* convictions, said yes, he would, and gratefully slaked his thirst.

After a long and harrowing journey to the east coast of India, Yogesh had to change trains again, for the one he was on was going to Calcutta. While eating at the junction, he became ill. It was not until late at night that he finally arrived at Bhubaneswar, and there in the railroad station he slept in an easy chair that a kindly stationmaster offered him. In the early morning, when the oxcarts came to the station, he got a ride into town, and there he found a small hotel made of rough stone. After taking a room, which he rented for several weeks, he cleaned up. Then, still carrying the basket of fruit, lighter now, for he had discarded some that had spoiled in the heat, he asked for directions to the Ramakrishna Math. Entering the monastery gates, Yogesh sat on the outside veranda. Just inside was the living room, and he could hear Swami Brahmananda talking with a *brahmacharin*.

The Swami said, "Someone has come; go and see."

The *brahmacharin* came outside and asked Yogesh what he wanted.

"I want to see Maharaj," Yogesh replied.

The *brahmacharin* relayed this information to Swami Brahmananda, who said, "Say he's not well. Say he cannot see anyone now. Tell him to come back in the afternoon."

The *brahmacharin* reported this to Yogesh, who gave him the basket of fruit and went away.

In the late afternoon, Yogesh returned to the Math only to find Swami Brahmananda going out for his evening walk. He looked in blooming health, was very finely dressed, and was twirling a cane. Yogesh followed him, and after a few steps the Swami turned and with the utmost courtesy asked the young man what he wanted.

"Sir," Yogesh said, "I came to see you in the morning." So Swami Brahmananda allowed Yogesh to follow him and asked him again what he wanted.

"Sir," Yogesh said, "I want to join the monastery."

"What? Belur Math?"

"Anywhere you are pleased to send me, sir."

Walking from the monastery building to the main gate, Swami Brahmananda asked Yogesh a number of questions about his family, his education, his spiritual practice. And then he said, "Do one thing: come to see me tomorrow morning."

"At what time, sir?"

"After I have read the mail."

"Can you tell me, sir, when that will be?"

"Eight o'clock. Come after eight o'clock."

The following morning Yogesh found Swami Brahmananda seated in his room in an easy chair, with a hubble-bubble beside him. He saluted him and sat at his feet. The Swami had read his mail and was about to read the newspaper. He asked Yogesh to arrange the paper for him, and Yogesh did so in a way he thought would be convenient. Maharaj (as Swami Brahmananda was generally called in the Order) read the paper and then closed his eyes and was quiet for a long time. Sitting there, Yogesh felt that his mind was being tugged by its roots, that it was being churned up and that everything within it was coming into view. When Swami Brahmananda finally opened his eyes, they were red. Then he said, "Very good. You will be in Bhubaneswar for a little while, will you not? I will write to some of the monasteries to see where they need workers." He was accepted!

While waiting for word to come from one monastery or another, Yogesh saw Maharaj once, if not twice, every day and would sit on the floor next to Maharaj's chair, seeing infinity in his eyes. Now and then Maharaj would smile at him or say a word or two. "Haven't I seen you before?" he once asked. And Yogesh told him that he had saluted him several times at Belur Math. He did not tell him that he had once asked through a third person to be admitted to the Order. That episode was best forgotten.

A letter came from Belur Math and one from Mayavati; both said they had no need for workers. Then after a week or so a telegram came from Madras: "Send him at once."

"Go to Madras," Swami Brahmananda said. "In five years your training will be over."

"Sir, how shall I dress in the monastery?" Yogesh asked.

"Purchase some white cloths; offer them on the altar to Sri Rama-krishna, and wear them." Coming from Swami Brahmananda, this was tantamount to the bestowal of *brahmacharya*, but Yogesh did not realize this at the time. "Make friends with a *brahmacharin* named Nirod," the Swami added. He also asked Yogesh to meditate on the beach at Madras, about half a mile from the monastery. Then he said, "I shall have to consult the almanac to find an auspicious day for you to leave for Madras."

On the last evening of Yogesh's stay at Bhubaneswar, he was sitting silently on the veranda with Swami Brahmananda. His train would leave later that night. After a long time, Swami Brahmananda said, "Son, do you mind if I go to bed now?" Astonished, Yogesh realized that the great Swami had been sitting up solely for his sake. He jumped to his feet, saying "Oh yes, sir! I didn't know you were sitting up for me!" "That is all right," Swami Brahmananda said affectionately, and bade him good night.[27]

IT WAS MAY OF 1920 when Yogesh arrived in Madras. He was, as it happened, greeted at the railway station by the *brahmacharin* named Nirod (who would later become Swami Akhilananda).

Yogesh had written to his mother, telling her that he was leaving his job in Poona, but he had said nothing about going to Bhubaneswar or about wanting to join the Order. About that, he wrote to her from Madras. A day or two after he sent the letter, he could hear her crying. Actually, when she received this letter from her beloved son, she fainted. When she regained consciousness, she cried and cried, heartbroken. Again she lost consciousness. Yogesh heard about the condition of his mother only later, but in his heart he had known, and he was deeply upset. Then one day as he climbed the stairs to the shrine, he felt the hand of Sri Ramakrishna pass over his chest, and at once all his sorrow disappeared. Sri Ramakrishna seemed to say to him, "Why are you thinking of such things? You have renounced the world!" His mother soon became reconciled to the inevitable and blessed him. After all, she had always known that he would become a monk. Yogesh would see her only twice again. (His brother-in-law, the husband of his sister Monohorini, for whom he had provided a dowry, agreed to take care of his mother for the rest of her life. And later when he was in America, Swami Ashokananda paid for the education of this sister's son with money that devotees had given him through the years.)

After his distress over his mother's grief subsided, Yogesh felt, as he later said, that "Sri Ramakrishna was the mother bird, with her wings outstretched over me, and I was the little offspring. I *literally* felt it all the time. I did not try to feel it or to imagine it. It was not 'as though'—Sri Ramakrishna *was* the mother bird."

He slept in a small room with two other monks. They slept on mats on the floor, and one of them snored very loudly. "One could hear him a block away," Swami Ashokananda recalled. Somehow, he was able to ignore this nightly racket. But one night there was a loud explosion that woke up all the monks in the Math. "What is it? What is it?" It took some time for them to figure out that one among them had sneezed. Such was life in a monastery—sweeter by far to the young novice than any other.

And this was despite the fact that at first Yogesh was ill in Madras. He had headaches (mild compared with his earlier marathon three-year headache, but headaches nonetheless) and attacks of flu once a month, which left him feeling as though he could not control his brain. Then very suddenly that feeling would lift. One of the monks asked a doctor to prescribe some medicine for him. He was given a mixture of cod-liver oil and phosphates, which he took by the bottleful for many months. Slowly he became well. The spicy food of South India, though, gave him a painful stomach ulcer that was not diagnosed for many years and that was never cured. But all that is by the way.

There was always a lot of work to do around the monastery, and sometimes Yogesh was assigned to take care of the Math cow. There was an incident connected with this that found its way at least once into Swami Ashokananda's lectures. The cow gave birth to a calf, which she of course dearly loved. But within a few months the calf died. "I have never heard such heartrending cries as that cow made," the Swami recalled later. "I can still hear it!" He went on to say that it was customary in Indian villages to skin a calf when it died young and to stuff the skin with straw so that it looked something like the real thing. This was done in the Madras Math, and the cow did not know the difference. She licked the skin as though it were her baby returned, and she thought the milking of her was her calf drinking. "So I say," the Swami concluded, "that all our cries, all our smiles, all our groans are in the name of the skin"—and one recalls his childhood insight into the unbearable meaninglessness of life and so-called love.

In addition to such odd jobs, Yogesh was given the task of counting words for the magazine *Vedanta Kesari*. He resolved to put his heart and soul into this and do the best counting possible. But soon some further editorial work came his way. It so happened that the editor swami was not given to his work. Each month, he approved the manuscripts with barely a glance at them, and inevitably, as Yogesh counted their words, the innumerable errors they contained would, as it were, shout at him. Although he had determined to simply count words, the deplorable state of the articles was too much to overlook, and almost every month, unknown to everyone, he carefully corrected the manuscripts before they went to the printer. Almost every month.

At this time, the swami in charge of the monastery—Swami Sharvananda, a great favorite of Swami Brahmananda's—was holding a class for the monks on the Brahmasutras. ("Two big volumes we had to study," Swami Ashokananda later recalled. "Commentary on commentary, arguments, counterarguments, all kinds of things. It was a wonderful experience. After the class we would feel as if we had come from a deep meditation.") The class was being serially published in *Vedanta Kesari*, and Yogesh would correct it along with everything else. One month, however, he grew impatient and decided that he would let the whole thing go as it was. After all, it was not his job or responsibility to correct the manuscripts. So Swami Sharvananda's class was published as it was. There was consternation in the Math: Swami Sharvananda was horrified, and the editor, much abashed. The next month Yogesh quietly resumed his self-imposed task of copy editor.

As time went on, Yogesh found that the ideas that had grown and developed within him since he had first discovered Swamiji in high school differed from those of his brother monks, many of whom, if not all of whom, he greatly admired. He said nothing. He thought he would watch and wait to see whether his ideas really differed from those of the others. He found that they did, and slowly he lost his self-confidence. Were his ideas, derived from his intense and thorough study of Sri Ramakrishna and Swami Vivekananda and confirmed by his own spiritual experiences in high school and college and during his two years of teaching in Sylhet and Shaistaganj—not least of all his experience of God through the service of the village of outcastes—were those ideas and convictions, which had become a part of his very being, all wrong? He began to subject them to a rigorous pounding of reason, examining them from all angles, ruthlessly exposing them to all kinds of questioning and logical battering, turning them this way and that, honing them, polishing them, testing them with the touchstone of scripture, always ready to give them up if they proved false. Throughout the years that Yogesh was in Madras, he went on examining his thoughts, which had been so spontaneous and natural to him before, until finally, although they still differed from those of others, he began to feel sure of them. It was not that ideas no longer came to him spontaneously; indeed, such experiences, such flashes of insight increased.

In later years, he told of a flood of knowledge he had had on the beach at Madras, where he had gone to meditate. "Suddenly," he said, "a part of my mind opened up, and through that part raced in quick succession ideas I had never thought of or read of, or even dreamed of before—the most extraordinary thoughts; I stood aghast. It just went on and on. I wanted to write those thoughts down, but I had no paper or pencil. By the time I got back to the monastery, I had forgotten most of them. After that, I used to carry a pencil and a pad of paper, but it never happened again." He subjected even those new ideas—those that he could remember—to scrutiny, along with the old. This rigorous examination of his thought was a long process. And, of course, it did not all take place in silence.

In those days, Swami Brahmananda permitted an old devotee to live in the monastery. "He is saturated with God," the Swami told Yogesh. Everyone loved the old man, and his room was a meeting ground for the monks. Here rousing discussions occurred, in which, one can be sure, Yogesh was a lively participant. Indeed, the old devotee, who gave nicknames to all the monks, gave him the name "the Argumentative Swami."[28] And thus Yogesh's convictions, ground and sifted through discussion and argument, through long thought and study of the scriptures, gradually became rock solid.

Recalling those days, Swami Rudrananda once said that Swami Ashokananda was much admired among the younger monks for his bold thought and his daring to question long-established ideas. Swami Rudrananda said modestly that he had been appointed editor of the Math's Tamil-language magazine only because he knew the language. "But I succeeded in that job," he added more modestly still, "because I simply translated Swami Ashokananda's ideas into Tamil."

One of Yogesh's tasks—not self-imposed but officially his—was particularly congenial to him. This was the worship of Sri Ramakrishna. He had the job for a year or two and found ritualistic worship immensely rewarding. Many years later he said of those days, "When I did worship in India, offering all the different elements to God, I felt that each had been absorbed back into the Infinite. The whole world seemed to disappear, to dissolve into a vast silence. I did not have to philosophize about it. I actually felt it. That is worship: you can actually offer a flower to the Infinite." And there was the Personal God, too. Of the same period he would now and then tell of two experiences he had had.

"In the afternoon, between one and four o'clock, Sri Ramakrishna's picture was 'retired.' In South India everyone takes a siesta in the afternoon. Sri Ramakrishna's bedroom adjoined the shrine room, and the picture was put on the bed or cot. One afternoon I dreamt that ants were crawling all over the Master's bed. This disturbed me very much, so I got up to see. One was not supposed to go into that bedroom between one and four o'clock. But, after bathing and changing my clothes, I went in anyway. There were no ants or any such thing, but I was overwhelmed by Sri Ramakrishna's vivid, powerful presence. It was exactly as though he were lying stretched out on the bed. I always felt his presence in that room, but never before as powerfully as this.

"In the same chapel Holy Mother and Swamiji were also worshiped. Swamiji's picture hung on one wall. This was the photograph of Swamiji taken before he came to America, seated in meditation posture, wearing a turban, his eyes wide open, a slight beard. I had performed Sri Ramakrishna's worship. Then I took the tray with the utensils and things on it and worshiped Holy Mother, next Swamiji. Symbolically, I placed a flower on Swamiji's head by putting it on top of the frame. The flower fell off, and I saw Swamiji's eyes blaze in anger and reproach. It was as though he said, 'You cannot do even a simple thing rightly!' His eyes actually flashed; it was not imagination."

"Why should it not be real?" he once said. "Why do you think God is so far off? If you have devotion, you will find living consciousness in whatever you worship."

For that matter, one may find it even where there is no worship. Not far from the Math there was an abandoned temple of Shiva. No one ever went there, and it was in a state of decay. One day Yogesh and some of the other monks went to visit that ruined and presumably empty shrine. And there he felt the vivid, living presence of Shiva. Comparing notes, he found that the others had also felt it. "There is no telling," he said as he related this, "where and how God will feel like manifesting Himself."

There was another Shiva temple closer to the Math, which was very much in use. Four times a day music was played there—appropriate *ragas* for dawn, noon, sunset, and midnight. Once a year a procession of priests would go from the temple carrying the image of Shiva and chanting the Vedas. Here, too, the presence of Shiva was vivid. Yogesh once gave the priest a coconut to be offered, and he felt exalted, as though Shiva Himself had accepted it.

In the years when he himself was not performing the worship, he used to prepare *payash* for the special celebrations. The brunt of the preparations fell on Swami Akhilananda, who would rise at four in the morning, having gone to bed at two. A part of Yogesh's task was to procure a bucket of milk, and to make sure the milk was not watered, he himself would go for it to the cowherd's house. Back at the Math, he would heat the milk, stirring and stirring, until it became thick. Then he would add a handful of rice and again cook and stir until the rice melted away. He would then add rose leaves and rose water, all the while his mind in deep concentration.

Mangoes were also offered from the trees in the garden. The monks would watch carefully over the fruit, waiting for them to get exactly ripe enough; then whoever was doing the worship would offer them to Sri Ramakrishna. "It was not playacting! His presence would be vivid!" Swami Ashokananda said in reply to an unvoiced comment. "It was like offering food to a living being. He was there, warm and loving."

One year, Yogesh (perhaps by then Brahmachari Prajna Chaitanya) performed the worship of Kali—a long elaborate worship that gave him deep satisfaction.

But there was one task that Yogesh had no heart for, even though Swami Brahmananda himself asked him to undertake it. Maharaj loved gardens and gardening, and when he and Swami Shivananda came to Madras in 1921, he had two frangipanis planted, one on either side of the driveway. Yogesh and others were standing nearby, and Maharaj asked Yogesh to water the plants. But while Yogesh had always responded to the beauty and wonder of nature, and loved flowers and plants and trees, he had no feeling for gardening. Evidently Maharaj sensed this, probably from the lack of enthusiasm in the young monk's response, so he added, "occasionally." As it happened, Yogesh watered the plants once. Maharaj apparently overlooked this negligence, and, in spite of it, the frangipanis thrived. Yogesh, however, did not forget his fault. "I am having my punishment now," he said many years later in California. "Endless gardening!" He was referring to the gardens of the San Francisco and Berkeley temples and the massive and interminable preparation of the soil of the Sacramento temple grounds before anything lasting could be grown in it. And there was always the regret of not having done as Maharaj had asked—even though the frangipanis did not, in fact, need much water.

Yogesh also had cause for regret in connection with Swami Shivananda. Telling of this, he said, "There had been a celebration; many people had been in the courtyard eating. The next morning Swami Shivananda asked me to hose off the yard. I knew that in a little while Swami Brahmananda would come to walk there, as was his custom in the mornings, and I thought it would be too bad if the yard was wet. I explained this to Swami Shivananda. He didn't say anything. That was very wrong of me. I should have said, 'Yes, surely, sir, I will wash it down; but could I wait until Maharaj has had his walk?' But he never held it against me. When I came to Belur Math, he was all graciousness towards me." But if Yogesh had said the right thing—and there must have been many times that he did—he would not have so sharply remembered that tiny incident, magnified a hundredfold by the greatness of the Swami.

"The way you think, the way you see things, cannot be applicable to these great ones who are enlightened," Swami Ashokananda once said when speaking of the direct disciples. "Their sense of time is very different from our sense of time. You have to learn their idiom. It took me quite a while to understand this about the disciples of Sri Ramakrishna, who were all knowers of God. In their presence, a little person like myself feels very much awed and becomes conscious of his frailties; he becomes self-conscious. But after some time it occurred to me that they never think ill of people like me. They do not see our faults. It is not that they never see them; occasionally, when it is necessary for our good, they will see our faults and speak of them to us. But in general that is not what they see. They see our potentialities, what we really are. And they shower their affection upon us."

Far from holding Yogesh's neglect of the frangipani plants against him, Swami Brahmananda was pleased by the young novice's application to another task—one that was more congenial to him than gardening. This was to translate into English Part 2 of M's five-part *Kathamrita*. (M had himself translated Part 1 from his original Bengali.) Yogesh wrote out his translation of Part 2 on sheets of brown wrapping paper cut to page size, and that is how it went to the printer.[29] It was an absorbing work, he said, like a deep meditation. The Bengali songs and the possible English translations of them used to go through his head all day; all day he brooded over them. Swami Brahmananda, who was in Madras at the time, once looked into the room where Yogesh was working. "What are you doing?" he asked, and when Yogesh told him, he said, "*Very* good!" That encouragement was one of the many blessings Yogesh had from Swami Brahmananda in Madras.

Indeed, the most memorable events during Yogesh's five-year stay at the Madras monastery were the visits of Swami Brahmananda in the summer and fall of 1921. Actually, it was one long visit, divided in two by the Swami's trip in midsummer to Bangalore. The first part of his stay in Madras was on the occasion of the dedication of the new Students' Home. The Swami, accompanied by Swami Shivananda and a number of other monks, came first to the monastery and then later moved to the Students' Home, which was about a mile away from the Math, and there he lived for some time. It was summer, and most of the students had gone home. The Swami particularly liked one wing of the building, and there in a long veranda-like room he made his quarters; he slept at one end and worked or received people at the other.

Perhaps the best way to relate Swami Ashokananda's further memories of Swami Brahmananda at Madras is to tell them in his own words, as given in his booklet *Swami Brahmananda*.[30] I shall just add here and there other incidents that he told elsewhere.

I had been living in the Madras monastery for a year when Swami Brahmananda came to visit, and now I had an opportunity of serving him occasionally, having conversations with him, and receiving instruction from him. Truly speaking, this was when I came to know him intimately.

As you know, he was looked upon in the Order as the actual representation of Sri Ramakrishna, and they say that seen from the back he even looked like Sri Ramakrishna. I was always fascinated to see him that way. There was such a kindliness about that view of him, such a fatherly attitude, as if your own elderly father were walking ahead of you. . . . Though he rarely gave it outward expression, there was no question of his infinite love. In the kind of love that people ordinarily feel for one another there is a great deal of attachment, which spoils it. But there is a love so unselfish and so pure that once you taste it—and it is something very distinct—you cannot doubt it, and you will never forget it.

While Swami Brahmananda was in Madras I began to feel that love more and more tangibly, and at the same time I began to have an extraordinary experience of him. I naturally saw his form; yet I could never see the clear outline of his body. Just as anything written on paper with ink and exposed to the rain loses its clarity of outline, so his form appeared to me diffused at the edges, as if it were melting into formlessness. . . . And why should it not have been so? He lived perpetually absorbed in Brahman. . . .

The custom of the monks was to salute him every morning and evening and to sit near him for a while. He used to sit in his room in a reclining chair; he would lean back, his eyes half closed, rubbing his fingers together slowly, his mind obviously on the verge of the infinite; then he would get up and pace back and forth and then again sit. Sometimes he would talk to us; sometimes he would just remain silent, absorbed in his own mood. If you had any worry or problem, you might have a little struggle with your mind for one or two minutes, but then you would become serene, calm. His very presence did that.

On the day he arrived I had cause for being unhappy. When I went to salute him the next morning, he called me by name, and all my sorrow immediately vanished, and that was not a solitary instance. The same thing happened to me on several occasions, he would just say a word or two, and my sadness would be dispelled. Once I was feeling depressed and worthless. In the early morning I walked over a bridge and stood looking at the water. When I came back to the Math I was sulky. I passed Swami Brahmananda's room and saluted briefly and went on without speaking. He called after me—so sweetly. I didn't answer. Then he called my name again, and my depression just fell off. He must have known all about it and removed it. Such love he had! As I have mentioned before, I received only the very kindest—I must say, rather, the most affectionate—treatment from him.

When he first arrived at Madras he was not pleased with the spiritual condition of the members of the monastery. After the dedication of the Students' Home [on May 10, 1921], he sometimes scolded very severely, but we never felt any absence of his love. Yes, he would scold and correct faults like a mother who becomes exasperated with a naughty child. But what has that to do with loving? We were his children. We always felt his love.

He used to get up very early and take a two-mile walk and then go to the Math. On this walk he found a vegetable store where fine, fresh vegetables were sold. Once he scolded a monk: "Why don't you buy good vegetables for offering? *I* found where to buy them. Why can't *you* go there?" Another time a man brought a basket of litchi nuts. Swami Brahmananda looked at them and sent them to the room where everything went that was to be offered. Before they had been offered, some of the monks gave them away to people outside the Math. In a few days Swami Brahmananda asked for the litchi nuts. There was hemming and hawing. He insisted on knowing where they were. Then his attendant told him what had happened, and Swami Brahmananda was so angry that he gave him a hard slap on the back. His scoldings were not just for the immediate offense, they were meant to correct other things, and also were meant not just for the person to whom they were directed, but for others also.

The monks used to visit him, mainly in the evening when their work was done. Swami Brahmananda felt at that time that he should point out all that was wrong with the monastery and with the individual monks. He did not mince matters. Whenever we would go to see him, he would bring up our faults and scold us. He said that there was only one boy in whom he found a light burning, however dimly. All the others were dark. Of course, all did not take it well. But, however that might be, it is wonderful to be told one's faults by a person of the caliber of Swami Brahmananda. One evening several of us . . . went to visit Maharaj in the Students' Home, and he gave us a long discourse on how a monk should behave. . . . Another occasion I remember was an afternoon when he spoke to us about the importance of spiritual practice.

Apart from setting the monks right and dedicating the Students' Home, Maharaj did not have what you might call business in Madras; so days passed in unalloyed spiritual joy. He loved music, and it was his practice always to have some musicians with him. Listening to them, he would become rapt in ecstasy. In Madras there was a group of singers devoted to the Divine Mother. Their leader was a great devotee who composed beautiful songs. This group would sometimes come to the Math to sing, and Swami Brahmananda and the other great swamis would sit for hours listening to them. A large crowd would gather. And it was not devotional music alone that Maharaj loved; he was a great connoisseur of music in general.

Many times when I was alone with him, he told me of his own accord certain things which at the time didn't seem relevant. Now I find his words had great meaning. They have oftentimes directed my life and are a source of strength and support to me. . . . The words of so great a soul arise from a deep source, a divine source. . . .

Once, for instance, I was walking along behind him, and he suddenly turned around and said to me, "Look, there are periods in life when the gods, as it were, turn their face away, and whatever you do, you do not succeed. But there comes another time when they turn their face towards you, and whether you do something or not, you are just pushed ahead." Now, why he told me that, I don't know. But I have treasured it. I have found it is a truth applicable to our own existence, because everything is rhythm—rise and fall, rise and fall. You cannot deny it. One morning I went to the Students' Home and found him alone. He himself began to speak about my spiritual practice. I told him what I did. He approved and added here and there, advising me to continue with this amended practice. He laid great emphasis on japa. If I remember rightly, it was on this occasion that he asked me how regularly I meditated. When I told him I meditated regularly except when I was ill, he solemnly said in English, "You are a monk. You have no right to think of the body."

It was no doubt on one of the occasions when Yogesh was alone with Maharaj that he told him of his initiation from Swami Vivekananda during a meditation, saying that perhaps it had been a hallucination. Should he not be initiated by him (Maharaj)? Swami Brahmananda answered, "Swamiji initiated you and you think it was an hallucination. If *I* initiate you, why will you not think *that* was an hallucination?"

That was the third assurance of the reality of his initiation by Swamiji from a direct disciple of Sri Ramakrishna that Yogesh received. But it would take one more (and then some) before his heart would be fully at rest.

After a time, Swami Brahmananda went for a stay in Bangalore, where it was cooler. When he came back to Madras he was a completely different person—full of jollity and laughter. There was no more scolding. All the monks enjoyed him. He would tell stories and

Madras, 1922. *Front row, left to right:* Two unidentified monks, Swami Sharvananda, Swami Shivananda, Swami Brahmananda, Swami Nirmalananda, Swami Anantananda, and two unidentified monks. *Middle row:* Brahmachari Yogesh (later Swami Ashokananda) is the sixth from the far left, and Brahmachari Abani (later Swami Prabhavananda) is the seventh.

laugh like a boy, or like a small child. Everyone was happy. Swami Ashokananda's written account continues:

During [this] latter part of Swami Brahmananda's stay in Madras, after the two worships of the Divine Mother were over, several novices asked him for sannyas, and he consented. On the morning before the ceremony I went to salute him, and he said, "You are also going to have sannyas, are you not?"

Foolishly I replied, "Sir, I shall receive only the novitiate vows." The general rule is that one is not eligible for sannyas until five years after receiving brahmacharya. But Swami Brahmananda could, of course, bestow sannyas upon whomever he wished, whenever he wished. I was told later by his attendant that he had wanted to give me sannyas that day and that I ought to have said, "Sir, since you say so, of course I shall." But I didn't have enough wisdom. . . . Nor did I dream that he would not live much longer. Of course, I was fortunate enough to receive sannyas the following year from Swami Shivananda, and so there is really no reason to regret that lost opportunity.

But it is difficult for me not to feel sorrowful for another reason. Before he left Madras [on November 19, 1921], Maharaj told me twice, "I will stay for a while at Belur Math, but as soon as I go back to Bhubaneswar, you will come there and live with me." Alas, that was not to be. He was never to return to Bhubaneswar from Calcutta. It did not occur to me then, or to anyone else, that Maharaj would die soon. We expected him to live for years; his health was good, his body firm, and he was not yet sixty.

Swami Brahmananda passed away on April 22, 1922. This was, of course, a great blow to Yogesh, because he had been devoted to him and had received so much love and encouragement from him. "I felt," he once said in later years, "that my bridge to eternity had disappeared."

With the disappearance of that bridge, the old doubt once again beset Yogesh, or Prajna Chaitanya, as we shall call him for a while. In September of 1922 he wrote to Swami Shivananda, who was then president of the Ramakrishna Order, telling him of his initiation and of his dream that Swamiji came to his village home and seemed to be his guru. He told him of his periodic uncertainty concerning the whole thing. Was it real? Should he be initiated again? And so on. On September 23, Swami Shivananda replied. This time Prajna Chaitanya did not burn the letter; the days of that wholesale holocaust were over. So Mahapurusha's letter, written in Bengali, still exists.

The envelope was addressed "Br. Prajna Chaitanya, Sri Ramakrishna Math, Mylapore P.O., Madras." The letter read, as translated from the Bengali:

Sri Ramakrishna: The Math Belur, Howrah, Bengal
He is my refuge   23/9/22

Dear Yogesh—

I was not present for two weeks in the Math, hence the delay in replying to your letter. I have read your letter very well, and it occurs to my mind that you do not have any need of taking any other initiation. A person like Swamiji, who is divine in nature, and who is like an incarnation of God, since he has shown all these things in dream [the confirmation of his having been given initiation], then I look upon all this as absolutely true. Sharvananda asked you to take initiation from Maharaj, and you tried for that; but as things happened, that also did not take place. Then you must understand that you do not have any need to take initiation from anybody. Therefore, you carry on as you had done before, without any anxiety. Know it for certain that at Sri Ramakrishna's will Swamiji has been leading you in the right path and will continue to lead on. Please know my earnest affection and blessing. Now everybody is very busy on account of the Divine Mother's worship. Ah, last year about this time we spent in great joy amongst you all in the company of Maharaj in Bangalore and Madras. All of you accept my affection—Ramu, Ramanuja, Rangaswami and other devotees.

This was the fourth confirmation from a direct disciple of Sri Ramakrishna that Prajna Chaitanya had received. Interestingly, it said practically the same thing that Swami Turiyananda's letter had said, and it gave Yogesh much comfort. But it was going to take a further word from Swami Shivananda before the last vestige of doubt was removed from his mind.

Now Prajna Chaitanya wrote again to Swami Shivananda, asking if he would kindly give him *sannyas*. The Swami replied, "Certainly. Come at once."

And so Prajna Chaitanya began to prepare to go to Belur Math. He got together a little money, and so on. But he failed to tell Swami Sharvananda that he was going. There was an uncomfortable relationship between these two swamis. At first it had been very cordial. Indeed, Swami Sharvananda had highly praised Yogesh to Swami Brahmananda when the latter first came to Madras in 1921, saying that he had one of the most brilliant minds in the Order. But later he took offense at something Yogesh had said, or had not said. Thus, when he learned that he was going to Belur Math for *sannyas,* he said to him, "Well, I won't give you any passage money!" "His attitude was a great puzzle to me for a long time," Swami Ashokananda once said in speaking of Swami Sharvananda, whom he much admired. "You see, you have to be awfully thoughtful, and I was not very thoughtful in those days. If I knew something to be true, I would just speak it out; and if I knew something to be false, I would at once say, 'That is wrong! That is not right!' I may have said things like that and hurt Swami Sharvananda somewhere. He was a proud man, and very touchy. I learned later that he thought I looked down upon him. I was careless. Tactfulness is an art one has to learn; if you haven't the art, then at any time you can say the wrong thing. Later, when I understood, I felt bad about it."

However that may be, Brahmachari Prajna Chaitanya (paying his own way) went to Belur Math in the latter part of 1922, and in February of 1923, on the birthday of Sri Ramakrishna, became Swami Ashokananda. (He was first given the name Aseshananda, which was soon changed to Ashokananda.)

IN THOSE DAYS Belur Math was a quiet place, still vibrant with the presence, if not the physical forms, of Swami Vivekananda, Swami Brahmananda, Swami Premananda, and Holy Mother, the last of whom had often come there. Her temple, recently built, faced the Ganges. Swami Vivekananda's temple, still one story high, was to its south, and Swami Brahmananda's, still under construction, to its north. The old Math, where Swamiji had had his room, was further north still. The only other building at that far north end of the Math grounds was the two-story shrine building, which accommodated a dining hall and kitchen on its ground level. An open field, on which a few cows grazed, extended to the south gate and to the small Mission office building. Further south stood an even smaller building, where Josephine MacLeod would later stay. To the west was jungly land. Only a few *gerua*-clad monks strode about the grounds, intent on one duty or another; and now that Swami Premananda was no longer there, even fewer were the devotees who came to visit. On the east the Ganges flowed by silently, serenely; country boats now and then quietly glided by, propelled by oars or poles or coasting with the tide. On the opposite shore only a few small temples and one-story houses overlooked the river; the rest was jungle and, here and there, a ghat.

Swami Ashokananda took his place among the other young monks, some of whom he knew. In the dining hall at Belur Math there was great freedom and camaraderie among the young swamis and *brahmacharins*—particularly (and perhaps only) when the older swamis were not present. If one wanted to defend oneself, fine; one would do so calmly and quietly. If not, one would just swallow whatever gibe was thrown one's way. One day Swami Vijayananda was criticizing the way the monks sang the evening *arati* in the worship hall: some monks did not sing out well enough. He indicated Yogesh Maharaj (in India a monk is often called by his premonastic name followed by the honorific *Maharaj*) and said with great sarcasm, "Here is this mahatma from Madras. He doesn't bother to open his mouth!" Swami Ashokananda said nothing; the taunt was not worth replying to. But later on, Swami Vishwananda, who had known Swami in Madras, went up to the offending swami in anger. "Why did you speak to him like that? Do you know who you were talking to? Do you know who he is?" The young Swami Ashokananda, surprised and touched by this championship, remained silent. Swami Vijayananda backed down; he did not apologize, but other swamis apologized for him. "Don't mind what he says." "He is just like that." "Don't pay any attention." And so on.

Thus Swami Ashokananda came to know and to be somewhat

known among his peers. But nearer to his heart were his solitary hours of meditation on the veranda outside Swamiji's room in the Math building. "It would be a deep meditation," he recalled, "steeped in sweetness." The experience of receiving *sannyas* was profound for him, as it was for many others whose minds had reached that state of renunciation, bringing about a definite exaltation.

When he returned to Madras, he found that there was even a physical change: his skin, ordinarily dark, had become golden. But more than this, he perceived things in a different light—literally. "There was a friend of mine," he once said, "a monk, who around eight or nine in the morning used to stand outside the Madras monastery in the garden. And one day the western sky suddenly appeared to him as if it were a honeycomb from which golden honey was just pouring out. The whole sky was filled with His smile, and one part of it seemed heavy with honey. That was just half of his experience; the other half was that he felt his whole soul was bathed in the utmost sweetness. It was like that every day for many days." Though he had not known it at the time, such an experience is spoken of in a chapter of the *Chhandogya Upanishad* called "Madhuvidya" (The Science of Honey). That sense of extraordinary sweetness stayed with him throughout the rest of his life. Indeed, it was always palpable to those who knew him—whether he was talking informally, laughing, lecturing publicly, scolding, being anything but sweet—it was always there.

DURING HIS LAST YEARS in Madras, Swami Ashokananda and Swami Akhilananda went off on a tour through South India in order to get subscriptions for *Vedanta Kesari* and *Sri Ramakrishna Vijoyam*, the latter a Tamil-language magazine published by the Madras Math. In later years he told of this tour: "We traveled all over to large counties in southern India for two months, going from village to village, staying three or four days in each one. We knew the names of current subscribers and would seek them out. They would become our hosts and would themselves talk to prospective subscribers. In that way, we would get thirty or forty new subscriptions in each village. Wherever we went the people greeted us with great warmth and respect. Everyone we asked subscribed, and people would invite us to dinner, and so on. We could not speak the Tamil language, but it was not necessary, because almost everyone could speak English. Of course they also spoke among themselves in Tamil when we were there. In one village there was a brahmin who invited us to dinner. He showed me a book he was working on—a Tamil encyclopedia. Every day, after his regular work, he would work on the encyclopedia. Little by little he had finished hundreds of pages. That is the way to work!"

"Akhilananda," Swami said, "was all the time talking about Mahatma Gandhi, and I would hurry him along. We covered a large territory, going from one town to another by train. In the towns themselves, we walked. We canvassed for one or two months and got quite a number of new subscribers for both the magazines."

Despite all he had experienced spiritually, Swami Ashokananda in those days occasionally had bouts of depression. One of these struck him while he was on this tour. He was sitting in front of a temple thinking that he was worthless and that God did not know he existed; he couldn't do anything, and so on. Later that day he went to a community outside the town to get subscriptions, and lo! everyone was at once taken by him, made a big fuss over him, and subscribed to the magazines. It was just as though, he said, God had heard him and was showing him that he was worth something and that He *did* know he existed. "In little ways," he said when telling of this incident, "God lets us know that He is paying attention."

"Towards the end of our trip," he related another time, "I discovered that I could understand everything that was said in Tamil. I had not learned the language, but I instinctively understood the sense of what was being said. It was as though the thoughts were communicated to my mind. If one hears a language enough, that happens.

"I am not good at learning languages. Sanskrit came easily to me and also English. But otherwise I have no aptitude for languages. I can't learn them and don't like to study them."

It was a successful tour. The two swamis must have increased the subscriptions to *Vedanta Kesari* and to the Tamil magazine by hundreds, if not thousands. And certainly they enjoyed themselves, for they got on well together, loved one another.

A little later they decided to go for a visit to Belur Math. But on the morning of the day they were to take the train for Howrah, Swami Akhilananda came down with a bad attack of jaundice and told Swami Ashokananda to go without him. Swami Ashokananda would not go; he stayed in Madras and nursed his monastic brother, who became extremely ill. For a time his life was in danger. Convalescing, he had to learn to walk again and for a day or two could take only one step. After he had recovered, he and Swami Ashokananda decided to go to Kodaikanal, a health-resort town in the mountains of South India a few hundred miles from Madras. They went by train from Madras to Madurai, then by bus across the burning plains and up seven thousand feet into the cool mountains to Kodaikanal. There on the top of a knoll was a bungalow that belonged to a Hindu friend. It was not occupied, and the owner had lent it to the swamis to stay in.

The first night in that house, Swami Ashokananda neglected to tuck in his bedcovers, and cold air came up through the cracks in the floor and through the loose blankets. This seriously aggravated the stomach trouble that he had contracted in Madras. He could eat nothing at all, and now Swami Akhilananda, who was supposed to be the ailing one, had to take care of him. After a few days, when Swami's condition did not improve, they went to a government doctor.

"Yes, Swami," said the doctor, "I could cure you. But you wouldn't follow my prescription."

"What is it?"

"To eat meat."

Being from North India, Swami Ashokananda was not averse to eating meat. But how to procure it? In South India it would be considered a disgrace for *sannyasins* to eat meat.

Swami Akhilananda declared that he would go to the kitchen of the European hotel in the town and ask for meat. Swami Ashokananda told him that he would do no such thing. If it became known that a *sannyasin* was asking for meat, it would create a scandal. "You cannot go there in your *gerua* cloth," he said.

"I don't care about the scandal," Swami Akhilananda replied. "I shall go!"

"Brother," said Swami Ashokananda, "whether you care or not, you cannot go!"

It so happened that they knew a man in the town who was a devotee of Sri Ramakrishna. He was a veterinarian and had charge of inspecting the meat at the slaughterhouse and officially stamping it. The swamis told him the problem.

"Surely, swamis," the man said. "I can get you some meat every day. You can pick it up at my office."

So every day the man brought a package of lamb for the young swamis, and every day they picked it up on the way back from their walk. They cooked it in a special cooker they had, arranging it in the morning with charcoal and water and pans one on top of the other. Then they went for a walk. When they returned in an hour or so, their meal would be ready. The first meal of lamb cured Swami Ashokananda's pain.

The walk the swamis took was along a road that followed the contours of a semicircle of hills. There was a bench a mile or so along the way. Here one could sit and look out over the valley. "Just below we could see the plains, hundreds and hundreds of miles of them. And we could see clouds floating below us. They arose from nowhere—from a small whiff of fog the whole valley would quickly fill with clouds. All we could see were these fleecy clouds floating under us. They rarely came above where we were sitting. I knew that it was dark in the plains below; the sun had been blotted out. But we were in the perpetual sun."

Seeing those clouds above the plains in South India reminded Swami Ashokananda of the days during his second year of college in Sylhet, when he had actually had an experience of going beyond the realm of death. Often during his later life, he used the analogy of the valley of clouds to describe that experience, which, he insisted, is available to everyone.

"Like that," he would say, "you literally come to a point where you can say, 'Here ends the kingdom of death, and here I enter into the realm of immortality.' It is almost as demarkable as that. You could almost look at your watch and say, 'Ah, here I have gone beyond the pale of death—today, at this hour, at this moment.' And whatever might happen to the body thereafter, you would not feel anything. For you, death has been conquered for good."

In that South Indian town of Kodaikanal there were (apart from a number of Jesuit priests and many Protestant missionaries) some devotees of Sri Ramakrishna and Swami Vivekananda, who had formed a Vivekananda club. They asked the swamis to give a lecture. Swami Akhilananda was not yet strong enough (nor did he want to lecture), but Swami Ashokananda agreed. It was the first lecture he had ever given. He lectured in English and took as his subject the life of Sri Ramakrishna. The devotees asked a high court judge (a Hindu) to preside over the meeting. A little earlier, this man had had an altercation with the Math in Madras and was not feeling friendly toward Ramakrishna monks. There had been a big flood in South India, and the swamis from Madras had gone to give emergency relief and, later, general relief. (This was where and how Swami Akhilananda had contracted jaundice.) The judge had allocated government funds for relief work, some of which had gone to the Math, but a difference had arisen between him and the Madras swamis. The difficulty was that the judge had been proven wrong and thus had lost face. But the devotees at Kodaikanal had no inkling of this when they asked him to preside at the lecture.

Swami Ashokananda lectured for an hour and a half, but only half finished his subject. At the end he said that he would give another lecture and finish. The judge decided that next time he would ask a Christian missionary to introduce the Swami.

When the day came, a week later, the hall was full of white faces, many of them Protestant ministers. They had come to see the fun, hoping to see the missionary put a swami in his place. But just before the lecture, a devotee came running up to Swami Ashokananda to tell him of this scheme.

"Nothing doing!" said the Swami. "I know his [the judge's] mischief."

So he went to the hall and, looking neither right nor left, strode up to the podium and began his lecture, giving no one a chance to introduce him. After all, this was a continuation of the previous lecture: no introduction was necessary.

This lecture was also an hour and a half long. During the course of it, the Swami, in this second lecture of his life, declared, "Sleep is a disease!" whereupon an English woman burst out laughing. Engrossed in his subject and surprised at the laughter, the Swami repeated strongly, "Sleep *is* a disease." And the laughter stopped. When he finished, the Swami turned to the judge and saw that he was crying. The judge said, "I have read a lot about Sri Ramakrishna, but I have never read anything like this!" Swami demurred, "No, no." But the judge would not be put off. He insisted, "No! I mean it! I am not just saying it. I *mean* it!" He was entirely won over.

This second lecture on Sri Ramakrishna was given the day before the swamis left Kodaikanal. The judge asked Swami Ashokananda to give a lecture on Swami Vivekananda, but there was no time.

The swamis had stayed a month in this mountain place. A few days before leaving, Swami Ashokananda took a plunge into a rushing stream at the foot of their knoll. The mountain water was icy. "My whole body felt filled with new life," he later said. "Completely energized." But there was no chance to repeat this restoring swim, for they had to leave.

Back in the Madras Math, Swami Ashokananda continued to hone his philosophical ideas, discarding those that did not stand up to assault, reexamining for flaws those that did. Indeed, many of his brother monks provided a sort of washboard on which he scrubbed his ideas again and again until they became free of dross and crystal clear. He did not in the least dislike opposition, for while his brothers brought home to him the fact that there were other ways of thinking, this also forced him to clarify and strengthen his way. By the time he left Madras, there was hardly any aspect of the Vedanta philosophy and of Swamiji's teachings that he had not thought through again and again. Whether his conclusions were right or not was, however, still open to question in his mind; his self-confidence was not yet restored.

Perhaps this showed somewhat. In any case, Swami Sharvananda wrote to Swami Shivananda that Ashokananda and Akhilananda were not happy in Madras because of the opposition to their ideas. Swami Shivananda at once called the two "unhappy" swamis to Belur Math. Although they cared not at all about the "opposition," the two swamis were not unwilling to leave Madras for Belur Math at Swami Shivananda's call. And thus, in May of 1925, almost exactly five years to the day since Swami Brahmananda had sent him there, Swami Ashokananda's training at the Madras Math came to an end. It had been an extremely fruitful time, primarily because it had brought him close to both Swami Brahmananda and Swami Shivananda; he had known the blessing of their company for many months, had served them and had felt their love—particularly that of Swami Brahmananda, whose presence in Madras had been like a sun, giving warmth, light, and nourishment continuously.

The train trip to Howrah took a day and a night. The swamis traveled in an intermediate class between first and second. Swami Ashokananda had with him a blanket and a pillow covered with *gerua*. In the compartment was a blustery man who posed as a religious preacher. He asked the Swami to lend him his pillow. Swami said, "It is not right for you to use *gerua* cloth." Whereupon the man said, "Mentally I am a *sannyasin*." Swami replied, "All right; enjoy the pillow mentally!" Everyone in the compartment laughed, for everyone knew the man had no right to ask for the pillow in the first place; it was a sanctified pillow. The man was much provoked, and he abused the Swami right and left. Despite this, Swami Ashokananda later felt badly that he had denied the man the comfort of his pillow and had, moreover, said something to hurt him. It was one of those things that would bother him for many years.

Once again at Belur Math, Swami Ashokananda found that his un-diagnosed stomach pain was still severe. He could not get meat at the Math, so he was sent to live at Advaita Ashrama in Calcutta, where special food was cooked for him. It was, in any case, a fitting place, for the Swami would soon be assigned to the main center of Advaita Ashrama in the Himalayas. Several other swamis lived at the Calcutta branch, and there were of course lively discussions at dinner time. Once the talk was about Swamiji. Swami Nityaswarupananda asked Swami Nirvedananda, who was senior to them all, a question. In the course of his reply, Swami Nirvedananda said that Swamiji had once said his London work was the most important of all his Western work. What could this mean, given that the London center had failed?

At this point Swami Ashokananda said, "There is no esoteric mean-ing. At the time Swamiji said that, the London work was flourishing. It was the most important work at that time. Later the London people lost interest. It's as simple as that."

Swami Nirvedananda bristled and coldly said, "We don't indulge in such higher criticism."

Swami Ashokananda was not at all squelched. He replied, "What higher criticism? It is just a simple fact."

Everyone at the table was aghast that this young swami should thus speak up to Swami Nirvedananda.

Later, Swami Dayananda came to Swami Ashokananda's room up-stairs and gravely said that he should not have spoken that way. He told him that Swami Nirvedananda was an authority on Swami Viveka-nanda. Swami Ashokananda failed to be impressed. "I, too, have read Swamiji," he said.

A few days later Swami Ashokananda visited his mother, who was then living with his married sister (the one whose dowry he had pro-vided) and her husband, an attorney. It happened that one of the

Swami's Sylhet students (the future Swami Shantaswarupananda) was staying at a nearby ashrama, which he and others had founded. So teacher and student, the latter of whom had grown a mustache, again met. Rather than stay with his family, Yogesh Maharaj moved to that ashrama, although it had very few conveniences.

"Those were nice days," Swami Shantaswarupananda much later recalled; "again I was close to him. And then he said, 'You will have to come with me and go to the Math. You will have to join the Order!' He almost compelled me. But by that time I was almost ready to join. Earlier, Swami Ashokananda had made arrangements for the livelihood of my mother, and I was free to become a monk. So then and there it was decided that I should go straight to Calcutta and meet him there. Meanwhile, he went to his native village to visit some friends. Then we met in Calcutta and went together to Belur Math, and I was accepted by Swami Shivananda.

"Swami Shivananda used to show great favor to Swami Ashokananda, very great! When he was in Madras and Swami Shivananda visited the Madras center, he became very familiar with him. And so when Swami Ashokananda told Swami Shivananda that I would rather go to a certain center instead of the one he had assigned me to, Swami Shivananda said, 'All right. Whatever you say. If they require a man, let him go there.' So there I went, and there I stayed for nine years."

When Swami Ashokananda returned to Belur Math, he found to his surprise that the Advaita Ashrama incident, which he had by then forgotten, had caused a commotion. Only Swami Abhayananda, much later universally known as Bharat Maharaj, was delighted with the fearless stand this "audacious" young swami had taken. He would soon be glad to learn that so free a thinker had been asked to go as a worker to the Himalayan center at Mayavati, where he himself was stationed. It was at this time that Swami Ashokananda first met Bharat Maharaj. The two were to become lifelong friends.

4

REFUTING GANDHI'S VIEWS

Now a new chapter in Swami Ashokananda's life began that would create a furor and reveal his mettle. In October of 1925, assigned to Mayavati, he went alone by train to the ashrama in the Himalayan foothills. Swami Vivekananda's English disciples James and Charlotte Sevier had founded the ashrama at his request, and from there one of the Order's English-language magazines, *Prabuddha Bharata,* was edited and published. Swami Vivekananda himself had only twenty-five years earlier visited the ashrama and had dedicated it once and for all to the study and practice of Advaita Vedanta. Nestled in the Kumayun Hills, at over six thousand feet of altitude, it was one of the most coveted posts of the Order—for those monks, at least, who liked solitude and contemplation.

Usually swamis coming from the plains walked from the railway station at Tanakpur to Mayavati, a long trek through deep forests and up and down steep mountains along winding paths. Since Yogesh Maharaj was not in good health, a servant with a pony was sent for him; even then the trek took two days and a night. At the ashrama, Swami Ashokananda found Swami Pavitrananda and Swami Vividisha-nanda, who was then the editor of *Prabuddha Bharata.* These two swamis, it turned out, were both admirers of Mahatma Gandhi's views and policies, whereas Swami Ashokananda was not.

Swami Ashokananda as a young monk at Mayavati (prior to 1930)

Before long, this difference of opinion led to ringing arguments in Bengali. In Madras, Swami Ashokananda had noticed that in every February issue, *Prabuddha Bharata* commented on the annual meeting of the National Congress that had been held the previous December. It had seemed to him that these February editorials were simply echoes of Gandhi and lacked the grandeur of Swami Vivekananda's thought. He had said to himself, "We have much more to say to people than this! Our thought should be of a much higher order!" He now said this aloud and tried to point out the impracticality of Gandhi's economic policy. That was the tenor of his side of the discussions with the two swamis at Mayavati, discussions that were never conclusive. The swamis, shocked at Yogesh Maharaj's views of Gandhi, would go off, he said, on a tangent; he was never able to complete his argument, nor would they listen.

One day in January 1926, the newspapers in which the meeting of the December National Congress was discussed reached Mayavati. To Swami Ashokananda's thorough disgust, Swami Pavitrananda and Swami Vividishananda were all praise for the stand Mahatma Gandhi had taken. "I gave the two swamis a blast," he said. Whereupon Swami Vividishananda mildly asked, "Why don't you write it down?"

"All right!" Swami Ashokananda replied. And then and there he went to his room and steadily wrote the burden of his ideas, giving all the reasons behind them and for once finishing his argument. His paper amounted to a refutation of Gandhi's views as presented at the National Congress of December 1925. Swami Pavitrananda and Swami Vividishananda read it and were silent.

Then, after a time, Swami Vividishananda asked, "Can we have it for the February [1926] editorial?"

Swami Ashokananda said, "Certainly."

It was a courageous move on Swami Vividishananda's part. While Swami Ashokananda only once mentioned Mahatma Gandhi specifically, there could be no question of whose policy the article was criticizing. The nation's hero was being taken to task. The editorial was entitled "Religion in Indian Politics" and read in part,

There is a subtle law which operates in all planes of life. Stated in general terms, it comes to this: Lower interests fulfil themselves by serving the higher ones; the latter in their turn attain fruition by declining to be exploited for lower profits; always the small for the great, never the great for the small.

This is true equally of individuals and nations. No nation can with impunity exploit its higher powers for lesser gains. To do so is to commit a Himalayan blunder, and though it may at first yield success, the end is always disastrous.

We are afraid the Indian National Congress has been guilty of the identical error in its policy and activities during the past few years. It has sought to exploit religion for political ends. And not

a little of the consequent failure and confusion is due to this un-
natural and reverse policy. Up till 1919 . . . the Congress had been
a purely political organization. The special Calcutta session inaugurated the policy of non-violent non-cooperation. This gave
the Congress, in effect and practice, a religious colouring. It
assumed a philosophical tone and preached a certain gospel of
life. . . . Altogether the movement looked more religious than political. Thus was religion made a hand-maiden of politics.

The editorial went on to enumerate and describe the undesirable
consequences, one of which was bitter communal struggles and in-
ternecine quarrels. It then continued,

> The fact is, we are not yet in a position to spiritualise politics.
> Spiritualisation presupposes that every individual should be-
> come conscious of his spiritual nature and make it active in every
> detail of his life. Only when such individuals engage in politics,
> does politics become spiritualised. Spiritualisation of politics
> therefore requires a spiritual reform of stupendous magnitude as
> a preliminary condition. . . . We are aware that there are some
> who can, by virtue of their spiritual eminence, even now take a
> spiritual view of politics. They are Karma Yogins, they have
> spiritualised their whole life. . . . The whole nation or the major-
> ity at least must become such Karma Yogins before Gandhi's
> spiritual politics can be actualised and made a mass movement.
> We cannot manufacture Karma Yogins by the simple passing of
> a resolution!
> We invite the nation to divert its attention from mere political
> agitations to silent and steady works of national reconstruction.
> Let each devote his whole soul to constructive work, not forget-
> ting his spiritual ideal. . . . There are things which the nation has
> cherished with greater love and care than political freedom. To
> their augmentation let our best energies be devoted. In spite

of our cult of non-violence and soul-force, we are yet far from regaining the true spiritual outlook. Let us strive hard to attain the true vision, and if we are sincere, the truth shall reveal itself.

The editorial, short though it was, created an uproar. It was highly praised or irately criticized in intellectual and political circles. The *Modern Review*, a prestigious magazine in Calcutta, quoted extensively from it and gave it much praise. At Belur Math, many swamis, among them Swami Gnaneswarananda and Swami Vishwananda, objected to the temerity of criticizing Mahatma Gandhi. While Gandhi was not yet looked upon as Bapu, the father of his country, he was already highly revered and his ideas were in some quarters considered to be gospel. It was almost a sacrilege to refute him, an outrage for a young unknown swami to openly oppose his views. But for the first time *Prabuddha Bharata* was a voice to be reckoned with. Thenceforth, both Swami Pavitrananda and Swami Vividishananda began to listen to Swami Ashokananda's ideas without brushing them aside. He was more often than not able at least to complete his arguments. More important, his own self-confidence, which had taken such a tumble in Madras, began to come back—now with his prolonged and exacting reflections behind it.

Meanwhile, in the winter of 1925–26, the swamis had decided to have a sort of Sunday meeting. The original purpose was to give Swami Vividishananda practice in lecturing, for in those days he was a painfully slow "public" speaker. At first only four swamis participated: Swami Ashokananda, Swami Vividishananda, Swami Pavitrananda, and one other. They started having impromptu talks, and this developed into Sunday afternoon assemblies, held on the long veranda of the bungalow where the Seviers had lived, down the hill from the main Math building. In the spring of 1926, Swami Pavitrananda returned to Calcutta, where he was manager of the Advaita Ashrama branch. (He would not return to Mayavati until 1930.) But in that same spring, other swamis came up to Mayavati, and most of them attended the meetings, which by then had taken on a well-structured form. On alternate Sundays there would be extemporaneous lectures. One unsuspecting swami would be called upon to speak then and there on a subject secretly chosen for him. He had five minutes to gather his thoughts. Then he had to lecture on the subject from the highest standpoint and to the best of his ability. When he was finished, the others would bombard him with criticism, and he would have to stand his ground. On the other Sundays, the ordeal was not quite as horrendous: one of the swamis would give a prepared talk on a subject chosen six weeks in advance. The others would also have boned up on the same subject and were prepared to question him.

Among the swamis who came to Mayavati in the spring of 1926 were Swami Shuddhananda, a great scholar and assistant secretary of the Order; Swami Madhavananda, then president of Advaita Ashrama and also a great scholar; Swami Nikhilananda, who had just distinguished himself by his good work at the first convention of the Order; Swami Vijayananda; and several others. One Sunday, it was Swami Ashokananda's turn to give the prepared talk. The Swami's subject was cosmology in the Vedanta and Sankhya philosophies. "I described each system," Swami Ashokananda told us, "and raised the question whether or not these were based on direct experience, and if so, why they differed. I pointed out that Swamiji had described the steps of creation, or evolution and dissolution, from direct experience in his poems." At the end, when Swami Shuddhananda, who was presiding, gave his closing talk, he said very gravely, "Today I have learned many new things." Swami Ashokananda's self-confidence went up another notch.

WHILE SWAMI MADHAVANANDA was at Mayavati, Swami Vividishananda, whose term as editor of *Prabuddha Bharata* was up and who from the start had a fondness for Yogesh Maharaj, suggested that he become the next editor. He had, after all, proved his ability with his "Religion in Indian Politics." Swami Madhavananda agreed. And thus Swami Ashokananda took over the editorship of the magazine in June of 1926.

He found it to be a monumental task. The editor was responsible for writing almost one-third of each issue and for editing and often rewriting the contributed articles. He of course wrote the editorials; also, he translated from Bengali and Sanskrit and wrote book reviews, the section entitled "Notes and Comments," and other articles as well. The first issue under his editorship came out in August of 1926. It surprised almost everyone.

While in Madras Swami Ashokananda's brother monks had come to know him, at Belur Math and Mayavati, except for a few, they knew him not at all. He seemed witty, friendly, but a maverick in his thinking and outspoken about it. Beyond that, nothing was known. He seemed to have no spirituality, no practicality, nothing but intellect, which some found too sharp for comfort. But lo! here was a deeply thoughtful, spiritually oriented, yet down-to-earth editor!

Shortly after the August 1926 issue of *Prabuddha Bharata* appeared, Swami Ashokananda's work with Romain Rolland began—a tremendous task on top of his editorial duties. As is well known, Romain Rolland had become acquainted with Sri Ramakrishna through Dhan Gopal Mukherjee and with Swami Vivekananda through Josephine MacLeod. The vivid accounts of these extraordinary souls by these two enthusiasts had fired Rolland to write their biographies. He wrote to Swami Shivananda for information, and Swami Shivananda, in turn, directed him to Swami Ashokananda. Thus a prolonged correspondence began, in which Romain Rolland would ask questions and Swami Ashokananda would reply in detailed letters, which sometimes ran to forty or fifty typing-paper-size pages (in India such pages are almost legal size in length). He wrote in longhand and made longhand copies of every letter.[31]

A few comments regarding this correspondence can be found in

Rolland's published journal for 1915–43, entitled *Inde*. Two excerpts, as translated from the French by Maryse Bader, read,

> October 1927.—A very lengthy and interesting letter from Swami Ashokananda (11 September) on the current development of the Ramakrishna Mission, and on the position taken by the Order in view of the current social problems of the present time. A whole chapter, precise and documented, most intelligent, which I will use in the conclusion of my future work. I answer the Swami, October 4th. On one point, question his thought. He believes that the link which reveals itself between the Vedantic ideas and certain ideas or tendencies in the Occident, comes totally from the modern-time spreading of Vedantic thoughts. In truth, I told him, "This thought, this link rests on the identical foundation of human nature, and especially of the vast Indo-European family." I recall Pascal's words: "You would not be looking for me, had you not already found me."

> December 1927.—Continuing correspondence with the Ramakrishna Mission. Swami Ashokananda is a man of admirable activity, with a precision which is not Oriental. Not only does he give answers to all my questions, with thorough articles full of documentation, but he also puts me in contact with other remarkable personalities of the Order. It is thus that I receive letters from Sister Christine and from the sage Boshi Sen, who has taken the trouble to gather for me all the parts of Vivekananda's writings, defining his attitude with regard to science.[32]

The correspondence continued until Rolland's book *(Prophets of the New India)* was finished in 1930 and published by Advaita Ashrama, turning out to be a landmark in Indian bookmaking.[33]

When he became editor of *Prabuddha Bharata*, Swami Ashokananda wanted to enlarge the format of the magazine so it could accommodate more material—two-thirds more. At first this idea was opposed by the president of Advaita Ashrama, who was then Swami Vireswarananda, but the trustees of the Order approved of it, and in January 1929 the new format with larger pages and two columns to a page appeared. Its frontispiece was a facsimile of Swami Shivananda's benediction in his own hand: "My blessings on the Prabuddha Bharata in its new form. May Swamiji's message reach through it a wider public." Until the present day, *Prabuddha Bharata* has retained this more generous format.

In his editorial in the February 1929 issue, Swami Ashokananda took up the urgent and huge question of how India could enter the modern world and yet retain her spirituality. The editorial was entitled "Spiritualising Nationalism." It was, in a sense, a reply to Mahatma Gandhi's policy of home weaving and so on, but it was also in itself a stirring, well-reasoned, well-written exposition of how India could wade in the materialism inevitably attendant upon industrialization and national prosperity without soiling her ideals; how she could, in short, grow in spirituality while growing in material strength and well-being. Let us quote a little. He asked,

> Shall we sacrifice our national ideals for the sake of India's external prosperity? *No, that cannot be.* Are we then to spiritualise politics? How can that be accomplished? This, then, is the crucial question.

He looked at all angles of this question, explored how it had been answered in the past and elucidated how it must be answered in the present and future. He pointed out the inadequacy of Mahatma Gandhi's policy and, finally, he set forth and clarified at length Swami Vivekananda's solution to this complicated but deeply critical problem. In brief,

> Swamiji believed that the industrialism of the West will have its full sway in India, however vicious it might be; and he believed that India would become a great industrial nation. . . . He

felt all the iniquities of present-day industrialism, with its degradation of the mind and exploitation of the weak. But he also felt that, good or evil, India cannot escape it, and the best thing for her would be to face it and make the best of it. . . . Modern India thus finds a strong support in Swamiji in her bid for industrial greatness. . . .

Did he also want the political emancipation of his country? Certainly he did. His ideal of freedom was absolute, as he often declared: it must be the freedom of the spirit, of the mind and also of the body. All these he wanted for his country. He devoutly wished that India should be great materially, intellectually, politically, and above all spiritually. Surely Indian nationalism also seeks as much. . . .

His support of nationalism does not mean that he also advocated the means that are employed by our politicians in imitation of the West. The aspirations of modern India find place in Swamiji's vision, but their means do not. . . . He prescribed a new motive of service and struggle—the struggle for self-realisation. Every man and woman of India must be filled with a burning enthusiasm for spiritual self-realisation. And when they will, with such a motive, devote themselves to the service of India, they will not only achieve materially and intellectually, but also spiritually. . . .

Let self-realisation be the battle-cry of New India. The self is endowed with infinite power, illumination and joy—let this be brought home to every man and woman, every boy and girl of India. Let them feel that life's only quest is this self-realisation and let everyone start from wherever one is at present, towards the goal. Let the consciousness of this inherent power and greatness spur everyone on his way.

Naturally this consciousness will not in all or even most cases, appear as a struggle for spiritual self-realisation. That will only be in cases of a minority, at least in the beginning. To most men, it will be a consciousness of the power of endurance, concrete material achievement and fearlessness. To many others it will be the incentive to high intellectual and cultural achievements. But if the consciousness of the real nature of the self be there—and we should never cease to proclaim it to all and keep it ever before the nation—this crude self-realisation will not be the last item of achievement; the original motive will by its very impetuosity impel and drive us on to higher and higher self-realisation, till we reach the very heart of the Eternal. *It all depends on the original impetus.* This alone will determine the direction of our progress and its destination. On this again depends how much we can be affected by the evils that infest the material aspects of nationalism. If the original impetus be not powerful enough to take us beyond the planes of politics or industrialism, there is every danger of our being stuck in the morass of moral complications which are so luridly evident in Western nationalism. So the proclaiming of the glory of the Atman is one of the ways of reconciling politics, etc., with the spiritual ideas of India.

Swami Ashokananda went on to speak of the need for the practice of *karma yoga,* of practical spirituality, of the service of man as the worship of God, and the necessity for men of spiritual realization to lead the country. "And thus," he concluded, "shall the nation advance, realising all the phases of the self, material, mental and spiritual, avoiding evils and consuming them where necessary, towards that Summit where the light of Heaven kisses the crown of India."

Under the editorship of Swami Ashokananda, *Prabuddha Bharata* became widely read and acclaimed. His editorials were directed toward India's highest spiritual ideals and at the same time were stirring calls to the country to awake and take her place in the stream of modernity and the congress of nations—to become active, strong, and progressive. In open opposition to the views of Mahatma Gandhi, the Swami believed firmly that both spirituality and industrialization were possible. With care and vigilance, they could go hand in hand to the glory of the nation. In this he followed Swami Vivekananda and urged everyone to do the same. Like the first editorial that Swami Ashokananda wrote in 1926, the succeeding ones were highly praised and extensively quoted from by the *Modern Review*. They came as bombshells not only to the intellectuals of India but, as one young swami would later discover, to the village people as well. They were read assiduously, discussed, and even written about.

But while Swami Ashokananda's editorials were perhaps the most impressive contributions to *Prabuddha Bharata*, they were only a small part of each issue. The other material was of great interest and, perhaps thanks in some part to the editor, well written and always readable. This was of course in the days when everything about the Ramakrishna movement was new; there was an abundance of unpublished material of immense value. Each issue was a feast—and a well-balanced one. There were articles of historical, philosophical, and topical interest written by eminent scholars, both lay and monastic; there were monographs on a variety of subjects written by Swami Ashokananda himself, and book reviews, also written by the editor, in which he praised (sometimes highly) or demolished (sometimes scathingly) some current book. There were English translations of Sanskrit scriptures—notably, *Vedantasara* and *Ashtavakra Samhita*—and scholarly dissertations on Indian philosophy. There was something for everyone, and all of it was good reading and full of substance.

One book to receive the Swami's particular scorn was Katherine Mayo's infamous *Mother India*, which threw venom over the face of India with its many lurid and scurrilous falsehoods.[34] Not only did Swami Ashokananda hold it up to ridicule and the light of hard, indisputable facts, but so also did other writers. They had a field day with this book, until it lay in shreds. Another book went to the opposite extreme, glamorizing India and the life of Sri Ramakrishna beyond all reason. This was Dhan Gopal Mukherjee's *The Face of Silence*, which had served as one of Romain Rolland's inspirations.[35] In an article entitled "A Biographical Fiction?" Swami Ashokananda highly commended Mukherjee's plan of presentation and then went on to say in part, "Never have we been so sorely disappointed as in this book. It has been like looking on a fair face fraught with insanity. . . . The book is a strange medley of facts and unjustifiable fancies."

The Swami's own reading was, as always, extensive. At Mayavati he had access to many Western magazines, such as *Harper's Magazine*, the *Century*, *American Weekly*, the *Forum* of New York, and the *Realist* of London. Through such reading he had his finger on the pulse of world thought; it gave him an overall view of Western life and ideas as they were then. He plumbed the shallowness of the West's best thinkers, including Bertrand Russell and George Bernard Shaw, and sensed the depths of the West's spiritual hunger.

In March 1929, there appeared in *Prabuddha Bharata* under the title "The Thought of Mahatma Gandhi" a three-and-a-half-column review of a book written by an Englishman in praise of Gandhi's policy of home weaving.[36] Using this book as a springboard, the Swami discussed the impracticality, inappropriateness, and inadequacy of Gandhi's economic program.

Mahatma Gandhi's reply (urged by his Bombay followers) came out the following July in his paper *Young India*. "He should not have answered," Swami Ashokananda would later remark. "It was not a good reply." Among other less-than-strong points, Gandhi deplored as "sacrilege" Swami Ashokananda's quotations from Swami Vivekananda. In "Notes and Comments" of the September issue of *Prabuddha Bharata*, to the shock of some and the delight and serious reflection of others, Swami Ashokananda devastated Gandhi's article.

In the September issue of *Young India*, Mahatma Gandhi replied again in an article entitled "Reason v. Authority." Again, he did not address the main issue of the spinning wheel versus the industrialization of India. Rather, he devoted his reply to a continuation of his criticism of Swami Ashokananda's "inferential invocation of the authority of the illustrious dead in a reasoned discussion, [which] should be regarded as sacrilege," and went on to enlarge upon this thesis. In the November issue of *Prabuddha Bharata,* Swami Ashokananda made short work of Gandhi's reply. And in the November and December issues of the magazine there appeared a long two-part article by "A Seeker of Truth," entitled "Politico-Economic Reconstruction of India," in which the truth-seeker's ideas (suspiciously similar to the editor's) were clearly set forth. In the first three months of 1930 Swami Ashokananda produced collections of quotations from Swami Vivekananda's *Complete Works,* in which Swamiji had stated his belief that India should be industrialized.

In the April and May 1930 issues of the magazine there appeared two articles by a professor of economics, Shiv Chandra Datta, entitled "Gandhi and the Economic Problems of India." These articles, as the editor explained, minutely and completely set forth Mahatma Gandhi's economic policies without comment (and with a perfectly straight face). It was a "dispassionate account." "Our readers know," the editor wrote, "that *Prabuddha Bharata* has not found it possible to support the economic policy of Mahatma Gandhi in toto. But it is due to that great soul that we give our readers an idea of what that economic policy is."

In the November issue of 1930, a balancing article, or editorial, appeared, entitled "The Economic Policies of Swami Vivekananda." And there the matter rested, both sides aired. Many years later, Sankari Prasad Basu wrote of this historic exchange in his book *Economic and Political Ideas: Vivekananda, Gandhi, Subhas Bose:* "Going through all the articles of Ashokananda and replies of Gandhiji, we [have] to admit that the latter's expositions were no match for Ashokananda's sturdy and comprehensive intellect. Gandhiji simply reiterated his faith with great sincerity, and that is all. Ashokananda in his turn was also an idealist, a man of religion, but spirituality did not obstruct him to see and understand the material needs of the millions."[37]

Meanwhile, Volume 2 of Mahatma Gandhi's *My Experiments with*

Truth had come out in 1929 and was reviewed in the March 1930 issue of *Prabuddha Bharata*. Swami Ashokananda had high praise for the book and great admiration for the man. "Many of the conclusions arrived at by Gandhiji through his experiments may not coincide with the experiments of others," he wrote; "but the rigidity with which he could stick to his purpose will be an object-lesson to all idealists, to all who want to live their lives to a purpose and not wallow in the mire of sense-enjoyment. . . . His autobiography . . . will be read with reverence as long as noble ideas do not fail to inspire human beings." Although Swami Ashokananda would always object to Gandhiji's policies, the sacrifice and dedication of the man touched him so deeply that years later, when Gandhiji was assassinated, for one week he could not restrain his tears from often welling up into his eyes and running down his cheeks.

Swami Ashokananda's method of writing editorials was almost never laborious. For four or five days before the actual writing, his mind would gravitate around a subject. In later years, for the benefit of his disciples who were trying to write, he explained his procedure: "I would let my mind gather around one subject, and I would dwell on it. Then I would think of an opening sentence. In the morning when I woke up I would go at once to my desk and start writing. I would write on and on until the editorial was finished. It would then be about twelve o'clock noon. I would have lunch with the other swamis, and in the afternoon I would read over what I had written. Only a word here and there would need changing. I would send the manuscript (of five or six thousand words) just as I had written it to Calcutta. The galley proofs were sent to Mayavati for correction. The page proofs were corrected in Calcutta; Swami Vijayananda [the swami who had taunted him at Belur Math] was the proofreader."

It was, though, not Swami Vijayananda but Swami Vishwananda (who earlier had come to Yogesh Maharaj's defense on another matter) who now objected strenuously to his criticism of Gandhi's policies. He was now head of the Bombay center and wrote directly to Swami

Shuddhananda, then general secretary of the Order. He told him to instruct Swami Ashokananda to stop his outrageous criticism of Gandhi. Swami Vishwananda's letter referred specifically to the review of the book on home weaving, which had appeared in the March 1929 issue of *Prabuddha Bharata.*

In the autumn of 1929, when Swami Ashokananda came down from Mayavati to Calcutta, Swami Shuddhananda showed him Swami Vishwananda's letter. They were standing on the veranda outside Swamiji's room at Belur Math. The letter was like a spark to an explosive. His eyes flashing and his stance regal (as they were when years later he related this incident), Swami Ashokananda said, "Swami Vishwananda has no right to interfere with what I do! I am not expressing my own personal opinion in *Prabuddha Bharata,* but writing for the Order, which is far greater than Gandhiji!"

Swami Shuddhananda said nothing. As for Swami Shivananda, although he regularly read *Prabuddha Bharata,* he made no comment about its criticism of Mahatma Gandhi's policies, thus tacitly giving his approval. And the young editor went on as before.

5

FIRE SONG

In the 1920s Mayavati was a place of tigers (some man-eaters), black bears (some very big and fierce), and wild boars. Now and then this wildlife played its part in the life of the ashrama. There was, for instance, Bharat Maharaj's encounter with a tiger, the story of which has become famous in the annals of Mayavati. Swami Ashokananda, who was there at the time, used to tell it, and through it his disciples came to know Swami Abhayananda—"Fearless Swami"—long before any of them met him. One day he was walking along a trail through the forest. Rounding a curve, he found a huge tiger lying square in his path. He and the tiger looked one another in the eye. Bharat Maharaj, a thorough monist and even then an *atmajnani* [a knower of God], wondered whether his body was reacting to the threat of death. He put his hand inside his tunic to feel his heart, and was filled with joy to discover that it was beating at its normal pace. He had indeed conquered fear! He and the tiger continued to appraise one another, and at length the tiger got up and walked away. Bharat Maharaj himself once told the present writer this story. "I will never forget the joy of that encounter!" he said.

As for the bears, in the years when the acorns were thick on the oaks, they used to come around the ashrama in large numbers. At night

Swami Abhayananda (Bharat Maharaj) at Mayavati, 1927

they would climb the trees, and all night one could hear them fighting and growling. In the daytime they would hide. But once "Fearless Swami" and Swami Ashokananda saw two black bears on the hillside across the deep gorge by the ashrama. "They were huge!" Swami recalled. "Although they were some distance away, one could see how enormous they were. And the black bears at Mayavati were known for their fierceness." To provide bear meat for the ashrama, Swami Abhayananda at once took off after them with a gun, despite Swami Ashokananda's alarmed protests. Unable to stop him, Swami sent two armed servants after him. But by the time Bharat Maharaj reached the other side of the gorge, the bears, to his disappointment, had gone. He was convinced that the noisy servants had driven them away. (As an addendum to this story, Bharat Maharaj told the present writer that on the way back he and the servants found a piece of jewelry lying by the trail, a pendant, that Josephine MacLeod, to her intense and vociferous dismay, had lost. This was not just any piece of jewelry, but the Lalique reliquary she had had made to hold a single hair of Swamiji's, more precious to her than diamonds.)

There were not only tigers and bears, there were also their prey. One autumn day, Swami Ashokananda could hear a deer being chased by a tiger in the gorge below. He heard the deer running, then a scream and a gurgling sound, and he knew the tiger had caught the deer. A man who was working as the postman at the ashrama—a disciple of one of the great swamis, though not a monk—also heard this drama taking place, and went out with his gun and dog. Seeing this, Swami Ashokananda called to Bharat Maharaj, "That man is insane! We must go after him!" So they, and others, went after the postman. They found the deer, which the tiger had had time only to kill, not to eat, and they cut up the meat, knowing that the tiger was nearby, furious and intent, watching them. It was dangerous work. They held the dog so that the tiger would not have that small recompense for its stolen meal.

"A tiger does not deserve any moral consideration!" Swami Ashokananda later declared when accused of having robbed the tiger of its rightful quarry. "A tiger is a murderer!" And so the swamis had venison without a qualm, perhaps remembering the tiger stories current at Mayavati in which man-eaters had many a time killed unwary villagers going home at night, and perhaps thinking they had served the tiger well.

And there were rats, big furry rats that came out of the woods into the houses, including the editorial office, which was separate from the main building and where Swami Ashokananda worked and, to save time, also slept. He waged, he said, an intensive campaign against these rats, setting many traps. "And I killed them. You will not like that, but I had to do it. It was the only way." After a while the rats learned that the editorial office was not a wholesome rendezvous, and they stopped coming.

Mayavati was also a place of deodars and wild rhododendrons that turned the hillside across from the ashrama flaming red. Beyond the Seviers' bungalow was a double line of huge deodar trees on either side of a wide path that followed the contour of the hill. The thick branches, reaching toward one another, formed a roof, making the path a sort of cloister. Here Swami Ashokananda used to walk in the afternoons, sometimes with other monks, talking, enjoying the loveliness of the hills and trees. One day when he came to walk there, he found to his horror that the lower branches of the deodars had all been cut and were lying on the ground. It was a scene of devastation. The natural thick roof was gone. He learned that a European who had been staying at the ashrama had persuaded the monks to cut the branches so that knots would not be formed in the wood and the trees, therefore, would have more value as lumber. The knots had of course been formed long since, and the aesthetic value of the trees had apparently not occurred to anyone, not even, it would seem, to Bharat Maharaj, who was responsible for the gardens and grounds. In those days Bharat Maharaj, though older than Swami Ashokananda, was a young monk who could be overridden by his seniors, and perhaps he had been. In any case, the roofed-over path was destroyed forever.

On some of his solitary walks along the hilly trails, Swami Ashokananda would pick yellow berries from bushes that grew along the way. He also picked ripe peaches, apples, and mangoes from the ashrama's orchards and took them to the editorial office, where he would peel and eat the luscious fruit, some of which was bat-bitten but (he assured his listeners) uncontaminated. This was probably the only food he could eat, for he still had severe stomach pain and indigestion. But it occurred to him that he was being selfish in taking the fruit as it ripened, and so he stopped.

The wildflowers were profuse. One year Swami Ashokananda in-
stigated a wildflower show—an exhibit of every kind of wildflower
the monks could find, and there were hundreds. These were gathered,
identified, labeled, and displayed in the library and living room of the
ashrama in whatever vessels could hold water. It was a joyful celebration of spring. They had a special feast on the exhibit day and vowed to
have another such celebration the following year. (Whether a repeat
exhibit took place or not, one does not know.)

"We had lots of fun!" Swami Vividishananda later recalled. On
beautiful clear days, the monks went on picnics to a lookout place up
the mountain. There Swami Ashokananda would read aloud Bengali
dramas, which they all enjoyed. From that lookout spot, the scenery
was, of course, spectacular, particularly in autumn, when the sunlight
was golden and the distant mountains, foothills of the snow peaks,
were mauve, range on range. On most autumn days the snow peaks
were clearly visible, towering in the north behind the lower mountains
like massive white thunderclouds, their outline sharply etched against
a blue sky, far too high to be part of the earth. Yet, incredibly, earthly
mountains they are—or, perhaps, divine presences brooding over
India, aloof and yet sheltering.

And then would come the winter, precluding picnics and wildflower
exhibits. The days and nights would be freezing cold, the only heat
coming from the open fireplace in the main building. But the surroundings were no less beautiful in their wintery way than in the spring and
autumn. In his editorial in the January 1927 issue of *Prabuddha Bharata*
(his second winter in Mayavati), Swami Ashokananda wrote of the
snow:

> As we write these lines, the snows are falling, falling steadily
> round us in the midst of a preternatural silence. The hills have
> become all white and the plants are covered and overladen with
> the white flakes. There is not the slightest breath of wind, and the
> silence is so profoundly deep that we seem almost to hear the

whispers of the gods, and to gaze on the effulgent white form of the Great God Shiva in the innermost depths of meditation. We are no longer on the earth, we seem transported into the very heart of the Absolute! . . .

The long range of snows, spread before our windows for a continuous three hundred miles, is a magic field of colours. Scarcely does the dawn peep through the dark upon our side of the mortal world when the snow-mountains flash light pink. And lo! In a few moments the pointed crest of Trisul, white and burnished like a silver tabernacle, is shot with dazzling fire, and in a trice the whole range is flooded with gold. Then as the sun rises high, the snows grow whiter and whiter, looking the very emblem of Divine purity and majesty against the deep blue of the sky. By and by the day declines and the evening sun enwraps them with its golden rays and the golden mountains hang between heaven and earth like a mystic dream become real.

There was more than natural beauty at Mayavati—much more. At least once, Swami Ashokananda felt the vivid, living presence of Shiva everywhere, inside and outside, day and night. The experience lasted about two weeks, and through it he understood what is meant when it is said that the Himalayas are filled with the presence of God.

And Swami Vivekananda, too, was there. At Mayavati, Swami Ashokananda had one of his very vivid dreams of him, in which Swamiji confirmed his initiation. "In the dream I would not ask him," Swami Ashokananda said, "although it was in my mind." Then he saw Swamiji nod, and he said, "But how did you know what I was thinking?" Swamiji replied, "Oh, I know what you are wondering. Yes, it is true, I did give you initiation. Now, let me teach you how to sing; you have a good voice." He taught him the Fire Song, a song that when sung well makes everything burst into flame. "You don't believe it?" Swami Ashokananda challenged his listeners. "Yes, that song could generate tremendous power! Well, in my dream Swamiji taught me to sing it. We sang it together. Such power was created that it woke me up! My dream broke."

AT THE END of 1927, Swami Ashokananda went down to the plains. He had, as he said later, been carrying a heavy burden in his mind. What that burden was he did not say, but his mind was troubled with unhappy thoughts, which he could not throw off. Worse, he had failed to tell Swami Shivananda of this mental state when, in 1925, he left Belur Math for Mayavati, and this, too, bothered him. So in November of 1926, he wrote a long letter to the Swami, telling him of the condition of his mind, asking him to forgive him for having silently entertained such a state for so long, and asking permission to come to see him. Swami Shivananda answered immediately with a loving letter, in which he asked him to come to visit him in Benares, where he was recuperating from an illness. As soon as Swami Ashokananda read that letter, everything that had been oppressing him cleared from his mind—never to return. Such was the graciousness and greatness of Mahapurush Maharaj. Although the clouds lifted, Swami Ashokananda went anyhow to Benares in the Christmas season of 1927. At that time he had no private talks with Swami Shivananda, for everything had been said in their correspondence. But he went with the other monks to see the Swami in the mornings and evenings, and the Swami was very gracious to him. The beauty and spiritual atmosphere of Benares impressed Swami Ashokananda deeply. Many years later, while holding a class on the *Manisa Pancikam*, he spoke of the wonder of that ancient city:

"It is a great delight to come to the Ganga in Benares. One winds one's way along the narrow lanes, which are flanked on both sides by little temples and shrines. And there it is! The Ganga itself is tremendously wide; it is curved like a crescent moon, and you find the whole city standing on the bank, tiptoe in expectation, as if seeing its own face in the calm waters. It is colorful and beautiful. There is not a single city in the world that has such a display of the religious sense as the city of Benares."

From Benares he went to Calcutta, where Swami Shivananda had also gone, and at that time he saw him privately and could ask questions of him. One of these was whether, if he were ever asked, he should go to a foreign country. Evidently Swami Shivananda then said yes, for that is indeed what he would say later.

While he was in Benares, Swami Ashokananda had gone to Swami Satprakashananda's room. The Swami had been staying in Benares holding classes on the Gita. When Swami Ashokananda entered his room, he saw him sitting erect, reading some scripture or another and holding a towel to his face. The towel was covered with blood! The Swami was having a terrible nosebleed. Swami Ashokananda was horrified. "What are you doing!" he exclaimed. He learned that Swami Satprakashananda was quite ill.

"You must leave Benares!" Swami Ashokananda said. But Swami Satprakashananda replied that it was a great good fortune to teach the Gita in Benares. "You will have to forgo your good fortune!" Swami Ashokananda replied, and insisted that Swami Satprakashananda come with him to Mayavati and work on the *Prabuddha Bharata*. And Swami Ashokananda had his way.

In the spring, the two swamis set off from Calcutta to Mayavati. The train trip was fine and beautiful. For miles and miles there were red-flowering trees in bloom on each side of the tracks. But when they left the train, the situation changed. The village of Tanakpur at the foot of the hills, where one generally stopped for the night on the way to Mayavati, was infected with bubonic plague, and the travelers were advised not to stop there but to continue up the mountain. It was a journey of two days and a night, but because of the prevalence of tigers, which, if they were not man-eaters, were fond of horses, one could not travel at night, and Swami Ashokananda knew from experience that they must reach a certain inn before dark. They stopped to have lunch by the road. Swami Satprakashananda ate very slowly and methodically and "with a great deal of deliberation." He had heard that one must chew each mouthful a certain number of times and then wait a certain number of minutes before swallowing. "I told him he must hurry," Swami Ashokananda later recalled. "But he would not." Thus it was that as night was beginning to fall they had to pass through a dark and melancholy forest in a valley between two mountains. It was full of tigers and bears, and probably other wild animals looking for dinner. It would have been suicide to spend the night in the open. Finally, they managed to get through the forest and reach the inn on the next mountain.

"It was in order to get here before nightfall that I asked you to hurry," Swami Ashokananda finally explained, afraid earlier to push his brother too much. The latter was already much upset, for not only had he been hurried at lunch but his large bundle of books, all annotated and invaluable to him, had been inadvertently left behind during a transfer in Lucknow from a carriage to a train.

At Mayavati, though Swami badly needed an assistant, he did not put pressure on Swami Satprakashananda to do much work, for the Swami was visibly ill. The following year, another assistant editor came—Swami Nityaswarupananda. But he, too, did not do much work as an assistant, for at that time he could not see that intellectual endeavors, such as bringing out the *Prabuddha Bharata*, were of any use. "He wanted just to meditate," Swami Ashokananda related. "He was like a mule," he added affectionately. Once Swami Ashokananda asked the younger swami how he would like best to spend his time. "In meditation," Swami Nityaswarupananda replied, "meditation and talk about God." Swami Ashokananda said he would like only meditation and listening to devotional music. Both swamis, as it happened, spent the rest of their lives engaged in strenuous activity.

"Swami Nityaswarupananda used to bring a big alarm clock to the editorial office in the morning," Swami Ashokananda recalled, "and when it was ten o'clock, he would leave." He was then working on his translation of the *Ashtavakra Samhita* under the direction of Swami Madhavananda.[38] He used to consult Swami Ashokananda about it regularly, and Swami would make him rewrite things endlessly, "not by telling him how to revise what he had written, but, rather, by making the revision come from him. It would take a long time—sentence by sentence wrung from him. He used to talk back, too. I was so fond of him, he felt free to do that." With Swami Ashokananda's encouragement, he finally finished his translation of the *Ashtavakra Samhita*, which appeared monthly in *Prabuddha Bharata* from January 1929 to December 1931. He also wrote some beautiful articles—one on the life of Swami Premananda, for the October and November 1929 issues.

During 1929, the young Swami Nityaswarupananda went back to the plains and to East Bengal and Assam to get subscriptions for the magazine. "It brought about a revolution in his thinking," Swami Ashokananda said. "He found that the people in the villages who subscribed to *Prabuddha Bharata* and whom the Swami visited in order to get names of prospective subscribers were deeply impressed with the editorials. They had read them and reread them, underscored many passages, made notes in the margins, and wanted to talk about them. They wanted to know what the editor was like. 'Is he a very old swami?' they asked." From all this Swami Nityaswarupananda realized that intellectual work went far in influencing people. He wrote two long letters to Swami Ashokananda about it. The latter did not save them.

In the late autumn of 1928 Swami Ashokananda again went down to Calcutta. He stayed at Advaita Ashrama, which at that time was housed in a rented building at 182A Muktaram Babu Street, next to a junkyard. It was very hot and very noisy, and perhaps for the first time in his life, he found it hard to write. He obtained permission to move to another place, and there, with Swami Shantaswarupananda, who was now a *sannyasin*, as his attendant, he moved to a sort of hut—a crude place with no desk and very little other furniture. Here, too, he could not write. But he forced out a long editorial on a political question, which he felt was not good. Because of this dismal experience, he would later undertake a sort of editorial marathon, of which more later.

It may have been during that same year of 1928 that for three days he was too ill when he came from Mayavati to Calcutta to go to Belur Math to pay his respects to Swami Shivananda. Many of his friends told him that when he did go he would receive a scolding for taking so long. But when, after three days, he finally went to Belur Math, Swami Shivananda took one affectionate look at him, and the first thing he said was, "Oh, you will be cured. In two weeks you will be cured!" And in two weeks Swami Ashokananda was well. "Just endless kindness!" he later said.

It was no doubt at the close of 1928 that Swami Shivananda asked Yogesh Maharaj to write a book on spiritual practice and serialize it in *Prabuddha Bharata*. Swami Ashokananda protested his unworthiness, but when Swami Shivananda persisted, he agreed to try to write such a book under a pseudonym. And thus "The Practice of Religion" by Ananda ran serially in *Prabuddha Bharata* from January 1929 to March 1930. It was an extra task on top of everything else. The articles later became a book, entitled *Spiritual Practice,* which is still being published, now under the author's name.[39]

Probably around this time—in the latter part of 1928—a young man, who would later become Swami Hiranmayananda, was introduced by Swami Pavitrananda to Swami Ashokananda. In 1970, at the request of one of Swami Ashokananda's monastic disciples, he would write his reminiscences of the Swami as he knew him at the Calcutta Advaita Ashrama. He wrote in part,

> The Swami received me kindly. His bed was on the floor; in those days, because of lack of space, there was no cot at the Advaita Ashrama. He was surrounded with books and papers. He had an intellectual forehead, bright eyes and very pleasing manners. But I also found out that in arguments he was extremely uncompromising and slashing in his remarks. He was also quite witty and at times full of satirical humour. From the first meeting I felt myself very much drawn to him. My associa-

tion with him continued from 1928 to 1931 when he left for America. During this period I used to visit him quite frequently. Though he was very busy in those days with the editing of the *Prabuddha Bharata* he had always time for me. He would discuss with me various topics about which he was writing or thinking.

At our very first meeting, he wanted to know about my political views. In those days I was reading books on Indian revolutionary activities as well as those on the Irish Freedom Movement. I had some superficial acquaintance with some Bengali revolutionaries. So I spoke to him about armed revolution and the cult of the bomb as the only way for liberating the country from the thraldom of the British. The Swami listened to me patiently and called me a firebrand politician. But later through many talks and arguments he began to direct my mind towards the teachings of Swamiji and wean me away from politics. . . . Under his guidance I began to study the various books on Swamiji and Sri Ramakrishna, and the little insight that I have comes from him. Whenever he would speak about Swamiji he would become supremely eloquent and inspiring. He told me once, "I believe in no love except love at first sight. Fall in love with Swamiji!" I was from my ninth or tenth year drawn towards Swamiji, but these inspiring words left an indelible impression on my mind, and all my life I have been trying to love Swamiji.

The Swami in those days was writing some of the most learned articles in the *Prabuddha Bharata* and they were receiving wide acclamation everywhere. He would sometimes ask for my opinion about these, though I was a callow young student, and would freely discuss with me all subjects.

Once he wrote an article on the economics of *charkha* (the spinning wheel) and pleaded for adoption of industrialisation. But this led to a controversy between him and Mahatma Gandhi. The Swami held his own ground quite tenaciously and logically. Mahatmaji had the worst of it in argument. I was in those days a student of B.A. class and my subject was economics. So we used to have nice discussions with him about this subject. I, with my newly acquired knowledge from books, would support the Swami and the Swami used to be very pleased.

The Swami not only guided me in my intellectual pursuit, but also helped me in my spiritual life. He used to watch me without my knowledge and one day asked me suddenly why was it that I had been restless for some time. It was true that for some time I was not feeling inner peace. But I did not know what it was due to. So I told him the same. He said that it happened to people sometimes and what I needed was Diksha (initiation). He also related how in his life such restlessness had come and how the study of Tagore's work had helped him. He asked me to read Tagore's book, *Santiniketan*. I asked him how and from whom I was to have initiation. He told me that he would send me to Mahapurush Maharaj. So he sent me with Swami Vimuktananda to the Math, and Swami Omkarananda took me to Mahapurush Maharaj. That is how in my spiritual life I am deeply indebted to Swami Ashokananda. . . .

Besides the direct disciples he is the one Swami who most profoundly influenced my life.

DURING SWAMI ASHOKANANDA'S STAY in Calcutta in the winter of 1928–29, Sarvepalli Radhakrishnan, impressed by *Prabuddha Bharata*'s strong stand against Mahatma Gandhi's economic policies, came to see him. The two men hit it off wonderfully. Dr. Radhakrishnan praised the Swami's editorials. "You are the only person in India," he told him, "who has dared to say such things publicly against Gandhiji's policy." The admiration was mutual, for Swami Ashokananda, though he disagreed on some philosophical points with Radhakrishnan, greatly liked his books. During the next years, he went often to see him in Calcutta, and they had many talks together. Once, years later, when discussing the philosophy of Advaita Vedanta, Swami Ashokananda recalled his differences with the professor:

One day, I remember, I went to visit him in Calcutta. . . . I was hounding him to give me an article. He was too slippery in that respect. When I would come to Calcutta from the Himalayas I sometimes used to go and see him. He was very friendly. In the magazine I had reviewed his second volume of Indian philosophy, particularly the section on Gaudapada. And he asked me one question, very seriously. He said, "Do you think there can be a subject without an object?" I said yes. He was taken aback. You see, this is the whole basis of monistic Vedanta: There can be the pure subject; of course you don't call it "subject" then. But that which is the subject, the knower of objects in ordinary life, that in its true nature is the pure subject; that is to say, it is the pure self-conscious being, without any need of objects, not even itself. We do not know ourselves, you see. There is no such process as knowing ourselves through a subject-object relationship, as the language would imply.

Monistic Vedantists are awfully careful about that. They insist it is a wrong statement to say you know yourself. They say that this ultimate, this Atman or Brahman, is all consciousness. It does not require something else by which it becomes conscious; no process is involved in it. Any process would of course nullify its eternity; process always makes time. There is no time in Brahman; therefore there is no process.

Professor Radhakrishnan doesn't seem to accept that. He is a monist, but whenever he interprets monism he compromises it, he gets frightened of it. In India, almost all monistic Vedantic scholars have felt that Radhakrishnan really doesn't grasp the ultimate of monistic Vedanta.[40]

The Swami and the professor, with mutual esteem, argued this point when they came together. One year, seeing the Swami in the gallery of a lecture hall, Radhakrishnan beckoned to him from the stage to come down. But the Swami shook his head, for he knew he would be asked to speak and saw no reason for it.

When Swami Ashokananda was asked in later years what Professor Radhakrishnan had thought of him, he replied, "I don't know about it." And that was the end of it. But one learned from other sources that when the Swami left the country, Radhakrishnan said, "There goes the best brain in India." And later on, when Radhakrishnan was in France, visiting the Vedanta Society at Gretz, he said to the swami then in charge, Swami Siddheswarananda, "In India there are just two or three original thinkers—just two or three, and Swami Ashokananda is one of them." Indeed, Swami Ashokananda's fame spread wide in his motherland. Once an American woman said to Jawaharlal Nehru, "You should send us intellectual, educated Hindus—philosophers and savants." And Nehru replied, "But there is such a one in America—Swami Ashokananda."

On the trip back to Mayavati in 1929, Swami Ashokananda was met at the Tanakpur station by a servant with small horses. But it was raining torrentially, so he stayed at an inn in the village, now free of plague. The most difficult part about this was that all Swami Ashokananda had to read was *The Intelligent Woman's Guide to Socialism* by George Bernard Shaw, in which he was not particularly interested. After several days the servant told him that the clouds were thinning and they could start out the following morning. It snowed heavily on the way to Mayavati, and the Swami had no warm clothes—but in respect to discomfort, the trek was not unusual.

That summer, the summer of 1930, knowing he would be returning to Calcutta in the fall, and knowing he would again not be able to write because of the noise of the junkyard and the general atmosphere of the city, Swami Ashokananda decided to write at Mayavati all the remaining editorials for that year, which would be his last year as editor of *Prabuddha Bharata*. So he set to it. Each day he wrote one editorial, and by the end of a week he had finished seven. (Some say that he wrote nine in nine days—the number is not known for certain.) When he had written sufficient editorials to cover the remainder of his work at Mayavati, his brain, he said, was tired out. "The day I finished I mentioned at the dining table that I had completed the year's editorials.

Mayavati, 1930. *Seated in the front row, left to right:* Swami Vireswarananda, Swami Satprakashananda, Swami Ashokananda, and Swami Yogatmananda. *Standing behind, left to right:* Swami Prematmananda and Swami Pavitrananda.

Swami Pavitrananda was there, having returned at the beginning of the year from Calcutta. (He was supposed to take one year's rest and then take over the editorship in January of 1931.) When I said what I had done, he was very annoyed. I still do not know why. He was so annoyed! But, then, people are different from one another. He is different from me, and I am different from him. He is a very nice swami—meditative."

In any case the editorials were done, and when Swami Ashokananda went down to Calcutta in mid-June of 1930, it was with a free mind. There was much other work to do for *Prabuddha Bharata,* but not the concentrated work of writing editorials. One of the remaining tasks was to bring out Romain Rolland's book *Prophets of the New India* (the life of Sri Ramakrishna and the life of Vivekananda). The Swami was now seeing the English translation through the press and attending to every detail of typesetting and composition. The latter job was an especially difficult and demanding one, for Rolland had written an abundance of long footnotes that were extremely hard to fit to the corresponding text. By the time the book was off the press, it was considered to constitute a typographical revolution in printing at Advaita Ashrama.

It was also at this time that Swami Ashokananda wrote a reply to Rolland's contention that the spread of Vedantic ideas in the Western world was due not to the modern-day diffusion of Vedantic thought but, rather, to "the unity of thought and laws that govern the [human] spirit." Swami Ashokananda's reply took the form of a pamphlet entitled *The Influence of Indian Thought on the Thought of the West*, in which he traced the influence of Vedantic philosophy from very early times up to the twentieth century.[41]

An event of greater, life-changing magnitude took place in early 1931 in Calcutta. One day when Swami Ashokananda was working at Advaita Ashrama, a monk came with a message from the trustees of the Order. Like a schoolboy, Swami was startled, thinking he might have written something wrong in *Prabuddha Bharata* and was being called to task for it. But the message was more epoch-making than that. The trustees had decided that he was to go to San Francisco as assistant to Swami Vividishananda, who was about to take over the leadership of the Vedanta Society there. Swami Ashokananda asked for a few days to think it over, and during those few days decided he was not suited to work in the West. So he went to Belur Math to tell his decision to Swami Madhavananda, then assistant general secretary. It was Bharat Maharaj who had recommended him as the best swami for the post. Now Swami Madhavananda said to Bharat Maharaj, "Just see! Your 'best swami' has refused to go!" Bharat Maharaj was stunned and, knowing that Swami Ashokananda was leaving the Math for Calcutta, ran out to the road to catch him before he could board a bus. The Math's secondary entrance was then to the north of the Math building, little more than a footpath through the jungle. Bharat Maharaj sped up this path to the Grand Trunk Road, and there he found his friend waiting for a bus. Without wasting words, he told him he must go to the West and there preach Vedanta, and he gave him all the reasons for which he was the best man for the post. Swami Ashokananda was adamant in his refusal, and the two swamis walked up and down the Grand Trunk Road, while bus after bus went by on the way to Calcutta.

It was because he could not, in the long run, refuse a call from Sri Ramakrishna that Swami Ashokananda eventually agreed. But because he was deeply exhausted from his long and strenuous editorial work, he asked Swami Madhavananda to give him first a three-month vacation. He longed to meditate in the Himalayas. Swami Madhavananda refused, because Swami Dayananda, who was then the head of the San Francisco center, was coming back to India, his agreed-upon five-year stint in the West at an end. Since he had accepted, Swami Ashokananda felt that he had no choice but to leave India for the West as soon as possible. "Maybe my personal desire would turn out to be a bad thing," he once said in this connection. "So I came right away. You do not know whether your own preference is right or not."

During the few weeks that were left in India to Swami Ashokananda, he often went from Calcutta in the early afternoons to pay his respects to Swami Shivananda. Because of the heat, only a few people would be there at that time. Once he found the Swami walking in the courtyard outside the Math building. The weather that day was pleasant, not too hot. Mahapurush was ill, and Swami Ashokananda asked him how he was. He did not reply in regard to his physical health, but very emphatically he said that it had become very easy for him to have spiritual realization. What had taken him a long time and much effort to realize earlier he could now realize within a short time. Indeed, he

Swami Ashokananda in Calcutta, before coming to America, 1931

said, it comes of itself. He also said that soon the doctors would ask him not to come downstairs any more. He would have to remain upstairs.

On another day, Swami Ashokananda asked Swami Shivananda, "Sir, when people in the West ask me for spiritual instruction, what shall I tell them?" The Swami was silent for a few moments, and then he said, "I won't tell you now. Go to San Francisco, and then write to me what those people ask about, and I shall give you the necessary instruction for them." "So after I had been in America for a little while I wrote to him," Swami Ashokananda related. "I think it was in October or November of 1931. And I received a long reply. He told me to give certain instruction to certain people of certain spiritual aptitude. It covered the needs of almost everyone. There have been a few special cases, of which I later wrote to the Swami, and he always very kindly advised me. In the first letter he ended by saying that he would stand behind me and that whatever instruction I would give to anyone would do him or her good."

A few days before Swami Ashokananda left India, a sumptuous dinner, complete with a speech of farewell, was given for him at Advaita Ashrama in Calcutta. He ate well, but, unbeknownst to him, Swami Shivananda had arranged another feast for him the next day at Belur Math. Unfortunately, for the first time in quite a long while, he had stomach trouble from the Advaita Ashrama dinner, and the next day he phoned to Belur to say he would not be coming to the Math that day. It was then that he learned of the feast Swami Shivananda had had prepared. It was too late. He said he would surely come the next day. The next day Swami Shivananda sent some monks to obtain a special kind of fish and again had a feast prepared for Swami Ashokananda. But this time Swami Shivananda was himself ill and could not come down from the second floor of the monastery. He sent for Swami Ashokananda to come to his room. Before this, he had bestowed many blessings upon the Swami during a private session. Among other things, he had told him that he (Swami Ashokananda) was in the state described in the Gita, "He by whom the world is not afflicted and whom the world cannot afflict, he who is free from joy and anger, fear and anxiety—he is dear to me."[42]

Telling of it, the Swami said in later years, still much moved, "Of course, he meant that that was the ideal. But he heaped blessings upon me, as from an ocean of jewels! One big blessing after another. Such wonderful things! Tremendous blessings. He just showered them on me. He was so kind! So very kind!" And he made the sound he used to make when he was deeply affected—perhaps a Bengali sound: "Ah hahah!"

Two attendants of Swami Shivananda's were sometimes present when Swami Ashokananda would come to see him. Many years later one of them (Swami Apurvananda) wrote to Swami Ashokananda and told him that once when he (Swami Ashokananda) had left Swami Shivananda's room, Swami Shivananda, looking after him, had said, "There goes a nugget of pure gold!" and he had gone on to say, "Swamiji liked Swami Sadananda so much because he could write a little. He thought highly of him. But if he had known Ashokananda he would have always kept him close in his heart." Another attendant (Swami Shraddhananda) told a monastic disciple of Swami Ashokananda's (also years later) that Swami Shivananda had just poured blessings on Swami Ashokananda. He said that in all his years with Swami Shivananda he had never seen him bless anyone with so much intensity and so much feeling.[43]

This same swami related another time: "I remember the occasion when Swami Ashokananda first left India to come to this country [America]. Swami Shivananda was so kind and encouraging. He said, 'I know what work you will do there. I know. The only thing that concerns me is your health. But, you see, my boy, I am also suffering. This body is so weak, and you see how much work Sri Ramakrishna is having done through this body! The same thing will happen to you. Sri Ramakrishna will work out whatever he has to do through you in spite of your bad health.' And he blessed him. 'I know, my boy. You go.

Make one great leap across the ocean like Hanuman. Leap from India to the United States. You are going on the work of God. It was Rama's power that enabled him to make that jump. So remember that it is Sri Ramakrishna's power that is behind you, and everything will be all right.' So many encouraging words he said!"

And now, calling him to his room from the feast he had given him, Swami Shivananda, who was lying ill upon his bed, said simply, "You are Swamiji's disciple, isn't it?"

"Yes, sir," Swami Ashokananda replied.

Those were the last words the great Swami Shivananda ever spoke to him, and they dispelled the last wisp of his doubt. He knew that he was indeed Swami Vivekananda's disciple.

PART 2

A HEART POURED OUT

SAN FRANCISCO, 1931–59

6

GROWING WINGS

S wami Ashokananda was seasick during almost his entire voyage
to San Francisco. He had a second-class cabin near water level;
when the waves were rough, the seas would pound against the porthole, and, seemingly, against his head. It was an old Japanese ship, the
Taiyo Maru, left over from the Victorian era, dirty and threadbare. His
cabin mate was a Hindu who had been to America before and had spent
several years there.

At Rangoon the Swami bought some mangosteens and found them
not only delicious but soothing to his stomach. At the next port, Singapore, he bought a whole basket of them and ate nothing else during
much of the voyage. It was also at Singapore that a Christian missionary from Japan with his wife and their two children (a girl, twelve, and
a boy, ten) boarded the ship. In his goodness of heart the missionary
took care of the young monk, and they became friends.

"He told me that in the Bible it said that Jesus was the only Incarnation," Swami Ashokananda recalled. "I told him that in the Hindu
scriptures it is said that there were others, and I showed him the Gita.
He became thoughtful, and he admitted, 'Yes, Sri Krishna says he is an
Incarnation of God.' He read the Gita all night long. He did not know
what to say. He was not a philosopher; he was a man of faith. If he had

been philosophically inclined, he would have been very much upset. There was also a proud professor with a big intellect on board. He said to me about the missionary, 'I hate those fellows. They try to save souls!' " But throughout the long voyage the missionary never once tried to save the Swami's soul.

The next port was Hong Kong, where the ship stopped over for a week. Here the Swami stayed with a doctor who was friendly toward the Ramakrishna Mission. One day his host persuaded him to attend a dinner that was being given by a community of rich silk merchants. At the end of the dinner crème de menthe was served, and the doctor urged the Swami to drink it, telling him it was good for the digestion. He did not tell him that the liqueur was also alcoholic. The Swami drank about a teaspoonful of the sweet green stuff and felt no effect. But the next morning he awoke with a full-blown hangover and a head-ache that kept him in bed all day.

Then through rough seas and stormy weather to Hawaii. Here the Swami was looked after by a federal district judge—Judge Christy—and his wife. The judge's niece, whom the Swami had met in India, had arranged for her uncle to take care of Swami Ashokananda during his one-day stopover in Honolulu. When the ship docked, the Swami and his cabin mate, whom he had refused to leave behind, waited patiently at the rail, looking for their hosts, who did not appear. Finally the two men went ashore. There Judge and Mrs. Christy were waiting—and had been waiting for nearly an hour. Their annoyance was ill con-cealed, but soon, charmed by their guests, they themselves became charming. "Americans can be wonderful people," the Swami said years later, recalling this time. "They have a special quality that no other people have—so generous and open. The judge and his wife were like that. They gave over their whole day to us." They took the Swami and his friend to lunch at one of the large hotels on the beach at Waikiki and then took them sightseeing. "I had my first smell of the West in Honolulu," the Swami would later recall; the general atmosphere, he said, "seemed too thick to breathe."

Then the Christys took their guests to their home. Before dinner, the Swami was introduced to their young daughter, who was in bed with a cold, reading a murder mystery. At once, Swami and the little girl became friends and talked happily about Sherlock Holmes until dinnertime.

Mrs. Christy had learned from Swami Ashokananda's sympathetic cabin mate that the Swami was having very bad stomach trouble, and so, being a kindly, motherly sort of woman, she took great care to get the right food for his dinner. She asked the friend what the Swami would like, and he told her curry, not knowing that spices were the worst possible thing. So Mrs. Christy made lamb curry for their dinner, and the Swami, knowing that she had gone to much trouble to please him, ate it. Besides, could the pain he was having day and night get any worse?

After dinner, Mrs. Christy, who was interested in astrology, palmistry, and such things, read the Swami's palm and told him that he was a very practical man. "Oh, no!" Swami Ashokananda said. "If you ask them in India, they will tell you that I am not at all practical—just intellectual and full of theories." Indeed, the Swami himself had come to believe this. "No," Mrs. Christy insisted, "you are practical!" And as the years passed, she would prove to have been right.

She was also right in another regard. As a departure gift, she and the judge gave him a large basket of avocados. He had never seen such fruit before, and even his cabin mate, who had spent a long time in California, had never before set eyes on an avocado. When the ship sailed, the Swami tried one and found it "absolutely tasteless," and thinking that the fruit might have spoiled, he threw the whole lot overboard. Only later did he learn how good for his stomach avocados could be and that they had, moreover, a taste.

Mrs. Christy, having consulted an astrological almanac, had told her two guests that the ship would run into a severe storm between Honolulu and San Francisco. Again, she was right. The seas ran high and the ship made slow headway. "I was again very seasick," the Swami related. "The missionary used to come every day and ask if there was anything he could do for me. He asked if he could help pack my bags. It is my belief that there are many good people like that, whom you would not know about until you came close to them. When we parted, he said that he would pray for me. I said, 'Thank you. That is very nice. But please pray that God takes me to Him in His own way. Don't tell Him how.' He said yes, very good; he would do that. He was a very nice man. I have always been sorry that I didn't get his address."

The SS *Taiyo Maru* was scheduled to dock on July 3, 1931, a date without meaning. Swami Ashokananda wished it could be July 4, significant to both India and America, and lo! the storm delayed the ship a full twenty-four hours; it was not until the historic and auspicious morning of July 4 that the *Taiyo Maru* sailed through the Golden Gate. When the Swami awoke that morning, he found that he felt better than he had since he embarked. The ship was not rolling; he looked out the porthole and found that the sky and sea were brilliantly blue. The hills of Marin County were emerald green, the earth of the cliffs was red. He had arrived at San Francisco, where he would rapidly develop into a teacher, a builder, and a leader, and where he was to live the rest of his life.

THE VEDANTA SOCIETY of San Francisco was one of the two that Swami Vivekananda had founded during his visits to America. The first, which still exists, he started in New York in November of 1894. In April of 1900, during his second visit to America, he founded the Vedanta Society of San Francisco. Before he returned to India, he appointed his brother disciple Swami Turiyananda to take charge of the Society and to establish an ashrama on 160 acres of land in San Antone Valley, some sixty miles south of San Francisco, which had been donated to him. Obedient to his beloved brother, Swami Turiyananda established the ashrama, named it Shanti Ashrama,[44] and for the larger part of two years lived there, sometimes with students, sometimes with only Gurudas as a companion. (Gurudas [later Swami Atulananda] was a *brahmacharin* disciple of Swami Abhedananda. He had come from New York to stay at Shanti Ashrama in December of 1900.)

In June of 1902, illness forced Swami Turiyananda to return to India. He never came back to the West. But before Swami Vivekananda passed away in July 1902, he had appointed Swami Trigunatita, also a direct disciple of Sri Ramakrishna, to carry on the San Francisco work. Swami Trigunatita was minister of the Society from 1903 until his untimely and tragic death in 1915, during which time he established the Society on a firm footing. After him, his assistant, Swami Prakashananda, a disciple of Swamiji's, took charge. Swami Prakashananda died in 1927. He was followed in fairly rapid succession by Swami Dayananda, Swami Madhavananda, and again Swami Dayananda, assisted by Swami Vividishananda. In 1931, many of Swami Trigunatita's disciples were still alive and active in the Society, and although the work was not flourishing, it was not moribund. The membership stood at forty-four.

Mr. Ernest C. Brown, a disciple of Swami Trigunatita's and vice president of the Society, managed to board the *Taiyo Maru* before it docked. "He wanted to make things easy for me and to attend to everything," the Swami said later, "but there wasn't much to do. He seemed a very nice person." Mr. Brown was not unknown to Swami Ashokananda. The former had written a long (and, according to some of his fellow disciples, inaccurate) account of Swami Trigunatita's life and work in the West for *Prabuddha Bharata* and in the course of it had corresponded with the editor, then Swami Ashokananda. He had also quarreled with him, for the Swami had deleted his long and elaborate descriptions of the Temple (then known as the Hindu Temple), which Swami Trigunatita had built, because without accompanying photographs, written descriptions of that oddly complicated, polyarchitectural building were unintelligible. Mr. Brown had been incensed—to no avail. His history was serialized in *Prabuddha Bharata* throughout 1928, minus elaborate architectural descriptions.

Swami Ashokananda in America, 1931.
(He arrived wearing this suit.)

Waiting on the wharf to greet the Swami was a welcoming committee, which seemed to consist primarily of a number of formidably
large women, such as he had never before seen. "Western dress," he
would later observe, "emphasizes a woman's largeness, whereas Indian
dress conceals it." Among these women were Mrs. Thomas Allan, Mrs.
Albert Wollberg, Mrs. Lartigau, and Mrs. Mae Weber. Standing beside
them were Swami Dayananda, Swami Vividishananda, and the hus-
bands, one of whom, Thomas Allan, was then president of the Vedanta
Society. Swami Ashokananda stood at the rail in the only spot available—behind a post, where he could see but could not be seen. The
members of the welcoming committee thought he was hiding from

The original temple (later called the Old Temple) in San Francisco,
Vedanta Society of Northern California

them, as well he might have been, for to Indian eyes, the women on the
wharf were an intimidating sight. But the Swami was not hiding.

Greetings over, they took him to the Temple on the corner of Webster and Filbert Streets. It was a strange building, part Victorian, part
Moorish, with towers in the form of three or four Hindu temples and
one crenellated castle. It was painted a yellowish cream color, towers
and all. On its narrow Webster Street front there were two glass-paned
entrance doors, flanked by Ionic columns. The door on the left opened
directly onto a steep and narrow staircase that led to the two upper
floors. The door on the right led into the vestry part of the Temple.
Here, immediately on the right, was a room that served as an office and

reception room. Its two wide windows looked onto Webster Street. A little farther down, the hall widened, at the expense of the next room on the right, which was used as a bedroom. The hall then narrowed again. Here, also on the right, was another room, used perhaps as a second bedroom; on the left was a bathroom and beyond it a light well, which Swami Trigunatita had converted into a small kitchen. At the end of the hall a door opened onto the platform of the auditorium, the main entrance of which was on Filbert Street.

It would have been clear to a newcomer that the hallway and the three rooms on its right had not been redecorated or even repainted since Swami Trigunatita's time. The walls were of plaster with an embossed dado about waist high, dark with the passage of many years. The carpets in the front office and hallway were threadbare, and the brownish linoleum in the other rooms was worn in heavily trafficked areas to its base. The furniture consisted of unrelated odds and ends donated by devotees. The only substantial pieces were in the front room, where Swami Trigunatita's old rolltop desk and a comfortable rocking chair were still used by the swamis. In this room, a shelf supporting unprepossessing holy pictures and nondescript objects extended around the wall at eye level. In the wall itself were many light sockets, unused now, but once, perhaps, bringing electricity to a multitude of lamps spaced along the shelf at intervals. The other rooms, used as bedrooms, were sparsely furnished; they were, after all, for the use of monks.

Although nothing much in the way of decor had changed since the Temple was built, Swami Dayananda had made two significant improvements. The auditorium seats were no longer movable chairs, as they had been in Swami Trigunatita's and Swami Prakashananda's time. Enterprisingly, Swami Dayananda had bought at a demolition sale a hundred or so old theater seats and had had them installed in the auditorium, their padded seats folding when necessary against their wooden backs, their iron frames welded together in rows and (tradition has it) bolted to the floor by the Swami himself—nine rows of six seats on the left of the central (and only) aisle and seven on the right. Swami Dayananda had also installed a steam-heat system throughout the building.

In Swami Trigunatita's time, the second floor of the Temple had been occupied by Mr. and Mrs. Carl Petersen, both of whom had served the Swami and the Society with full attention and love. After the death of Mr. Petersen (Mrs. Petersen died in 1916, Mr. Petersen in 1924) the second floor was rented out to devotees and at the time of our story was still occupied by tenants. The third floor had always been a monastery and was used for swamis, both resident and visiting. Two aged monks—Mr. Page and Mr. Anderson—lived in the towers.

For several days after Swami Ashokananda's arrival, the weather in San Francisco was beautiful and bright. "The sky was very blue," he recalled, "so blue it hurt me." Still, he found the atmosphere of the city even thicker than that of Honolulu—at least at first. The world into which he had entered was indeed far removed from the one he had left. True, Swami Vivekananda had introduced Vedanta to America not long before. But while Swamiji was still vivid in the memories of those who had seen him and heard him, the general public had forgotten him. He had come and gone, as though a wave had crashed over the land and had receded. The powerful seeds it had left behind were unseen, unsuspected. On the surface, America went on its way, as though nothing extraordinary had happened.

Nor did the climate of the Temple compensate for the general thickness of the air. In this small enclave, Mr. and Mrs. Allan (and Mr. Brown) were lords. Not only were they veteran disciples of Swami Trigunatita, but they had known Swami Vivekananda—had seen him, talked with him. Consequently, although the Society's bulletin for July had spoken highly of the coming swami, these old-timers looked upon him as small fry, barely worth his title. In March, in a report read in the Society's 1931 annual meeting, Mr. Brown, in his capacity of chairman of the activities committee, had announced Swami Ashokananda's imminent coming and had gone on to say enigmatically, "Don't forget that a real Swami is going from our Society to India . . . to stay and work there."

Fortunately, Swami Ashokananda had friends at the Temple who spoke his own language. In residence, there was not only Swami Dayananda, the "real" swami who was about to depart for India, but Swami Vividishananda, who would take Swami Dayananda's place as head of the Society. Also, visiting San Francisco were Swami Akhilananda, Swami Ashokananda's close friend from his Madras days, who had now started a Vedanta center in Providence, Rhode Island, and Swami Prabhavananda, who on July 6 had come from Los Angeles to visit.

Swami Prabhavananda had been in America for some time. He had first started work in San Francisco in the early twenties as an assistant to Swami Prakashananda and had held a well-attended class on the Gita. But, perhaps because of his youth, he had not been allowed to lecture or give interviews. Frustrated, he had gone to Portland to open a center of his own, but this venture had not succeeded. So, after sending to India in 1929 for Swami Vividishananda to take over the failing Portland center, he successfully established a Vedanta society in Hollywood with the help of one of Swami Vivekananda's old friends, Mrs. Carrie Wykoff. Now, visiting San Francisco in a happy, buoyant mood, Swami Prabhavananda took his four brothers on an excursion to Golden Gate Park. There is a photograph of the group of five swamis in the park, with Swami Prabhavananda in the middle gleefully offering a cigarette in a holder to Swami Vividishananda, who wants no part of it. Swami Ashokananda is smiling at this foolery, but he seems nonetheless strained, as indeed he felt.

"I couldn't seem to make an association with anything," he later said. "Did you feel homesick?" a disciple asked. "No," he replied, "it wasn't that. I never felt that I shouldn't have left India or that I wanted to be back there. It was just that I couldn't feel associated with the surroundings here. I couldn't make a connection. It was at least a year before things stopped seeming strange."

Swami Ashokananda with brother monks in San Francisco
shortly after his arrival, 1931. *Left to right:* Swami Vividishananda,
Swami Dayananda, Swami Prabhavananda, Swami Akhilananda,
and Swami Ashokananda.

Even apart from the alien culture, things at first were indeed passing
strange. One day while talking over the phone with Mr. Allan in the
hearing of Swami Ashokananda, Swami Prabhavananda turned to his
brother monk and said, "Mr. Allan has invited you and me to dinner
tonight." Swami Ashokananda thought that if Mr. Allan, president of
the Society, had invited him, it was only polite to accept, so accept he
did. Too late, he learned that what Mr. Allan had actually said to
Swami Prabhavananda was "We have room for only two swamis. You
choose who the other will be." "If I had known the invitation was like
that," he would later say, "I would have refused."

The dinner itself had an Alice-in-Wonderland quality. Mr. Allan, a

Mr. and Mrs. Thomas Allan at the Alameda Hotel, April 26, 1942.
(The same palm tree was there in 1900 during Swami Vivekananda's
residence at the Home of Truth, which then occupied the site.)

burly Scotsman in his late sixties, presided at the head of the small
table, with Mrs. Allan, stout and looming, on his right and Swami
Ashokananda on his left. Swami Prabhavananda sat opposite the host.
Almost at once the conversation turned to criticism of a swami of another center, and suddenly, during the course of this talk, odd in itself,
Mr. Allan, his elbow on the table, shook his fist in Swami Ashokananda's face and said in threatening tones, "We have been accustomed
to putting the swamis on a pedestal. That is going to stop! You swamis

won't have any say in running the Society. The board of directors will have the authority!" Speechless, Swami Ashokananda did not reply—not then.

On the whole, the new swami was not made to feel welcome. After all, he was not Swami Vivekananda; he was not even Swami Trigunatita. He was a young, boyish-looking monk who, to be sure, may have edited *Prabuddha Bharata,* but what of that? This distinction could have somehow been even to his discredit. One evening after Swami Dayananda had lectured, Mrs. Allan came to the front room, where Swami Ashokananda was talking with a visitor, possibly about Vedanta and the current state of civilization. After listening briefly, Mrs. Allan said to the walls, "Well! He is busy saving the world!" Curiouser and curiouser. But before long, all that would change.

On July 12, the Swami gave his first lecture in the Temple. It was entitled—or had been entitled for him in the July bulletin—"My First Message." Mr. Allan introduced him by saying, "I don't know him. We will have to wait and see what he is like." "It was like a slap in the face," Swami Ashokananda later said. There is no record of his talk, and one does not know how it was received. The auditorium was packed, but that was because a new swami straight from India was speaking.

A few days later, Swami Ashokananda went with a young student (possibly Adolph Gschwend, who was Swami Vividishananda's disciple) to Shanti Ashrama, where Swami Turiyananda had stayed for nearly two years trying to establish a year-round ashrama. Swami Trigunatita had later used the property to hold annual monthlong highly structured and extremely popular retreats. The spiritual atmosphere those two great disciples of Sri Ramakrishna had generated was palpable in that arid, austerely beautiful valley, where the summers were broiling hot and the winters freezing cold. Broiling hot it was when Swami Ashokananda stayed for almost two weeks in one of the five cabins that had been built in Swami Trigunatita's time and that the Society had maintained through the years. "My brains boiled," he would later say of this vacation—he who was accustomed to the burning summers of Bengal. But there were compensations. Swami Trigunatita once said (Mrs. Allan later reported) that Swami Turiyananda had consecrated the ashrama and had left an atmosphere there that would last for 250 years.

What spiritual experiences Swami Ashokananda had at Shanti Ashrama that summer of 1931, we don't know, but one quite ordinary incident that occurred while he was there would have bearing on the most outward part of his life in the West—his clothes. He was walking one day along the road with the student; both men were dressed with extreme casualness. Indeed, Swami Ashokananda had as yet no proper Western clothes at all, let alone country clothes. Tired, he and the student sat a while by the roadside. Two visiting devotees from some other Vedanta center walked by, and one said scornfully to the other, "What are these tramps doing here?" Shocked, Swami realized that foreigners, particularly (he thought) people of dark skin, were judged by their clothes. And thenceforth, throughout his life in the West, he was careful of how he dressed. Casual his clothes might often have been, but they would be always meticulously tailored and spotless.

Before Swami Ashokananda left India, Swami Madhavananda had taken him to a Calcutta store, where they had chosen some very good gray suit material. But another swami, who was thought to be an authority on Western clothes, was given the task of buying him a hat and an overcoat. He bought him a dark brown hat of a fuzzy material and an overcoat for five dollars. He then took him to a Muslim tailor, who cut two ill-fitting suits out of the gray material. Swami Ashokananda had no choice but to wear the suits. He himself did not know how bad they were until, on the voyage to the West, he noticed the oblique looks of his fellow passengers, and possibly of his various hosts along the way. In America the truth was even more obvious, and the Shanti Ashrama experience made the matter urgent. Returning to San Francisco, he told Swami Dayananda that he would have to have a new overcoat and a new hat. Swami Dayananda took him to a discount store and there, although neither of them had the least knowledge of

Swami Ashokananda wearing his clerical collar

Western styles, they somehow chose a presentable blue-gray hat and a good brown overcoat. As for suits, Swami Ashokananda continued to wear the Indian-made ones.

After Swami Dayananda left, Swami Akhilananda, who was visiting and who understood the problem, offered to buy Swami Vividishananda and Swami Ashokananda each a new suit and an overcoat. The three swamis went shopping. They could find no ready-made black suits, so they went to a good tailor and had suits made, each with two vests—one for a clerical collar and the other for a shirt and necktie. And thus, at least for city wear, the problem of Western clothes was solved. Later, Swami Ashokananda discovered sports jackets and shirts for casual wear. When he lectured, he wore a tailored robe, dyed a terra-cotta or dark *gerua* color and loosely sashed, such as Swami Vivekananda had worn in the West. For as long as he lived, this was the kind of robe he and his assistants would wear when they lectured or held classes. Otherwise, they dressed in Western style. (Until the seventies a *gerua* robe on the streets of San Francisco would have created a sensation—and that was the last thing Swami Ashokananda wanted to do.)

On Sunday, August 14, 1931, Swami Dayananda was given a farewell reception in the Temple. Four swamis took part in it: Swami Dayananda, Swami Akhilananda, who would also soon be leaving San Francisco, Swami Vividishananda, who would be taking charge of the Society, and Swami Ashokananda, the newcomer. About a week later, Swami Dayananda left for India.

Now Swami Vividishananda was in charge, but regular work would not start until September of that year. Swami Madhavananda, then assistant secretary of the Ramakrishna Order, had agreed (in lieu of three months in the Himalayas) that Swami Ashokananda would not have to start his work in the West immediately. Such was the arrangement also in Swami Vividishananda's case, for both swamis were badly in need of rest.

Summer vacations had never been in order at the Vedanta Society, Sunday lectures continuing nonstop throughout the year. Accordingly, Mr. Brown and Swami Akhilananda gave the Sunday lectures in August of 1931, while the two resident swamis continued to rest. Not until Wednesday evening, September 2, did Swami Ashokananda give his first regular lecture. It was entitled "What Vedanta Can Do for You." And with that, his work in the West began. On September 4, he started to hold the Friday evening Upanishad class. On the Sunday morning of September 6, Swami Vividishananda gave his first lecture as head of the Society and on the following Tuesday held his first evening Gita class. The swamis settled into this routine, each giving one lecture and one class during the week. The attendance was good—around eighty people came to both the Sunday and Wednesday lectures, and around thirty-five to the Tuesday and Friday classes.

From the start, Swami Vividishananda was not well. When in 1929 he had come from India to take over the Portland work, there had been hardly any work to take over. At length, after trying his best, he had given up and had asked Swami Dayananda if he could work with him as an assistant in San Francisco. Swami Dayananda was delighted, so Swami Vividishananda closed down the Portland center and came to California. By that time his health was extremely poor. Swami Dayananda sent him to a doctor, and it was found that he had severe anemia. The doctor, a surgeon rather than a general practitioner, prescribed rest and rich food. Such was the situation when Swami Ashokananda arrived. For the next year he cooked for his ailing brother—among other things, chicken curry and *kichori* made of moong dal and rice—and cared for him as best he could. But Swami Vividishananda remained physically weak and, because of his lack of lecturing skills in those days, he was depressed as well. Actually, the attendance at Swami Vividishananda's Sunday morning lectures was larger than at the lectures of the swamis who had immediately preceded him and slightly larger than at those of his assistant. Even so, the attendance on Sunday mornings should, he felt, have been much larger than it was.

On the whole, the circumstances were not heartening. Seldom did anyone come to the Temple for interviews. There was no work to do, except for cooking and housework. Now and then Swami Ashokananda wondered why there was need of an assistant at all, except as a matter of tradition. In the daytime the two swamis took long streetcar rides around the city, seeing the sights or simply enjoying the ride, or they would walk along the Marina or go to Golden Gate Park. In the evenings they sometimes went to a movie at the neighborhood theater, which they highly enjoyed. Known nostalgically today as golden oldies, those movies of the 1930s not only were entertaining but were an education of sorts in the mores and culture of America. The swamis also had an education from the audience. There was, for instance, the fat woman who sat in front of them during the film *The Greeks Had a Word for Them*. In sheer enjoyment, she kept exclaiming, "Oh, boy! Oh, boy! Oh, boy!" "Every time something pleased her she said that," Swami Ashokananda recalled years later. He had puzzled over it. "Now, what is the meaning of 'Oh, boy'?" Thus it was that he learned Americanisms firsthand.

Despite the slowness of the work, Swami Ashokananda felt in those days of pioneering a tremendous mental vitality. A great eagerness was stirring in his heart to spread the message of Vedanta far and wide, to get the work going and to expand it. He gave much thought to the best way of doing this: not, perhaps, by lecturing throughout the country, as Swami Abhedananda had done and as Swami Paramananda was then doing, but, rather, by building up a following in nearby communities and by simultaneously strengthening and deepening the home center. Before he left India, he had asked Swami Shivananda whether, in his post as assistant swami, he could act with some degree of independence. Swami Shivananda had said yes, surely. Swami Ashokananda had also asked Swami Madhavananda whether he could have the right to work in his own way, and Swami Madhavananda and the other trustees of the Order had assented. So now, eager as a young racehorse at the starting gate, Swami Ashokananda felt free to act on his own initiative, and Swami Vividishananda, far from objecting, gave his full-hearted consent.

In the Society's November 1931 bulletin, one finds Swami Ashokananda's thoughts at this time about the importance of the work and the necessity for expansion. The bulletin, a mimeographed leaflet of two pages, had been started in June of 1931. It had at first a homey flavor but later on became more formal and impersonal. It gave the calendar of events for the month and other general information. If there was room, a scriptural quotation or a short essay by one of the swamis would be included. In November of 1931, the bulletin was produced on legal-size paper to accommodate the following essay, which could well have been written fifty years later and whose authorship was unmistakable:

Do the students of Vedanta realize that they have great responsibility on their shoulders? None can deny that humanity is just now passing through a period of great storm and stress, when every ideal is being remodeled, old ideas are being challenged and accustomed ways of doing things are being questioned. Economically, politically, culturally, spiritually, in every respect, the human mind and affairs are undergoing great changes. We are finding that every aspect of life has to be conceived in terms of the entire humanity. Take the economic problem itself. It is being increasingly realized that if the people of the world are to escape depression and unemployment, the economic system of each nation has to be adjusted in reference to the needs of the other nations. In fact, there has to be one interrelated economic system throughout the world. We can no longer remain self-contained and self-sufficient. Every nation has to learn from and teach the other nations, and there is no doubt that the intermingling of cultures that is going on so rapidly at the present time will eventually lead to a universal culture in which the whole of humanity will participate. Religion, too, is aiming at that universality. The future is surely going to reveal a universal religion of which the different creeds will be parts. This universality is going to be the keynote of future mankind. And man's honest efforts at the present time should be to actualize this much-desired future as early as possible. For on this depends the peace and prosperity and the spiritual welfare of mankind.

But prejudice dies hard. We are too timid. We are loath to give up our mental narrowness. When the rising sun is calling us into the open to bathe in its golden rays, we are still moping in the dark corners of our hovels. This is the tragedy. We are afraid of the new things that are happening and are going to happen. But, of course, we have to change and remodel ourselves after the future ideals. And herein lies the great responsibility of the Vedanta students. Vedanta stands above all for universality, oneness, synthesis, harmony, and infinite affirmation. Vedanta is a philosophy and religion of infinite hope. It promises infinite glory to mankind. It invites men to march forward from one achievement to another, till the very highest is attained. It stands for the unity of mankind. All true students of Vedanta have to feel and realize this fact. They have, above all, to be all-inclusive and harmonious. By their life they have to prove to the timid world the beauty of the new ideals towards which humanity is reaching. . . . They have to demonstrate to others that these new ideals are infinitely more helpful than the older creedal and sectarian ideals. Do they feel that they are the forerunners of the new age? Those who feel so, will surely prove a valuable asset to humanity. None may know of them, they may be looked upon as ordinary; yet the high potency of their thought and life will bring about revolutionary changes in the mental plane of humanity and will eventually set forces in motion which will greatly alter also the outer life.

The challenge of Vedanta is tremendous. The weak may shrink from it, but those who have any strength in them will take it up and rise to the required heights. It is of these that Jesus said they were the salt of the earth. Let the best (and everyone has got the best in him or her) in us come out, let the Divine in us shine forth! Let the light in us be a beacon to the blundering world!

FROM THE VERY START of his ministry in the West, Swami Ashokananda expected to make spiritual heroes and heroines out of those who called themselves Vedantists. As he saw it, his primary service to Swami Vivekananda was to develop men and women fit to do his work and fit to realize God.

In later years he once said during a class, "One of the functions of Swami Vivekananda's mission was to create a large number of men and women in the world who would live and act in the consciousness of their own spiritual nature—free, divine, perfect in their Self, strong, fighting those tendencies which are unspiritual, which are against their own nature, just as one fights evil dreams knowing that they are not part of oneself. [If many such people existed] the whole world would be filled with a spirit of cooperation, people helping each other, doing unselfish service. That is the kind of thing Swami Vivekananda wanted, and I have not the least doubt that it will take place." To help bring it about, the Swami decided that whatever needed to be done for the work he would do. And he kept this resolve to the end of his days. "If the work is to succeed," he would later say to a young monastic disciple, "the heart must be poured out—*poured out!*" And pour out his heart he would—in full.

He could not wait long in idleness for prospective students to come to the door. While it is said to be a spiritual law that a person who is ready for spiritual life will find the right teacher, it is not said that the teacher should hide himself in an obscure corner waiting to be found—particularly not in America, where almost no one had ever heard of spiritual teachers in the Eastern sense or, for that matter, of spirituality as distinct from creedal religion. True, the swamis' lectures were advertised in a few local newspapers, but the attendance was not growing. Something more was needed.

The earlier swamis in San Francisco had made little effort to expand the work to other cities and towns. Indeed, one school of thought at Belur Math was not to expand the work in the West at all but, rather, to strengthen and deepen the centers already established. Swami Trigunatita had taken several steps in this latter direction. He had started a monastery, started a convent, inaugurated a magazine, conducted

annual monthlong retreats at Shanti Ashrama, and tried to establish a
Vedanta colony on a 160-acre tract of land at Concord in the East Bay.
But while the traditions that he had established in the Vedanta Society
remained vital, the institutions he had started had all but vanished.
Even before his death, the convent was disbanded; soon after his death,
the magazine, *The Voice of Freedom,* was terminated; the colony was
abandoned; and the annual retreats at Shanti Ashrama were gradually
given up. As for the monastery, it dwindled to a minimum.

Whatever the authorities at far-off Belur Math might think, Swami
Ashokananda was certain that expanding the work to nearby towns
would not in any way diminish the strength of the home center. On the
contrary, it would increase the membership, spread the message of
Vedanta throughout the community, and thereby not only gradually
introduce Vedanta into the mainstream of Western life but spiritually
benefit growing numbers of individual men and women. As early as
December 6 of 1931, he began to give Sunday evening talks in Oakland
at 536 53rd Street, the home of Mrs. Charles E. (Lila) Martin, a member of the San Francisco Vedanta Society. He would go there alone by
streetcar and ferry and then electric train and return the same way. But
this was not the Swami's first excursion across the bay.

Since the beginning of November, he had been going once a week
for voice lessons to a woman in Berkeley named Miss McCue—a
friend of Sarah Fox's who needed financial help. Sarah and her sister
Rebecca had been to India, where they had become disciples of Swami
Saradananda and where Swami Ashokananda had first met them. (The
younger sister, Fredrika, would later become his disciple.) Swami was
delighted to meet Sarah again (Rebecca had died) and often said that
she was one of the most spiritually advanced people he knew in the
West. Dumpy, friendly, bubbling with joy, yet withal emanating an immense dignity, Sarah Fox felt that the voice lessons, for which she paid,
would help both Swami and her friend, Miss McCue. And so they did.
In those days before microphones and loudspeakers, the Swami had
difficulty in projecting his voice to the back rows of the Temple audi-

torium. Miss McCue, an excellent teacher, taught him to control his breath and to make his voice carry. He took notes of her instructions and faithfully practiced. She told him that she would make him a fine opera singer, but he was content simply to be heard in the back rows of the Temple's nine-row hall.

This weekly trip across the bay was an ordeal for the shy, unassuming young man. He had been confused by the newness of everything and, lacking a sense of direction, often had difficulty finding Miss McCue's house, a small cottage hidden behind larger houses and reached by a narrow walkway. After his lesson he would visit Sarah Fox's house on 55th Street in Oakland and again become lost. He would have dinner with Sarah, who occupied the upper floor of her two-story house, renting out the lower floor. Starting in December, the Swami would give a talk on Sunday evenings at Mrs. Martin's house, which was near Sarah's. The attendance at Lila Martin's rapidly grew, and in a month or so it was advisable to find a larger place.

Swami Vividishananda, Swami Ashokananda, Mrs. Martin, Mrs. Weber, and Dr. Flambert, the last two of whom were members of the board of the Vedanta Society, looked for lecture halls in downtown Oakland. None were satisfactory: some were shabby, some barnlike, some too small, some too large. At length, they settled on the auditorium of the Ebell Club. After the arrangements had been made, though, it was learned that one Yogi Hamid Bay, a teacher of "Hindu magic" and occult practices, would be lecturing on Sundays throughout March in the very hall the Society had engaged for that month. So Swami Ashokananda, Mrs. Martin, and Dr. Flambert went to the Leamington Hotel and engaged the Castilian Room on the ground floor for Sunday meetings in February and March. They also looked at smaller rooms upstairs for a possible classroom. Somehow Yogi Hamid Bay got wind of this and phoned Swami to inform him that he (Yogi) was going to lecture at the Leamington Hotel during February and March and would begin on February 26 in the hotel lobby with his lecture and show.

Swami was unperturbed. But when he came to give his first lecture at the hotel on Sunday evening, February 7, he found that the hall had not been properly prepared. Although chairs had been set up for the audience, there was neither a rug nor a special chair on the platform, and the table was covered with a white cloth, kitchen style. The ventilation was poor; a heap of tables was piled up behind a screen at the far end of the hall, and a small linen closet served as a dressing room where the Swami could, with difficulty, change to his robe. As time went on, however, these faults were corrected, and, gradually, even though the audience had to pass through Yogi Hamid Bay's elaborate show before entering the Castillian Room, the place became presentable. The lecture attendance at the Leamington rapidly increased to over one hundred. But, to the consternation of Lila Martin, who noted the fact in her diary, the collection was always meager.

In all this, the Swami attended to the smallest details—the design and placement of posters, the light over the entrance door, the cloth on the table, the drapes on the windows, the wording of the ads in the newspapers, better arrangements for dressing—everything. There was nothing he could do, however, about Yogi Hamid Bay, who habitually moved the Vedanta Society's rugs, chairs, and screen to another hall in the hotel for his own use; nor was there anything he could do about the more-or-less-constant noise of banquets, dance parties, pipe organs, and metallic bangings in the garage underneath the lecture hall.

Despite these disturbances, Swami Ashokananda did not stop with Sunday lectures. On Thursday evening, March 3, 1932, he started a class in the Argyle Room on the mezzanine of the Leamington Hotel; at least, that is what he had arranged to do. But when he and Mrs. Martin and the others arrived at the hotel, they found that the hotel manager had forgotten about the class and had rented the Argyle Room to a banquet party for that night. Fortunately, another room close by was available. But this bit of negligence on the part of the hotel was too much, and a search for another hall in Oakland was undertaken. None could be found.

Finally, the Masonic Temple on Madison Street was hit upon, and at the beginning of April, Swami's lectures and classes (the latter now on Mondays) were moved there. The hall at the Masonic Temple, however, was not particularly pleasant, and, for one reason or another, the attendance began to drop off. The rent was steadily raised, the janitor was noticeably hostile, and the place was not always clean or in order. So, again, a search was made for a better hall, and at length, Ebell Hall was given another try. On Sunday, October 1, 1933, after a summer's vacation, Swami opened his lectures and classes there. Although Ebell Hall had its drawbacks, it was, as long search had proved, the best in Oakland, and Swami lectured there for six years, until October 15, 1939, when, as we shall see, another move was made—this time, a momentous one.

But to return to the early days of 1932, the Swami's trip across the bay and back continued to be arduous. There were three trips a week now, for on Tuesday evening, October 10, he started to lecture once a week at the Berkeley Women's City Club. After these East Bay lectures and classes his body would be icy cold—even to the touch. Still, the ferry ride back to San Francisco was restful, and sometimes, when there was moonlight on the water, it was beautiful. Finally, when the cold became too severe, he asked a close and relatively wealthy member of the Society—Elise Taylor—to buy him a warm overcoat. She bought him a dark blue camel-hair coat, which served him well to the end of his life. Around the same time, Adolph Gschwend, who was soon to become a member of the monastery, suggested that he drive him to and fro across the bay, taking the auto-ferry, which of course eliminated many streetcar and train rides each way. "I was surprised this made such a big difference," the Swami later said; "I felt much less tired!"

Meanwhile, things were beginning to stir in San Francisco. A young woman named Carol Weston, a professional violinist, and a group of her friends were desperately searching in one metaphysical book after another (the choice in those days was limited) for they knew not what—and not finding it. One day in 1931 Carol said to one of this

group, Edith Soulé, a concert singer with whom she had often performed, "Have you read a new book called *Prophets of the New
India?*"[45] Edith Soulé had not heard of it, and Carol said, "I think you
will find something in that book to interest you." Around this time, in
the late months of 1931, Carol had been asked by the officers of the
Young Women's Christian Association, of which she was a member, to
arrange a course of study that would interest young people. The officers of the YWCA had in mind a course of music, but Carol thought
that a course in comparative religions would draw more people. She
found an obscure Buddhist and also someone who could speak for the
Catholic Church, and knowing (through Mrs. Allan, with whom
she was acquainted) that in San Francisco there was a Hindu temple,
she went there.

Swami Ashokananda opened the door, asked her in, introduced her
to Swami Vividishananda, and after amiably agreeing to speak at the
YWCA on Hinduism, handed her his card. Looking at it, she was
stunned speechless. As soon as she could, she phoned Edith and said
(or probably shouted), "Do you know who we've got here in town?
The man who is mentioned all the way through the book by Romain
Rolland!"

Then came the YWCA lecture. It is not possible today to discover
the exact date of this, but it must have been toward the end of 1931 or
in the early part of 1932. Edith had the flu and didn't go, but her highly
intellectual and skeptical husband, Douglas, dutifully attended. On his
return he was ecstatic. "It was a remarkable talk!" he told his wife. "It
was the first time I've heard any sense spoken by a minister." The
Swami's lecture, "An Overview of Hinduism," led to classes at the Y,
and these, in turn, led to increased attendance at the Temple.

Sometime in early 1932, Mrs. Allan asked Carol to play the violin on
Easter Sunday at the Temple and asked her whether she knew someone
who could sing on that day. Carol mentioned her friend Edith Soulé,
whose parents, it turned out, Mrs. Allan had known. Edith agreed and,
with no time to prepare a religious song, sang a German love song—a

song being a song. Her voice was exquisitely beautiful and pure—a far cry from the voice of the Christian missionary whom the Swami had heard in his boyhood. But in the congregation there happened to be a German woman who understood the romantic words. After the service, this formidable woman said with severity to Swami Ashokananda (who was lecturing on Sunday mornings that April of 1932), "Do you know what you had this morning? It was a scandal! You had a woman singing a German love song!" Swami Ashokananda merely smiled.

Edith felt drawn to this young and obviously saintly Hindu, but she remained wary and aloof. Only at Carol's insistence did she again attend a lecture at the Temple, and then she went yet again—this third time without being urged. Finally, in June 1932, she asked the Swami whether she might come to see him. He said certainly.

It was perhaps at this first interview that the Swami asked Edith why she was interested in Vedanta, what her ideal was, her goals. She told him of her interest in Christian Science and of her idea that the healing part of Christ's mission was of great importance, and she explained that she thought that perhaps she could develop the art of healing and thereby help people. He looked at her for some time and then said, "Oh? And would you buy a five-cent loaf of bread with diamonds?" Startled, Edith then and there gave up her idea of healing. But she shot at him a barrage of questions about Christ, to whom she was devoted. After answering a good many of these, the Swami suddenly leaned back in his chair and said with finality, "You will have to read a lot of our books." He wrote a list for her, which included the *Complete Works of Swami Vivekananda.* Dutifully, she started with *Jnana Yoga* and before long was absorbed.[46] When she came to Swami Vivekananda's double-barreled lecture "The Cosmos," the answers to her many questions were answered, and, to the vast amusement of Carol and her other friends, she went "out of her mind for joy." At her next interview, she asked Swami Ashokananda to teach her meditation.

"Do you really want it?" he asked.

"Of course."

"You have to make a promise—that every day of your life for as long as you live you will never neglect it."

Edith Soulé did not make promises easily, but this promise she made.

And then, as she related in later years, "the discipline began. Every time I was egotistical, I got slapped down so hard that my breath would be taken away! One of the first things he said to me when I cried over something that seemed unjust was 'Look here, if you think I work logically, you will think I'm a madman. I work *psychologically;* remember that!'"

When she asked him what exactly was meant by obedience, he replied, "Can you do whatever I tell you to do?" "Of course," she said. "Then open the window and throw that tray you are carrying into the street." Without hesitation, Edith opened the window and threw the tray and its glass of water into the bushes outside.

"Now," Swami said soberly, "go and get it." She did so. Swami nodded.

Soon Mrs. Allan retired from her position of chief temple singer, and Edith began to sing regularly at the Sunday services. An acclaimed concert singer, spirited and independent, she was not used to being told how to sing. "Nobody can understand your words!" Swami admonished her. There were many other little comments, until one day, talking over the phone to her about her singing, Swami began, "Mrs. Allan said . . ." Edith had had enough. "Look, Swami," she replied, "I don't have to sing there. *Do* have Mrs. Allan sing; it is all right with me. If I sing, I will do it my own way; I don't know what else to do. I just don't have to sing at the Temple at all!"

There was a long silence, and finally Swami said coldly and with devastating evenness of tone, "That is not the kind of answer I expected."[47] That was the first step in Edith's transformation from a concert singer to a disciple, a process not as easy as throwing a tray out a window. She continued to sing at the Temple and continued to receive, and finally to accept, criticism. Not for several years did she learn that

Swami had known from the beginning that she had a magnificent voice. "Incomparable," he said to another, who told her.

By now, a few other students had appeared—most of them young schoolteachers or nurses. There was Mara Lane, who had come first to an Oakland lecture at the Leamington Hotel; Kathleen Davis, who had first heard Swami speak in 1932 at the YWCA; Lila Chandra; Mary Lou Flambert; Thelma Fine; Eve Bunch, a registered nurse; Leona Smith, Kathleen's close friend; and Dorothy Madison, a young high school teacher from the East Bay, who would soon bring several of her students to the Temple.

In the early part of 1932, Swami Vividishananda had developed a bad case of pleurisy and had gone to see Dr. Lartigau, the doctor who had diagnosed his anemia. The doctor now told Swami Ashokananda that his brother monk should not remain in America, that he could not thrive here. Swami Ashokananda did not convey this unpleasant news to Swami Vividishananda; nor did the doctor. Rather, the latter told Swami Vividishananda that he should live in the country, not the city, for the city's climate, generally cold and damp, was slowly sapping his strength. The only country then available to the swamis of San Francisco, though, was Shanti Ashrama, which was out of the question. Aside from its severe extremes of heat and cold, the ashrama was isolated and far from any supplies; it had no electricity or gas, no running hot water, very little running cold water, only the most primitive plumbing—if it could be called that—and, of course, no telephone. It was an ideal place for desert fathers, but not a place where an ailing monk could regain his health. So it was decided that Swami Vividishananda should cross the continent to Providence, Rhode Island, where he had a standing invitation from Swami Akhilananda.

In April of 1932, Swami Vividishananda lectured on Wednesday evenings rather than on Sunday mornings; in May he lectured not at all, and his Gita classes were closed. On Sunday, June 5, 1932, he gave a farewell address that packed the hall, and on the following day he departed from San Francisco for Providence, leaving the Society in charge of Swami Ashokananda. He had been loved in San Francisco, and later on, he would come to the Temple every summer, visiting his disciples, his brother monk, and the latter's disciples, who looked upon him as a beloved uncle.

7

TAKING FLIGHT

So a new era began. The membership of the Society now numbered fifty-seven and was growing, the attendance at the lectures was generally around eighty and was also growing, there was $242.60 in the bank, and yearly receipts and disbursements amounted to around $4,000. Things began to return to the days of Swami Trigunatita, when the spiritual leader of the Society was the authority in all matters—even small ones. At first, there was a slight tussle. There had been, for instance, the time a few days before the annual meeting of March 1932 when Mr. Brown had said to Swami Vividishananda, "Well, Swami, we must decide who to nominate for the board of directors."

"Never mind, Mr. Brown," Swami Ashokananda had said quickly, not giving his monastic brother a chance to agree; "the swamis will decide about it."

Mr. Brown's face had turned red with anger. "Swami," he said to Swami Ashokananda with immense disapproval, "you are the first swami since Swami Trigunatita to exercise authority!"

"Mr. Brown," Swami Ashokananda replied evenly, "who should exercise authority if not the swamis? Would anyone come to the lectures if it were not for the swamis? Do they come here for the board of directors? Who would become a member of the Society if it were not for the swamis? Tell me!" Mr. Brown had been silenced, but after that, he did not speak to Swami Ashokananda for a month or so.

"If I had not proved successful in lecturing," the Swami once said, "they [the old guard] would have crushed me." But as it was, he held his own, even prevailing upon the board not to cut the swamis' weekly allowance of twenty-five dollars in half after Swami Vividishananda left.

Many years later, in a special meeting of the members, Swami Ashokananda had occasion to speak of the position of the swami-in-charge in relation to the students:

When I first came here in 1931, I found a peculiar state of things. There were quite a few original students here, that is to say, disciples of Swami Trigunatita and also disciples of Swami Prakashananda. They seemed to think that they had no other duty now than to lay down the law for others, including the swamis. That was the main purpose of their existence. So I talked with some of the old students—students of Swami Trigunatita. I said, "You must remember this: It is true that the members of the board of directors or the members of the Society in an annual meeting or in any other meeting have a right to stand up and challenge the swami and tell him some bitter things, as it occurs to you. And so you do it. The next morning you come to him and ask him for some spiritual advice. . . . Just imagine what kind of attitude you have taken towards the swami the day before. And today, if you ask him something, will you be able to accept what he tells you? How will you benefit from his spiritual advice? You cannot do both of those things. So you have to make up your mind. Are you going to fight in the meetings and find fault with the swami all the days of your life, or are you going to benefit spiritually from him? *Is this Society for spiritual purposes or for something else?*" Of course they all agreed it was for a spiritual purpose. And it is to their credit, I must say, they agreed that they would not go on fighting the swamis in meetings any more. They did not, for which I am grateful. During the years I have been here, I have had no trouble from the members. The work has had its own trouble, but the members have not caused me any trouble.[48]

Thus at the very outset Swami Ashokananda made his relationship with the members of the Society clear, and even the strong-willed, opinionated disciples of Swami Trigunatita understood and bowed to him—figuratively. The Indian tradition of *pranams* and other cultural mannerisms adopted by Western students was anathema to him. "Vedanta in America," he once said, "should not make fifth-rate Hindus out of you; it should make first-rate Americans!"

With the departure of Swami Vividishananda, Swami Ashokananda's work naturally increased. He gave now both the Sunday morning and Wednesday evening lectures at the Temple and held the Friday evening class. The attendance quickly grew at both lectures, and soon the audience would fill the standing room at the back of the auditorium and cascade down the auditorium stairs to press against the entrance door.

At the first annual meeting of his ministry (in March of 1933), Swami Ashokananda spoke of moving the Sunday lectures to a larger hall. He spoke also, the minutes read, "of expansion and of sending of the Vedantic message to all quarters of the globe. . . . Vedanta, he declared, was not meant for a handful of people only." During this same talk to the members of the Society, the Swami spoke of publishing a magazine and of establishing a monastery for men and a convent for women.

Though his health was not good, his acute and almost constant stomach pain still with him, the Swami's energy seemed unbounded. After giving a lecture in Oakland at the Leamington Hotel on a Sunday evening, he would hold a class there on the following Monday evening. On Tuesday evening he would hold a class in Berkeley; on Wednesday

Swami Ashokananda in charge of the Vedanta Society
of Northern California, 1933

evening he would give a lecture in San Francisco; on Thursday evening, as we shall see a little later, he would give a lecture in Burlingame, a town south of San Francisco; and on Friday evening, he
would hold a class in San Francisco. His weekly schedule would vary
from time to time, but for several years there was scarcely a day of the
week (except Saturday) that he did not either deliver a lecture or hold a
class, giving two lectures on Sundays. Nor were these lectures and
classes such as a college professor or political orator might deliver day
after day. They required an enormous expenditure of spiritual energy,
which was, in a way, as invigorating to him as to his listeners, but also,
because he gave so much at such a high pitch, was physically exhaust-
ing. He always spoke extemporaneously, pouring his heart and soul
into his words, wanting with his whole being to give his listeners
the great truths of Vedanta. During his lectures he would seem transported, even awesome; one could not imagine approaching him. Yet in
the most philosophical or vigorously upbraiding of his talks, the
sweetness of his concern would come through in his voice, his manner.
Indeed, throughout his mission in the West, until he could speak no
more, he delivered lectures and held classes as though he were performing profound acts of worship. And so he was.

In the early days he had the "knack," as he called it, of lecturing for
exactly one hour without counting the time. When he finished, he
would look at the clock and find that sixty minutes had passed, no
more, no less. "Later, I lost that knack," he said. Indeed, later, his lectures and classes, when there were only four a week, would run to an
hour and a half or two hours, his listeners absorbed to the end. But at
the meditation session that preceded the Friday evening Upanishad
class, he would meditate exactly twenty-three minutes. When Edith
Soulé, who noted this precision, asked him how he could know the
time, he said, "One gets accustomed to a certain mental routine." But
there was no routine or set pattern about his lecturing: it sometimes
flowed straight on, carrying everything with it; sometimes it mean-
dered like a stream through rocky land; sometimes, though rarely, it

was leisurely; and sometimes it was torrential. Whatever its pace, one thing it never did was bog down.

He held interviews every day, one after the other—often without stopping for lunch—with individual men and women who wanted to know more about Vedanta, or who simply wanted to tell of their spiritual experiences or of their ongoing personal hells. Sometimes those who came for an interview wanting to know more about Vedanta would wordlessly cry and cry in his presence, feeling his compassion flow over them like a warm current. Often, they would end up wanting spiritual instruction. "Interviews," he once said, "are the most tiring of all. One has to try to enter the minds of others, to understand things from their point of view. It is sometimes a great strain." After hours of back-to-back interviews, he would become so physically exhausted that in the late afternoon, when the last seeker had left and he walked up the block to Union Street to buy his groceries, he would stagger with fatigue. One evening as he zigzagged up the street in his clericals, a respectable and upright man who was walking toward him looked at him with disgust. "No doubt he was thinking," Swami said, amused, "that here was a Negro preacher so drunk he could not walk straight!"

Sometimes his exhausted excursions to the stores on Union Street a block away gave him a glimpse deep into the American religious psyche. One day, when he lingered in a bakery, selecting a treat for his dessert, two large and well-corseted housewives watched him closely. When he made his selection, one said to the other in patronizing tones, "The reverend has a sweet tooth." The words sent a warning chill down his spine, calling up a vision of the suffocating arms of American churchwomen in which they embraced their pastors and controlled them. To that danger he would not open the door a crack. And a danger it was: in the eyes of many of its members, the Vedanta Society was a church like any other, with a genial and pliable minister—except that it had an Eastern slant and substituted Sri Ramakrishna for Jesus Christ.

He found that the members, young and old, had very little conception of Vedanta. "When I first came to San Francisco," he once said,

"I could not distinguish between Vedantists and Christian Scientists. Only a few 'Vedantists' had some idea of what Vedanta was. Even then, they did not have a very clear idea. They had devotion; that is all." But there were also those who wanted seriously to undertake spiritual practice, and to give them instruction was, to the Swami's mind, the most important aspect of his work. In early bulletins, the following paragraph began to appear:

> The Swami considers practical instruction as the most important part of his activity. He is glad to give practical instruction for spiritual development to those who sincerely want it. They also are invited to make appointments with the Swami for interviews—for practical instruction can be given only privately and personally.

More and more earnest seekers came. Though often physically exhausted, Swami Ashokananda always felt in those early days a great upsurge of mental energy. "I was enthusiastic all the time," he later said. "I needed very little food or sleep. I would have a glass of milk for breakfast, another for lunch—if I remembered—and for dinner two lamb chops and a can of peas [cooked in the small kitchen on the ground floor of the Temple]. That was all." "There was the tiredness of lecturing," he said at another time, "but everything looked fresh; nothing sat heavy on my shoulders. There was no responsibility."

In those days the Society's finances were in good shape, and a good thing, for these were the years of the Great Depression in America. No one had money to spare for church donations, and many people had no money at all. Almost every day gaunt and shabbily dressed men, clearly hungry, would beg at the temple door for a dime or so. Invariably Swami would give them some money. But the requests became so frequent that it occurred to him that the Temple had become known as a good place for a handout. His allowance, moreover, was becoming depleted. One day he turned a man away. It was only after the man left that he realized he had been well dressed and had an air of culture about him. He was not an ordinary beggar, but must have met with some dire reversal of fortune. Swami asked two devotees who were working in the Temple at the time to run after the man, and he gave them some money for him. They ran and searched in every direction, but the man was nowhere to be found. Swami Ashokananda never forgot that dignified and gentle man whom he had turned away, nor did he ever cease to regret having done so.

In November and December of 1932, Swami delivered a series of four Tuesday evening lectures in a rented hall in downtown San Francisco (Sorosis Hall). Leaflets with the announcement "Four Lectures by Swami Ashokananda" were printed, and in small type beneath the banner line was the parenthesis "Disciple of Swami Vivekananda." This was the first public statement of his discipleship. Perhaps thinking that there were many people still living in San Francisco who had heard Swami Vivekananda speak in 1900 and who would therefore be drawn to attend lectures of a disciple of his, he had thought it wise. It may well have drawn people; indeed, the attendance was so great at Sorosis Hall that at the beginning of 1933 the Sunday morning lectures were moved there. Because of this, the parenthesis was inserted in the Society's January and February 1933 bulletins, and once again in October, when he would lecture in Burlingame. But in the Burlingame flyer for November 1933 the mention of his discipleship was omitted. It had, in fact, been ill advised, bringing forth the derision of at least one of his brother monks. Until the last years of his life, he did not again reveal the identity of his guru. Even many of his close disciples did not know. But the Swami was what he was. The attendance at Sorosis Hall remained high, double what it had been in the Temple. The Sunday evening lectures in Oakland were also proving highly successful, regularly drawing over a hundred people—then a record number for a Vedanta society in America, where Eastern religions were thought to be both life-denying and loony.

———

IN MARCH OF 1933 Edith Soulé gave a party for the Swami. Edith lived with her husband, Douglas, and small daughter, Anne, in a large house in Forest Hill, an affluent and wooded neighborhood in the southwestern part of the city. The Soulés' money, which came from Douglas's side, was soon to be entirely lost. But in early 1933, the Soulés' house and its beautiful furniture and appointments were still solidly their own. Douglas's family was prominent socially in the Bay Area, and in her own right, Edith had good social connections in the city, largely among wealthy Jewish families who moved in the same musical circles as she did and appreciated the beauty of her voice and her musicianship. Moreover, many of these influential, highly cultured people knew Edith's mining-engineer father, Edward Benjamin, in a business capacity.

Early in 1933 one of San Francisco's wealthy social leaders, Noël Sullivan, a patron of many artists and a champion of many causes, had given a dinner to introduce the young Krishnamurti to San Francisco. He had invited Edith Soulé. The dinner is memorable to us because during the course of it, Edith conceived the idea of having a similar party for Swami Ashokananda.

Edith Soulé seldom conceived an idea without at once putting it into action. The Swami was consulted and was agreeable, and a date was set—March 16. Three hundred invitations went out, and all was ready. Then, shortly before the event, Edith proudly showed a printed invitation to Swami. He read it and looked at her with dismay. "Do you know what we have done?" he asked. "This is the date of the Society's annual business meeting!" Edith had visions of contacting all three hundred people to advise them of a change of date. But with characteristic common sense, Swami Ashokananda unhesitatingly postponed the traditional (and all but sacred) date of the Society's annual meeting. The fifty-seven members were so advised, and on the evening of the third Thursday in March of 1933 Edith Soulé gave her party, whose purpose was to introduce Swami Ashokananda to the intellectual and cultural cream of San Francisco. This it did—but this was not its only or its most important achievement.

The Soulé house was an ideal setting for the occasion. Its living room was spacious and was overlooked by a balcony, which could seat many additional people. Edith and Douglas moved the furniture out of the living room and balcony and moved in three hundred or more rented chairs. In the dining room, after-lecture refreshments were set out on a big round table laid with fine linen and gleaming china. There was coffee, tea, fruit juices, sandwiches, and small cakes. Conspicuous to every guest, except the guest of honor, was the absence of a variety of liquors.

By eight o'clock over two hundred people in evening dress had arrived—not quite the three hundred who had received invitations, but the gathering was large. They had come primarily because the occasion would no doubt prove to be unusual. It was possible in the 1930s that even among that cultured group some may have come to have their futures read in a crystal ball or to hear about mahatmas flying in the Himalayas. When everyone was seated and looking expectant, Douglas brought Swami Ashokananda into the living room. The Swami sat in the front row next to Edith. "Douglas was nervous," Edith recalled, "but he introduced Swami very nicely," and then "this young, dark, slight, *tender* man," as Edith would describe him, wearing a dark, well-tailored business suit, rose to face an audience of society leaders, professional men and women, military men, university professors, and business tycoons. As the Swami stood up, Edith saw that his hands were slightly shaking. "What have I done!" she thought, appalled. "I have made him face a bunch of worldly people! To what end?" The Swami's nervousness was only momentary. He was soon at ease and master of the situation. He highlighted Hinduism's basic points—the doctrines of karma and reincarnation, the cyclic theory of creation, the Vedantic view of consciousness, the divinity of man, the ultimate goal of life, and so on. He spoke for about thirty minutes, and at the end he said, "I understand that some of you would like to ask questions." They would indeed.

For the next hour and a half the Swami answered question after question. "The questions just poured out," Edith recalled. "One question I remember. A man said, 'You've talked about consciousness, Swami. What happens if a man is knocked on the head. Doesn't he lose consciousness? You have said you can't lose it.' Swami's answer was, 'He has lost contact with consciousness.' I don't think the man was satisfied. Then in the balcony Noël Sullivan asked, 'Swami, does an animal have a soul?' Swami said, 'Of course!' And Noël, a Catholic, said with great feeling, 'Thank you, Swami!'"

The questions went on and on. Eventually, the Swami left and was driven back to the Temple by Adolph. The party continued, the refreshments were consumed, and the guests talked animatedly among themselves. The evening was a success: the Swami's talk had aroused intense interest. But perhaps only a very few knew what they had heard. Among those few, one of San Francisco's prominent patrons of music asked her hostess, awestruck, "Do these people know that they have heard another Moses?" And Josephine Stanbury, visibly moved, said to Edith, "Why weren't these people all on their knees!" In the audience was a young man named Alfred Clifton. He had been induced to come by a Junius Cravens, a locally well known artist, who was then living with the Soulés and had heard the Swami earlier. It was for the sake of Cravens that Alfred Clifton had attended the lecture. From then on he never left Swami Ashokananda's side.

Josephine Stanbury and her friend Helen Sutherland were partners in an interior decorating business. (Helen did the decorating, and Josephine attended to the business.) Edith Soulé knew both young women and had one day gone into the Sutherland-Stanbury shop to pay a visit. Josephine had laughingly said to her, "We want to know what makes you look so high and mighty. What are you so happy about nowadays?" Edith had replied, "Come and find out!" And she invited them to the party. Like Alfred Clifton, Jo and Helen thenceforth never left Swami Ashokananda.

Beautiful Jo! Tall, with black hair and blue eyes, a commanding presence and a warm heart, she worked untiringly with a devotion as

Josephine Stanbury and Helen Sutherland

pure as it was fierce. Helen, small and elfin, watched over Jo even as Jo watched over Swami and fumed that Jo worked too hard, although she herself would do all that Swami asked. And Al, the young and energetic son of an army officer, knew how to take orders as well as to give them and had no other goal but to follow the commands of his guru, one of which was that he become a saint. For the rest of their lives, those three—Al, Jo, and Helen—were among Swami Ashokananda's closest, most helpful, and most loyal disciples, even helping to support the Society long after he himself had gone.

The lassoing of those three was the main accomplishment of Edith Soulé's party. But as she had intended, the two hundred or so guests knew thereafter that the Vedanta Society and its spiritual leader were not representative of some strange, unwholesome cult; that one could respectably go to the weird-looking temple on the corner of Webster and Filbert Streets and listen to lectures and classes delivered by an orange-robed Hindu; that one could even become a disciple of that Hindu and count oneself lucky. As time went on, though, most of the people whom Edith's party had brought to the Temple dropped away; only Al Clifton, Josephine Stanbury, and Helen Sutherland made Vedanta an all-absorbing part of their lives—indeed, the whole of their lives. It is quite possible that even without the party, those three would have found their way to Vedanta and to Swami Ashokananda, and in that respect the outcome might have been the same—but who knows?

The Soulés' party had taken place just in time. Shortly afterward, due to the slump in the national economy and bad management on the part of Douglas Soulé's family, Edith and Douglas lost their entire fortune, including their house and car. Edith, counting as usual on a more than ample monthly income, had paid their bills and without a thought had let their bank account drop to twelve dollars. It was then that she received the news from their lawyer that everything was lost. Twelve dollars was all that was left of Douglas Soulé's not inconsiderable fortune. One day when Edith was feeling extremely low, sitting in the beautiful living room, with its huge fireplace, its balcony, its Oriental carpets, knowing it was all as good as gone, the phone rang. It was Swami. He said, as if he didn't know, "What are you doing?" "If you must know," she replied, "I think I'm crying." "Why?" "Well—you know what's happened to us: the house is going, the automobile has gone . . ." Without offering the least sympathy and without hesitation, Swami Ashokananda said commandingly and bracingly, "Be a monk! Be a monk!" "That was enough," Edith later said. "I felt as if someone had given me a hard blow and a shot of energy. I said, 'All right, sir, I'll try.' And that was that. From then on I didn't let down. I felt badly; I did a lot of hard things; I had to go around and sell china and silver and carpets and whatnot; but the awful feeling of loss was gone. He was so strong! And just like that—on the phone, when one needed it. It was uncanny."

For his part, Douglas, who seemed effete and incapable of getting a job, let alone of holding one down, surprised even his wife by quickly applying for work at the City College of San Francisco. Having had an extensive and thorough education in the humanities, Dr. Soulé was qualified to teach a large number of subjects, among them English literature, the Romance languages, Greek and Latin, the history of Western thought, ancient and medieval history, and philosophy in its elementary phases. He was readily accepted as a teacher of several junior college courses and was steadily able to support himself, his wife, and his daughter—not in the style to which they were accustomed, but in a style that most people would find comfortable.

IN JUNE OF 1933 Swami Ashokananda went for a vacation to the East Coast, where he visited the Vedanta centers in New York, Boston, and Providence. He also visited the center in Chicago, where Swami Gnaneswarananda was in charge. In each center he lectured at least once at the behest of his brother monks, who show no mercy to their own.

During his absence, the ground floor of the Temple was refurbished. To the Vedanta Society's great good fortune, Josephine Stanbury and Helen Sutherland took on the job of cleaning, painting, and redecorating the auditorium and the three ground-floor rooms, the middle one of which Swami used as his bedroom. They donated their services as interior decorators and supplied all materials and furnishings at cost, as they would do for the rest of their lives. Many of the members pitched in to pay for whatever expense there was. Thus, on his return from the East Coast, Swami came back to refreshed and redecorated rooms. But the most welcoming part of his homecoming had nothing to do with the decor. When he entered his bedroom and saluted the photograph of Sri Ramakrishna on his dresser, he saw the figure actually moving with joy to have him back.

The devotees celebrated his return with a picnic at Shanti Ashrama. Then in mid-August of 1933 the Swami's work started again. The Sunday morning lectures were now given at the Century Club, a women's club on the corner of Franklin and Sutter Streets, the hall of which could accommodate some three hundred people. If there were people

Shanti Ashrama, 1933. *Seated on the ground in front, left to right:*
Adolph Gschwend, Mr. Groeting, Al Clifton, Mary Lou Flambert,
and Elise Taylor. *Standing, left to right:* Edith Soulé, Thomas Allan,
Swami Ashokananda, Mae Weber, and Ernest C. Brown.

outside of San Francisco and Oakland ready to receive what he had to
give, Swami Ashokananda was ready to go to them. And soon, possibly through some of the guests at the Soulés' party, he was asked to
give lectures in the town of Burlingame, where many members of the
city's highest social circles had their summer homes as well as their
year-round mansions, their polo fields, their swimming pools and tennis courts. Indeed, Burlingame was in itself a sort of large and highly
exclusive country club—an unlikely place to hold an Upanishad or a
Gita class. But the Swami, still unaware of that, agreed to lecture at the
Burlingame Women's Club on Thursday evenings, starting on October 5. He rented a house in the nearby town of Belmont, where he and
very likely Adolph could stay on the night of the lecture, returning to
the city the following morning.

The Burlingame lectures were well attended—most of the time.

The Swami noticed that while sometimes eighty or ninety people would come, on other Thursdays there would be only five or six. After a time he asked one of the regulars why this was so. He was informed of the nature of Burlingame: "It is a social town; whenever there is a party, everyone will go to it." Everyone, that is, except the five or six faithfuls who were not a part of the social whirligig. Swami Ashokananda saw that there was no hope in such an environment and gave his last lecture in Burlingame on November 23. He had given eight lectures altogether. He did not regret those evenings. In connection with them, he once said, "One must scatter seeds here and there like Johnny Appleseed did. One never knows what will come of it." And to be sure, the Burlingame venture did not go to waste. One person (Evelyn Zeiss) became a disciple, a student of Sanskrit, and a member of the Vedanta Society for the rest of her life.

In December of 1933 Swami Ashokananda went to southern California for four days and called it a rest. When he returned, his heavy lecture program (minus Burlingame) continued as before until he fell really ill and despite himself had to remain in bed. During most of March and April of 1934, he gave no lectures or classes in the Temple or anywhere else. Edith Soulé thought it was the news of Swami Shivananda's death that had been too much for him. And perhaps, on top of a relentless schedule, it was.

He had learned of the great Swami's *mahasamadhi* on February 20, 1934, when Edith was in the Temple for an appointment. "I remember he was silent," she recalled, "and then he said, 'Swami Shivananda has gone,' and he left the front room. When he came back, I said, 'Swami, would you let me drive you down to the Marina, just to get into the air?' He didn't answer, but he got his hat. He was silent, completely silent. I think it hit him very hard. And I wouldn't be a bit surprised that his illness a little while later came from that experience." After that, Edith often drove Swami to the Marina, where he would sit in the car looking at the water or at the hills of Marin County across the Golden Gate. Or she would drive him through Golden Gate Park to the ocean and along the sand-duned shore. Such outings rested him, and he would talk almost to himself of his plans for developing, nurturing, and expanding the work.

Certainly Swami Shivananda's death was a severe blow to Swami Ashokananda, but his subsequent illness seems to have been more physical than psychological, requiring prolonged medical care. His medical bill was high, and, even more telling, his failure to appear on the platform for almost two months was a sure sign that he was ill indeed. He did, however, attend the Society's annual meeting, which was held on the evening of March 15. This was the second annual meeting during his ministry, and it was his first opportunity to amend the Society's constitution and bylaws, which, as they then stood, invested unchecked power in the board of directors.

No doubt remembering Mr. Allan's and Mr. Brown's early belligerence in this regard and possibly having discussed the matter with his fellow swamis during his visits with them in June of 1933, Swami Ashokananda deemed it essential that his position vis-à-vis the board of directors be made legally clear. To have pressed the point a year earlier at the first annual meeting of his ministry would have risked unleashing the still-churning opposition and created unnecessary unpleasantness. But by March of 1934 Mr. Allan had considerably modified his views in regard to this young swami. As early as December 15, 1933, he had written the following paragraphs in a letter to Swami Shivananda:

> We of the Vedanta Society of San Francisco feel very grateful to you for sending us such a wonderful Swami as Swami Ashokananda. He reminds us, we older ones, of the Older Swamis who came to the west shortly after Swamiji was here. Swami Ashokananda has no mercy on his body, and some of us wonder whether he will be able to keep his health if he continues to work so hard and at such high pressure. His addresses are marvelous, his life and example are sublime, his oratory is beyond description, and

he is so human that he does not talk away over our heads. He is beloved by all, old and young. It is interesting to see small children go to him, when he is standing conversing, and throw their small arms around his legs in a loving embrace.

Last month (November) his public lectures, each week, were as follows: in San Francisco, three; in Oakland, in Berkeley, and in Burlingame, one each; six public lectures each week, besides the many private individual lessons he gives every day.

Under his leadership the society has grown in numbers and in importance in the community. In San Francisco the average attendance at the public meetings is about one hundred and sixty. His lectures are enjoyed by rich and poor, by intellectuals and also by the common people.

Mrs. Allan, too, had changed her tune. After Swami Ashokananda's first Wednesday night lecture, she developed a hand-wringing fear of him. "I am so afraid of him," she confided to a friend, "that during an interview I cannot sit still." Her fear later turned to deep respect and affection. In October of 1946 she wrote to the same friend, Ida Ansell, "I sometimes call Swami Ashokananda on the phone just to hear him speak, and he is kind enough to speak to me though he is so busy with many many things to do. I am very fond of him." Again to Ida Ansell after an interview with him in 1947:

> I felt truly thankful that the Lord had sent Swami Ashokananda to this Temple. . . . I walked on air for a few days and gradually came down to good old Mother Earth again, but as I write to you about it I feel all aglow. . . . He is really a wonderful Swami! Most brilliant and fearless.

Nevertheless, there was no guarantee in 1934 that the directors would remain amenable or that Swami Ashokananda's successor (whoever he might be) would be able to control them. The primary trouble with the existing bylaws was that they gave the swami-in-residence no authority at all. Since Swami Trigunatita's time, the bylaws had scarcely mentioned the swami, except as a sort of resident doctor of souls, tolerated, even respected, but in temporal matters of no consequence. The board of directors could do practically anything it chose with respect to the operation of the Society, with or without the approval of the swami, who, if he happened to have a retiring nature, could be steamrolled by the board with not a word to say. Swami Ashokananda amended almost every article of these insidious bylaws to include the phrase "with the sanction of the Resident Swami" or "under the approval of the Resident Swami." It was now clear that the resident swami was by unanimous consent in charge all along the line, de jure as well as de facto. Everyone could have a say, but the swami would have the last say. As far as is known, the amended bylaws were passed without demur. (Later, the term *Resident Swami* was changed to the more accurate *Swami-in-Charge*.)

While Swami Ashokananda may have discussed the Society's bylaws with his confreres in America, it is not likely that he consulted the trustees at Belur Math about changing them. The Indian swamis knew nothing about the cultural environment that shaped, and sometimes obstructed, the American work, much as the contour of a countryside shapes a river flowing through it. Nor were the bylaws a concern of the trustees. In temporal matters, the American Vedanta societies were strictly (and rather fiercely) autonomous.

EVEN AFTER HE RECOVERED from his illness and started lecturing again in May of 1934, Swami Ashokananda felt the need of a rest and of a place in the country where he could vacation for at least one month. He asked Edith Soulé, whom he had finally agreed to call Ediben (the name she was best known by to her friends) rather than the formal Mrs. Soulé, to search the newspaper ads for a likely spot. The place she found was a house at Huntington Lake in the Sierras, approximately 80

Huntington Lake, 1934. *Seated, left to right:* Edith Soulé and Sarah Fox. *Standing, left to right:* Al Clifton and Swami Ashokananda.

miles southwest of Yosemite Valley and about 120 miles southeast of San Francisco, which was available for a month or two. It was built of stone and had several bedrooms, a large living room, and a patio, a portion of which was glassed in and used for dining. Stone steps led from the patio down to the lake. It was a beautiful spot, serene and quiet.

Swami, the Soulés, Adolph Gschwend, Al Clifton, who, along with Adolph, was by now in the monastery, and Sarah Fox made up the party that went to Huntington Lake. Sarah had burst into tears when Ediben asked her to come and had said, "You mean you want *me?*" "Yes," Ediben had replied, "We want you and need you." And in the long quiet days at Huntington Lake, Swami and Sarah would sit on the patio and reminisce about India and Swami Saradananda, Sarah's guru, while Ediben, Douglas, Al, and Adolph went swimming. Once when they were all sitting on the patio after lunch, a bird flew straight through and banged into the clear glass on the other side. It fell to the ground, and Ediben rushed to pick it up. It wasn't dead, but Swami was much moved. "You see," he said, "it is like life. You think your way is clear, and you go right for it, and suddenly you hit a barricade that you had thought was an open path. You hadn't seen it, but it was there—a false view of an open way. Don't shoot too hard for something you think is real; it may be a false view; it may stop you." It was an almost prophetic remark, for toward the close of his life, Swami Ashokananda was to find his way obstructed by more than one unexpected barricade.

At Huntington Lake, Swami's health and energy soon returned, and he began to miss his other students. He would wonder out loud, Ediben recalled, what this one or that one was doing. "And finally," she said, "we realized that he had had enough rest and wanted to get back."

For Douglas Soulé the return trip was terrifying, infuriating, and altogether memorable. He and Adolph drove together, Adolph at the wheel. Suddenly, driving along the relatively crowded highway, Adolph, imbued with Advaita Vedanta, shouted, "So 'hum! So 'hum!" (I am He! I am He!), and with a burst of maniacal speed, weaving in and out, tore down the road. This was in the days before expressways, when two-lane, two-way highways were laced with crossroads, many without signs or stoplights. Paying no heed, Adolph, the Self, was king of the road; everyone else could get out of his way. Fortunately, everyone did. But Douglas talked crossly about that drive for years thereafter.

———

WHILE HIS STAY at Huntington Lake had benefited Swami, he needed more rest. He had worked almost nonstop since his arrival in San Francisco, and besides, he was wanting to once again see Belur Math. Belur Math! It was to him the holiest of holy places. Three of the great swamis from whom he had received so many blessings were now gone—Swami Premananda, Swami Brahmananda, and Swami Shivananda—but perhaps because of their memories, sacred to him, he longed now to visit the places where he had known them.

Who would go with him: Al Clifton or Adolph Gschwend, the latter of whom had been in Vedanta longer? Adolph settled the matter by giving Al his savings so he could afford the trip. For Al the trip was momentous, not only because all trips to India are momentous for the American devotee, not only because he made the trip with his guru, but because while he was there, in January of 1935, Swami Virajananda, then general secretary of the Order, gave him the vows of *brahmacharya* and the monastic name Bhrigu. This was kept a secret for many years; indeed, not until Al received the vows of *sannyas* in 1962 and became Swami Chidrupananda did anyone realize that he had been a *brahmacharin* for nearly thirty years.

Swami Ashokananda was slow in giving vows. He wanted to be entirely sure that the disciple was ready to live up to them, for he felt that spiritual harm would come if the monastic should break his vows or feel a sense of guilt in not being able to keep them perfectly. It was not until 1959 that other members of the monastery would receive *brahmacharya*. For the vows of *sannyas,* they went much later to India.

Before leaving San Francisco for India in 1934, Swami Ashokananda made certain that things would go on with as little hitch as possible during his absence. As we saw earlier, at the annual meeting of 1933 he had expressed the need for a monastery and a convent. In 1934 he mentioned these needs again. The monastery started by Swami Trigunatita in 1908 had two members living in the towers: the old man Mr. Anderson, and the faithful Henry Page of Swami Trigunatita's time. So, although all the other monastics under Swami Trigunatita or Swami Prakashananda had vanished, there was still a monastery. Later, Adolph Gschwend had joined, and later still, Al Clifton. Mr. Brown, who had been a monastic under Swami Trigunatita and who had left to marry and was now a widower with a grown daughter, was permitted to return to the monastery by Swami Ashokananda. But, insofar as these four or five monks earned their own living, the monastery was not what Swami Ashokananda had in mind.

As for a convent—the convent that Swami Trigunatita had started had been disbanded even in his time, and nothing had taken its place. But the establishment of a convent was as dear to Swami Ashokananda's heart as was that of a monastery, and before he left for India, he sent up a trial balloon. Mae Weber, known also as Nirupama, was a student of Swami Prakashananda's and secretary of the Society when Swami Ashokananda first came from India. When her husband died in 1934, the Swami asked her to rent a flat in the neighborhood and there live a monastic life with other women. She found a place—the lower floor of a two-family building—on Green Street, between Webster and Buchanan, less than three blocks from the Temple.

Two young women (both thirty years old) were chosen to live there with her. One of them, Thelma Fine, was one of Swami Ashokananda's first students; she was, in fact, a member of the Society when he came, having learned of Vedanta a little while before. She worked as a companion to another devotee's elderly mother, and soon developed a relationship with Swami Ashokananda that was like that of a child to its father. "When you feel the sunshine on your face," he would say to her, "think that it is the Lord caressing you. When an animal looks at you, think it is the Lord looking through the creature's eyes."[49] Thelma would cook for him. She also helped Mr. Page arrange the flowers in the Temple and attended to the mimeographing of the monthly bulletins. She had a pure, simple, and loving nature—making her a perfect candidate for a convent. The other young woman, Mary Lou Flambert, a nursing school student, was not as dedicated a devotee

as Thelma, but Swami Ashokananda saw in her great spiritual potential and encouraged her to practice deeply. She did so. One day the fur-
nace in the convent house would explode, and for a dazzling moment
she would think she had realized God.

On Durga Puja of September 1934, Swami held a dedication ceremony in the shrine room of the fledgling convent. He had had an altar
built and had brought relics from the Temple for the occasion. That
day he taught the three resident women, and also Edith Soulé and Mara
Lane, who were present, how to perform ritualistic worship. And thus
the second convent of the San Francisco Vedanta Society was started.
Edith Soulé was appointed guardian—that is to say, while Swami was
in India, she was to visit the Green Street convent every weekend and
report to him how things were going. Mara Lane spent weekend nights
on the couch in the living room; Mrs. Weber had one of the two bedrooms, and Thelma and Mary Lou shared the other. There were no
rules or routine to speak of, but morning worship was done in the
shrine, each of the three residents taking a turn at it. Then, after breakfast, the two younger women would go off to their separate jobs.
Nirupama, who had a private income, stayed home and kept house.
Kathleen Davis, who taught elementary school, came often to visit,
as did Leona Smith. Another young woman who often visited was Eve
Bunch. And thus it went on—for a while.

On his way to India, Swami wrote to Thelma Fine:

On Board *Tatsuta Maru*   Nov. 25, 1934
Dear Thelma,

   I hope you got the joint letter I sent to Ediben. I have very
little news to give. The sea has been fairly good, so I have not
suffered from any seasickness yet. But I have felt very weak from
the very first and that makes me keep to bed for long hours every
day. I often feel dizzy and very weak. I am hoping this will pass
off gradually. Two or three days before reaching Honolulu and
till yesterday after leaving there, it has been very warm, even

hot. Today it is cool. Japan will be cold. The sky is often blue, but there are clouds, too. Yesterday and today there were gorgeous sunsets. The boat is nice and they give excellent service. I have almost all my meals in the cabin, and do not dress until 11 a.m. Every morning at 7 some toast and milk, at 9 regular breakfast, around 12:30 lunch which I eat very little, and at 6:30 dinner. I read a little of philosophy and a little of history and a little of detective story, and often talk with Al. Thus passes the day. I have not made any acquaintance in the boat and do not hope to. Sometimes I lie for hours in the deck chair. That's all.

How are you doing? Are you maintaining the improvement? Do not find too many faults with yourself. You are fine, even as your name is. Be happy and cheerful. No child of mine shd be unhappy. The Lord is with you always. Why shd you worry? Don't bother if you fail sometimes. We all do. Have you been going to Mr. Flambert's office? How do you find it? Is he satisfied?

I hope Dec. bulletin is ready by now. In case you do not get copy by right time, phone Mr. Allan and ask him to send it.

Please do not think about yourself too much. Think of the Lord. Does Mara come weekends? Does Kathleen visit you? Tell her all my news and give her my love. How is Leona? Give her my love and accept it yourself. I have often scolded you and treated you hard. That is because you are my child. Don't remember these. You are all very good. Otherwise you would not have come to Sri R. Take very good care of yourself. I hope to see you much stronger when I return. If you need any money, ask of Ediben. I have left some with her for that purpose.

> No more today. Love and affection.
> Ever yours in the Lord,
> Ashokananda

The Swami felt that he would need forty dollars a month in India, and to offset that amount, so it would not burden the Society, he had

Dinner at the Century Club given by the Vedanta Society
in honor of Swami Ashokananda, November 13, 1934

the ground-floor telephone disconnected, the newspaper advertise-
ments reduced in size, and the amount of petty cash lessened to ten
dollars. "The [Society's] expenditure in my estimate," he wrote in a
memorandum, "will not be more than $140 per month; whereas in-
come should be at least $225. Therefore I hope there will be a monthly
surplus of income."

On the eve of Swami Ashokananda's departure for India, the
Vedanta Society gave him a banquet. Held in the Century Club on
Tuesday evening, November 13, the party was a great success. It was
photographed, and thereby the now burgeoning and vital Society—
old guard and new, young and old, embarking together on a pioneering
journey—was immortalized. Even without its swami, the—dare one
say it?—orphaned Society would carry on nobly, keeping faith for
seven long months.

In preparation for his absence, Swami Ashokananda had written detailed instructions to the Society's executive committee and appointed
subcommittees for every department—the Sunday and Wednesday
services, music, bulletins, advertising, Shanti Ashrama, and so on.

Shanti Ashrama was taken care of by a devotee, Arthur Bryan, who
lived there year-round. His needs were few, amounting in all to about

twenty dollars a month—not counting the purchase and care of a horse he had asked for and the complications attendant upon it. (Mr. Bryan had soon fallen off the horse and dislocated his shoulder, an injury that required medical treatment and his transportation to Livermore to receive it.) There were other expenses at Shanti Ashrama: a new water pump was installed, the windmill was checked and greased, and there were annual taxes (which, after repeated efforts, Mr. Allan succeeded in getting reduced by about $2.50). The cabins, most of them built in Swami Trigunatita's time, needed constant repair. During Swami's absence, the Shanti Ashrama Committee would attend to such matters, and would also grant permission to devotees to visit the place and would advise Mr. Bryan of their coming.

A committee called the Service Committee consisted entirely of old-timers, one of whom crustily remarked, "When he needs us, he takes us off the shelf!" But not all felt that way, nor was it true. Swami Ashokananda had deep regard for the disciples of Swami Trigunatita and for those of Swami Prakashananda as well, and he was careful not to wound their feelings. "I feel their passing away as a personal loss," he would say on the death of old Mr. Anderson in 1935.[50] For their part, the old-timers had come not only to respect Swami Ashokananda, but to love him—even those who at first had scorned him. Most of them understood that to be on the Service Committee was not a consolation prize but an honor. Their task was to keep the Sunday and Wednesday services going with the reading of a lecture of Swami Vivekananda's or of another swami, preceded and followed by music and Sanskrit chanting. It was no small responsibility, for the services were the heartbeat of the Society. Much later, Mrs. Allan wrote to her friend Ida Ansell, "Before Swami Ashokananda went to India . . . he had each of us who were to keep the meetings going to see him privately. . . . I remarked, 'Swami, we will be like children without a Mother.' He said, 'You dare to say that! I tell you, Mrs. Allan, that Sri Ramakrishna is in this Temple in a very special way.' And I told him that I believed it."[51]

Not only the committees but each member of the Society was

expected to maintain a sense of responsibility. In an open letter addressed to the students of Vedanta, he appealed to each member to keep faith, not grimly, but just as though he were there. Dated November 7, 1934, it read,

Dear Students,

I would like to address a few words to you before I leave for India for a visit. I wish I could talk to you individually, but it has not been possible. Kindly receive these words as earnestly as if they were my spoken words.

Every student of Vedanta has, in my opinion, two distinct duties. One is to live and practice the principles of Vedanta, realize the Truth through self-discipline and meditation and prove in his own life that Vedanta is not empty forms. The other is to help maintain the Vedanta movement from which he has derived so much benefit himself, so that similar benefit can be extended to more and more men and women. I have so far tried to help you to do your duties in both these respects as far as my limited powers have allowed me. Now that I am going to be away from you for some time, the responsibility of performing these dual duties rests fully on your shoulders. I sincerely hope that none of you will fail in any respect.

I earnestly request you to continue self-discipline and meditation with full vigour and courage. And I earnestly pray that you continue attending the Sunday and Wednesday services as regularly as you have always been doing. For if in my absence you neglect your personal spiritual practice, you are bound to lose the strength of mind and growing clarity of vision. And if you do not attend the services, not only will you deprive yourselves of their benefit, but you will do profound damage to the growing volume of power for well-being which has been developing in the Society during the past years, since without persons to be benefitted, the power to benefit shrinks.

I am sorry that I have to leave my post of duty even for a short while. But I have every faith that you will, by your earnest efforts, keep the fire ablaze during my absence. The teacher is the strength of the students, and the students are the strength of the teacher.

I do not want you to feel the burden of these responsibilities. Take them naturally and you will find that you have the strength to discharge them fully. Never forget that if you have derived any good from being here, it has been directly from God Himself and not from me. I am but a most imperfect instrument in His hands. My absence, therefore, will not take away from you the invisible Divine Substance which has always been yours. It ought rather to awaken further your self-confidence and faith in the eternal. Then it would be, instead of a loss, a source of great good to you all.

Though I shall be away, my heart will be with you all. May I suggest that you all write to me regularly, telling me how you are doing? I would very much like to know. I, however, do not promise that I shall reply to your letters except when I consider it urgently needed, for you must admit that to maintain an extensive correspondence would be a heavy task, and I want, above all, to have some rest. But your letters will be eagerly awaited and read. My address in India will be:

Sri Ramakrishna Math

P.O. Belur Math

Howrah, Bengal, India

May the Lord bless you all and lead you to the illumined life in Himself is the earnest prayer of

Swami Ashokananda

8

LION DANCE

Swami Ashokananda's visit to India satisfied his need to see his motherland once again. He stayed at Belur Math in what was then the guest house (now the president's quarters). He visited his mother for the last time. And standing on the bank of the Ganges just north of the Math grounds, he was splashed by a wave of divinity—not water, but pure divinity. Thus the Ganges proved to him firsthand that she was indeed divine. At Belur Math, with the consent of the then president of the Order, Swami Akhandananda, he acquired for the San Francisco altar, and the altars of temples that might later be built, relics of Sri Ramakrishna, Holy Mother, and Swami Vivekananda. He renewed many friendships, and when he left for Madras, he found that his brother monks had covered the walls of his train compartment with hundreds of lotus blossoms—an expression of affection that deeply touched him. The visit was a sort of completion. He would never again return to India, partly because his work in the West would never again allow him to, and partly because the yearning of his heart for his motherland had been stilled.

During Swami Ashokananda's seven-month absence in India— from November 15, 1934, to June 26, 1935—things went on at the Vedanta Society without incident of note. The Upanishad classes were

suspended, but the Sunday and Wednesday services were faithfully
held in the Temple, with one or another member of the Service Committee reading a lecture, generally one of Swami Vivekananda's. The
birthdays of Sri Ramakrishna and Swami Vivekananda were duly celebrated, Mr. Page quietly working his usual wonders with the flower
decorations. As far as can be judged by the Society's minutes for the
period, Arthur Bryan's "accident with his horse" was the only mishap.

But the young convent had not fared as well as had the Society.
When he returned on June 26, 1935, the Swami learned that at least one
member, Mary Lou Flambert, had lost her zeal, having found interests
that conflicted with convent life. She often stayed away from the Green
Street house and defied the rules that Swami had laid down. Equally
disruptive had been a close friend of Mae Weber's, who came often
to visit her and attempted to discourage her (unsuccessfully but dis-
turbingly) from living a monastic life. All in all, things were not going
well.

Swami Ashokananda did his best to bring enthusiasm back into the
hearts of the fledgling nuns, speaking to them as a group. There exist
a few notes of his talks when Ediben and the four would-be nuns—
Mae Weber, Thelma Fine, Mary Lou Flambert, and Mara Lane—were
present. Mara's notes read,

> You people are very unfortunate. The presence of God is here
> and you do not feel it. It is as if God has come and you turn away
> and say, "No!" Practice, practice seeing God! Think that He is
> not body, not mind; He is the Divine One.
>
> If you walk, there is danger; if you go slowly, there are tigers
> and lions on the way, but if you run, you will be safe!
>
> What will you do to further the work? Are you willing to be a
> maidservant, to serve the children of Sri Ramakrishna? First,
> feel that you are nothing, that you will dedicate yourself to this
> building up of a monastery. How? By loving and serving each
> one as a child of Sri Ramakrishna's. If each one gives you ten

kicks each morning, will you serve them just the same? You see when you have the attitude that you have given your life to Sri Ramakrishna, things said to you might hurt, but you'll just set it aside and say, "This does not concern me."

Remember, renunciation is the way—love and renunciation. Who will become the leader? He who will sacrifice his head!

This you can do in earnest: feel that you are serving the children of Sri Ramakrishna, but there will be no reward for you. Otherwise, you can just come over on weekends and go home feeling very pious and comfortable and become a crusty old maid!

The teacher has to overlook the faults of others. Don't think you are all angels with clipped wings; you are not. Feel that you are privileged to serve the children of Sri Ramakrishna. Even those great souls, the direct disciples, served the monks at the monastery. I myself feel that I am a servant, and every day I feel blessed to be in this Order! I am glad to be a servant even to the brahmacharins in the Order. Feel that you are a sacrifice on the altar of the Lord!

Again, on July 4 of 1935—the anniversary of Swami Vivekananda's *mahasamadhi* in 1902 and of Swami Ashokananda's arrival in San Francisco in 1931, to say nothing of America's independence—that day at the Temple when Thelma, Mary Lou, and Mara were present, Swami almost pled with these three young women to carry on with the convent. Mara's notes continued,

Make a resolution today to do the very best you can. . . . The next two years will be very difficult; there will be many obstacles to overcome. Don't feel discouraged for any reason or think yourself unworthy for this life. Just think how difficult it is to control and conquer the senses. . . . Even great souls have a tremendous struggle to conquer the senses. . . .

You three are young; you have your whole life before you. What will you do? Either you have to lead a worldly life or a spiritual life. Each one of you came here through your own choice; no one lured you here. You came seeking Truth, guided by Sri Ramakrishna. (Swami told the story of the man who went through all difficulties to swim a flooded river and scale a wall to meet his mistress.) You see, this mind is so difficult to control. You may have been good before, but as you take up spiritual life, you become much worse! There are so many latent samskaras [tendencies] in the mind which were dormant and these continually rise up—terrible things; you have no idea! A monk in India told me that every time he would begin to meditate on his spiritual ideal, he would see himself spitting on it. Just imagine this! After you have sought the help of a wise, all-knowing one, he can be of help in clearing away these difficulties.

Don't think of each other's faults. Each one consider yourself a servant to the others. Be an elder sister to the others.

So much time wasted thinking about this body! A time will come when you who think you are so pretty now, so attractive in form, will become wrinkled; your skin will be dried, your hands will become shriveled, and you will look just like *witches*! . . .

I tell you, each one of you could realize Truth. I know this. I *see* it! Only you will have to pay the price and make great effort and sacrifice.

I think I have been as indulgent as any parent. I have given you everything—a shrine room, an altar. I am willing to give you anything, but that would spoil you. That I won't do! I have laid myself at your feet, but please don't trample on me!

Do you know what a privilege is yours? The chance to build something that will be a source of inspiration and joy to others. If you hold on, all the difficulties will be overcome. You will be capable of undreamed-of activities. You have no idea now. . . .

Have a little faith in me. I personally am nothing but the

instrument. If my personal happiness means anything to you, I tell you it will make me happy to see this undertaking progress. This is all I ask. I want nothing in return, but it will make me happy to see you devote yourselves to the purpose for which Swamiji laid down his life on this day.

Two days later Swami came to the Green Street house to take the relics from the shrine—not by way of disbanding the convent, but simply because it was time for the borrowed relics to return to the Temple. On that day he again spoke to the women—all of them—and again it was Mara who wrote down his words:

> You are all children of immortality! The presence of Sri Ramakrishna is surely here. When I first joined the monastery, I used to feel surrounded by the protecting care of Sri Ramakrishna. Day and night this went on for months. Just as a great mother bird puts out her wings and protects, so the Lord is protecting and guiding each of you. Have faith; all difficulties will be removed. The presence of the Lord is here; it is real, not imaginary. . . . Go ahead! Keep steadily on. Be grim about it, like a soldier.

He not only cajoled. At least once he fiercely scolded the recalcitrant Mary Lou Flambert. Afterward, when she left the Temple and walked down the street crying, he watched her from the little oval window in the front room (then his office) and sorrowfully shook his head. "I had to do it," he said. "I had to do it!"

But even that did not move Mary Lou—at least not at the time. Never fully committed, she came to the decision that she was not really interested in continuing on at the Green Street house and would like an apartment of her own. That was the end. Swami could not maintain the house for only two rent-paying women, and thus in September of 1935 he disbanded the convent. The experiment had been premature, as he later remarked. He did not abandon his hope that someday there would be a Vedanta convent in San Francisco, for he was convinced that both monasteries and convents connected with the Ramakrishna Order were a necessity if the Vedanta movement in the West was to deepen and grow strong. In the minutes of the Society's annual meeting on March 19, 1936, he is reported to have said, "No religious body can survive unless such body supports and protects those truths as it professes by having a group of spiritual aspirants who have vowed their life to the ideals of the truths of the society." He was also convinced that there were many young men and women in America ready for Vedanta and ready to renounce the world. Where were they to turn if there were no Vedanta monasteries and convents?

For the time being, the experiment had failed. Not only that: Mary Lou Flambert, in whom Swami had seen spiritual potential and to whom he had given a great deal of his attention, urging her to go deep into spiritual practice—this disciple to whom he gave his heart not only left the convent, but left Vedanta altogether. That was probably the first blow of its kind that Swami Ashokananda received. It would by no means be the last.

Swami dissolved the Green Street convent on September 8, 1935, exactly one year after its beginning. Eventually he would move the altar he had had made for the women to the monastery chapel on the second floor of the Temple. But before the chapel was ready to receive it, he asked Ediben to give it an interim home. Ediben and Douglas were now living in a small house on Green Street only a few blocks from the convent house. "I will never forget my experience," Ediben said, "as I watched that altar come up the hill in the back of a little pickup truck. It was covered with a cloth, and it looked exactly like Sri Ramakrishna with a shawl over him. Later, I told that experience to Swami Akhilananda. He looked at me so wisely and kindly, and he said, 'But, my dear Ediben, it *was* Sri Ramakrishna.'"

———

THAT SUMMER CAROL WESTON and Ediben drove up to Lake Tahoe, two hundred miles northeast of San Francisco in the high Sierras. They were looking for a place where Swami could rest before taking up his work. At Brockway, a town on the California side of the lake, they found a cabin connected to a resort hotel. It was a shacklike cottage on the water's edge, large enough to accommodate several people. Swami liked Ediben's description of it, and so he, the Soulés, and Adolph drove up to Lake Tahoe. Al Clifton was to follow in his own car. Anxious about this young man, dear as a son to him, Swami wondered when he would arrive, and Ediben, knowing that Al would be eager to get there, said he would appear in four hours. Swami bet that it would be much later, for the drive was long and, in those days, arduous. As it happened, Al arrived just as Ediben had predicted. Hiding his pleasure, Swami exclaimed with great disapproval, "Why did that boy have to drive so fast!" But Ediben won the bet—*Vivekachudamani,* a book she thenceforth cherished.

At Brockway, they had their meals served in the cottage rather than in the public dining room. Once Swami very much wanted to eat a lake bass, so Al and Adolph fished for a bass, caught a large one, and had the hotel cook it. It was served, head and all, at the cottage. "You people in the West," Swami said, "don't know anything about a fish unless you eat the head. It is delicious." Offering the head to Douglas, he said, "You try it." Looking at the baleful eye of the fish, Douglas said to his wife, "You have it, dear." "So I tried," Ediben related, "but I could hardly get it down; it was so oily. To me it was repulsive. But that was Swami's favorite dish, and every time we had fish, there had to be the head."

Swami waited that year until mid-September before resuming his Sunday lectures at the Century Club and his Wednesday evening lectures in the Temple auditorium. Not until October did he restart the Friday evening Upanishad classes. From then on, as long as his health permitted, and often when it didn't, he gave lectures and held classes in San Francisco with a spontaneous intensity that never diminished. Ediben remembered that one Wednesday evening, when he had been very ill from an ulcer attack, he insisted on getting up from his bed to lecture. Ediben begged him to let someone read instead, but he paid no attention. He rose, donned his robe, and gave a magnificent lecture. There was no sign of physical weakness as his words, perfectly organized, precise, and at the same time spontaneous and filled with fire, poured forth. At the end he shot a look at Ediben, who was sitting in the front row. "It was the most I-told-you-so look I have ever seen!" she recalled, laughing. "So never again did I say, 'Please don't.'"

Not only were the Swami's lectures informative in regard to the philosophical concepts of Vedanta, they lifted his listeners (for the time being at least) into a higher state of consciousness. At their close, everyone looked exalted, transformed, as though having achieved some spiritual height. In later years, his lectures would run almost invariably to over an hour and a half, sometimes two hours, his audience absorbed to the end. He did not spare his listeners. He never assumed that Western audiences could not understand the rigors of Vedanta philosophy; he never talked down to them. On the other hand, he made the most difficult of philosophical concepts seem simple and broke the tension from time to time with sidesplitting humor. In the days before a microphone chained him to the podium, he would move energetically about the platform as though propelled by some inner force.

There is a brief black-and-white silent film of Swami Ashokananda lecturing at the Century Club, in which he seems to be doing a kind of lion dance—striding back and forth, gesticulating. ("Once in the picture," a student's notes read, "Swami was hammering with his fist on the lectern. Watching the film, Swami said, 'Now what do you suppose that was for?'") But at the time, his striding and pounding seemed entirely natural, and the audience, caught up in his fire, barely noticed. Nor did those who were used to it notice his accent, which was sometimes difficult for newcomers. He would now and then stress the wrong syllable, as in "cannery woman" for a woman who would bestow all her love upon a canary. Or he would say "pur-'ga-tory" or "mon-'as-tery." He was a past master of the use of American slang, employing it with the precision and aptness of a native born. Like a dash of cold water, it would come as a surprise and then as a source of vast amusement in moments grown too tense. He never misused it. He had trouble, however, with singulars and plurals and sometimes with articles and prepositions, which irregularities added to everyone's delight. "To get down to the brass tack," he would say, or "Your family and friends will tell you, 'Don't go the deep end!'" Repudiating some solemn idea, he would say, "Fiddlestick!" Although he often asked that his English be corrected, no one told him of these small mistakes. And he could well afford them: his English was otherwise flawless and exceedingly eloquent. His choice of words was always just right, often startlingly so. Sometimes passages of his lectures or classes were like poems in their beauty and imagery, somehow conveying the transcendental reality of his subject.

To Swami Ashokananda the *tat tvam asi*—the "thou art That"—of Advaita Vedanta was not the last word of religion; it was the *first* word. It was the ground to stand on at the very beginning of one's spiritual journey—a rock-sure foothold to go forward from, following any path one wished, in the firm conviction of the solidity of the ground under one's feet, until conviction became realization. To Swami, the final truth, the full realization of the oneness and divinity of all being, was the beginning, the middle, and the end of religion, and he never compromised that truth. And yet he was as full-hearted a devotee as the most fervent of *bhaktas*. His lectures on devotion were as rich in their love for the Personal God as his lectures on monism were luminous with *jnana*—the knowledge of the Absolute Brahman, the Reality beyond name, beyond form, beyond time and space, beyond God Himself. How could he not love the Personal God, the human mind's highest reading of the Absolute, as real as, or as unreal as, the universe itself? Swami Vivekananda's sentence in *Inspired Talks* "Do not seek for Him, just see Him" had struck him forcibly when he had first read it in his youth, and it still held for him the very crux of religion. *He is in everything, He is everything. It is all He, and thou art That!*

Swami Ashokananda was thought by some to be uncompromisingly monistic and stern in his interpretation of Vedanta. And, indeed, since his first reading of Swami Vivekananda in his boyhood and his first spiritual experiences in Sylhet, there had been no doubt in his mind as to the truth of Advaitic Vedanta. To realize the oneness of all being was to him the ultimate goal of all life and, even more important, that same oneness was the present fact of existence as it is here and now.

He was not, however, rigid in regard to the means of such realization. Like Swami Vivekananda, he prescribed any path, or all of them combined. The path of devotion was to him not only a path to the realization of the Personal God, but also a direct path to the realization of the Absolute Brahman. In fact, devotion was bound to end in the oneness of the lover and the Beloved. As he said in one of his lectures, "It is possible to realize the monistic ideal through love. And when I think that it can be realized either through reason or through love I am inclined to think that the path of the dualist or the qualified monist remains incomplete until it has ended in this incomparable Love, indescribable Love, which is the same thing as Consciousness."[52]

He emphasized monism, but not as a purely rationalistic truth. Rather, he emphasized it as the Truth underlying all paths: the ground upon which they gently wound or from which they boldly leapt their way upward, and the goal to which they all led. There was nothing dry or cold about his teaching of monism; it emphasized the divinity of all life far more strongly than the unreality of the world.

But it followed that the renunciation of the world was necessary to realize one's own divinity and that of others. He never brushed that prerequisite aside or downplayed it. Renunciation meant the practice of chastity, poverty, asceticism, and, if one meant business, obedience. One of his recurrent lecture titles was "I Am Not the Body; I Am Not the Mind," and—the lecture would go on—if you are not the body, then stop acting as though you were the body. It was as simple as that.

This was like saying from the platform (with great emphasis), "This is the steep price of spiritual realization. Be warned!" He never compromised that statement or twisted it. It was true that individual capacity and circumstance made a difference in individual practice, but as a general instruction, the need for renunciation, in any path, was an absolute—for monastics and nonmonastics alike. This was not a prescription to live in a cave. He was keenly, indeed prophetically, aware of the world's push into a new age of material knowledge and power. All the more reason for stressing the divinity of man, as Swami Vivekananda had done. Man as an animal with almost unlimited power in his hands would inevitably destroy himself; man as divine, with the material means to nourish and uplift his fellow men, could, *must*, become godlike. It was an exalted and a challenging theme. It was not popular. It never had been—not in any religion. But Swami Ashokananda did not propound one kind of religion for those who were serious and another for popular approval and practice. Vedanta was a religion for the serious, period. Many people, bright enough to understand what they were getting into, heard one or two lectures and never came back. Fine.

This is not the place to speak in any detail of Swami Ashokananda's teaching of Vedanta, which, though it did not deviate from Vedantic texts, was richly original in expression, exposition, and practical counsel. His published lectures and classes speak for him. It is enough to say here what has already been said: the basis of his teaching was always *tat tvam asi*—"thou art That"—ever pure, ever perfect, ever free. In the beginning, in the middle, and in the end, whatever he said was luminous with the knowledge of the divinity of the Self. And it was not only in his lectures and classes that he taught and manifested that truth. It was an integral part of his being; no part of his life was not vibrant with it. One never felt, being with him, that he ever for a moment lost that awareness, that knowledge. In pain, in illness, in grief, in anxiety, the joy and the sweetness of it was always with him. No darkness could blot it out.

There was a hugeness about him. In the most ordinary of times, Swami's presence seemed immense, but there were occasions when it seemed as though some extra power entered into him. When he lectured, it was like that; one would then feel awed by him. One never spoke to him as to an ordinary person, but at those special times one barely dared speak to him at all. Ediben related an experience she had had when she once met him at the Oakland mole, or railway depot. He had come from one of the northern centers, probably Seattle, where he had been visiting Swami Devatmananda. "I walked down the long train," she said, "watching for him to come out. And when he came, I will never forget my impression: *This is not Swami; it's Swami Vivekananda!* He hadn't had his hair cut, so it was a bit long, and for some unknown reason he seemed a giant as he got out and walked down that train. I thought, 'I can't go up to him as I usually do.' So I went up and did *namaskar*, and he just looked at me and went right on walking. A king had arrived; I mean it was something more than Swami. He just strode the length of that train, and I went toddling after him until he got to the car. And then in the car he was Swami again. It was as though he had been so completely tied up with Swami Vivekananda or whatever he'd gone through—some meditation or something—that he was still in it as he got off the train. It was not just a human contact; it was something *tremendous*. I'll never forget what he looked like, never! It was really Swamiji walking down that train."

SOON AFTER HIS RETURN from India in the summer of 1935, Swami resumed his Oakland lectures at Ebell Hall. It had been over a year since he had last lectured in Oakland, having stopped when he became ill in March of 1934. Although a notice of his return was placed in the Oakland papers, he thought no one would come, everyone having by now forgotten him. When he stepped onto the platform, though, an audience of over 150 stood up and applauded. He was astonished by the number of people and much moved by their unexpected and spontaneous greeting. His lectures, being in the nature of religious services, were customarily never applauded, nor was he, the minister, given ovations. But this was different: it was by way of welcoming a beloved father returned home after a long absence.

The Oakland attendance at the Sunday evening lectures remained steady at around one hundred throughout the following years. In 1936 the Swami again started a class at Ebell Hall, which was highly popular, drawing, despite a charge of two dollars, between forty and forty-five people—a large number in those days for an Upanishad class, even when admission was free. Indeed, the enthusiasm of some of the Oakland people would lead Swami Ashokananda to the first ambitious venture of his ministry.

Meanwhile, changes were taking place in the Temple in San Francisco. In October and November of 1935, the directors (and, of course, Swami) decided to do some renovation. The first floor had already been renovated in 1933. It was now decided to transform the front room, which had been the Swami's office and reception room, into a library. His bedroom—the small middle room on the first floor—would become his office. The back room on the first floor would become the Society's office, where all clerical work would be done and in which the secretary would have her desk. In addition to these changes, the second floor of the Temple, which the tenants had now vacated, would be refurbished and become a monastery, in the chapel of which the erstwhile convent altar would find a permanent home. The third floor, already used as a monastery, would also be refurbished, and Swami would thenceforth have his bedroom there—the same room in which Swami Trigunatita had slept until he could no longer climb the stairs.

The establishment of a library was very dear to Swami Ashokananda's heart. He had brought many books from India for the purpose, and, with Ediben to chauffeur him, scoured the Bay Area for more. "He would look through book catalogues, and I would drive him to the stores," Ediben later said. "We went to every secondhand bookstore in San Francisco, Oakland, Berkeley—everywhere. He knew exactly what he wanted. He chose practically every book that went into the Temple library. It was a sort of obsession with him for the time being." He built up a religious and philosophical library of rare books, many of them long out of print and irreplaceable. The Society's board of directors did not demur. On the contrary, by March of 1937, Mr. Wollberg, then president of the Society, announced in the annual meeting, "Thanks to Swami Ashokananda's tireless efforts and to the contributions [made by members and friends of the Society] our library now boasts a total of some 1,300 volumes covering various fields of philosophy and religion, the philosophy of science, Indian history, art, and culture."

To this point, Ediben seemed to have been Swami Ashokananda's sole driver. As time went on, other of Swami's disciples, both men and women who had cars and leisure time, drove him here and there—to Sacramento, Berkeley, Tahoe, and Sausalito. He never learned to drive. He applied twice for a driver's license and both times failed to pass the driving test. After that he gave up, which probably was a good thing— and this not only because it gave his disciples a chance to drive him. His passenger-seat driving (he always sat in the front seat, unless there was a guest swami) was an indication of what his own driving might have been like. "Can't you go a little faster?" he would say on a two-lane winding mountain road, as the road to Tahoe was until the late 1960s. Or on a blind curve, "Pass that fellow!" These were perhaps the only times his disciples deliberately failed to obey him. "Go! Go!" he once ordered Josephine Stanbury at a busy intersection, with cars coming from right and left. "What do you want me to do?" Jo asked. "Go *under* them?"

Most of the time he rode in silence, fingering his beads in a pocket of his coat or perhaps singing softly to himself. In the early part of 1954, when he began to go to Olema every Monday to stay one or two days, he had a young monk of the San Francisco monastery drive him there and back. "He used to sing all the way," this monk later recalled. "But when I had to stop at a red light, his singing would at once stop; when the light turned green and we drove on, he would start singing again. I never understood why it was, but invariably he would stop singing at a red light and start again when the traffic moved." Perhaps it was because he did not want to draw the attention of other drivers to himself. Once he said to a woman devotee who was fairly well known in San Francisco, "What will your friends think if they see you driving a black man?"—to which she replied that she could not care less.

NINETEEN THIRTY-SIX was the centenary year of Sri Ramakrishna's birth. Swami Ashokananda celebrated the day, indeed the week, with all-out grandeur. On Monday, February 24, he conducted a special *puja* in the new chapel on the second floor of the Temple. The room was filled with flowers sent by devotees and also, no doubt, bought by the Society itself. The worship was private. But that evening there was a meeting in the auditorium attended by invited students, friends, and members of the Society. There was chanting, music, and a talk by Swami on Sri Ramakrishna, after which everyone was invited to see the new library in the office part of the Temple. When they all had returned to their seats in the auditorium, slides of Belur Math were shown—photos taken by Al Clifton during his sojourn in India. And then came refreshments—which meant a fairly large Indian meal, perhaps of *kichori*, chutney, and *payash*. Jo Stanbury, who all her early life had heartily disliked anything to do with a kitchen, was now, to her astonishment, becoming proficient in Indian cooking, following Swami's recipes, which he, in turn, had learned from his mother.

The *puja* on Monday was by no means the end of the celebration. On Wednesday evening the auditorium was again profusely decorated with flowers. There was special music, the best the Society could offer, and Swami gave another lecture on Sri Ramakrishna. Refreshments were again served—cooked in advance at the home of a devotee and served from a small room in the back of the auditorium. The service of some two hundred people crowding the auditorium was a masterpiece of organization. Until the end of her life, this cooking and serving of food to the devotees would be one of Jo's departments of work, as would be anything connected with the flower room and the altar.

The final celebration of the centenary came the following Sunday at the Century Club, where the Sunday morning lectures were usually held. That day the morning lecture was canceled, and the celebration took place that afternoon. The rather bare and mundane hall was made as festive and beautiful as possible. An old theater screen that Carol Weston knew of was resurrected from the basement of the YWCA, cleaned, and hung as a backdrop on the stage. Against this was a life-size photograph of Sri Ramakrishna, adorned and flanked by flowers and greens. Again there was music and a talk by Swami. After this, a pamphlet that Swami had written, entitled *Sri Ramakrishna: The God-man of India*, was distributed to all three hundred people of the audience.[53]

The week of celebration was a huge success, everything done to perfection. No detail had escaped Swami Ashokananda. Once in later years when some minor thing had gone wrong during one celebration or another, he stormed into the flower room at the back of the Temple auditorium, where a number of students were working. "He came up the aisle like a gigantic wave of power," one student remembered, and he furiously declared, "You are all neet-weets!"—a rendition of *nitwits*, hilarious, but also petrifying in its fury.

Perhaps because of the intense spiritual atmosphere that was created during Sri Ramakrishna's centenary celebration, Swami Ashokananda decided to add to the number of annual celebrations, which heretofore had been confined to the birthdays of Sri Ramakrishna, Christ, and Swami Vivekananda. In December of 1936 Christmas was celebrated as usual. But if Christ, then why not Buddha? In Gump's, a San Francisco store of expensive household furnishings and impedimenta, Jo had discovered a statue of a young and slender Buddha that Swami liked immensely. Typically, wanting nothing but the best, he commissioned the photographer Ansel Adams, famous for his stunning photographs of Yosemite Valley, to photograph the statue. On Buddha's birthday (or on the day his birthday was observed) the large photo was centered in the backdrop of the chancel and profusely decorated with flowers. The evening of the celebration was Wednesday, May 26, 1937. That morning there would be a private *puja*.

Swami was having grave doubts as to the wisdom of so many celebrations and so much ritualism. It was not that he did not himself pay reverent homage to the great Incarnations, nor was it that he had the slightest objection to devotional worship, and certainly not to devotion itself as a religious practice. Rather, he felt that there was a great danger that Vedanta, Advaita Vedanta as Swami Vivekananda had given it to the West, could easily slide into a dualistic religion of grace or become externalized if there was too much emphasis on ritual. Was he not starting a current that could dilute the heady waters of Advaita Vedanta and that he would not be able to stop? In presenting Vedanta to the Western world, his effort was to follow Swami Vivekananda's lead in every respect, and Swamiji had never initiated any kind of worship in the West. He had emphasized above all else the sovereignty, the divinity of the individual Spirit.

As Swami Ashokananda dressed that morning, preparing to go to the second floor for the private *puja*, he was filled with misgivings. But as he came down the stairs, he was almost overwhelmed by the strong, palpable, and joyful presence of Lord Buddha. All that day he felt Buddha's vivid presence permeating the Temple. His doubts were totally dispelled. The evening celebration drew a crowd of 220 people— a record to that date. Many of the people, overflowing onto the sidewalk, were seated in the hallway behind the chancel. And thus, the celebration of Lord Buddha's birthday became, like Christmas, a traditional observance of the Society. Then in October of 1939, there was a celebration and worship for Sri Krishna, which also became a tradition.

In deference to Sri Sarada Devi's lifelong modesty and reticence, Swami Ashokananda had forborne from celebrating her birthday publicly in San Francisco. But as Holy Mother became more and more known in the West and more and more loved by Western Vedantists, he would perform an annual public *puja* for her in Berkeley. Kali Puja he performed privately in San Francisco, and Durga Puja publicly in Berkeley. Although Swami Ashokananda instituted all these *pujas*, which punctuated the year and satisfied the hearts of the devotionally inclined—indeed, the hearts of the majority of Vedantists—his worships were simple, consisting primarily of meditation. Only on very special occasions, such as the dedication of the Berkeley Temple and, twenty years later, the dedication of the New Temple in San Francisco, did he go all out, omitting no item of ritual worship. On each occasion the respective temple seemed to vibrate with the footsteps of Durga Herself, come to bless it. And in each temple She stayed. But we are way ahead of ourselves.

On July 16 of 1936 Swami received word that his mother had died. He had stopped by Ediben's house on Green Street that day to talk. "When he came in he looked very serious and tired," Ediben said. "Perhaps it was because he had just walked up the hill, or perhaps it was because he guessed what was in the cable he had received as he had left the Temple. He had stuck it in his pocket unread. He sat down in our little sitting room and then he pulled out the cable and read it. He said only, 'Ah hah,' and was silent. In a little while he said, touching the cable, 'This is the death of my mother.' I didn't know what to say. I felt dreadful, and he looked dreadful. After a moment I said, 'Swami, would you care to go up to my shrine?' The altar he had had made for the convent was there. He left the room without saying anything and went up. He didn't stay long, and when he came down he just picked up his hat and said, 'I will be going now,' and he left. He never again mentioned anything about it."

That summer of 1936 Swami Akhilananda paid one of his visits to San Francisco, and Swami Ashokananda decided that it would be a good time to visit Yosemite Valley. The Society had recently come into possession of a new Chrysler sedan for the Swami's use, and the Soulés had bought a Plymouth roadster. They set out—the two swamis and

Swami Akhilananda *(left)* with Swami Ashokananda
in the back seat of the Chrysler, 1936

the Soulés in the Chrysler, and Al Clifton and Adolph Gschwend in the Plymouth. In those days it was necessary to break in new cars, driving them not faster than forty-five miles per hour for some five hundred miles. So at first the drive was stately, the Chrysler leading. But Adolph, who was driving the Plymouth, was soon unable to stand this funereal pace and zoomed past the Chrysler, going, as Ediben recalled, "lickety-split." Disgusted, Swami said, "Catch up with that fool!" So the new Chrysler had also to be driven faster than it should have been. Adolph was overtaken, pulled over to the side, and thoroughly berated. The caravan proceeded with measured speed, the Chrysler again leading.

At Yosemite the party stayed at the Awahnee, a luxurious hotel on the floor of the valley. The first morning at breakfast in the dining room, Swami Akhilananda, knowing that Ediben was subject to allergies, removed a large vase of goldenrod to another table. Ediben thanked him profusely. After breakfast the two swamis, Al Clifton, and

Ediben went on a sightseeing tour through the spectacular valley, where Ediben had spent many wonder-struck summers. Swami Ashokananda and Al sat in the back of the Chrysler, Swami Akhilananda and Ediben in front. Ediben, who knew Yosemite by heart, was driving and acting as guide. Throughout the drive, ignoring the two passengers in the back seat, she gave Swami Akhilananda her full attention, pointing out to him the glories of her Yosemite: the towering cliffs, the spectacular uninterrupted waterfalls, some the highest in the world— sights that people would come thousands of miles to see. Passing El Capitan, the famous monolith of solid granite, she finally turned to Swami Ashokananda and said, "Look, Swami, here is that huge rock of granite!"

It was too late. Silently, Swami Ashokananda picked up the newspaper lying beside him and, holding it in front of his face, began to read. Ediben tried again. Pointing to a distant cliff, she said, "Look, Swami, there's Glacier Point, where I used to sing." Al then asked her to tell the story of how she sang at the nightly fire-fall from the top of that great cliff, her voice filling the valley.[54] Swami showed no interest. He continued to read the paper. Ediben, hurt, said reprehensibly, "Well, Swami, what a pity! You're not seeing Yosemite at all!" Swami refolded the paper and became absorbed in another page.

Swami Akhilananda, fully understanding the situation on both its superficial and deeper levels, began to shake with suppressed laughter. He knew that Swami Ashokananda was extremely sensitive to a slight or an affront, but he also knew that personal hurt, although sometimes keen, was momentary and never triggered in him an angry or defensive response. Disrespect to the guru, however, was another matter altogether. No responsible teacher would ever countenance it. It was a blow that could shatter the delicate structure of spiritual guidance and growth—an affront that far exceeded any personal insult.

They finished the drive and returned to the Awahnee Hotel, not speaking. The next morning they drove in silence to Lake Tahoe over Tioga Pass, a mountain road through the high, extremely scenic

Sierras. That night at Brockway, Ediben, wanting to clear the air, tried to say good night to Swami, who was again engrossed in his newspaper. Still highly amused at his brother's droll behavior, Swami Akhilananda intervened. "Swaaaami," he said, "Ediben is saying good night to you." The newspaper came down and Swami Ashokananda looked up as though nothing had been wrong. "Hmmm," he said. "Good night." Peace restored, the next day they returned to San Francisco.

The Temple had been newly painted in their absence and was now a pale gray with gold-color trim. While this color scheme was less nondescript than yellowish cream, it missed by far the impressiveness and dignity it no doubt aimed at. Jo and Helen, now the Society's official interior decorators, had not yet become its exterior decorators. It was not until the late summer of 1948 that the Temple was painted an arresting dark bluish gray with vermilion towers and balcony walls, which became the color of its dress for as long as Helen lived.

That autumn Swami Ashokananda's severe stomach pain was diagnosed in part as appendicitis. Rather than fuss with more doctors and more medical opinions, he agreed to an operation, indeed insisted upon it, much against Ediben's nonmedical judgment. She did not trust the doctor. The operation took place in early October at Dante's, the small hospital where Swami Trigunatita had first been treated after his fatal accident. Swami Ashokananda's operation, which was indeed necessary, went well, and he was delighted to find that he had the same nurse who had tended Swami Trigunatita some twenty years earlier. He was also cared for by one of his own disciples, Eve Bunch, a trained nurse who watched over him from start to finish with an eagle eye. He was soon well enough to come back to the Temple. Al Clifton and Adolph made a seat of their hands to carry him up to his bedroom on the third floor, Ediben trailing. At the top of the first flight of stairs, Adolph stumbled a little, which led Swami to think that he was too heavy for the young men, and he declared that he would walk up the second flight on his own. Ediben and the two monks strenuously objected. In those days, it was believed that after a major operation the patient should not exert himself for many weeks, should not even walk, let alone climb stairs. Paying no attention to their cautionary cries, Swami climbed the steep stairs, Ediben weeping at the foot. He was none the worse for the exertion and in late November was back lecturing.

The operation had on the whole improved his health, but it was at least a year before he felt really strong again. Meanwhile, when he sat on the platform before lecturing, his right leg would tremble uncontrollably. Only by using great willpower could he stop the tremor. Once, on his way to the podium, his leg buckled under him and he fell. He picked himself up and proceeded as though nothing had happened. He used to grow very tired, he said, and would sometimes feel that his nerves would burst—particularly during long and troublesome interviews. He remembered one such occasion.

A young woman and two men had come to the Wednesday evening lecture and had asked to see the Swami afterward. He received them in the library. They asked him whether he believed in divine incarnations and whether he thought there would be other incarnations, and so on. Although the woman was a little on the aggressive side, she seemed well educated and very earnest. When she asked for a private interview, Swami granted it. On the appointed day she told him with some intensity that one of the men who had been with her was a divine incarnation and that he had clearly seen that Swami himself was an incarnation of Indra. She went on to ask that the Vedanta Society be used as a platform from which her friend, the divine incarnation, could communicate to the world. "That was their game," Swami later said. "They wanted to enlist various societies in their cause rather than start their own organization. If my nerves had been in a normal state, I would have just laughed or made polite fun, putting her off. But I couldn't bear it." When the plot became clear to him, Swami stood up and speechlessly pointed to the door. The woman turned red with anger. "You will suffer for this," she cried. Swami thrust his finger again at the door and this time, indeed like an incarnation of Indra,

The cabin near Meyers, Lake Tahoe, where
Swami Ashokananda spent a week in 1937

boomed, "Get out!" And out she got. "That man was using her," he
said, looking back. "She believed in him. My! Such strange things happen in this world."

IN THE SUMMER of 1937 Ediben decided to buy a house near Lake Tahoe
where Swami could stay during the Society's now-customary summer
recess. At the south end of the lake on the Nevada side near the town of
Meyers, she discovered a large, sparsely wooded and boulder-strewn
valley set back from the lake and widely scattered with small houses.
One of the houses, lovingly built by its owner, who wanted to sell it,
overlooked a running stream. Swami, going to inspect it, at once liked
it, and the Soulés bought it. At his request, they left him alone for one
week in that little house. There were no close neighbors. He had a coal

Swami Ashokananda standing on the porch of the cabin

stove and a small gasoline stove. A vegetable wagon would come by every day, and also a milk wagon. He was entirely free to do as he pleased, with no demands upon him, no appointments to keep, no lectures to give. He could meditate all day, sing or chant, or dwell upon God in silence. "It was the happiest time I have ever spent," he later said. That week was probably the one retreat in his entire life when in relatively good health he could go deep within himself without giving a thought to the passage of time. There would be vacations at Lake Tahoe almost every year after that, but never again would he be alone for days on end, and never again without a care. Perhaps that week made up a little for the three months he had wanted in the Himalayas before leaving India the first time. In any case, it came just on the eve of his plunge into an era of intensive building, expansion, and trouble.

When the week was up, the Soulés returned to the lake with two visiting swamis—Swami Gnaneswarananda from Chicago and Swami Vividishananda, who was now trying to establish a center in Denver. Swami Ashokananda's two brother monks moved in with him, and the Soulés took a house on a ridge above. The two households communicated at night by flashlight, letting each other know that all was well. The valley was beautiful, quiet, and serene. But it was shut in. "It is a pity," Swami said one day, "to be surrounded by hills when the lake is so close. We ought to get a spot on the water, not only for the swamis but for a future ashrama." And thus Ediben went again on a searching tour.

She set out in her Plymouth from Meyers and drove north along the road that circles the lake, hugging its shore. Working her way around the lake, which is twenty-two miles long and twelve miles wide, she turned into every road that looked as though it might lead to property overlooking a wide expanse of blue water. After several days of search, she was almost exactly halfway around, on the California side, more north than south. And there, near a town called Carnelian Bay, she found about twenty acres of land in a parklike development called Ridgewood. The property was more or less secluded, the road leading into it was good, it had a narrow view of the water, and it was bordered on the north by a running creek. It seemed ideal, and it was for sale.

The next day she took Swami to see it; he very much liked it and decided that it should be bought. Working now with a real estate agent named Mr. Kilner, Ediben put down a deposit. The sale was almost closed when Mr. Kilner, suddenly punctilious, decided to read the contract with close attention. Sure enough, he found a clause that bluntly stated, "No non-Caucasian or organization led by a non-Caucasian can own the property." Ediben explained that Hindus are Caucasians. "They may be in your book," Mr. Kilner replied. "But I could never get the real estate board to go along with it. I have to stop the sale." So Ediben and Al took back the deposit. "You made a great mistake," Swami said when he heard of it. "You should have left the deposit and fought it through." "In good conscience, I couldn't," Ediben said. "To hell with your conscience!" replied Swami, once more taking her breath away. But, as it turned out, Ediben was right.

A day later, Mr. Kilner began to talk about a large adjoining piece of land on the north, just across the creek, on which there were no restrictions of ownership. The road leading into this property of two hundred acres was steep and rough, but once up the hill, one came upon a sweeping view of the lake. Mountains, sparsely forested because of earlier lumbering, rose seemingly straight up from the farther, eastern shore. The land extended westward, back from the lake, into a thick and deep forest of pine and fir. Swami liked this property as well as, if not better than, the first. Its size and wildness did not faze him, and suddenly he became a canny businessman. "Tell Kilner you don't want it," he instructed Al and Ediben. They assured Kilner to this effect, and he came down on the price. They again said, "No; we really want a smaller piece." He said, "If you take the whole piece, you can have it for the price of the first one."

When this was reported to Swami, who was now back in San Francisco, he sent Ediben, Al, and Adolph to thoroughly explore the land, saying to Ediben before they left something that she would always treasure: "You will be going with these two young men: they are your sons." She and her two "sons" stayed at the lake with an aunt of Dora Blaney—a close friend of Carol Weston's and a member of the Vedanta Society. For several days they tramped through the rough forestland of towering pine, fir, and occasional cedar, crashing through thick underbrush, climbing hills, following deer trails, taking measurements, and photographing the lovely vistas, lake views, and clearings that they came upon. They reported everything to Swami, and at length the property was bought in Ediben's name. A donation for the purchase was made by two devotees who intended to turn over the land to the Vedanta Society on certain conditions. The matter was presented to the Society's Executive Committee on November 10, 1937, and the following letter to Swami Ashokananda from the two donors, who wanted to remain anonymous, was read:

Dear Swami:

We the undersigned have for a long time felt the urgent necessity of your having a complete rest and period of retirement every summer. As you will doubtless recall, we have discussed the matter with you on many occasions. We feel very strongly that there should be a place for this purpose in the high mountains, yet within easy access of San Francisco, where you can recoup the strength which you expend so completely during the year and which is so necessary for the carrying on of your teaching work here.

We are extremely glad to inform you that we now find the realization of that scheme has become possible, with the help which you yourself have promised toward that end. We are donating a piece of property at Lake Tahoe for this purpose to the Vedanta Society of San Francisco, of which you are the teacher. This property has been purchased in the name of Mrs. H.D.B. Soulé [Edith Benjamin Soulé], and we hope next year to build a suitable house on it for your use.

The property is located on a beautiful site overlooking the greater part of the lake and is very quiet and secluded. We consider that it is well suited to the purpose for which it is intended. Before completing the arrangements for transfer of the property to the Vedanta Society, however, we wish to outline certain conditions which we wish to impose upon its acceptance by the trustees of the Society, and we should like to know whether the trustees will accept the gift subject to these conditions. . . .

1. The property is to be used by Swami Ashokananda, as long

as and whenever he wishes, so long as he remains in this country, and after him, by the swami who will subsequently be in charge of the Vedanta Society of San Francisco.

2. The members of the Vedanta Society of San Francisco shall have no claim for use of this property.

3. Swami Ashokananda, and after his departure from this country, the swami subsequently in charge of the Vedanta Society of San Francisco, shall have full freedom and right to invite anyone to the place as his guest.

4. The property is to be held in trust by the trustees of the Vedanta Society of San Francisco solely as a place of retirement for Swami Ashokananda, and after his departure from this country, for the swami subsequently in charge of the Society, except that the swami may use it at any time for other purposes if he so desires.

5. The property is not to be sold, leased, mortgaged, or otherwise disposed of without the written consent of Swami Ashokananda, and after his death, that of the swami who may be the head teacher of the Vedanta Society of San Francisco. If the property is sold, the proceeds of the sale shall be devoted to the purpose of acquiring other property for the purposes outlined above. In case the money is not so used, it shall be used for some religious purpose or purposes as Swami Ashokananda may designate, or in the event of his death, it shall be sent to the trustees of the Ramakrishna Math, Belur, Howrah, Bengal, India, to be used by them for any religious purpose. In the event of the dissolution of the Vedanta Society of San Francisco, the property shall be sold and the proceeds forwarded to the trustees of the Ramakrishna Math, Belur, Howrah, Bengal, India, for such use by it in its religious work as the said trustees may determine.

In conclusion, we wish to declare that this project will in no way become a liability to the Vedanta Society. A balance is still due on the purchase price of the property, but this is being paid off in monthly installments. We pledge ourselves to liquidate this entire balance on the land, and also to bear all expenses of the building and furnishing of a suitable house.

For the present, we request that you withhold our names from the trustees. However, we feel it is only right that you mention to them the condition which you have all along made in connection with this project: namely that if it materializes, you wished to bear a portion of the cost yourself.

The letter was discussed fully by the Executive Committee, and Mr. Allan moved that the offer be accepted along with its conditions. The motion was seconded and unanimously passed. Swami would add his allowance of $1,300 a year to the anonymous donations until the land and house were fully paid for.

And so the building of Swami's cabin began at the new site. Ediben recommended the architect who had built the Soulés' house—Mr. Henry H. Gutterson, a Christian Scientist, whom Swami would come very much to like. He designed a simple but strong and thoroughly convenient cabin, giving Swami the long ridgepole he wanted to support heavy snows. There was a large living room, with Swami's bedroom and bath at the north end and a loft above for guests; at the south end was another bedroom and a large kitchen–dining room. A wide porch ran the length of the building on the side that faced the rising sun and an unobstructed expanse of shining blue water.

The new cabin was ready to be dedicated in early August of 1938. That summer five swamis visited Swami Ashokananda, both at San Francisco and in the old cabin near Meyers—Swamis Akhilananda, Devatmananda, Prabhavananda, Satprakashananda, and Vividishananda. All five attended the dedication, as did whichever devotees happened to be at or near Lake Tahoe at the time. There was also a young probationer of the San Francisco monastery, Francis Chamberlain (later, Swami Bhaktimayananda). There were only six beds in the Swami's house, so one of the seven men would have to sleep on the

Swami's newly built cabin at Carnelian Bay, Lake Tahoe, 1938

Senior monks attending the dedication of the new cabin at
the Lake Tahoe retreat, 1938. *Standing, left to right:* Swami
Devatmananda, Swami Ashokananda, Swami Satprakashananda,
Swami Prabhavananda, Swami Vividishananda,
and Swami Akhilananda.

Swami Ashokananda worshiping Sri Ramakrishna on the property
of the Lake Tahoe retreat, 1938

floor. One would think it would have been the probationer—but no, it
was the host, Swami Ashokananda. And none of the others, least of all
Francis, could dissuade him.

The ceremonies took place on August 8 in the living room in front
of the fireplace, in which Swami Akhilananda performed a *homa* fire
ceremony. There were bountiful food offerings, and at the end, the
devotees who were present made their own offerings of flowers. At
one time or another during that summer of 1938, Swami Ashokananda
performed a worship on the property. One knows this because there is
a photograph of him, deeply absorbed, worshiping Sri Ramakrishna
somewhere in the piney woods. And thus the Tahoe retreat came into
existence. Through years of use it would acquire more and more holiness, so that the entire property would become, it seemed, steeped in a
golden haze of spirituality.

Private dedication ceremony in the woods at the Lake Tahoe retreat, 1938. *Seated in front, left to right:* Helen Sutherland, Josephine Stanbury, and Swami Ashokananda. *Standing behind:* Ernest C. Brown.

On one side of Swami's cabin, about a hundred yards to the south, the Soulés built their own much smaller cabin in 1940. Ediben designed it herself and left off the inside walls because, apart from the matter of expense, she had heard that in the wintertime mice got trapped inside the walls and died there. On the other side of Swami's cabin, at a little greater distance, Jo and Helen had built their own small cabin a year earlier, with an inner lining of tongue-and-groove knotty pine. As far as one knows, mice never died between those walls.[55]

After the dedication of the cabin, Swami Ashokananda went there during the summer (whenever his work permitted) for a stay of six weeks or so for about thirty years. He loved the place, and the clean rarefied mountain air (Lake Tahoe is at about the same altitude as Mayavati—6,250 feet) would restore his energy, which would be thoroughly depleted after ten months of steady work. He could walk freely over the extensive and secluded forests, which would not have been possible on the first property he had thought of buying, where the available land was limited and surrounded by what would later turn out to be an enclave of wealthy WASPs. The present land afforded total privacy and freedom to wander in the deep forest, to chant, to sing, to worship God. He roamed as freely as did the ranging deer, which he loved to see. He had a large block of salt bought for them and had it placed near his house, where he could watch them through his kitchen window when they came for a lick.

At his request, and to the alarm of the locals, the county gave the name Shivagiri (the mountain of Shiva, or of God) to the hill's near-impassable road. But while that sublime forest retreat was indeed a haven from the world, during his stays there Swami never lost touch with the work in the city or with the devotees. For many years the only phone was at the foot of the hill, down by the lake—a pay phone on a corner of the grocery store porch, at which he would stand, rain or shine, to talk for what seemed hours. The Carnelian Bay post office was also in the grocery store. Indeed, the grocery store *was* Carnelian Bay—at least the downtown part of it.

9

DRAMA IN BERKELEY

At the same time that the Swami's Tahoe cabin was being constructed, a suspenseful drama was unfolding in the East Bay. The attendance at Swami Ashokananda's lectures and classes in Oakland had been consistently high, the Sunday evening lectures almost always drawing over a hundred people. One hundred may not seem like much in relation to Christian congregations, but in relation to American Vedanta congregations in the 1930s, it was large. Probably in relation to first-century Christian gatherings it was also a figure high enough to be remarked upon. Still, Swami was not satisfied with the quality of the Oakland audience; it was constantly changing and, for the most part, was not receptive to the exalted ideas he was pouring out. Some few people, however, were steadfast and had become earnest students of Vedanta. It was for them that Swami felt the East Bay congregation should have a place of its own.

"The work either goes forward, or it dies out," he said in this regard. Nor did he like lecturing in a rented hall, where who knew what went on during the week. The Ebell Club, which had earlier been a prominent women's club, was running down. Other clubs in better neighborhoods were taking its place, and on Saturday nights the hall was rented out indiscriminately. One Sunday the janitor told Swami that the state of things on early Sunday mornings "was a mess—empty beer bottles all over the place." And to be sure, on Sunday evenings the hall had a barroom atmosphere hard to speak of God in. Nor was the commercial city of Oakland a particularly good environment for a temple. The nearby town of Berkeley, the seat of the University of California, seemed far more appropriate.

On the evening of April 24, 1938, an Easter Sunday, Swami asked all those who were really interested in the philosophy he preached to remain after the lecture. About fifty people remained. He then asked those who would be interested in forming an organization that would continue to present the Vedanta philosophy to please rise. About half of the fifty rose. Of those twenty-five or so, he asked how many would be willing to attend lectures in Berkeley. About fifteen assented. But a Mrs. Huey, who was more than willing to follow him, knew that most of those fifteen would soon fade away. She said to him that he was exchanging the Oakland congregation for one and a half people— meaning herself and the diminutive Sarah Fox. "There will be more," he replied.

Confidently he set out to search for a house in Berkeley that could be converted into a Vedanta society and temple. On the southeast corner of Dwight Way and Piedmont Avenue, he found the very thing—a large Victorian house, surrounded by trees. It was a good location and a good house. Swami asked Mr. Gutterson to see whether the house could be remodeled. Yes, he said, for around $20,000. Swami was not deterred. The Vedanta Society obtained approval from the Berkeley Planning Commission to buy the house and remodel it. The Berkeley City Council gave its blessings, and the process of transferring the property to the Society was under way.

But at that point, an article relating these events appeared in the *Berkeley Daily Gazette* and came to the notice of a prominent real estate agent, whose name was Mr. Sherman. Mr. Sherman lived across the street from the proposed site. He was outraged. What! A Hindu church moving into the neighborhood! A heathen community invading Berkeley! Property values would sink; civilization as Berkeley knew it

Mr. Henry Gutterson *(left)* inspecting the Berkeley
property with Swami Ashokananda, 1938

would be destroyed! Not only did the wealthy and influential Mr. Sherman bring this impending disaster to the attention of the city council,
he had handbills of warning printed and distributed throughout the
city, he sent a petition of fifty names to the city council protesting the
diabolic intrusion of a Hindu church upon the town of Berkeley, he
had scurrilous articles published in the Berkeley newspapers, and altogether he waged a fierce and vituperative campaign against Hinduism
and the Vedanta Society, about neither of which he knew a thing.

The neighborhood surrounding the property in question was soon
seething with anger and fear. In this atmosphere, a meeting of the
Berkeley City Council was held on May 15, in which its blessings were
withdrawn and the matter given back to the planning commission for
further investigation. In San Francisco, Swami Ashokananda and a few

interested devotees held several meetings and decided to get out a petition themselves and secure as many signatures of Berkeley residents as possible. Several devotees living in Berkeley, notably Bob Utter, one of Swami's young college student disciples, and Mrs. Gladys Harvey, also a disciple, took on the job. The battle was on.

Another hearing was held before the planning commission on June 9. Mr. Gutterson's blueprints were on display. About 150 people attended, most of them from the opposing forces. There were only five speakers for the Vedanta Society, including Mrs. Hansbrough from southern California, but those five were dignified and strong, and, as anyone could see, the very soul of respectability. An elderly gentleman from no one knew where arose to say that in a closing session of the English Parliament, the prime minister had said that he considered the Vedanta movement throughout the world to be the greatest event since the coming of Christ.

Few people were listening: the opposition, which consisted primarily of influential property owners, was strong, loud, irrational, and absorbed in its own panic. Although the ostensible objection was that a church—any church—would be an invasion of the neighborhood, it was clear to everyone that the real reason for the opposition was racial. After deliberating for two hours, the relatively sane planning commission decided that there was, after all, nothing detrimental in the Vedanta Society's proposal. The matter was then referred back to the city council for a final decision. The city council hearing was to be held on June 14, but on that date the opposition was not well represented, and Mr. Sherman, the opposer-in-chief, requested a rehearing. Over the objection of the Society's lawyer, the meeting was postponed to June 20.

Mrs. Lila Martin, the Berkeley devotee in whose house Swami had first held classes in the East Bay, was keeping a diary of these events. Her entry for June 14 reads,

> Council seems more influenced by the property owners than by the merits of the case (politics, of course). The truth [is that]

the main cause of opposition is the race question; one of the opponents when privately interviewed said he did not want a Hindu
coming into the neighborhood. (Strange indeed! Just think!
These people of Berkeley!) . . . The opponents have among them
some who are unscrupulous people; many things have come to
light, misrepresentations, etc. A handbill of some sort was
printed and distributed around; many lies have been told—just
any kind of a thing to influence against the Vedanta So.

On June 20 at 7:30 p.m. the hall was packed. The debate had become
a civic sensation. Members from both groups spoke, and this time, after
a short debate among themselves, the members of the Berkeley City
Council unanimously voted to deny the recommendation of the planning commission. And that was that. The Vedanta Society had some
satisfaction in knowing that its petition had been signed by 437 Berkeley citizens, some of whom were prominent professors and teachers.
But that was small consolation. The Society had lost.

Swami Ashokananda had no intention of giving up a Vedanta center in Berkeley, particularly since its rejection from a community
would be an inauspicious beginning to his plans for expansion in the
area. On June 30 he met with the Berkeley group (Sarah Fox, Mrs.
Harvey, Mrs. Huey, Mrs. Watkins, Mr. and Mrs. Martin, and Bob
Utter) and decided that Mrs. Martin and Mrs. Harvey should search the
town for another suitable location.

Swami Ashokananda was by now exhausted. He had worked all
winter and spring, lecturing and holding classes in San Francisco, Oakland, and Berkeley, to say nothing of giving innumerable interviews
to spiritual seekers, keeping an eye on the construction work at Lake
Tahoe, and paying keen attention to the Berkeley battle, some details
of which he would rather not have known. One Sunday evening his
exhaustion was so great that, sitting in the dressing room at Ebell Hall,
waiting to go onto the platform, he felt he could not rise from his chair.
He forced himself to the platform, but standing there, no words came.
Then suddenly he was aware of a voice delivering a lecture, and he

listened to the whole thing. Afterward he was told by several members of the audience that his lecture had been among the grandest and most inspiring he had ever given.

That may have been his last lecture of the Oakland season, which closed on June 26, 1938. The San Francisco work closed for the summer on June 29, and on the weekend of July 7 to 10, Swami Ashokananda went to Los Angeles to attend the dedication of the temple there that Swami Prabhavananda had built. He brought back with him Swamis Akhilananda and Vividishananda, the former of whom returned to Hollywood after a few days' stay in San Francisco. Swami Vividishananda accompanied Swami Ashokananda and Adolph on July 19 to the cabin at Meyers. As we saw earlier, the house at Carnelian Bay, then under construction, was completed that summer and dedicated on August 8. Swami and his guests moved into the new house for the remainder of the summer, Al Clifton joining them a week later. But during most of the two remaining weeks of vacation Swami Ashokananda was acutely ill, his digestive system completely upset. He returned to the city on August 29, and, well or ill, opened the San Francisco lectures on the evening of Wednesday, September 7.

Meanwhile, the search had been going on for another temple site in Berkeley. "Numerous sites have been considered," Mrs. Martin wrote in her diary for October, "but none seem to answer the purpose." Swami and Ediben took up the search, and at length they found a lot for sale on the corner of Haste and Bowditch Streets. The land, a mud hole, was occupied by a tall deodar tree and a ramshackle house. College students habitually used the place for a parking lot. The old house would have to be demolished. But the location seemed ideal: it was close to the university campus, and the intersection of Haste and Bowditch was not too busy. Mr. Gutterson again drew up plans, and an application was again made at Berkeley City Hall.

The Berkeley Planning Commission took up the matter on November 10. Although the meeting was crowded, there were only two protests: one from a woman belonging to the Christian Science church that adjoined the property on the south, and the other from the owner of Head's School for Girls, which stood on the corner of Haste and Bowditch Streets catercorner from the lot. But despite these two complaints, the planning commission unanimously approved the plans and again recommended the Vedanta Society's proposal to the city council.

By now, Mr. Sherman, the powerful real estate man, was more incensed than before, riled by the Society's persistence. Although the Hindus no longer threatened to invade his particular domain, he used his influence in an attempt to have them stopped altogether. Anticipating this, Swami had directed Ediben to knock at every door within two hundred yards of the new site. (According to Berkeley ordinances, only owners of property within two hundred yards of a proposed new building were entitled to protest.) Ediben's task was to convince the neighbors that Vedanta was an ancient and highly venerated religion and philosophy and that the Vedanta Society was a respectable, well-established American organization. She carried with her a roll of Mr. Gutterson's blueprints. But the splenetic campaign of the opposition had been effective. Some doors were slammed in Ediben's face—sometimes directly, sometimes by means of an upstairs lever. (Swami laughed. "Very good, very good," he said. "Let the doors slam!")

One man who opened a door to Ediben looked at her meaningfully and said in a low voice that he had heard the church was a sex cult. "How about it?" he asked. Because the man was prominent on the city council, Ediben did not slap his face; she simply told him with immense dignity that he was misinformed and walked away. When she related that adventure to Swami, he did not laugh. But neither did he relieve her of the onerous job of ringing doorbells. "To gain anything in this world," he said, "you have to wade through mud. You will weather it. But from now on, take someone with you." Ediben chose Gladys Harvey to be her fellow campaigner. Mrs. Harvey, stalwart and dedicated, would later become secretary of the Berkeley Vedanta Society, a post she would hold for many years.

Things were not all unfavorable. Many of the neighbors signed statements saying that they had no objection to the Vedanta Society's proposal. There were even a few enthusiastic and influential supporters: for instance, the president of a well-known school for deaf and mute children, who happened to know Swami Ashokananda. There were two brothers on Bowditch Street who were lawyers and whose mother assured Ediben that her sons would help. Then there was Professor Utter, the father of Bob Utter and a good friend of a member of the board of the city council, a Dr. French. The Vedanta Society also had the petition that had been signed earlier by 437 citizens of Berkeley—now minus some.

The opposition had also been at work. They had organized their forces, engaged a lawyer, and convinced several of the people who had signed the Vedanta Society's petition to withdraw their signatures. Many deliberate and scurrilous lies were circulated in the neighborhood to discredit the Society. Even the Christian Science church, whose property was, it thought, at risk, was responsible for much of the false propaganda.

Thus it was that when hearings were held before the city council, the odds were greatly stacked against the Society. It was during the course of these hearings that the true nature of the opposition became abundantly clear. "You can have no idea of how terrible they were," Swami Ashokananda said at a much later date. "A regular witch-hunting mentality had taken hold of them. The community seems to be cultured, but scratch it a little, and just underneath it is savage— no culture, no refinement, no understanding, nothing."

At the first hearing, held on November 22, the hall was crowded and the hostility intense. Ediben read a paper explaining the nature and aims of the Vedanta Society. Facing a sea of stony faces (only the people in the back row were Vedantists), she said that she was glad her comments were on paper as then she could not, this time, be misquoted—whereupon she was hissed. Anna Webster, a staunch devotee who had been raised in Boston and had every earmark of Bostonian forthrightness and respectability, also spoke for the Society, as did the college student Bob Utter and the architect Mr. Gutterson.

In speaking in favor of the Society, Mr. Gutterson was going directly against the stand of his church, for which he was severely censured by the church board. Nevertheless, he stuck by the Vedanta Society, and urged Swami Ashokananda to appear at the hearings. There would, he said, be no resisting Swami's obvious goodness and holiness. "Swami," he implored, "if you would just stand up and smile, there would be no one against you." "Mr. Gutterson," Swami replied, "I don't feel that way about it. I wish to stay in the background." Not only did Swami wish to stay in the background, other friends had advised him not to make an appearance, since strong racial prejudice, as well as a blind fear of the Hindu religion, or what was thought to be the Hindu religion, was the force behind the opposition.

"[The attorney for the opponents,] as dirty-minded a low-down thing as ever drew breath," Mrs. Martin commented in her diary, "made pornographic insinuations during this meeting in the Council chambers and in this way put forth the immorality charge against the Vedanta Society and Hinduism in general." The fear of the Hindu invasion was so great that the principal of the neighboring school for girls became hysterical over the impending danger to his charges as they went to and fro. He circulated a story that there was a ship in the harbor waiting to take young girls to India to be sold into slavery. The Society's lawyer, Morse Erskine, asked this man how, precisely, the Hindus would molest and capture the girls. Would they hide behind the trees, perhaps, and jump out? To make the hearing complete, there was the usual crank that attends such meetings. This particular man came carrying many books on Hinduism, from which he read out at length and in scandalized tones Sri Krishna's life with the *gopis*.

When finally the matter came up for the first vote, the air was charged. There were nine council members, but of these Professor Utter's friend Dr. French was that day absent. After a heated debate, the vote was four to four. At the next and final hearing, held on November 29, the hall was again packed. And suddenly at that last moment, the wind changed. Dr. French was not only present but had taken the trouble to inform himself thoroughly about every aspect of the matter, and he gave a stunning talk, in the course of which he ex-coriated his fellow citizens for their intolerance and lack of American spirit. The two young lawyers, who had been friendly from the start, also spoke strongly in favor of the Society. In addition, the lawyer for the opponents thoroughly discredited himself by speaking with undis-guised prejudice and rancor.

When the councilmen and councilwomen returned from their de-liberations, one of the women looked squarely at Ediben and winked. It was the first ray of hope. Then the verdict was announced: six to three in favor of the Society! Ediben nearly fainted, whereupon a kindly-looking woman sitting beside her, a Christian Scientist, pulled away to protect herself from the malicious animal magnetism (MAM) she said Ediben was emanating.[56]

As Ediben left the hall, accompanied by Sarah Fox and full of ela-tion, the little man with the books on Sri Krishna accosted her, shook his finger in her face, and said with venom, "You are a wicked woman." To Sarah's boundless delight, Ediben promptly put her index finger on his forehead and replied, "And you are a stupid little man." Then she phoned Swami, who, in San Francisco, was anxiously awaiting the ver-dict, and cried, "We've won!"

After the Vedanta Society's victory, the people of Berkeley could not be cordial enough. Ediben was invited to teas and luncheons to an-swer questions and give talks. But the venom of the opposition had sickened Swami Ashokananda. He later said that he was never again quite the same after seeing into the abyss of ignorance and hatred in the everyday American mind. He felt, he said, that he had turned a cor-ner toward age. At the same time, he felt deeply appreciative of those who had helped, such as Dr. French and the two young lawyers, whom he kept in touch with for long afterward.

The primary anxiety now was money. There was nothing in the San Francisco Society's treasury called a "building fund." However, there was, Swami informed the members, enough in the form of pledged do-nations and interest-free loans to make at least a down payment on the property. The Vedanta Society agreed to assume the responsibility for the balance until the Berkeley center could fend for itself.

And now, with the Berkeley populace quieted down and money a possibility, Swami immediately started planning the Berkeley Temple with Mr. Gutterson. However, before anything was done, any ground broken, he went to the site with the photographs of Sri Ramakrishna, Holy Mother, and Swamiji and, giving the photograph of Holy Mother to Ediben, walked through the mud over every inch of the lot. He stood reverently where he thought the altar would be, holding Sri Ramakrishna and Swamiji, Ediben holding Holy Mother. He consecrated the whole property with those holy photographs. Only then could construction begin.

In January 1939, a building permit was issued (not without a member of the city council asking with innuendos why a bedroom had been included in the plans), the old house was demolished (in exchange for its lumber), and construction work was begun. From start to finish, from the breaking of ground until the last chair in the auditorium was placed and the last tree in the garden planted, there was no detail Swami Ashokananda did not know about in the building of that temple. Every day, often twice a day, he would be driven by Jo or Ediben across the new Bay Bridge to Berkeley to watch over the work. Sometimes he would have lunch among the college students in the town of Berkeley with one or another of his drivers, and then stay at the construction site throughout the afternoon. He watched the excavation (complicated by an underground stream); he watched the erection of the walls, the laying of the floors, the raising of the roof, the designing and building of the altar. (Just as out of reverence Swami Ashokananda forbore for many years from publicly celebrating Holy Mother's birthday, he did not expose her to public view on the Berkeley altar, most particularly perhaps because of the apparently prurient mind of the Berkeley public. Could he bear to have such eyes look upon her? In those days, her absence didn't seem strange, for few people in the West, or in India, for that matter, knew of her. But today her absence

Anna Webster, Edith Soulé, and Josephine Stanbury
at the construction site in Berkeley, 1939

on the Berkeley altar seems to many devotees to have been a grievous
oversight. It was not so.)

Swami supervised the planting of the garden; he went often to the
arboretum in Golden Gate Park, becoming fascinated with and enchanted by its many rare and beautiful trees and bushes. He visited
many nurseries, choosing bushes, flowers, and trees, studying their na-
tures. He became great friends with an old Japanese nurseryman,
walking with him through his nursery garden and talking with him
about trees and world affairs. He wanted a shade tree under which
Sarah Fox could sit as she grew older, and trees that would not lose all
their leaves in the winter. Often he stood in the pouring rain watching
the workers transplant a tree from an unsuitable spot to exactly the
right one. It was with the creation of the Berkeley garden that Swami
Ashokananda became an expert horticulturist, and it was probably
during this time that he first became enamored of camellias—a love
and fascination that lasted for many years.

By June 25, the building was ready for its finishing touches. The rose window over the entrance waited for its art glass, donated by the husband of one of Swami's students; the altar, with its paneling of rare hardwood, imported from England, was ready to be installed. The altar's design had been discussed by any devotees who, in Swami's opinion, had some aesthetic sense and who wanted to raise a voice. Indeed, the decor of the whole temple was open for discussion. This policy of Swami Ashokananda's to give many devotees a say in the decorating of the Society's buildings was hard on Helen Sutherland— but though frazzled by the cacophony of opinion, Helen always endured and prevailed. And the result satisfied everyone.

At last, on Sunday, October 15, Swami Ashokananda closed his lectures at Ebell Hall in Oakland and announced their removal to Berkeley, inviting the members of the Oakland audience (none of whom had responded to his low-key appeal for funds) to attend. On October 22, 1939, Vijaya Day, the Berkeley Temple was formally dedicated with a private worship in the morning, to which 220 people came, including three visiting swamis (Swami Prabhavananda, Swami Vividishananda, and Swami Devatmananda), and a public service in the evening, attended by 290 people. That Vijaya Day dedication was the climax of a four-day celebration of elaborate ritualistic worship, music, and talks by the swamis. It is said that at the close of the services, the presence of the Divine Mother was so palpable that everyone was awed.

"A monk was offering flowers to a picture of Durga," Swami Ashokananda once related of this occasion, referring of course to himself, "and the moment he touched the glass he felt as though a tremendous electric shock was going through him deep, deep down into the inmost recesses of his mind and heart. It went on digging, and he was thoroughly galvanized. Why should it not be? Why do you think God is so far off? If you have devotion, you will find living consciousness in whatever you worship." (Swami Ashokananda on occasion also told the story of a monk—Swami Nirvedananda—who, in India, once touched the feet of the statue of Sri Durga and felt warm, living flesh.) Even today, the auditorium of the Berkeley Temple seems to vibrate

Swami Ashokananda at the pulpit for the first public service
at the newly dedicated Berkeley Temple, October 22, 1939

with an atmosphere that says the Divine Mother is still there, will always be there.

And so the Berkeley Temple was established as a branch of the Vedanta Society of San Francisco. Swami Ashokananda would now give Sunday evening lectures and Thursday evening classes at this new center; Cara French, a disciple of Swami Trigunatita's, was made caretaker, and Hazel Messersmith, chief gardener. Gladys Harvey would soon become secretary and would remain in that position until her last days. In order to accommodate the East Bay center, new bylaws were drawn up in San Francisco, and the name of the main center was changed officially to Vedanta Society of Northern California. A group of nine San Francisco members who lived in Berkeley were transferred to the Berkeley center to get things started. The following year, the membership reached forty, and around forty it stayed year after year. If this slowness of growth disheartened some of the members, it did not dishearten Swami. "How do you expect to become great?" he asked a gathering of devotees in the Berkeley Temple library after one of his Sunday evening lectures, and continued,

> This is the way all centers are built up. Do you think the Lord will leave you in the lurch? Sri Ramakrishna and Swamiji will shower their blessings upon you. You go on until you reach a point where you cannot go a step further, and then something that has never opened up before will open up. You should so work that others seeing you will be glad of a chance to work along with you. Work through love. If you have the right spirit, everything will be all right. The Lord will pour strength into you. You will feel it in your arms and limbs, and you will feel that you are being blessed by the Lord.
>
> In India, when a host prepares a big dinner he calls all his closest friends and relations together, and they work all day long preparing a feast for others to come and enjoy. And probably when the day is done there is nothing for them to eat, but *they are closest to their host*. Do you think you have any will of your own? You have *not*! If you go away and do not work for the Lord, then you will have a will of your own, but not so long as you are working for Him. . . . Do you think He chooses anyone and everyone? He chose you to do this work. You should feel blessed.[57]

Gradually the center grew, and eventually it accommodated its own resident swami—Swami Shantaswarupananda, Swami Ashokananda's first assistant, who would come from India in 1948. For five years or so he would divide his time between Olema and Berkeley, until, in 1953, he would become the full-time resident swami in Berkeley, giving almost all the lectures and classes.

10

GURU SHAKTI

S wami Ashokananda once said that during his first years in San Francisco he felt he was undergoing a change. He did not say what the nature of that change was. But one has the temerity to guess that, quite apart from the mellowing of age, it was the effect of the *guru shakti* now pouring through him to his disciples. A great compassion and love was growing within him. He had always been of a loving nature, but the fiery, judgmental young teacher who would not speak to the secretary of the Sylhet school because he felt the man's philanthropy was motivated by self-interest was gone. Looking back, he now appreciated the man's goodness of heart, overlooking whatever self-interest there may have been. He no longer saw a person's faults, let alone condemned them, just as one does not see a blemish on a television screen while watching an absorbing show. One can zero in on the blemish, to be sure, in order to eliminate it, but otherwise it is of no real significance. Still, to the person who harbored it, a small flaw could be a dark cloud obscuring the sun; if so, Swami would go after it relentlessly. His scoldings were masterpieces. But he used great care: a student with an ego glaring to his other disciples would go scot-free, while another with what seemed to be only a small fault would be castigated for it within an inch of his or her life. Who knew his reasons?

Three photos of Swami Ashokananda
taken for his passport renewal

One only knew that the motive in both cases was love. Once, after fiercely scolding Al Clifton (now his right-hand man) in front of others, Swami said of him with the utmost love when Al had left the room, "I cannot let that boy develop an ego!"

"Swami pushed you," Al once later said without the slightest rancor, "just short of stripping your threads."

His purpose was not to destroy his disciples' sense of identity and self-confidence, but to reorient them. "I have great respect for people's egos," he once said, astonishingly. But then one realized that he looked upon the ego as a reflection of the Spirit in a dirt-covered and warped mirror. It was the mirror he would clean and straighten with full care and energy, not the light reflected there. As long as the disciple hung on, he himself never gave up polishing away, patiently, endlessly.

"There was never any self in Swami's scoldings," a monk-disciple once reminisced. "He could scold! But I found this out: if you stood next to him, close to him, you could feel the love coming out of him. It was like being in a glass house with a storm raging outside. There was never any edge of resentment or hostility or bitterness in his scoldings; they were all great, and they were all coming from a place above. That was my experience. His scoldings were all coming out of love. It was what I call 'tough love.' And many a time I felt uplifted afterward."

And another devotee once said that when Swami scolded her (and he often did, fiercely) she felt like moving close to him for protection against that onslaught. He was the raging storm and the secure haven, both at the same time.

It would seem (as it was meant to) as though he were furiously angry. But sometimes one would hear him berating a student in another room and his voice, though saying the most wrathful things, pulverizing the person into dust, would be as sweet and clear as a bell; there would be no anger in it at all, no guttural quality or thickish sound of personal ire. He might be saying with all the appropriate intonations and facial expressions—the curl of the lip, the pinch of the nostrils—"You are the most contemptible person I have ever known!" but in his voice there would be not a whisper of contempt. And if, while he was directing an apparently unleashed fury upon some hapless disciple, someone stopped by the door to greet him, he would turn to face the newcomer with a radiant smile, full of welcome. He would say a few affectionate words with total attention to the person in the doorway, and then, without missing a beat, would return to the scorching business at hand.

The words he used in scolding were inspired: exactly on the mark, surprisingly put together—all in an apparent fury. To those listening, and often many were, his turns of phrase were sometimes hilariously funny, though one did not dare laugh. But to the person at the receiving end they were devastating, as, indeed, they were meant to be. "Anyone who hasn't felt the sting of my paw," he once said, "won't be formed."

It was of course not only through scolding that the *guru shakti* operated. It was there all the time. He never preached, but he always taught. He would point out the inner meaning of some ordinary incident, explain some puzzling quirk of human nature, correct an unworthy attitude, or throw a dazzling spiritual light on what had seemed humdrum. One could not be in his presence and remain one's ordinary mundane self; without thinking about it, one stretched as high as one could to be the best one could be. Sometimes at a sign of weakness or self-pity

he would shoot out an admonishing and bracing "Hup!" Once that
"Hup!" was so forceful that the devotee it was aimed at fell backward
into a chair, whereupon he, the devotee, and an onlooker all burst out
laughing. Sometimes he probed at one's faults so lovingly and gently—
often playfully—that one scarcely knew that one had been overhauled
and cleansed. A fount of joy seemed to be always within him, ready to
overflow. He would throw back his head at some incongruous remark
or incident and his laughter would ring through the downstairs of the
Temple contagiously; everyone would start laughing just to hear him.

Even more enthralling was his singing. His voice was very sweet,
and he would softly sing devotional songs to himself as he worked or
when he walked through the hall to go upstairs. At any moment he
would sing, as though those songs were always running through his
head, ready to break out. One of the monks related that when Swami
came upstairs late at night, he would be softly singing. "I would hear
him coming up the stairs singing. His voice would stop when he would
salute at the shrine door, and then go on again as he climbed to the
third floor. What a blessing to hear that!" This same young man recalled Swami's singing while being driven in a car: "We were once
coming over the ridge to Olema," he said, "and suddenly he stopped
singing and he said to me, 'There is a profound security at the heart of
Reality.' And then he added, '—and a buoyancy.' I thought to myself,
'That's just the quality of Swami's singing—buoyancy.' It was bubbling up from within. These devotional songs were just welling up!"

But we have again gotten ahead of ourselves. He said a change had
come over him after he had been in San Francisco a few years. It could
have been the change from writer and editor of *Prabuddha Bharata* to
guru—all-loving guru.

There was nothing he said or did that was not conducive (consciously or unconsciously) to the good of his students. His whole
being was given to them, but from time to time he also let them know
that in a moment he could walk away; there was no attachment in his
love—nothing at all to hold him should he want to go.

Another thing that changed him was the Berkeley battle. For him it was like being doused in the dark side of the West without warning, and it repelled him, hurt him. Actually, he had been fortunate in regard to encounters with racial prejudice in America, which well into the 1960s was generally undisguised, shameless. There was a barber at Brockway who had refused to cut his hair, and there had been the non-Caucasian clause in the property contract at Lake Tahoe, but aside from those minor eruptions of a deep-lying cancer, he had not run into difficulty.

The neighborhood surrounding the Hindu Temple was composed largely of middle-class Italians, most of whom had known Swami Trigunatita and remembered him with respect and affection. There was no problem about accepting his successors; indeed, the Temple was looked upon as an asset to the community. Thus the virulence in Berkeley was totally unexpected. The prejudice toward his beloved country, toward his countrymen, the ignorance that still existed in the West in regard to India and Hinduism, stunned him. A veil had been lifted and behind it he saw, glaringly, the powerful current of religious and racial prejudice that Vedanta would have to breast. During the first two-thirds of the twentieth century, the swamis in America were working against a strong head wind all the way. They put their faith in Sri Ramakrishna and went ahead.

THE MEMBERSHIP IN SAN FRANCISCO now stood at one hundred minus the nine members who lived in Berkeley and who had been transferred to the new society there. Earnest students were coming, some of them to remain for their lifetimes; now and then someone in whom Swami had seen great spiritual potential would leave, in almost every case breaking his heart. After the convent was disbanded, Thelma Fine had spells of depression and finally left the Society. Later she married, but she remained a devotee always. Despite the occasional departure of workers, some of whom had held key posts, the Temple work maintained a definite, though always flexible, kind of organization.

Before 1939 individual members of the Society were customarily praised and thanked in the annual meetings for the work they had contributed during the previous year. But when Mr. Wollberg became president, this practice was stopped, Swami no doubt finding a change in president a good time to change this rather un-Vedantic policy. Without these annual acknowledgments, history suffers to some extent; after 1938 until a time so recent that it still exists in memory, we do not know, generally speaking, who was doing what. We do know, however, who the officers of the Society were from the beginning, and we know that sometimes, for reasons best known to Swami, devotees were assigned tasks they were ill suited for.

Ediben, for instance, became treasurer. It happened one day when she was driving Swami down the peninsula to San Jose, where he was going to see a man about building materials. Swami suddenly said, "I think I will make you treasurer," whereupon Ediben cried out in panic, "Oh no, Swami! I can't handle money and I can't keep books. I can't do that!" He said, "You can learn to do it." Ediben continued to protest, "I just can't, I can't! I can't!" He looked at her for a long moment and then was silent. Throughout the remainder of the trip he did not speak to her again. To San Jose, talking with the man about wood or tile, back to San Francisco, he said not one word to her. It was as though she weren't there. When they returned to the Temple and went inside, Ediben, trying not to cry, said, "Well, Swami, good-bye." He started into the back room and then turned and looked at her, and finally he spoke. "Swami Brahmananda," he remarked, "once said, 'To disagree with your guru is also a way.'"

With Ediben as treasurer, the balance sheet, no matter how long she worked over it, was always a few cents off. One day Swami stood in the door of the back office, watching her trying to type up a report. Finally he said with compassion, "It's torture, isn't it?" "It certainly is!" Ediben replied. After that he asked Jo, who was good at figures, to help her. Once they worked until two in the morning trying to find an error Ediben had made. Jo at last found it. But despite her anguish over the

A rare portrait of Swami Ashokananda's austere "scolding" face

books—or was it because of it? ("If I didn't order you," Swami once said to her, "I couldn't control you")—Ediben remained treasurer from 1936 until 1942, when she was appointed secretary, a position that suited her well and that she held for many years.

Swami's ways of disciplining his disciples varied of course with the disciple, each of a different temperament and need. For one it would be a silence and a turning away, as though that person had ceased to exist for him—even in memory; for another it would be a gentle, almost playful reprimand; or he would scold some seasoned student at length, entirely for the benefit of another standing in wide-eyed innocence nearby, to whom he would not utter a word of reproach. For yet another there would be a torrent of fire.

There was, for instance, Adolph, who seemed always to draw fire to himself. One day, during the transformation of the front room into a library, Adolph suddenly got it into his head to varnish the handsome mahogany bookcases that Helen had had made. As he was happily going about this self-appointed task, Swami came into the room. "What are you doing! Who told you to do that?" he demanded. Adolph proudly said that he thought it was a good idea—whereupon Swami berated him so fiercely for having good ideas of his own in regard to Temple work that Adolph collapsed onto the floor. Swami's barrage of words fell now upon Adolph's prone body but did not lessen in either intensity or precision. The devotees who witnessed this episode were almost as stunned as Adolph himself.

Somehow (it was always a cause for amazement) his diverse ways with different disciples all worked together, like a well-choreographed ballet, or a drama written by a great master. Indeed, if the dramas that arose naturally did not in themselves provide enough occasion for training, he would create (one suspected) some tension or conflict that would invariably draw out someone's failing—and thereupon he would pounce.

He missed nothing connected with the work or with the doings of his disciples. Hazel Messersmith, who was in charge of the Berkeley garden, used to swear that he could read her mind, even across the bay. She was fluent in French and other languages that Swami did not know, so she decided she would think in French. This was no deterrent; he still knew her mind—inside out. And he knew not only the minds of all his students but also their ways. He once said to Jo, who prided herself on her good housekeeping, that she should always tuck in the sheets of her bed. Indignantly, she said that she always did. "Hmm," Swami said. When she returned home that day, she found the top sheet of her bed hanging out below the covers.

And there was the young devotee who had always sung devotional songs to herself when she was sure no one could hear; it was a correspondence between herself and God alone. One day, out of the blue,

Swami gently asked her, "Do you sing to yourself?" "How do you know?" she exclaimed. "Oh," he said, smiling, "a little bird [pronounced 'leetle bard'] told me." He went on to encourage her to sing to the Lord as a regular spiritual practice.

Though he knew all that his disciples did or didn't do, he rarely said anything about it, lest they become uncomfortable (to say the least). And yet, one did not want to hide anything from him. Better that he know every fault and correct it than that he not know. He once said gently to a student who was smarting under a reprimand, "Isn't it better to have your guru, who loves you, correct your faults than to have life do it by dealing out suffering again and again? If the guru doesn't do it, rest assured, life will."

He alleviated suffering whenever he could, generally by natural means but sometimes by what seemed to be sheer prescience. Once the widowed mother of one of his young disciples lost her job and because of her age could not by any means get another. There was no money. Seeing no other way, her daughter wanted to leave college and go to work to support them both, but the mother would have none of it. One day when the mother was staying at Lake Tahoe with friends, she phoned Swami, who was also staying at the lake, and told him the whole unhappy situation. He said simply, "Be sure to be home next Saturday." She at once returned to San Francisco, and on Saturday an old friend, whom she had not seen for many years, phoned to offer her a job. She did not tell that tale until long after, perhaps because Swami asked her not to, lest a legend grow. But such miracles did happen.

As a rule, however, by simple human kindness, by a loving smile, a sweetness of greeting, or a show of interest in a person's welfare, he would turn a state of gloom into one of cheer. Or if he himself had brought about the state of gloom by a scolding, he would often phone the afflicted person before nightfall. "What are you doing?" he would ask in the most dulcet of tones, and go on with words of comfort. Despair would vanish.

He seemed ever alert to his disciples' needs—whether they were physical, psychological, or spiritual. He somehow knew of their sudden depressions or illnesses; wherever they might be or whatever the hour, he would phone: "What is the matter with you?" If the trouble needed immediate care, he would arrange to have someone go to help. Sometimes he himself would go, even though it was the middle of the night. He once aroused Ediben to drive him across the bay at two in the morning to bring peace to a disturbed mind. Wherever there was distress, he was there, healing, comforting, restoring a distraught soul to serenity—if not by his actual presence, then by his powerful thought. He often brought material help, such as food or medicine or warm clothing, or, where it was needed, furniture collected from other devotees, or a set of dishes from his own kitchen. Again, he would pay for a young man's college tuition or see that another had proper medical care. Whatever the gift, it never carried any obligation; it came as from a loving parent.

A letter (long cherished) exists that he wrote from Lake Tahoe to Mae Weber in the summer of 1945, when she was not well:

Carnelian Bay
Lake Tahoe, Calif   Aug. 25, 1945
Dear Nirupama,

I was very glad to receive your kind letter & to learn that you are feeling better & having an appetite. I hope you gain in strength too & all is well with you soon & completely. Let us hope the doctor's examination at St. Helena turns out reassuring.

I am resting as much as I can. The weather is very helpful. Today is vigil at Jaya & Vijaya's [longtime devotees—an all-night vigil was held in their house once a year]. Hope it has gone on as in other years, & the Lord has been as gracious as ever.

I am glad you still like that property. Seeing it in the summer I felt pretty disappointed. And of course Mr. Thomas has been tiresome. Let us see what the Lord wills.

I want to give you a little sum, when I return to the city,

toward the expense of your operation, as I said before. It is not because you may need it, but because it will give me great satisfaction to be allowed to do it. I hope you will not refuse.

I hope to return to S.F. the second week of Sept.

Affectionate regards to yourself & Miss Baker.

Affly,

Ashokananda

Unbalanced people would often come to the Temple to sit in the library—just to sit there. He never turned anyone away. "Where will they go," he would say, "if they cannot come to Sri Ramakrishna?" One night after a Friday class, one such lost person, a regular, came to the library. Unfortunately, a devotee was rude to her, and the woman, gentle, if off center, went into the bathroom and there cried her heart out, using yards of toilet paper to blow her nose. After she left the Temple, Swami learned with dismay of what had happened. He told several devotees to go to her home *at once* and apologize to her. She lived alone, five or six blocks away. The delegation—Jo, Ediben, Kathleen, Mara, and others—rang her bell, but she had by then gone to bed. They persisted in ringing. Finally she opened the door, and they made their apology, not insincerely. She was astonished and overjoyed that they had come. She warmly invited them in and showed them her shrine, and her hurt and heartbreak were healed.

After his lectures and classes Swami would almost always sit in the back office (or in the library of the Berkeley Temple) and talk to the devotees who would invariably gather around, standing in the doorway and (in San Francisco) sitting, often two to a chair, in the six or eight straight-backed wooden chairs that lined the walls. He would sit in a wooden armchair in a corner of the room, still in his robe, his mind raised to a particularly exalted state after an hour and a half or two hours of lecturing, and would answer questions or just talk on whatever aspect of spirituality came to his mind. Sitting there in his vivid robe, poking his thumb into his right side, where there was pain, he looked like a blazing fire. Sometimes he seemed to be in a state of ecstasy; in one of those times he said, as though seeing the actuality of his words, "It is alive! The whole universe is alive!" Another time someone asked him whether he always saw God. "That depends on what you mean by God," he said. "If you mean the utter reality in all things, yes, I see that."

The devotees, gathered around after a lecture or class, would not take their eyes from him, and he would be entirely unconscious of that steady, multiple gaze. He would talk, sometimes playful, sometimes serious. After an hour or so—sometimes two or three hours—he would say, laughing, "Well, I have given another lecture!" Even then the students would not let him go, but would ask more questions or say something that required an answer or a long commentary. And he would go on giving, without food, without rest. At last he would go upstairs to his room, softly singing to himself. If it was a Sunday, he would later go to Berkeley to give the Sunday evening lecture and afterward talk with the devotees in the Berkeley Temple library.

One evening in Berkeley a woman, looking around the library table where rapturous college students were assembled, said somewhat caustically, "Swami, all these young women are in love with you!" Swami smiled. "That is all right," he said benignly; "it won't hurt them." (He pronounced it "hart": "It won't hart them.")

Unfortunately, there are very few notes of Swami's after-lecture talks in San Francisco and Berkeley. Small tape recorders had not yet been invented, and everyone present was too engrossed to scribble, nor would it have seemed appropriate. But on going home, one or two of his students would sometimes write down what they had heard—or at least some of it—and thus there exist snatches of his informal talks as they welled up while he was in an exalted mood. The following paragraphs are from the notes of Marion Langerman (then a Berkeley student) written down in the late 1940s:

Berkeley, 1946. "My medicine is the Ganges water, and my doctor is the Lord Himself." When you know there is none else you depend on just God, and you have nothing else, then God surrenders Himself to you. You come close to God and He then allows Himself to be captured by you. Give up support on other beings, give up dependency on other things, money, etc. . . .

The Lord knows you, I mean you as an individual. He knows you and your problems. You think it is just a blank and that you just live in the blank space until you realize, but that is not so. The Lord is always with you. The Lord is with His devotees. It is said by Kabir, "Oh, where are you seeking me? I am right by thy side." The Lord is right by our side. Hmm? . . . You are all lazy people. The Lord has placed you in an easy position and you have some control over the mind and you are just enjoying life where you are and are not going on. You have so much and are so fortunate and the Lord is so gracious; you are just being pushed by the Lord. The Lord doesn't want to push anyone, He knows you will come to Him in time. Why should He push you? If you would just go on steadily, calmly, perseveringly, you would make great progress, tangible progress.

You are all pioneers. You would not have come here unless you were strong people. The Lord does not place responsibility on just any people. If you are in earnest . . . and want to build something that will be a place of peace for generations and generations of people, the Lord will make you perfect. Your earnestness is what is required. You think you just happened to come here, but that is not so. You are all special people. The Lord has brought you here. There is a Divine Providence in it. You do not know it now, but you will appreciate it more and more later on. But whether you know it or not, you are very fortunate. These things do not come easy. You are building a foundation.

The afternoon and after-lecture meetings in Berkeley came to a virtual end in 1952 when Swami Ashokananda became convinced that the Berkeley devotees wanted a swami of their own who would live in the Temple at least part of the time and give the Sunday lectures. He had heard some talk to this effect, and no one could persuade him that he

Swami Shantaswarupananda in California, 1940s

had surely misunderstood. Swami Shantaswarupananda, who had been giving a weekly class at Berkeley but spending most of his time directing the monastery at Olema, was now asked to spend the latter half of the week in Berkeley, giving not only a weekly class there but three Sunday evening lectures a month. Eventually, he became a full-time resident swami, and later still, when the Berkeley center became independent, he was its first swami-in-charge. In 1970 he returned to India, having, as he said, worked in America for over twenty years. He was sorely missed.

It was primarily the women devotees who gathered at the downstairs talks at the San Francisco Temple. The domain of the women workers was the first floor; the men occupied the second and third floors—the monastery and the swamis' quarters. In one sense, the women had the best of it. The Temple work took place downstairs: the accounting; the secretary's multiple duties; the preparing of the monthly bulletin; later, the various stages of getting out the magazine;

and the planning and furnishing of the temple in Sacramento and, later still, of the new temple in San Francisco.

In all these ventures Swami took both a directing and an active part; there was a constant exchange between him and the students involved in the work at hand, whatever it was—sometimes many things at once. A person having an appointment with him in his office would do well to expect a sensitive moment of confidence or instruction—the most important moment in his or her life—to be interrupted by a question about accounts, or by information about a sick student, or by someone on the phone. The phone conversations would be sometimes long and far afield. Until the 1950s the telephone was in the hallway, and those phone interruptions would seem calamitous to the suffering soul left alone on the verge of salvation. But when Swami came back to the student fuming across his desk, he would invariably and without hesitation take up the conversation exactly where he had left off. Then someone would stop in the doorway to greet him, or if the door was closed, someone would knock on it with business that couldn't wait. Still, nothing was lost. One had to have that faith.

He was always there for the disciple who had a problem, or who thought she had one. Generally, the problem, real or imagined, would simply disappear in his presence. Before one could articulate it, it would be gone; one would forget what one had come to cry about. Or if one remembered and could speak of it, he would listen gravely and then say, "Everything will be all right!"—and it would be. Or he would instantly give some advice or make some comment that cleared the skies. A devotee was once deeply upset because a friend of hers had spoken disparagingly to non-Vedantic acquaintances about the Vedanta Society. The devotee thought the Society would thereby be irreparably discredited in the eyes of the world. Swami listened. "Vedanta Society," he said when she had finished, "is not so del-ee-kate," and the problem vanished. Or there was Ediben, who came to him in tears over having lost the purity and beauty of her singing voice. He didn't take her sorrow lightly, but with the utmost sweetness and pathos he said to her, "Oh, Susanna, don't you cry." She was startled into laughter at hearing him quote an American folk song. Even though he later comforted her by telling her it was no great tragedy in spiritual life to lose one's voice, it was those words, "Oh, Susanna, don't you cry," that took the edge off her grief.

Whether one was a worker or a newcomer having a critical, lifesaving interview with Swami, the downstairs activity was an experience one rarely forgot. He paid minute attention to the way things were done, not only in the direct service of God but in everyday activity. He would never use a pencil that was not sharp, and if his desk was piled high with books and papers, as it generally was, there was an order to the jumble that he himself knew. He would not tolerate carelessness. If a button was missing from someone's coat or sweater, he would at a glance spot it. A devotee once hurriedly parked her car in front of the Temple with the back wheels farther from the curb than the front ones. He saw it, had her called from whatever she was doing, and told her to repark her car. This was not finickiness, but an insistence on an elegance and precision of living. "If you cannot live in eternity, then live in time gracefully," he once said to a student. And yet he was sometimes all compassion when someone blundered.

Or again, he was humorous with a wit that never missed its mark. One Thanksgiving, a devotee with a flair for the dramatic announced that she was fasting that day. "Ah," Swami said sweetly, "very good! Tomorrow morning there will be headlines: 'Dorot'y Fasts While Nation Feasts!'" To another, who had a princess complex, he once said, "At the least little thing you start smithering!" To one who did not hesitate to risk life and limb for the work but who tended toward platitudes, he once said with vehemence, "You are a mealy-mouthed tomboy!" To another of an opposite temperament, "You will soon become a dowager lolling in your easy chair flapping your fins." And to one who often went downtown on one personal errand or another, "You come to me with your robe dragging all the dirt of the city." There was no way to predict what he would say or do; yet, in retrospect, when one could see the big picture, one could see—at least sometimes—that his response to any given situation always made sense, was always right as rain.

Generally, over and above all illnesses and grudges, the student's need was deeply psychological; it was a need to turn his or her mind inside out, to uproot old habits of thought and action from their entrenchment in an ordinary view of the world and to reroot them in the wellsprings of the soul—in short, to transplant the roots of one's very being from the small self, which had been forming for who knew how many lifetimes, to the true Self. Such transplantation could be a long slow process. It needed both the delicate, compassionate, infinitely understanding and patient touch of the guru and the grace of God.

To be in his presence was to be stretched mentally, emotionally, spiritually. It was always joyful, but it was not all ice cream. Once a disciple who was often in his company pled with him that another be allowed to be with him, for the other grieved that she was often kept at a distance. "Do you think," Swami replied, "that she would last two minutes here? She thinks she would like it; but she would suffer intensely. Do you think it is easy to be in this atmosphere?" Still, it was not all stretching upward: there were also relaxed moments in which the talk became easy and general. Swami's laughter would ring through the rooms, and he would indeed sometimes send out for ice cream.

Yet, even in the most relaxed of moments, he would not tolerate a casual or "clubhouse" use of the Temple. It was, first and last, a holy place; one did not go there to socialize. Nor was the Temple "home" in the sense that one need not be at one's best. He heartily disliked the idea that he and his disciples formed a family with himself at the head; any flavor of domesticity repelled him. And yet, the Temple—those three small downstairs rooms and the tiny kitchen—*was* home: it was where one belonged without the least wish to be anywhere else.

Actually there were four rooms downstairs, for the hallway could be made into a music room. The doors of the library and offices would be closed so that no alarming Oriental sounds could escape into the neighborhood, and Swami and a few devotees (whoever was there at the time) would play recordings of Indian devotional songs by the hour. Marion Langerman ordered the records for him from India and from a store in San Francisco. She also brought him catalogues over which he would pore and from which he would make selections. "Marion," he once said during a music session, "is our musician in chief, our superintendent of music." At another time, on the Fourth of July, Marion's notes read,

> " 'My Lord is deep, deep down,' says Mirabai. 'Make me Thy servant in every life.' That is religion, that intense love. All else is just talk."
>
> Swami is in an unusual mood, shaking his head from side to side with his eyes closed and beating the rhythm with his fingers. From time to time he says, "Ah"—short Ah, not long Ahhhh. The song is about Sri Krishna and the Gopis. When the record ended he said, "Such love!" He played records from 9 p.m. to twelve midnight. It did not seem that long. He played a record of Ediben's singing and said, "She used to sing so beautifully!" He said it with such feeling that I think to myself, "Can God think of even such things as that—singing and how a person sings?" The wonder of it that He thinks of everything about us, each and every one, as being precious to Him!" These thoughts come into my mind. Later in the library Swami is standing by the books and looks at me and says, "You are a fool!" But through those words I did not feel ridicule or anything bad.

Unless he was ill, Swami was downstairs almost every day, mornings, afternoons, and very often evenings, sitting in his office or in one of the other two rooms (or in the hall, listening to Indian records). In his presence one knew that no harm could ever come. He was one's own; he loved each of his disciples unconditionally—and each was very sure of that. He was the road to God and the remover of all obstacles along that road. Yes, his disciples knew (for he told them again and again) that it was Sri Ramakrishna who was the Road and the Remover of Obstacles, but they were children in spiritual life, and with the implicit trust of children they looked upon him as their savior. Nor was that trust misplaced. "I'll never let you down," he once said to a new student. That was it: his love was eternal and sure. One remembers here his once saying out of the blue, "There is a profound security at the heart of Reality." Through him, his disciples were all cradled in that security—a security such as no earthly guide or mentor could ever give.

Although he sometimes told his disciples by way of admonition that he could leave them all and not look back, he would never have done so. Rumors once started among the membership that he was going back to India to become the president of the Order or to lead a retired life in the Himalayas. Such talk came to his ears, and thus more than once during his classes he reassured the devotees: "I have thrown in my lot with you. I will stay here until the very end doing this work and being of whatever help I can be to you."[58]

In his excellent book *Six Lighted Windows*, Swami Yogeshananda has given a picture of what went on upstairs and of Swami Ashokananda's relationship with the men.[59] The women knew very little of this, just as the men knew very little of what took place on the first floor. There was almost no contact between the men and the women, except for necessary talk about the work, and even then such talk was kept to a minimum and never verged on chitchat. The women addressed the men as Mr. So-and-so; similarly, the men addressed the women as Miss or Mrs. So-and-so. All this formality, of course, was because the men were monks, but Swami also treated the women as nuns, and trained them as such—convent or no convent. His belief was that without renunciation there could be no, or very little, spiritual development. He was strict about this, and there was no use telling him that in America there was an easy, platonic relationship between men and women—perfectly innocent and safe on both sides. One might as well have tried to explain to him that in America fire did not burn.

11

DEFERRED DREAMS

S wami Ashokananda had been aware of the need for a new and
larger temple in San Francisco from the beginning of his ministry; he had mentioned it in almost every annual meeting. But the existing temple, built lovingly by Swami Trigunatita, was so vibrant with
that great swami's spiritual power and with the vivid presence of Sri
Ramakrishna that Swami Ashokananda felt he could not on his own
move the Society's headquarters away from it. Toward the close of
1932 he had written to Swami Shivananda, asking for his counsel in the
matter. Swami Shivananda had promptly replied. The relevant passage
of his letter, dated January 6, 1933, and translated for the membership
by Swami Ashokananda, read,

> I fully approve of the removal of the Temple to a better loca-
> tion in the city. When Swami Trigunatita built this Temple he
> surely desired its continuous prosperity. Why should we think
> that the Temple should remain where it is without any further
> growth? What he thought best suited to the times, he did. Work
> has been done in that place for many years. Now, if the place is
> inadequate, he surely, if he were living, would have transferred
> the Temple elsewhere. If you transfer it, you will receive his

blessings on your efforts from the very first. He would indeed be pleased. As regards the spiritual power and presence which you have mentioned, this will also appear in the new temple, because it will be the extension of the same presence and power. The bricks and wood of the temple are only its outward covering. If, however, you still have some doubts in your mind, then I am saying that through the grace of our Lord, wherever you move the Temple, this spiritual power and presence will be manifest and will attract the minds and hearts of people more, rather than decreasing or being lost. You build the Temple in your chosen place, according to your chosen plans.

It was a go-ahead signal and blessing for whenever the time was ripe, and by 1940 the time seemed ripe. Even on Wednesday and Friday nights the audience was overflowing into the aisle, and, much against the city's fire ordinances, folding chairs were set up, barely leaving room for passage. From the platform, Swami Ashokananda had been unable to see the people who regularly crowded the entrance stairs, but those sitting in the aisle he couldn't miss. In order to thin out the crowd, he began to make his evening lectures highly philosophical. This worked—indeed, it established a sort of tradition: the Wednesday evening lectures were thenceforth always on the philosophical side, difficult for casual listeners, who, therefore, stopped coming. But to discourage people from coming on Wednesday and Friday nights was not a real solution to the problem, nor was to rent a hall on Sunday mornings to accommodate them. At the Society's annual meeting of March 20, 1941, Swami put the matter before the membership.

He began by saying that the financial situation of the society was very good—there was even a higher surplus than usual. He then went on to explain the need for a temple large enough to accommodate the crowds that were now being frightened off on Wednesday and Friday evenings by his rigorously philosophical discourses and on Sunday mornings were being shunted to a hired hall of dubious atmosphere, neither a solution that was worthy of the Society. "We should feel obliged," he said, "to have a worthy place to worship the Lord." And he asked the members whether or not they intended to do anything about it. He went on to describe exactly what needed to be done.

First, the present temple could not be expanded, as it already filled every inch of the present lot. Besides, the Temple was deteriorating. An adequate lot must be purchased and a substantial temple built upon it, spacious enough to satisfy the needs of several decades. Such a temple would develop sacred traditions and generate a spiritual atmosphere through many years of worship and meditation. Second, the location of the new temple was important. It should be in a neighborhood not apt to deteriorate, easily accessible to all parts of the city but not favorable to through-traffic arterials.

He spoke of what a large auditorium and shrine would involve: flower rooms, kitchens, rest rooms, a foyer, storerooms, office rooms, a library, space to develop a magazine, space for a garden and toolshed, and, above all, space for a monastery. In short, a new temple would not be a flimsy project. Indeed, the magnitude of the work, as he envisioned it, was staggering.

In addition to enumerating the practical advantages of building a new temple, he pointed out that all the members would gain greater confidence and wider vision by undertaking and carrying through this work. "Those who have the strength of soul," he said in conclusion, "let them stand up and range themselves by my side!"

Of course, all the members supported Swami, and a search was undertaken for property that would meet the requirements. Actually, Swami Ashokananda had been searching for the past seven years for a suitable lot, looking at every corner of San Francisco that offered the slightest possibility. He had found two: one was near the Presidio, and the other, more suitable, was on a steep northern slope of the posh residential district known as Pacific Heights. The lot was on the corner of Vallejo and Fillmore Streets, three blocks south (uphill) and one block west of the existing temple. The view was breathtaking—the waters of the Golden Gate, its splendid new red bridge, and, beyond, the hills of Marin County. The transportation was good: a bus stopped a block away, and in this hilly neighborhood there was little likelihood of arterial traffic developing nearby.

The Executive Committee of the Society voted to purchase the property. Swami Ashokananda engaged Mr. Gutterson to draw up tentative plans and asked him to have borings made of the terrain to see upon what kind of foundation the new temple would be built. This was an especially important point, given San Francisco's proclivity to earthquakes. Indeed, one of Swami Ashokananda's reasons for wanting a new temple was his conviction that another major quake, like the one of 1906, would send the third floor and the towers of the existing temple sliding into the street. (Long after another temple was built, however, he continued to live in the precariously perched, or so he thought, third floor of the old one.) The borings showed that the proposed lot was composed of solid rock, so that anything built on it would most likely stand firm in a quake. Accordingly, the board of directors voted in July of 1941 to buy the lot. The purchase price was $18,500.

In the same year, additional land was purchased adjoining the Tahoe property, as was also a lot adjacent to the Temple in Berkeley. The original donors contributed the extra Tahoe expense, and Swami donated three times the amount of his annual allowance to that purpose, the extra money having come, no doubt, from the accumulated gifts of his disciples and friends. As for Berkeley, the additional expense was covered by Sarah Fox's earlier donation of her Oakland property. Thus the Society had no debts, but neither did it have any money on hand—at least, none to speak of. Launching the huge project of building a large temple was an act of unbounded faith. The membership did not flinch. Indeed, in 1941 this tiny, impecunious, but courageous group managed to donate $76,676 to the proposed new temple. It was a beginning.

The resolution to build a new temple had brought an era to an end.

It was, indeed, coming to an end in any case. The old-timers, the staunch devotees of Swami Trigunatita's time, were beginning to die off. Mrs. Wollberg died in 1941, as did the faithful Henry Page, who at one time was the sole member of the monastery. Because of his unbroken residence, the monastery's continuity remained intact through the years, and by the time he died, there was no longer fear of its disappearance, since there were then three other monks: Mr. Brown (who had returned), Adolph Gschwend, and Al Clifton. While the monastery would live on without him, Mr. Page was sorely missed. He had been the temple gardener, taking care of all the potted plants and the outside strip of garden around the building; he had, as well, always decorated the altars for the birthday celebrations and had done it to perfection. Gentle, unassuming, he had been much loved. During the funeral cortege to the cemetery, Swami Ashokananda saw Sri Ramakrishna sitting on the roof of the hearse, as though claiming and protecting his own.

ASIDE FROM THE MOMENTOUS decision to build a new temple, the greatest event in the Vedanta Society in 1941 was the opening of the Sunday school on Swamiji's birthday. Ediben and Kathleen Davis were the school's first teachers, and there would never be a shortage of children. The main attraction was Swami himself, who would look in the door every Sunday morning. The children adored him; they knew, as children know these things, that he was not an ordinary person and that he respected and cared for them. Sunday school was held in the library, and when Swami came down the stairs from the monastery floors on his way to the auditorium, the children, hearing his approaching footfalls, would stand up to greet him. He would come through the door at the foot of the stairs and for a moment (for generally he was late) would enter the library. In later years, one of the little girls told the author that she always had the impression that he had to stoop way down in order to get through those doorways, he was so gigantic. He did not

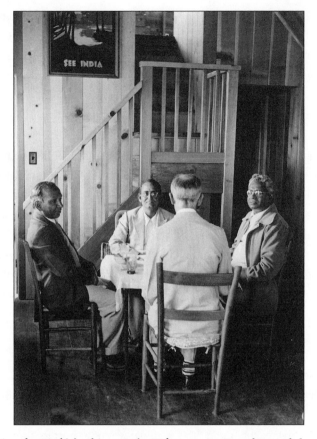

Visiting the Soulés' cabin at Lake Tahoe, 1941. *Seated around the table, left to right:* Swami Vividishananda, Swami Yatiswarananda, Swami Ashokananda, and Ernest C. Brown *(back to camera).*

treat the children with jovial condescension but with the solemn and attentive respect accorded to honored, full-witted grown-ups, and they, in turn, stood tall in his presence.

Another event of importance in 1941 was the beginning of a long visit by Swami Yatiswarananda, a senior and much-beloved monk of the Ramakrishna Order. Swami Ashokananda had known him in the Madras monastery, but not well; he now became deeply fond of him.

Indeed, Swami Yatiswarananda was one of the three brother monks whom Swami Ashokananda felt especially close to, along with Swami Akhilananda and Swami Vividishananda. Those three, in turn, had great affection for him. Swami Yatiswarananda arrived straight from Europe on July 15 and three days later went up to Lake Tahoe with Swami Ashokananda. Less than two weeks later he returned to San Francisco, and from there he went to Los Angeles for an extended visit with Swami Prabhavananda. He returned to San Francisco in November, and it was then that his long visit with Swami Ashokananda began.

Unfortunately, a few days after he had delivered the Christmas morning lecture in the Temple auditorium, Swami Yatiswarananda fell ill, first with rheumatic fever and then with measles.[60] He remained bedridden until March, staying on the third floor while Swami Ashokananda slept on a bedroll in his office downstairs. Not until May was Swami Yatiswarananda well enough to take part again in the activities of the Society. This he did with great generosity, giving lectures, talking with the students, with many of whom he had a warm relationship, and holding the Friday evening Gita class from May of 1942 through most of September (not counting a summer vacation at Tahoe). In November of that year he left San Francisco to establish a Vedanta center in Philadelphia.

In the summers of 1940, 1941, and 1942, other swamis had also visited San Francisco, generally on their way to and from the retreat at Lake Tahoe, where they stayed with Swami Ashokananda. There were Swami Nikhilananda, Swami Vividishananda, Swami Devatmananda, Swami Vishwananda (in 1943), and, briefly in May of 1942, Swami Prabhavananda. The last had been on his way to Seattle to attend, with Swami Ashokananda, the dedication of a new chapel in Swami Vividishananda's center. Because of an estrangement, familiar within Vedanta circles, between the two swamis—Swami Prabhavananda and Swami Ashokananda—this would be the former's last visit of more than a stopover in San Francisco for many years.

As far as can be ascertained, the estrangement came about like this: In March of 1944 Swami Prabhavananda published through the Vedanta Society of Southern California a now well known book on his great guru, entitled *The Eternal Companion: Spiritual Teaching of Swami Brahmananda*. Previously, probably in 1943, he had sent the manuscript to the swamis in America for their opinion. Swami Ashokananda read the work with great attention. He liked it, as he said, very much, and he made many suggestions and comments, among which was the following:

> This last point arises from what you have said or implied in several places regarding the relative positions of Swamiji and Maharaj.
>
> You seem to maintain that Maharaj, not Swamiji, was the successor of Sri Ramakrishna—an idea which you first mentioned in the jacket of "The Wisdom of God." On page 25 [of the present manuscript] you have written: "Naren took the hint and understood that the Master wanted Rakhal to be their leader. He lost no time in bringing this about." This interpretation of Sri Ramakrishna's words about Maharaj's royal intelligence and administrative abilities is justified neither by the words themselves nor by what actually happened. There is nothing to indicate that Swamiji thought the way you maintain he did. You say he soon proposed to others that Maharaj be called "our king," but the Bengali expression does not contain "our," and that makes a great difference in the meaning. Also it is well known that Swamiji was made the leader of all the young disciples by Sri Ramakrishna himself. Until his [Swamiji's] passing all his brother disciples faithfully obeyed Swamiji and carried out his instructions.[61]

There was more along the same lines—a questioning of the correctness of Swami Prabhavananda's facts and interpretations. Swami Prabhavananda was deeply hurt, much as though Swami Ashokananda had disparaged Maharaj, his beloved guru. His wounded feelings evolved into a personal enmity that surprised Swami Ashokananda and unfortunately drove a wedge between the two seminal Vedanta societies. It was not until November of 1965 that Swami Prabhavananda again paid more than a transient visit to San Francisco; the friendship between the two great swamis became renewed, almost as if it had never been interrupted.

SHORTLY AFTER the Society had resolved to build a new temple in the early 1940s, the Japanese bombed Pearl Harbor and the United States entered the war. The immediate effect of this on the Vedanta Society (apart from occasional blackouts during classes and lectures, which caused no ripple in the Swami's discourses) was the indefinite postponement of any idea of constructing a temple, let alone a reinforced concrete one. It was clear, therefore, that the existing temple would be in use for years to come—how many years, who knew? It was also clear that repainting outside and repairs inside were urgent. The roof was leaking badly into the third-floor rooms, plaster cornices were crumbling and falling off, and there were mysterious leaks in the ceiling of the second-floor dining room, which had for years defied repair. In addition, walls, foundations, and supports were secretly rotting away.

Extensive renovations and redecorating were undertaken in the fall of 1942, and all the decaying walls and foundations were repaired. The glaring lights and the lack of proper ventilation in the auditorium, both of which the membership had regularly complained about at annual meetings, were remedied. Handsome new mahogany altars, a mahogany entrance door with a lotus window, and new pictures of Swamiji and Holy Mother were installed. A large photograph of Swami Prakashananda was hung on the south wall of the platform, where it long remained, not only because Swami Ashokananda had a warm feeling toward Swami Prakashananda, but because many of that swami's students were still living and would have felt wounded had their guru, head of the Society for many years, not been honored. New folding chairs that could be set up to accommodate overflowing crowds were bought. The platform floor was replaced (the boards upon which Swami Trigunatita had trod and from which he had lectured were still retained under the new flooring), and a new green-velveteen hanging now covered the back wall behind the platform, replacing one that had had a peephole in it through which a swami waiting in the wings could view the audience, and through which the audience could see his peering eye.

The painting *Christ in the Wilderness,* which stemmed from Swami Trigunatita's time, was retained on the north wall of the auditorium—to the objections of some of the members, who in an annual meeting requested that it be disposed of. Aside from decrying its lack of artistic merit, one member questioned its historicity. "How do we know that Christ sat cross-legged?" she asked. Without hesitation Swami replied, "Do you think he dragged a chair into the wilderness?" (At this writing, almost sixty years later, *Christ in the Wilderness,* now well known in Vedanta circles, still hangs in its place on the north wall.)

Not only did the auditorium need remodeling, but so did the back office and the bathroom. All this took money, some of which had to be borrowed from the building fund, which meanwhile had been growing. Swami assured the members that more money would come. He had enormous faith in them, and in God. During the repair work, the Wednesday evening lectures were moved to the Century Club, and the Friday evening classes and Sunday school were postponed. But when the Society's lease with the Century Club came to an end and the rent was inevitably raised, Swami Ashokananda decided to move everything, including the Sunday morning lectures, back to the refurbished Temple, let come what may. It was then and for the next seventeen years that the inadequacy of the Temple became more and more pressing. Even the highly philosophical Wednesday evening lectures were crowded to the walls and overflowed beyond. One devotee remembers standing on the sidewalk with others on a Wednesday evening outside an auditorium window listening to the lecture. There was no help for it.

Aside from curtailing any thought of constructing a new temple in the near future because of the now-prohibitive cost of building materials, the outbreak of war had another effect upon the Society. The two young men then living in the monastery were drafted. At first, Al Clifton's claim of exemption was granted by the draft board. But in 1942 the second draft called men of Adolph's age, and the draft board questioned Al's right to exemption, there being no official record whatsoever that the Vedanta monastery was a recognized religious institution. To Swami Ashokananda it was unthinkable that his boys, Adolph and Al, who had dedicated their lives totally to God, should now go to war. He pulled every string available to him. All the influential educators, clergymen, and even army officers that he knew reasoned with the draft board; he himself and the president of the Society wrote statements to the effect that Adolph and Al were monks of one of the great world religions.

Despite all these efforts, Adolph was firmly classified as 1-A (which meant he was inducted) and Al Clifton was reclassified into the same group. Both young monks appealed vigorously to the state director of selective service, as did Morse Erskine, the prominent San Francisco attorney who had been the Society's friend in previous legal battles. At length, the state director was persuaded to appeal to the president of the United States (then Franklin D. Roosevelt). At this point, Swami Ashokananda offered to appear personally before the draft board. The board requested him to do so.

There is no record of what Swami Ashokananda said before that draft board. Perhaps it was not so much what he said that impressed those skeptical, war-minded men and women as it was his very presence—his charm, his air of holiness and total integrity, that would not have been lost on anyone not blinded by hysteria or fear. Whatever it was, within a few days, both Al Clifton and Adolph Gschwend were reclassified as 4-D (divinity students). After that victory, the Society's board of directors voted to support the monastery, Al Clifton and Adolph Gschwend gave up their outside jobs, and Swami Ashokananda asked that his monthly allowance be further reduced in order that the Society could meet the expense of supporting the young monks. Thus it was that the Vedanta Monastery of San Francisco, started by Swami Trigunatita in 1908, became in 1942 recognized by the United States government as a bona fide religious institution belonging to a real religion.

AT ALMOST EVERY annual meeting since he first took charge of the Society, Swami Ashokananda had mentioned his desire to start a magazine. He was waiting, he said, for the right person to come along—someone with writing and editorial ability. It would have to be a woman, of course. He did not allow the men and women to work together on any project. It was the women with whom he worked downstairs in the daytime, and since he would be closely involved in the production of the magazine, supervising every word from start to finish, it was the women with whom he would work. But where was the experienced and capable woman who could act as editor? She showed up in 1941, or at least her name first appears in the Society's membership list for that year—Florence Wenner. Very probably she had come sometime in 1940, for at the May 1942 monthly meeting of the directors, Swami Ashokananda announced that for over a year three students had been working under his supervision to prepare a full-fledged magazine and that on January 1 of 1942 one copy of the first trial issue had appeared very privately in typewritten form.

In 1938, Swami Prabhavananda had started a magazine in southern California, asking Swami Ashokananda to be its co-editor. For one reason or another, in January of 1940 that magazine, the name of which had been *Voice of India*, became the well-accepted *Vedanta and the West*. Now, Swami Ashokananda tried his hand at bringing out a magazine in the north, taking the old name *Voice of India* (and adding a *The*) for this new project.

Swami watched, tested, and trained Florence Wenner like a doting father. Not until early 1941, though, did he feel satisfied that she was the editor he had waited for. On Sri Ramakrishna's birthday, February 28 of 1941, he called three of his students into his office—Florence, Kathleen Davis, and Edna Zulch (see Appendix A). Kathleen had been one of the first students to come to him (in 1932); she could write well, had a fund of knowledge, and was 100 percent devoted. Edna had been a student for a long time. She was not a writer, but like Kathleen was almost a Miss Thistlebottom in persnickety editing. To their joy, Swami appointed these three as an editorial board, with Florence as editor in chief. As Swami Ashokananda envisioned it, the new *Voice of India* was to be characteristically immense. "The Swami stated," the minutes of the May 1942 meeting read, "that his idea was to bring out an edition of about 100 pages [8½-by-11-inch paper, single-spaced] or 42,000 words—of about the size of *Foreign Affairs*."

Each issue of *The Voice of India* was to cover all aspects of Vedanta—philosophical, devotional, biographical, anecdotal, practical, literary, and scriptural—making it a solidly researched magazine with sustenance for everyone. The reader was not to simply read it and toss it aside, but to *assimilate* it, to learn from it, and to be uplifted by it; it was to spread the message of Vedanta as taught by Swami Vivekananda throughout the West and to bring spiritual thought into the lives of its readers. Moreover, *The Voice of India* was to be an education in India's religious culture and her ancient, skull-cracking systems of philosophy—and, withal, it was to be readable, enjoyable.

The editorial board, along with other members of the Society who were recruited as writers, studied, wrote, edited, and consulted with Swami, who watched every word, every comma and semicolon. He read the submitted articles and, if he found them possible, made the authors rework them until they shone. "It hasn't jelled," he would say of an imperfect work, and back the author would go to his or her desk. To one writer who had worked endlessly over a piece until she felt it had reached perfection, he said, "Very good. Now polish it." She was incensed. "I will perish!" she exclaimed. Swami smiled. "Don't perish," he said; "just polish!"

In January of 1942 the first trial issue was completed and typewritten with a carbon copy. This was circulated privately (very privately), and over the next three years, trial issues were produced—thirty-one issues in all—before Swami considered the Vedanta Society capable of bringing out a presentable magazine. In January of 1945 *The Voice of India* made its first public appearance. Miriam Kennedy, a new worker at the Temple, cut the stencils in the back office; Jo Stanbury cranked out 150 mimeographed copies (the cost of professional mimeographing was prohibitive); Anna Webster and a Mr. Haste designed the cover, which was professionally printed; a number of capable students bound the copies in the back office; and behold! a magazine was born. Every other month, with the exception of the second summer, during which two issues were combined, the magazine came out.

The project was an all-consuming, concentrated, and demanding affair. Long paragraphs and long, meaty articles were typical of Swami Ashokananda. He would have had little patience with the short attention span of the present-day listener or reader. He expected human beings to be vast, capable of containing the whole universe, and he did not spare them. Although *The Voice of India* did not have a large subscription, still, for as long as it lasted, its scholarly articles were a great success among serious students of Vedanta. No one took credit (the editors and writers were all anonymous), but by the same token no one took responsibility—except, of course, Swami Ashokananda, who stood by every word in every issue, overseeing it all, working on it even during his vacations at Lake Tahoe. For the two years of its existence, *The Voice of India* was his love and his special offering to Sri Ramakrishna and Swami Vivekananda.

In November of 1946 the magazine came to an abrupt end. There had been in all eleven issues. The primary reason it folded was that

Florence Wenner disappeared. She did not merely resign; she left the Vedanta Society. It happened because a member of the Berkeley Society had told her, confidentially and falsely, that Swami was planning to give the editorship of the magazine to another of his students. This other student had come to Vedanta about the same time as Florence. She had a brilliant, quick, and well-informed mind. But she was not a writer and, while she had greatly contributed to the magazine, editing was not her forte. It is very unlikely that Swami Ashokananda dreamed for a moment of making her editor, but it was not possible for him, try as he would, to convince Florence Wenner that she (Florence) was the appointed editor in chief and would remain so. She grew more and more morose, more and more erratic, until one day she simply left and never came back. Swami Ashokananda, who had thought so highly of Florence and had relied upon her, was thunderstruck. He did not, as he would do later in the case of another of his departed students, try to win her back. He knew it would take an enormous amount of his time and energy to do so and would thereby deprive his other disciples, not of his love, but of his concentrated attention. Yet for many months, if not years, he grieved. As late as 1949 he was talking affectionately of Florence Wenner again and again.

In connection with the sudden (almost always it was sudden) departure of one of his disciples, all of whom were dear to him, Swami Ashokananda once said, "I sometimes think that when I die they will find my bones like those of Dhritarashtra, all full of holes. At first they thought it was because of the arrows that had been shot into him. But no, it was his grief for the loss of his hundred sons. My bones will be like that." "But Swami," a disciple said, "I thought monks were supposed to be detached!" "That *is* detachment," he replied, "when there is no self mixed up in it. Do you think detachment and hard-heartedness are the same thing?"

It was not only because of Florence's departure that *The Voice of India* was suspended. Another work was turning itself over in Swami's mind, taking most of his interest and time, not to speak of his heart.

Still, the idea of having a magazine did not leave his mind. In 1950 he once again had a group of his students bring out trial issues, which were, again, huge, intense, and comprehensive. This second batch of trials went on for about five years, and then, because they never quite got off the ground, came to a halt. That was the end of the magazine project.

I 2

THE OLEMA RETREAT

The development of the retreat property at Olema in Marin County was now predominant in Swami Ashokananda's mind. He had not been in the West for long before he felt a hunger among the people for spiritual retreats, secluded places where they could get away from the hectic life of the cities and think of God in the peace and serenity of wide and open country. Much later in a lecture he would speak of this need:

> I think that nowadays there is a great desire in the West for retreats—places where people can go and think about God. It is very necessary. You see, we have to fight constantly against other influences and prevail against them. And in this fight, we lose a great deal of our own positive spiritual energy. If we did not have to fight, then we could use this energy in our further progress; our meditation would be better, our spiritual growth would be quicker.[62]

Fifteen years before he spoke those words, Swami Ashokananda had in mind the needs not only of the Vedanta Society as a whole but, more urgently, of the monastery. The monks (whose number, Swami knew, would grow) were confined to the top floors of the Temple. Their only breath of fresh air was the small roof garden—an unhealthy situation not only physically but psychologically. The retreat property should be closer to the city, more easily accessible than Shanti Ashrama, and should provide a year-round climate that could be endured without strain. At first, the Swami's vision was modest: a place of some twenty acres—enough land to ensure privacy, but not so much as to be a burden. In order to find such a place, he and Ediben (or sometimes Jo) would take off on search-excursions in the East Bay, down the peninsula, and in Marin County, none of which were as solidly built up as they are today. Property was available, but nothing was suitable.

Then Swami asked Miss Iride Martini, a member of the Society who was in the real estate business in San Rafael, to search for a piece of land in Marin County, which seemed the most suitable area in respect to beauty and accessibility. Aware that Swami Vivekananda had spent a few weeks at Camp Taylor, Swami leaned in that direction—west, toward the Coast Range and the ocean. After presenting many pieces of property, which Swami explored and for one reason or another rejected, Miss Martini at last came up with a very large piece in the vicinity of Camp Taylor. It was near the tiny town of Olema, separated from the Pacific Ocean by a ridge of the forested Coast Range. The property was only seven or so miles from the place where Swami Vivekananda had camped. Its entrance was a long avenue bordered by towering hundred-year-old cypress and eucalyptus, from the latter of which hung long strips of bark like untidy festoons.

On a rainy day in April of 1946, Ediben drove Swami and Mr. Brown down that entrance avenue. "The vista," Ediben recalled, "was magnificent, even in the rain. Suddenly Swami, who was sitting in the front seat, turned to Mr. Brown in the back and said, "This is it, Mr. Brown! This is it!" Later, he would say that when they drove down that avenue, he felt that a cloud of deep peace and joy was coming at him, enveloping him. It turned out that the property was two thousand acres

Driveway to the Olema retreat, bordered with
cypress and eucalyptus trees

The original house at the Olema retreat
(now the Men's Retreat House)

of mostly thickly wooded and hilly land, but it contained wide, level meadows and fields and was watered with streams.

The entrance avenue had originally led to a late-Victorian house, a remnant of the Payne Shafter estate, to which the whole property had originally belonged. Mary Shafter, whom Ediben knew, and her sister still lived in the old house. Now, the avenue skirted the house and led to the barn area. Here an old barn and several sheds, painted the traditional barn red, were clustered around a horse corral. There were no other buildings on the property, nor were there any buildings on the spring green, oak-splattered hills to the east. Swami, Ediben, and Mr. Brown got out of the car and, in Ediben's words, "splashed around in the mud." They liked what they saw. The property was beautiful, quiet, and secluded, and yet it was a place where one could live indefinitely without frying or freezing, parching or starving. This was not, of course, the twenty-acre hideaway Swami Ashokananda had visualized; that modest dream had turned into a true Ashokananda project.

Still, Swami was not yet ready for the two thousand untamed acres that faced him.

Negotiations to buy five hundred acres of the property, which currently belonged to a Mr. Harvey, were set in motion immediately. The owner complained that the Vedanta Society wanted the very "heart of the ranch"——the meadows, surrounded by towering fir trees with a burbling creek running through them.

"No way," said Mr. Harvey. He would sell the entire two thousand acres or none of it. Swami and Ediben, and often Mr. Brown, made several trips of inspection to the Olema property, Swami becoming increasingly drawn to every part of it. Driving back from one of these trips, Ediben, practical and cautious, said, "Swami, it will be impossible for us to take care of two thousand acres, let alone buy it." Whereupon Swami replied, "Ediben, stop! Let me get hold of my mind! This is an incomparable piece of land!" "So I stopped thinking," Ediben recalled, "and just drove."

In July of 1946, the Vedanta Society bought the two thousand acres at Olema, the purchase price of which was $166,250. As Swami Ashokananda had pointed out to the membership, large pieces of land close to the city and suitable for a religious retreat were fast disappearing. The Society might never, indeed, *would* never, find another. But how could so small a society, with barely more than 120 members, most of whom were poor, hope to raise so large a sum? Somehow it did. The Society had a balance in its treasury, a large part of which was earmarked for a new temple, but the donors now agreed to transfer their donations to the Olema account. (Not that the San Francisco Temple project was given up. It was only postponed, as it had been in any case.) Many members made additional donations out of meager incomes; others made interest-free loans. It was therefore possible to make a sizable down payment on the Harvey Farm. Not only that, down payments on two small adjoining pieces of land were made, and monthly payments on the balance due on the three properties were arranged.

On July 26 of 1946, the papers were signed and recorded in San Rafael, the county seat. "That was a memorable day!" Ediben wrote in a diary of sorts. She continued,

It was a Saturday [Friday], and Swami wanted the negotiations to be over by noon.[63] I drove Swami, Mr. Brown and Mr. Clifton over to the courthouse in San Rafael where we were to sign the final papers. Suddenly we discovered that I had forgotten the Vedanta Society seal, which had to be stamped [actually embossed] on all official papers. What to do? I raced back to San Francisco in the old Cadillac, breaking all speed limits, and returned to the courthouse just before noon. When we pressed the seal on the deed, and the transaction was recorded, all the noon factory whistles and sirens blew and bells rang from the courthouse tower and from the churches. Swami's face became radiant, and he said, "Mr. Brown, the bells—the bells! Listen to them! This *is* an auspicious day!"

Then we started for *our* land. As we approached the beautiful entrance drive, Swami said, "Drive slowly," and he took out the three pictures of Sri Ramakrishna, Holy Mother, and Swami Vivekananda and held them against his heart, facing outward. The avenue was lined with devotees, who stood with bowed heads as the car passed.

A meadow was chosen, which today holds a small stake marking the actual spot where Swami placed the pictures and where we joined him in an informal worship and meditation. The stake bears a metal strip marked "July 26, 1946." Josephine Stanbury had prepared a picnic lunch, which she spread on a large cloth placed on the ground just to the north of the dedication spot.

Swami Ashokananda's vision of what the Vedanta Retreat at Olema would become was now huge. He spoke of it in the Society's annual meeting in March of 1947:

As you well know, the Olema property was acquired for two purposes: for the establishment of a monastery as a counterpart to the monastery already existent here [in San Francisco], and as a retreat for the lay members of the Society. Therefore, in order to serve these purposes, the whole property will have to be divided into four main sections or areas:

1. The Monastery
2. The Retreat
3. The Working Center
4. The Farm

He went on to say that the Vedanta movement in America, having a tremendous spiritual power behind it, was bound to grow. There would be huge demands made on the Society and a vastly increased use of the retreat. He then continued,

Eventually, you see, we shall have to establish colleges for study and training of the monks, as is always done in large monastic foundations. In formulating a general plan for our new property, we have taken all these things into consideration.

The second main area, the retreat, will itself consist of three subareas: one, residences for men devotees; two, residences for women devotees; and three, the area for the temple and its associated buildings, such as a library, a kitchen, dining halls, residences for attendant workers, offices, guest houses, and residence for the presiding swami.

Swami Ashokananda went on to reasonably rule out the possibility that members could build their own houses for permanent or semi-permanent residence on the property. He made it clear also that, while eventually there would be a convent in the city and another in the country, it was his "unalterable opinion that the rural convent should not be located on the Olema property." "The location of monastery and convent in the same area, no matter how vast," he stressed, "is un-desirable for obvious reasons."

For the same obvious reasons, he tentatively located the residence for women devotees (now called the Women's Retreat House) far from the existing monastery—and from any future monastery. (This was in the days when security was not a major concern, and women felt safe in remote areas.)

WORK ON THE OLEMA retreat began at the close of 1946—and never stopped. It was a matter of transforming jungle-like forests and marshes and overgrown meadows into more parklike terrains where devotees could roam, meditate, and think of God, or, if they wanted (and some did), loudly chant the Upanishads. Roads had to be built and kept open, cleared of fallen trees and mud slides; bridges needed seasonal repair; erosion prevention was an ongoing job; streams had to be periodically cleared of debris, and their banks, eaten by floods, re-stored; fallen trees were cut up for firewood, and other trees that stood in the way of future landscaping felled; enormous quantities of brush were uprooted, carted away, and burned in huge pyres; and swampland was drained by digging a mile of drainage ditches and creating a creek. Thick stands of alder and willow were felled; persistent purple thistles, tall and thick everywhere, had to be destroyed before they gave their thousands of seeds to the wind; other weeds (among them poison oak) were continuously battled; and retaining walls were built to prevent landslides during winter storms. Now and then a winter of torrential rains and floods would undo a year's hard labor of building bulwarks and dams—and the work would have to be redone.

Underground lines were laid for water and electricity, a well was dug, and a water tank was installed on the western slope of the ridge. After Swami obtained expert advice about earthquakes (the San An-dreas fault ran through the property), the largest barn, declared safe, was thoroughly cleaned with a rented industrial vacuum and made

Swami Ashokananda at Olema, 1947

ready to be remodeled into living quarters for the monks, and a "shed" was built by the men for the women workers, where they could rest, eat lunch, and wash up. The monks also built a larger shed to house all the equipment needed for transforming a wilderness into a parkland. Places of beauty were created: groves and meadows, and areas from which one could look eastward over pale gold, oak-splashed hills, where no house marred the serene expanse of countryside.

Swami Ashokananda took part in all this work, even in pouring rain, lending a hand at cutting down thistles, chopping trees, closely surveying the drainage of the marshland, and digging ditches himself. He would not ask anyone to do work that he himself had not done, and once or twice, to the consternation of those who watched, he used a bucking chain saw to attack trees. The work and the conditions of the land would remind him of some aspect of spiritual life or of some relationship between God and man, and the metaphors would find their way into his lectures or classes, hitting some nail precisely on the head or illuminating some difficult concept with a flood of familiar light. "Don't ever destroy a good form," he once said in the course of a class, "even though it appears to have lost its substance. You do not fill up the channel of a creek or a river because in the summer it has dried up; you know the water will come again. If you close the channel, the water will flood and create a swamp, so you leave the channel open."

The women's work crew, consisting of schoolteachers, librarians, nurses, office workers, and housewives, pitched into the work like a corps of Amazons, their muscles hardening as they used them. At least twice a week carloads of women devotees came from San Francisco and Berkeley to thrash the land into submission. They sprayed acres of weeds with the new miracle herbicide 2,4-D, cleared brush, and dug trenches. One summer the women established a camp on the property in an area known as Bear Valley and spent several weeks there, working long hours every day. Swami at times worked with them, and at other times simply by his presence cheered them on. A newcomer to Vedanta once stood with him on a hillside overlooking a field on which one of the monks was driving a tractor back and forth. After watching the distant farm machine in silence for a minute or two, Swami said, "*That* is *karma yoga*." It was all *karma yoga*.

After Rachel Carson's *Silent Spring* came out in 1962, there was a great deal of discussion among the devotees about their giddy use of 2,4-D. One day the leader of the Olema crew, a resolute Bostonian, put everyone's mind at rest by stoutly proclaiming that the herbicide was

Workers at Olema, 1950. *Standing, left to right:*
Jeanette Vollmer, Josephine Stanbury, Swami Ashokananda,
Anna Webster, and Marion Langerman.

perfectly safe, that she herself doused her arms and face with it regularly. Later still, when Swami was bedridden, another devotee gratuitously remarked to him that if he didn't stop spraying he would indeed have a silent spring in Olema. He made the only possible answer: he stuck out his tongue at his know-it-all disciple. But after the dangers of 2,4-D became generally known, the spraying decreased, and there was never a silent spring at the Olema retreat.

Aside from the unending physical development of the property, there were seemingly endless boundary disputes, which sometimes became violent. (Al Clifton once received a punch in the nose from an irate neighbor. Being a monk, he did not hit back.) No inch of the Olema property was taken for granted; no problem about it was let slide into the future for Swami Ashokananda's successors to solve. In the end, every boundary, every right-of-way, was legally secured and spelled out in writing; every possible tax exemption was obtained; nothing was left uncertain. And that was long before the very existence of the retreat would be challenged and rough battles waged and won. But of that, more later.

Suffice it to say for now that the retreat at Olema, an additional department of the Society's work, claimed Swami's full attention during the last half of 1946. Then in the spring of 1950 came the purchase of property in Sacramento and the beginning of the slow building of a temple there. Before we say more about Olema, Sacramento, and the new temple in San Francisco, it should be said that in Swami Ashokananda's mind, all these works, grand and necessary to the Vedanta movement though they were, were subordinate to what he considered to be his main job—the development of men and women of spirituality and character.

"I HAVE A FEELING sometimes, which I have expressed before," Swami Ashokananda began his address to the Society's annual meeting of 1948, "that character is much greater than even devotion and worship, although without these two, character probably cannot develop. And character cannot be developed unless we work together for a common cause." Then he continued,

All the little angularities and all the ugly hidden thoughts and feelings by which we are held down to this earthly level are rounded, exposed, and eliminated when we devote ourselves to a common cause, working with people of different temperaments.

Self-sacrifice is an action. You may become inactive only when you have reached a high state of spirituality. But you have to function where your reality is. If my reality is the world of action, it is there that I have to serve my ideal, through action; otherwise I am cheating. Yes, meditation will benefit, but it must be backed by work. Work has this danger, however, that in it you might become so absorbed and egotistic that it could be dragged down to a selfish level. But working together in groups, learning to be enduring, forgiving, and nonegotistic, appreciating others' good qualities, not noticing their faults—all this is the sacrifice of the lower self, and therefrom rises the consciousness of the deeper Self.

Do not, however, get the idea that you must not meditate; that of course you must do. During the days when the magazine was being prepared, the workers often worked day and night, but they would stop every hour and meditate for five minutes. I have seen this same thing being done at Olema, and have been proud that in this manner the Lord's work was carried on. . . . You have to become gigantic workers, so that the wellspring of work will not be this little self, but the Self which is in communion with God, which thus becomes the source of Divine power. In egotistic action the Lord never operates. He is not restless as we are. He is calm. We have to achieve a similar calmness. In this way work, and you will find you have become gigantic characters. Then it is only a step to become giants of spirituality, and in all this, I wish you Godspeed.

Important in themselves though the external, visible activities were, they were a theater of action, crucibles where the raw metal of human personalities was transformed—fired, beaten, ground, fine-honed, until at length the real person emerged. This, to Swami Ashokananda's mind, was his primary work; thus, while he gave his full attention to every detail of the Society's growth, he gave his deepest attention to the spiritual growth of his students.

It sometimes seemed that he made the work more difficult, more tense, than it need have been. He would, for instance, wait until the last moment to give someone a task with a deadline. The person had to exert himself or herself to the utmost. Nothing was leisurely, and yet he himself seemed never distraught or hurried, which was in itself a lesson. His disciples learned to work with full strength and with full attention and yet with detachment and composure. In those days of pioneering, when so much had to be done to build up a strong center in an alien and, on the whole, unsympathetic country, without in any way weakening or compromising the high ideals of Vedanta, *karma yogins* were needed.

As though in response, the Society's membership expanded in the 1940s. A number of young men and women who were financially independent and able to work full-time for the Society joined; others who had to work for a living gave whatever time and energy they could. Seldom did people come with a ready-made understanding of the meaning of selfless service, of discipline, of sacrifice. Those qualities had to be developed, and these two flowerings went hand in hand: the building of the Society and the development of men and women who were able—or who heroically tried—to carry it all out along spiritual lines, that is to say, without egotism, ambition, or snarling.

As early as 1934, before his trip to India, Swami had conceived the idea of a strong, dedicated group of primarily nonmonastic students and workers who would stand unwavering by the ideals of Vedanta and become an unobtrusive but indomitable core of the Society. He had roughly drafted a set of rules to guide such a group. They read,

1. No privilege: interviews like all others for personal instruction.
2. A few to be assigned duties here [at the Temple], on the performance of which they will depart and not tarry behind.
3. No gathering of a select few after lectures on Wednesday.
4. A selected group of men and women students to be formed, who would pledge to love one another, ignore one another's faults, would not be jealous of one another and would be absolutely devoted to Vedanta and to the Swami. They must never expect any return from the Swami, and must feel contented by serving the Cause. They must not gossip among

themselves. If they have to say anything against another, they must say it to him [or her] alone and to the Swami if necessary.

5. They must look upon the Swami not so much as a man as an embodiment of the Cause. *Imp.* The selected group must never make a difference between themselves and other students.

In his faith in the potential greatness of men and women, Swami had seen no reason that such a group of near-perfect beings could not be formed. And, indeed, it could be, but it would take time. In those early days, the very idea of a "selected group" had inevitably led to an inner-circle mentality, which he abhorred. At the first sign of it, he had abandoned the whole idea. Nevertheless, through his slow, persistent training of individuals, a body of students such as he had visualized grew of its own accord. Without self-consciousness, rules, or vows, without definition by itself or by others, a hard core of dedicated workers—mainly but not exclusively nonmonastics—who could work selflessly came into existence. Most of them, whether formally monastic or not, would live a monastic life in respect to frugality, chastity, service, and obedience—obedience to the guru, who had the light one wanted and who could open the way to it.

There was no feeling of "difference between themselves and other students." If a sense of superiority crept in, Swami would immediately squelch it. "You think you are big shots," he once said scornfully; "you are just BBs." And another time, "I have students much closer to me than any of you. Some of them live far away from here. Don't think that physical closeness means spiritual closeness!" By example and counsel, the members of this informal, thoroughly chastened group would train younger students in the traditions and ways of temple work, and thereby the group would perpetuate itself and give strength and coherence to the Society. But there was no guarantee that this would happen.

The future of the work was always on Swami's mind. He wanted, as far as he could, to make sure that the structure he had built up would not collapse once he had gone. Whoever his successor might be, there would be an inevitable turnover of workers; old ways and traditions would be lost, new ways not yet established. He did not believe in leaving these things entirely in the hands of God—not if he could somehow help the transition to flow smoothly. It was with this in mind that in 1956 he drafted a long letter, addressed to "The Workers of [the] Vedanta Society"—and it was, perhaps, with a sense that this letter was, after all, an unnecessary document that he discarded it. Essentially, the letter stated the need for the workers of the Society to become an organized group, with a sense of identity and responsibility to the work, so that whatever project was in progress and had already entailed the expenditure of large sums of money and great sacrifices on the part of the members would not be disrupted during a transitional period but would continue under the overall leadership of a new swami and the direct leadership of the workers to whom the project had been assigned and who had the experience and training to carry it through.

Although these thoughts of Swami Ashokananda were not made public, and although there was no formal organization of the workers and no official clarification of their position in the Society, they had become, as said above, a well-organized group and would, in loyalty to the work itself, if not to Swami, carry on even without him.

One night in December of 1945, he dreamt that a young man dressed all in white like a Hindu *brahmacharin* came into the downstairs hall and said to him, "Come; it is time to go." The dream was so vivid that the next morning he spent hours in his room putting his papers in order and writing his will and his last instructions. That afternoon when Ediben was driving him across the Bay Bridge to Berkeley, she said to him, "I have felt the nearness of death all day." He did not reply. He told no one of his dream at the time, but one of the papers he wrote that morning would become a sacred mandate to his disciples:

To all students & members
In case of my death, please stand by,
& help the cause of Vedanta by remaining
faithful to the work here & in Berkeley
Please help my successor or successors
with faithful & earnest cooperation & service.
May the blessings of the Lord be forever upon you.

Swami Ashokananda

Dec. 8, 1945

Twenty-four years and one week later, that short handwritten note became relevant and copies of it were distributed to all the members of the Society.

Aside from its value as a means to train individuals, the work of the Society was in keeping with the purpose of the Ramakrishna Order: *Atmano moksartham jagad dhitaya ca* ("For one's own salvation and the welfare of the world"). In his address to the Society's annual meeting of 1950, Swami touched on this point. His words, as paraphrased by the secretary in the minutes, read,

If we were only seeking God, life would become a little easier for us. But we feel that at the same time we have a responsibility to the spiritual movement of which we are a part and which we want to see spread and grow. Sometimes I think that in order to realize one's spiritual goal, one does not necessarily have to accept this responsibility. By becoming deeply spiritual and devoting oneself to God alone, without any thought to the furtherance of the Vedanta Society, one still becomes an asset to mankind. But from the very inception of this movement, the idea of responsibility has been injected . . . and I believe this ideal is in our blood, that we are not just to think of our own salvation, but that we are to remember to serve others. . . . This mode of spiritual practice is the responsibility bequeathed us as our heritage from Sri Ramakrishna and Swami Vivekananda. . . .

Swami Ashokananda's words had a way of entering into the souls of his disciples and sometimes brought about an overzealous reaction. It was possibly because of this that in his address to the annual meeting the next year (March 15, 1951) he said, as though in continuation,

> You must not think, as some of you might, that if you live this life of dedication and renunciation . . . poverty, misery, and suffering will be your lot. This is erroneous. I have never known anyone who has served God to suffer misery in this life as a consequence. Not anyone. There should not be any fear. Nor should you think that your sacrifice and service should excel your means. What the Lord wants is that we be filled with the true spirit of renunciation, not that we strain beyond our ability. After all, we are a very small group of people, yet I am amazed that during my stay here so much has been accomplished. And that amazement brings to me the assurance, if and when I need it, that behind this movement there is undoubtedly the hand and will of God. He is certainly guiding us; He wants us to grow, and He wants us to be His willing instruments. Let us all do the best we can. We need not torture ourselves in His service. Let there be a sense of triumph in us, a freedom from the bondages of lower life. That is what He wants.

And to a devotee who was totally disregarding her body in her eagerness to serve, he once said, "Don't abuse a horse from which you cannot dismount." He likened the body of another to the Society's pickup trucks, which needed care in order to be useful. That alone gave her pause.

I3

THE STRUGGLE OF
SACRAMENTO

The building of a temple at Sacramento, like the development of
the Vedanta Retreat at Olema, gave plenty of scope to serve. In
the autumn of 1949 a group of newcomers began to attend the Sunday
lectures in San Francisco, which were then being given at the Temple.
There were the brothers Emil and Theron Martin, their wives, and the
father of Emil's wife. A little later, the parents of Emil and Theron
Martin joined this group. Later still, Theron and Emil brought their
young children to Sunday school. They came regularly, all the way, it
turned out, from Sacramento, a drive of over two hours on what was
then a narrow two-lane highway. They had been interested in metaphysical literature of sorts and had somehow learned of the San Francisco Vedanta Society. Some say it was a Ouija board that guided them.
In any case, they came and continued to come.

One Sunday, Emil, who was by then enchanted by Swami and
Vedanta, asked whether he could take the lectures down on wire.
Swami agreed, and Emil set up his recording apparatus in the hall be-
hind the green curtain. After some weeks of recording, Emil said to
Swami, "You know, Swami, it is really too hard for all of us to com-
mute so far every week. Why can't we start something in Sacramento?
You can start in my house." In other words, the Swami could do the

commuting. But Swami himself did not think of the proposal in these terms. He readily agreed. "This is the way things start," he said to Ediben. "We'll go up there and see." Since Swami Shantaswarupananda was now holding the Thursday evening classes in Berkeley, Thursday evenings were free for Swami Ashokananda; so every Thursday evening Ediben drove Swami Ashokananda to Sacramento, where he held a class in the living room of Emil Martin's small house, which contained a built-in organ. Mrs. Martin sang, and a number of neighbors came in. After Swami's talk, refreshments were served, one of the wives having baked a cake. The group was very earnest.

Before many weeks had passed, Swami Ashokananda decided that the Emil Martins' house was not a good place for the meetings. The room used for the classes was too small and the setting too domestic. "We must look for some place that we can rent or buy," he said. And so in November of 1949 the group started scouring the city of Sacramento for a suitable house. Every time they found something that seemed acceptable, they would phone Swami, and he and Ediben or Jo would drive to Sacramento. This sometimes happened twice a week. But nothing that held a promise fulfilled it. At length, Swami said to Emil, "The only thing to do is to get a piece of land and build a place the way we want it!"

Emil found the lot on which the Sacramento Temple stands today—an empty and barren seven-acre lot, with a single oak tree at the far end. Nothing else grew on it except weeds. But it was a good buy, and in April of 1950 the lot was purchased. It would be a long time before the temple in its final form was dedicated. Although the work was slow, it was intense and concentrated and claimed the devoted labor of many students—men and women both.

It was the men, primarily five or six young monks from the monasteries at San Francisco and Olema, who did the building. At first they lived in tents, and then they moved into a barnlike structure that they had erected and that served also as toolshed, lumber room, and storage room. The first permanent building that went up, just west of the temporary "barn" and attached to it, was to become a chapel, at least for a time. Simultaneously, the ground around the future temple was prepared for a landscaped garden.

The existing soil of the lot was hard-packed clay, in which practically nothing could grow—and, if anything did grow, it would not endure for the centuries of use that Swami Ashokananda required of everything. A garden dedicated to Sri Ramakrishna, and where Sri Ramakrishna would walk, as Swami later said with certainty that he did, should be no ephemeral thing, blooming and fading overnight. Therefore, a complete change of soil and a drainage system were necessary. It was pointed out to Swami that nearby gardens were doing very well without all this trouble—to which he replied that they might be doing well *now*, but where would they be in a hundred years? He sought the kinds of trees, plants, and ground cover that would thrive in the burning summers and harsh winters of Sacramento, and in the course of his search he again visited innumerable nurseries.

Swami's love of trees and plants had started with his development of the Berkeley Temple garden. Now it grew into a veritable passion, particularly a passion for camellias. Their seemingly infinite variety, their perfection of form and exquisiteness of color fascinated him and reminded him, he said, of divinity. He read all the books on camellias that he could find, studied catalogues, and sent for the plants that most appealed to him. On the roof of the San Francisco Temple he converted the old greenhouse into a glassed-in hothouse, where he grew camellias and also rhododendrons. Later the camellias were moved to Olema, where, shaded by towering fir trees and tanbark oak, a fenced-in, deer-proof garden of more than one hundred camellia trees was planted. Despite the determined inroads of gophers, the trees are today large, seasonally full of bloom, and watched over by Lord Buddha, who sits in a small shrine in their midst.

Working at Sacramento, the Martins conceived the idea of building the temple of adobe bricks, made on the spot from the clay soil. Although Swami was not too keen about the idea, because of the homespun look handmade bricks might give the building, he let them try, and soon there was a small adobe-brick factory on the lot. Before this went too far, Mr. Gutterson, the architect, was brought in to design the temple. He went to work with great enthusiasm. Meetings were held periodically in the "barn," where a long makeshift table was set up for the display of blueprints. These were discussed by Swami and the devotees from San Francisco and Sacramento, were rejected or partly accepted, and, in either case, were sent back to Mr. Gutterson's drawing board.

At one of these meetings (in August of 1951) Mr. Gutterson presented what he felt was an inspired plan. He allowed no one to see it until, as though unveiling a statue or painting, he spread it out on the table. It was a beautiful, detailed drawing, complete with trees, shrubs, and people. The temple building was delicate, slightly ornate, and looked as though it had sprung from a Pre-Raphaelite concept of a medieval abbey. There were murmurs of delight and appreciation. Mr. Gutterson was himself so moved by his drawing that he trembled as he showed it. His wife, who had come along, beamed proudly. Mr. Gutterson pointed out his plan's various merits, answered questions, and accepted with humility the praise that came from all sides—all sides but one. Swami, watching Mr. Gutterson closely, was silent. At length, Mr. and Mrs. Gutterson left. It was then that Swami turned to the devotees. "You see," he said, "that just won't do! But I couldn't tell him. We've really got to start over. This is not it."

Later Swami spoke to Mr. Gutterson, explaining, consoling, and winning him over to his own idea, which was one of strength and solidity, and yet of grace. Eventually, a plan was drawn by Mr. Gutterson that incorporated Swami's idea of what a Vedanta country temple should be. Subsequently, discussions of the plans were held halfway between Sacramento and San Francisco on a large shoulder of the highway, backed by a half circle of tall eucalyptus trees. Here the Martins and the party from San Francisco would meet. The blueprints would be laid out on the hood of one of the cars and studied by flashlight, because these meetings generally took place at night after everyone's workday was done.

At length, a rudimentary plan was settled upon and the construction work was begun. A few things were done professionally, for instance, the planning of the drainage system and the laying of a part of the foundation for the building. The building of the wall along the road and the rest was done by monks, most of whom had to learn as they went. And learn they did: they became electricians, plumbers, carpenters, masons, and soil movers. They worked day and night for years. To the casual onlooker it must have appeared that various-colored mounds of soil were being mindlessly moved around. The process went on endlessly, day after day, as though it were some sort of yoga practice that Vedanta monks engaged in—and so it was. Swami Ashokananda kept in detailed touch with the work as inch by inch it progressed; he also kept his finger, as it were, on the pulse of the workers, worrying like a mother about their health, their comfort, their spiritual growth, but he was as stern as a disciplinarian father when he visited them, as he very often did.

The men worked hard, and the women, too. Dorothy Peters (later, Pravrajika Nirbhayaprana) became an authority on ground covers. After persistent and endless research, she and Swami found the best possible plant for the purpose—hardy, perennial, and attractive. Carloads of women devotees went weekly to Sacramento to install this miracle cover, vinca, little seedling by little seedling, over the entrance grounds. Fifty years later, the ground cover is still there, thick and thriving.

Also thriving is a double row of Italian cypress trees, which had not been in the original plan. While the temple and its grounds were taking shape in their timeless fashion, a country club abutting the south boundary arose almost overnight. It was complete with swimming pool, tennis courts, shouting revelers, and loudspeakers. Thus an emergency sound barrier of Italian cypress was planted, and today, while most other cypress trees in the neighborhood have long since died, this

Swami Ashokananda standing at the Sacramento construction site with
several members of the Martin family and Edith Soulé *(far right)*

line of trees stands tall and thick, effectively blocking the neighboring
ruckus.

Seasoned redwood beams were obtained from the dismantling
of the San Francisco International Exposition at Treasure Island, and
these, standing still unroofed, were carefully wrapped in brown paper
to protect them during the winter rains. These upright beams were
later sculpted to fit exactly the walls of the library, which were made of
the Martins' irregular adobe bricks. Everything was done with endless
care, with trial and error, sacrifice and triumph. But all the while, the
overall floor plan was still unsatisfactory. Somehow neither the flower
room that served the altar nor the foyer of the auditorium would go
where they should.

Mr. Gutterson had no satisfactory solution, and Swami puzzled
over the problem for days. Then one night he woke with a start and the
whole thing was clear: simply put the altar next to the flower room at
the near end and move the foyer to the far end. And that is the way it is

today: one walks down a loggia to the foyer entrance, passing a lawn on the way, and, in the foyer, one turns to the right to enter the auditorium.

Throughout these developments, the Martin families had sacrificed a great deal. In an annual meeting at Sacramento in 1952, Swami Ashokananda paid tribute to them:

> I cannot but feel that I am greatly responsible for the tremendous task you have undertaken in building up the center in Sacramento. Do not think that I do not appreciate how hard and how heavy your duties have been in this regard. But as I look back over my years of work in this country, I find that I have always assumed that every man and woman is capable of great achievements.
>
> From a common sense point of view, it is almost madness to have expected a small group who are busy in family life and earning a living to take on the responsibility of building up a center in such a short time. . . . When I think seriously about it, however, I realize [that] all this madness would not have seized us were it not for the working of a higher power behind us. If we can really build the library, rest rooms, and the swami's quarters, and invite people to attend discourses on spiritual topics, and if this center really helps those who have been seeking a spiritual life, then I think we will be right in concluding that from the inception of this venture we were impelled by divine power and divine intelligence. If the project breaks down and fails, then it might appear that it was based upon only the faith of a misguided enthusiast, and I shall feel very bad—not for myself but for those who have participated in the work and who may feel their labor has been futile. But my true conviction, which springs from realistic faith and realistic hope, is that you are growing and that we shall bring to completion what we have undertaken.
>
> When we started, I did not know where we would get even

one dollar, for there is no material fund behind us. But there is a fund, an inexhaustible fund, that is God's. . . .

We who have come to this country happen to be the instruments, the representatives of the power of Sri Ramakrishna, and we feel our responsibility keenly. We know that He whose banner we carry in our hands is in back of us. And I want to say to you who have become a part of this work that I have not the least doubt but that you are drawn through His deliberate will. I want you all to recognize this fact so you may feel how blessed you are.

I do not want you to take God's blessing lightly, for through it you get such strength and comfort in your heart that if a hundred million deaths were facing you, it would not faze you. The Lord's blessing is a burning blessing. If the Lord has chosen you, what alternative have you? But though it is a burning blessing, it is also a joyful one. As Christ himself said, "My yoke is light."[64]

The Lord recognizes your devotion, and if you give one cent from your heart, it is infinitely precious to Him. . . . In and behind these visible temples of the Lord are the invisible temples where people may come and be blessed. Because you are building through sacrifice and loving dedication and service, that inner temple is being built simultaneously, and when it is built I am quite sure that the Lord will be very glad to manifest Himself there.

Nevertheless, it was becoming clear to the Martins that they had bitten off more than they could chew. Indeed, they were stunned by the outcome of the modest meetings in their homes with which they had started their romance with Vedanta. Not exactly that they wanted out—not yet—but they definitely did not want the responsibility of the property, the proposed temple, the ambitious landscaping. The project had been named the Church of Universal Philosophy and Religion; now, toward the close of 1952, they asked that the whole thing be made a branch of the Vedanta Society of Northern California. At an October meeting, the board of directors of the San Francisco Society agreed, and accordingly the name of the proposed Sacramento center was changed to the Vedanta Society of Sacramento—a branch of the Vedanta Society of Northern California. Everyone was happy, and the Martins, who had faithfully played their part, were home free. After a time, they vanished from the world of Vedanta altogether.

Long before the temple was completed, the small building that would later become the entrance lobby of the future auditorium became the first chapel. It was dedicated on February 28, 1953, the birthday of Sri Chaitanya. Just before the dedication ceremony of this shrine, Swami Ashokananda's lingering doubts about the rightness of the Sacramento project were once and for all removed. The altar had been built and installed, and the photographs of Sri Ramakrishna, Swami Vivekananda, Buddha, and Christ had been selected, printed, and set in position. Swami went into the chapel, removed his shoes, and looked toward the altar, and suddenly he saw that the photograph of Sri Ramakrishna was vividly alive. From it a beam of light and great joy sped toward him and entered into him. He did not reveal the details of this experience until long after, saying at the time only that now he was sure and, when pressed, that "later on, later on" he would tell what had happened.

Swami had another experience in that small chapel that had to do not with Sri Ramakrishna but with Lord Buddha, who was one of the deities on the altar. One Thursday evening, when he had gone to Sacramento to hold a class and perform a simple worship at the altar, he felt Buddha pulling him to himself with an almost irresistible force. He had always felt strongly attracted to Buddha at that Sacramento altar, but this time the attraction was, in his own words, "overwhelming." "The pull was so great, I had to speak up," he said. His pleading words to Lord Buddha were "Please don't pull me like that! I belong to Sri Ramakrishna." At once the pull stopped, and never again did Buddha pull him to himself with that same insistence. But no doubt remained that Buddha had come to Sacramento, even as he had come to the San Francisco Temple.

The building, landscaping, and planting continued, until at length, in November of 1964, on Jagaddhatri Puja, more than fourteen years after the lot was purchased, the completed temple was dedicated. By that time, Swami Ashokananda was too ill to attend the ceremony, but he kept in touch by phone throughout the *puja*, demanding to know why things were taking so long.

The temple at Sacramento was the joy of his heart, even more than the Berkeley Temple. Indeed, it was a beautiful building. One story high, J-shaped around an open lawn, it was simple, unpretentious, and, as Swami wanted, strong. It looked as though it was there to stay. The entrance hall, auditorium, altar, monks' quarters, dining rooms, rest rooms, and kitchen form the long vertical stem of the J. The library and offices, the horizontal base, which faces the road, and the resident swami's quarters form the hook.

The Sacramento Temple was finished, but it had been a long struggle. Of this Swami spoke one September evening in 1962 in the cabins at Lake Tahoe; four devotees were gathered round him. He spoke that evening of the difficulties involved in the changing of the soil, work that was going on at the time. "To work for the Lord is never easy," he said; "there is always struggle. Always! There is no other way." And then he went on to say,

It is good to have a spirit of struggle. Out of that growth comes. If spiritual life is made devoid of struggle, there is a danger in it. The danger is twofold: first, there is the danger that the work will gradually peter out, and second, it will draw third-rate people who are seeking comfort and enjoyment. Those who have a little substance in them will find themselves in the minority and will go. Those who are pleasure-seeking will take the whole thing over. There is always that danger. If you continually provide entertainment, you will draw that kind of person. I am in favor of keeping things a little on the dry side. . . . If you have no background of strength, the right kind of people just won't come.

In front of the Sacramento Temple, 1966.
Standing, left to right: Swami Ashokananda, Swami
Shraddhananda, and Marie Louise Burke (the author).

Then, when you have learned to stand on your strength, there comes a joy. You rather like to struggle, you like to wrestle with the mind. It is as though you had climbed a steep mountain, you breathe pure air and see vast views all around. Also, you will find that you will draw good people. You are, as it were, tuned to the right wavelength.

I have a horror of this watering down just to make everyone feel comfortable. There is a trap there. We fall for the obvious and miss the deeper thing. . . .

Struggle! The struggle of a hero, not of a coward! Struggle without even a thought that there could be defeat in that struggle. There is no other way! It is not as though you could take an easy path and find that good meditation comes. There *is* no easy path. The mind sometimes will be difficult. When it is difficult, you have to rise up and give battle to it. Outside troubles come, inside troubles come; you have to rise up and be a conquering hero. There is no other way about it!

Certainly there was no other way in connection with building up the Vedanta Society. There were difficulties at every step—whether in Berkeley, Olema, Sacramento, or San Francisco. Now and then, Swami would say softly, as though to himself, "Hé Prabhu!" (Oh, Lord!)— a gentle sigh. But he made no other complaint, if complaint it was. Whatever the current difficulty, his method was to face it, to conquer it, and to become thereby stronger. His disciples followed along, sometimes holding their breath, sometimes straining every muscle, but, in his wake, never giving up.

14

BIRTH OF A CONVENT

By the end of 1964, the Vedanta Society's monastery had grown to around fourteen members, distributed in San Francisco, Olema, and Sacramento. Yet a convent was still a dream in Swami Ashokananda's mind. It was a persistent, demanding dream, but not until fifteen years after the first trial convent had failed did he make another attempt. He had been waiting, as he had once said, for a strong, spiritually advanced woman to act as a sort of mother superior, but no one who fit that role had appeared; so he started with what he had—a few earnest women devotees, eager to renounce, eager to become nuns. This time, two convents were started—one in San Francisco and the other in Oakland.

Just after the 1949 celebration of Sri Ramakrishna's birthday in the Berkeley Temple, Sarah Fox, then eighty-seven years old, fell and broke her hip—or broke her hip and fell. She never recovered from this accident and died three weeks later. Conducting her funeral service, Swami Ashokananda, for the first and only time that anyone knew of, could barely control his tears. In her will Sarah deeded her house in Oakland to the Vedanta Society, requesting that if possible it be used as a convent. At least the top floor was available, the ground floor still being rented. But who would be the nuns? A potential nun,

Marion Langerman, one of the charter members of the Berkeley Vedanta Society, was already living in Miss Fox's apartment, helping the elderly woman during the last seven months of her life with house-keeping and gardening. Swami Ashokananda asked her whether she would like to continue living there, along with Dorothy Peters, as though in a convent.

At that time, Dorothy Peters (a worker at the Berkeley Temple and later in charge of the Sacramento garden and ground-cover crew) was living with her parents in the East Bay. A monastic life had long been the dream of this very earnest, very devoted young woman, who had been Swami Ashokananda's student and a member of the Berkeley Vedanta Society since 1940. Marion, too, liked the idea. On Buddha's birthday, May 12, 1949, Ediben picked up Dorothy and her luggage at her parents' home and drove her to Miss Fox's erstwhile flat, already rich with a spiritual atmosphere. The flat had only one bedroom, which Marion was using. Dorothy had a bed in the dining room, and when Ediben came to stay overnight, as she did now and then, just as she had done in the first San Francisco convent, she slept in the living room. Sarah Fox had used a large closet with a window for a shrine, and this was retained. The whole flat, shrine and all, was adorned with Sarah's holy pictures, which were left just as she had had them.

There were no special rules in the budding Oakland convent, but the two young women established a routine. They rose early, bathed, and meditated. Marion performed a simple worship while Dorothy cooked breakfast. After breakfast, each went to her separate job in Berkeley—Dorothy to a post as science teacher at Head's School for Girls, across the street from the Berkeley Temple, and Marion as secretary for the Berkeley Public Schools. Work over, they returned to the convent. Marion, an excellent cook, prepared dinner. After dinner they read from *The Gospel of Sri Ramakrishna*, sang a holy song or two, and went to bed. That was the weekday schedule. On Thursday evenings Swami Ashokananda regularly held a class at the Berkeley Temple, after which he and Jo Stanbury (or Ediben) would drive the two nuns to their convent on the way back to San Francisco. Once a month or so, Swami and Jo would come for supper, and Swami would hold a short class for the three women.

After about one year, Dorothy and Marion were joined by a newcomer to Vedanta—Miriam King, a young graduate of Stanford University. While Miriam may have been a newcomer to Vedanta, she was not so to spiritual life. She had been a member of Gerald Heard's meditation-cum-retreat group at Trabuco Canyon in southern California, and afterward had searched on her own for a hermitlike place to live. In a remote town in the Sierra Nevada called Rough and Ready she found a poor apple farmer and his wife who had a small, run-down house to rent. There was no running water or electricity, and the rent was five dollars per month. This suited Miriam perfectly. She earned a little money picking apples and doing odd jobs for the local people; the rest of the time she meditated or studied under the trees, living on apples and cornflakes. After a while, she began to feel a need for spiritual guidance. She had heard of Swami Ashokananda from her professor of comparative religion at Stanford, so on a visit to San Francisco to visit an aunt, she went to the Old Temple.

Miriam was much moved by the Swami, and he was much impressed by her earnestness and spiritual potential. He quickly initiated her and gave her daily interviews. Soon, though, she returned to Rough and Ready, wanting to follow her own way, much against Swami's will, for it was a way of no particular tradition. He was not about to let this young woman of spiritual promise destroy herself, either physically or spiritually. He and Ediben drove to Rough and Ready, taking blankets for her and food. At this time, a second trial convent (of which more later) had been started in San Francisco, and Swami, after frequent visits to the small mountain town where Miriam lived, persuaded her to join it. But there was no room at the San Francisco convent; thus he sent her to the Oakland convent, where there was at least a bed in the living room, on which Ediben had sometimes spent the night. Still, he wanted to see her daily. So she commuted by train and streetcar every day between Oakland and San Francisco. Fortunately, the commuter train ran by the Oakland house and stopped not far away.

There were now three women in the Oakland convent, each of a diametrically different nature from the others. Fine. While Swami had laid down few convent rules, his reply to the question, asked by Dorothy, "What is the most important thing in monastic life?" was "To be able to live in a group of diverse people without being agitated by them and without agitating them." Embedded in that response were a number of hard-core disciplines: detachment, self-abnegation, forbearance, endurance, and, above all, selflessness. The Oakland convent (perhaps like any other convent worth its name) was a cauldron ready-made to produce spiritual virtues. It lasted for as long as the house belonged to the Vedanta Society—over two years. The surrounding neighborhood was running down; it was no longer a fit area for young women to live in, and in November of 1951 the house was sold. But this was not the end of Swami's dream.

The second trial convent in San Francisco had also been started in 1949. This time, Swami had not broached the idea. Rather, two women members of the Society had come to him, asking for a convent. One was Eve Bunch, who had nursed Swami when he had his appendix operation and had hovered on the outskirts of the first Green Street convent, drawn to monastic life. The other was Miriam Kennedy, who had been married and had a teenage son, old enough, she felt, to stand on his own feet. Strong willed and intrepid, she was determined to live a monastic life. Swami Ashokananda listened to the pleas of the two women. Tentatively, on the condition that they find three other single women who would join them, he agreed to start another convent in San Francisco.

Miriam Kennedy was at the time living with a devotee named Gladys Pilkington, a retired schoolteacher and librarian, sometimes described as Victorian in her manner and outlook. Beneath her lace and refinement, however, Gladys was a tough party, and when Miriam asked her to go along with the convent venture, she agreed. Eve Bunch recruited two other devotees: Maj Berger, who, on a teachers' tour from Sweden, had found Sri Ramakrishna in San Francisco and had never returned to her native land, and Florence Dunn, a devotee on the sentimental side. Like Gladys, she was in her sixties, but she still worked as a kindergarten teacher—a job that exhausted her. She spent the weekends in bed. Maj, at thirty-six, was the youngster of the group.

Unlikely as this quintet seemed, Swami accepted it as a start, and Miriam Kennedy set about finding a place in the neighborhood of the Temple. She finally found a house for rent at 2254 Green Street, between Steiner and Fillmore. And on Durga Puja of 1949, the second unofficial San Francisco convent was started. While he insisted on a kind of exclusiveness, Swami made it clear that these five women should not think of themselves as "special." "And don't think," he added, "that the swamis will be visiting here."

The house had two stories and a basement. On the first floor, the living room was converted into a shrine room and the dining room into a sitting room. Upstairs were three bedrooms. Maj and Gladys shared one; Miriam and Eve, another; and Florence had the smallest to herself. After a time, because of the difference in Miriam's and Eve's erratic outside-work schedules, there was difficulty in their rooming together. Miriam and Maj (who had a big-sister–little-sister relationship) undertook the conversion of a corner of the basement into another bedroom. Upon its completion, Miriam promptly moved in, and an awkward roommate problem was thus resolved. The five women, four of whom worked all day at outside jobs, more or less amicably shared the housekeeping, cooking, and gardening.

There were of course problems for the women other than that of having roommates; the trial convent, volatile as a two-year-old child, had its ups and downs, its smooth sailings, and its rough goings. There was the time when Swami, resting in Tahoe, heard of a particularly rough patch and rushed down to San Francisco to smooth it out. And there was the time when one infuriated member swatted another full force on the buttocks with the broadside of a butcher knife. Hearing of this episode, Swami threw back his head and laughed, but perhaps he was also not a little despairing. Indeed, more than once he thought of dissolving the entire experiment—but he waited to see.

By the time the Oakland house was sold, Marion Langerman had left the Oakland convent and Gladys Pilkington had left the San Francisco convent. Dorothy Peters and Miriam King were moved to San Francisco, and another young woman joined—Marilyn Pearce, the youngest of the would-be nuns. The convent now had six members, all of whom, except the newcomer, had held on for over two years. Although Swami was still waiting, he was pleased. He was watching one of his dearest dreams come true—maybe.

He gave individual instructions to these beginners in monastic life. Here are some notes taken at random from the diary of Maj Berger:

Swami (in regard to small annoying things that become trouble-some): Ignore certain traits, then you can enjoy the other sides of the person. She will change, but she cannot change overnight. . . . This is my advice: Don't pay attention. Don't listen. Think of something else. Go to your room, and when the storm is over, come downstairs.
Maj: Swami, I thought we were not to go to our rooms.
Swami: Yes. But there are many things you are not supposed to do, but you will still do them.
(Regarding the feeling within the group): You do not have to feel tied together like in a family. You do your part; they do theirs. Mutually dependent, which is no dependence at all.
(Regarding the feeling in the group in relation to the rest of society): Stay together when you appear outside the house. It is like two people who are engaged to be married, they do not go out with this one and that one; they stay together. In the same way, you stay with each other.

Swami asked me if [the convent members] were crowded. I said they were. He asked if I felt that anything was growing and taking form in the house. I said I did not know. He smiled very sweetly and said quietly, "Not yet. Spiritual life is a very dry life." I said, "Is it?" He smiled and said, "It is dry; afterwards it becomes juicy. 'Hold on yet a while.' Swamiji said that to one of his disciples. The roots will strike water, literally so. It is like a plant that has been planted in a desert and for a time it misses all those things. There is a layer that is dry. You have to work through that. Then you come to water, eternal water. Sri Rama-krishna filled all the vessels; he left no one empty. . . . Monastic life is the same as all other spiritual life, only intensified. A home is built up around a person. Householders have their wives, hus-bands, and children. Here God is put in the place of man. Sri Ramakrishna is the head of the household. You love each other and serve each other and stand up for each other, and think of all of you as Sri Ramakrishna's children, living under his protection and care. You have to cultivate that consciousness that he is real. If you say, 'He is not very real to me,' then think of times when he did seem real."

Maj: He never did.

Swami (laughing): Then think that you are living there to build up a special kind of life. Learn self-control, purity of mind, for-bearance, forgiveness. "I won't allow my mind to become upset." That would be a noble life. This is the second best to think, if you cannot do the first. Of course, one leads to the other.

You might think then: "Why should one choose monastic life over spiritual life lived individually?" Because you are sort of left alone. Friends and family can make no demands on you. Even [the] government grants certain freedoms. So, you are really free. Further, you have a spiritual environment. Every-thing reminds you of spiritual realities, whereas if you live by yourself you cannot avoid worldliness, even if you yourself are unworldly. Are you feeling more harmony towards each other now?

Maj: Oh, yes!

Swami: I am glad. That is a great achievement. That is the basis upon which convents are built. Think they are all nice people. Nobody is perfect, but we shall help each other. Learn loving patience. Then others who come will feel [they are] part of that harmony and will also learn to be perfect.

Maj: Does monastic life mean that one gives up friendships and contacts with others?

Swami: Yes.

Maj: Do you mean with devotees also?

Swami: Yes. Be quite restricted. You see, this is a different life. You try to keep your mind concentrated. If you mix with others who also do many other things, your mind will also want to do those things. It is a different life.

Maj: By householders, do you also mean those who live alone without marriage or family?

Swami: Yes. They live a life of compromise. It easily becomes a life of indulgence. They choose their friends, environments, objects of like and dislike, etc. In a monastery, you have nothing for yourself. Whoever comes, you accept as your own. Swamiji said that like the difference between a pond and the ocean, between an anthill and Mount Meru is the difference between monastic life and a householder's life. Compared to worldly people [spiritual householders] are wonderful, but compared to monastics they are far behind.

Maj: I want to live the kind of life that is most conducive to spiritual advancement, and I understand that this is it.

Swami: It is *the* way.

15

THE NEW TEMPLE

The building of a new temple in San Francisco was again being seriously considered. In January of 1952, the Society's board of directors voted to start with what was called "the first unit." This would consist of a first (or ground) floor, a second floor, and part of a third floor, the latter of which would accommodate two office rooms. The architect, still Mr. Gutterson, was asked to draw up plans. At the Society's annual meeting in March, Swami Ashokananda told the membership that the cost of this "first unit," including the finishing of the interior and the architect's fees, would probably come to $150,000. The once-substantial building fund that had been collected before World War II had been reduced by the purchase of the property at Olema to a few hundred dollars. One hundred and fifty thousand dollars was a huge, an overwhelming, amount! After this stunning announcement, Swami went on to say,

> Don't consider yourselves just a helpless handful! We follow one of the great systems of philosophy, if not the greatest the world has known. Millions have been inspired by it, and millions more will be. I have always said that if we do our best, the Lord will do the rest. We cannot capture the Infinite by just spreading

Drawing of the proposed new temple in San Francisco, 1952

a few crumbs for the sparrows. God is not a sparrow. To catch Him we have to be great and do great things. So I say we shall need $150,000, but I also say, do each of you your best, have no fear, and the temple will be built. . . . How will you learn dependence on God if you stop to calculate? But if you rise to the occasion, the Lord will push you forward. This is my faith, and if you share this faith, the job will be well done.

Who could say nay to that call? And so, after some difficulty with the city's planning commission, during which Swami one day declared, "City Hall is a rendezvous of morons!"—pronouncing the last word of this exasperated sentence "morones"—a building permit was secured. As dawn was breaking on October 16, 1953, he performed a short worship of Sri Ramakrishna on the property. At 8:15 a.m. the construction work began on the steep hill that climbed up Fillmore Street from Vallejo. A cavernous hole was dug for the foundation, creating a cliff thirty feet high at its back. The pouring of concrete started on Kali Puja, November 5. The steel bones to reinforce the concrete foundation were implanted that month. And on December 4, as the wet concrete was poured into its forms, Swami Shantaswarupananda buried in the northeast corner a small stainless steel cylinder that contained earth, pebbles, and leaves from Belur Math and other sacred places of India. By the end of 1953 the foundation for the first unit of the temple was completed. The walls of the second floor started to rise in January of 1954, and by December of that year the last of the concrete was poured and the forms were removed. The shell of what would be called the New Temple was standing free.

And now for the roof of the auditorium. This could not consist of the floor of the third story of the building, for the simple reason that a swami standing on the chancel at the podium would almost hit his head upon the ceiling. That, at least, was the practical reason. Another reason was that a low, flat ceiling in the auditorium would be an ugly thing. A vaulted roof with wide beams to support it was constructed. On the outside the roof was shingled with slate tiles. As it turned out, though, only secondhand tiles were available, and so some five thousand shingles were scrubbed into pristine offering condition by some of the monks and men devotees. These same workers also waterproofed all the lumber for the roof so that it would not be damaged or stained by the rains of winter before it could be covered over.

There was not an inch of the construction that Al Clifton did not oversee, reporting each step to Swami Ashokananda, and there was scarcely a day that Swami did not himself go to the temple site to watch the work as it progressed. Many a time he insisted that imperfect workmanship be done over, whatever effort this might involve. One might think that such demands for perfection would irritate the workmen— but it was not so. "Ordinarily," the foreman told Al Clifton, "people don't ask for our best work, so we don't give it. But you people know how things should be done and you care, and so we do our best for you. That makes us feel good."

Swami had his eye on a substantial three-story house immediately west of the temple site. The house belonged to a Mr. Harrigan, who had no intention of selling his property, least of all to the Vedanta Society, whose purchase of the lot next to him had not been to his liking. Once again, the fear of a Hindu invasion hovered like a miasmic fog over the Society's projects. But Swami Ashokananda was determined that the Vedanta Society should have the Harrigan House, as it came to be called. One day in March of 1952, discussing this matter in his office with Ediben and one or two other devotees, Swami said with force, "We *must* have that house! Ediben, go and phone Mr. Harrigan and make an appointment with that man." "Swami," Ediben said, "He will never sell to us. He doesn't like us . . ." "Just phone him," Swami replied.

The Society's only phone in those days was still in the hall. Ediben went into the hall, and just as she was about to pick up the phone, it rang. "This is Mr. Harrigan," a man's voice said, and promptly Ediben dropped the phone. After she had made amends—"Oh, yes, Mr. Harrigan. How *are* you?"—Mr. Harrigan went on to say, "Are you people still interested in buying my house? I am thinking of selling it." "Why, Mr. Harrigan," Ediben replied as calmly as she could, "I can't answer that so quickly. I don't know. It would have to go before the board . . ." Swami came into the hall and Ediben nodded emphatically to him. After she had hung up, he clapped his hands together: "You see! It's ours!" he exclaimed. Later, after members of the board had met with Mr. Harrigan and succeeded in getting the price lowered to a reasonable figure, the Society did indeed have the Harrigan House and its garden, which reached back up the hill as far as did the temple lot. Around the same time, the Society bought a narrow piece of property next to the Harrigan House on the west, and thus, even before the building started, the property for a new temple became commodiously wide.

At the beginning of 1955 the grading for the large garden behind the temple began, and it was completed within two months or so; the flagstones of the paths were laid according to the plans of the landscape architect, Mr. Butler Sturtevant. The main stairway of the temple was completed this same year, and the stonework of the main entrance was begun. The first unit was emerging.

The second unit, as planned, would be constructed in front of the Harrigan House, which was set back from the street, as well as over the adjoining lot on the west side and behind the house on the land that extended up the hill. All of this would accommodate garages, a library and reading room, more office rooms, and a monastery. The tentative plans for this second unit were approved by the city. The third unit would complete the temple, which in its finished form would be a grand and imposing building, climbing halfway up Fillmore Street.

This plan for the future required that the first unit contain elements that would eventually be used in the completed temple but that had no immediate function. For instance, there were the rudiments of a stairway and an elevator shaft under the chancel of the first unit. In the completed building, these would lead to a spacious auditorium on the fourth floor. Also leading to this envisioned floor was a stairway that rose from the third floor and presently led nowhere but into the ceiling.

One of the contractors once remarked with admiration that the building was like intricate clockwork, full of wheels within wheels. But as it turned out, the inner wheels would never turn; when the time came some forty years later to extend the building, the zoning laws and earthquake regulations had changed, and the early plans, into which so much thought and work had gone, were no longer acceptable to the city—nor were the needs of the Society quite the same. Indeed, the finished temple that Swami Ashokananda had envisioned, that Mr. Gutterson had meticulously blueprinted, and that the first unit had been made ready to receive and support would never rise.

Henry Gutterson died of cancer in August of 1954. Swami Ashokananda had much liked and admired him. He had recognized a deep calm in the architect during his terminal illness and knew that it came from his unshakable faith in his religion—Christian Science. Mr. Gutterson had worked for as long as he could, moving his office to his home in Saint Francis Wood, a far-off residential district of the city, and from time to time had come to oversee the building of the temple, pain showing in his face, but not in his eyes, which remained calm, clear. He saw the construction rise at least to the second floor.

In the Society's general meeting of March 15, 1955, in answer to a question of when the new temple would be finished, Swami said,

> That will depend upon funds. As funds come we will sign contracts until the whole thing is finished. . . . It might be four or even six years. Or it might be finished earlier. However, much more remains to be done. We have signed a contract for plastering and for the interior walls. After that comes the millwork and fine woodwork. Then comes the painting and metalwork, which will include the installation of stair railings. Floor covering has not yet been decided upon; light and plumbing equipment must go in and, most important of all, the chapel altar and furnishings must be designed. But if we can finish this project, we shall set a good example of trust in the Lord. We shall not only be happy in our accomplishment, but we shall grow in self-confidence and confidence in God. That would be one major outcome of this venture.

Meanwhile, the work at Olema went on unabated. And now, because so much Herculean labor went into clearing and planting, controlling the land, draining swamps, repairing storm damage, building bulwarks, and laying water pipes, the work was done with a master plan in view—a plan in pursuance of which a portion of paved road would later be built, leading from one level of land to a higher level. Because this graded piece of road was the most difficult engineering feat of the proposed landscaping, Swami did not want to leave it for his successor to wrestle with. But to the bewilderment of later retreatants, it today serves no apparent purpose, because Mr. Sturtevant's plan for the retreat did not materialize—at least not to date. Only that mysterious piece of pavement is there, curving up a hill to a dirt road.

At Sacramento, the temple and the landscaping were proceeding,

Swami Ashokananda taking a moment's
rest in his cabin at Lake Tahoe, 1957

with members of the monastery living on the grounds and working
there under Swami's constant care. He was on the phone to them almost every day, even during his stays at Lake Tahoe, at first standing in
the phone booth on the grocery store porch down the hill, and later

calling from a phone mercifully installed in his house in the summer of 1957.

These projects—the new temple, the development of the retreat at Olema, the center at Sacramento—were all undertaken with an eye to future centuries, not just future years. Swami Ashokananda was convinced that the great influx of spiritual power that Sri Ramakrishna had brought to the world would spread over the earth like a tidal wave, turning the minds of thousands of men and women to its light. He was convinced, as well, that the message of Sri Ramakrishna and Swami Vivekananda would provide an answer to the multifarious problems that the world would inevitably face in the coming age and that for generations devotees and monastics alike would flock to the temples and retreats where Vedanta was taught and practiced. It was for those unborn generations that he planned the three units of the temple in San Francisco, which, when completed, would include an auditorium large enough to hold hundreds of people; for them that he designed the landscaping of Olema, with its central temple, its retreat houses, and its monastery; and for them that he changed the soil at Sacramento so that it could support long-lived trees and remain a place of beauty and peace for centuries to come. And he thought, of course, also of the present and the immediate future.

At one point, when all these projects were going at once, Swami learned that some people were saying that his motive was self-aggrandizement. "Swami Ashokananda came into the [monastery] kitchen at the Old Temple one time when I was cooking the dinner," one of the monks told the present writer. "He said, 'People say I am doing all these things just to make myself a big man!' I could see he was really hurt. I'm not sure where those things were coming from, but they wounded Swami. I stopped my preparation of dinner and just stood there, because in Swami's presence you stopped what you were doing and were attentive to him. He stood and looked out the kitchen window for a few minutes, very pensively, lost in thought, and finally he said to me, 'Well, maybe so; but it is a noble work.'"[65]

Indeed it was, and in 1958 it was a work far from over. As Swami had told the assembled membership as early as March of 1955, the altar for the new temple had yet to be designed and built; the statues that were to be enshrined upon it were yet to be sculpted, a process that would take many months and endless trouble; floor coverings had to be chosen; and the color of the walls was yet to be decided upon. Two of the most demanding tasks were designing the bronze grilles for the entrance doors and designing the balustrade for the stairway that led from the entrance foyer to the auditorium floor and thence to the office floor.

All of these details were a setting, so to speak, for the altar—the focal point of the new temple. They would give the temple its individuality and charm, as well as its flavor. Through 1958 and most of 1959, Swami Ashokananda's office in the Old Temple, the library, and the back office looked, at least twice a week, like a decorator's studio. Floor tiles, paint samples, swatches of upholstery material, pieces of colored glass, mock-ups of interiors, and models of statues, altars, and grillwork were displayed in ever-changing patterns. They were pondered, discussed, and, in the long run, decided upon. Everyone with any discernment was consulted, and Helen Sutherland, the true interior decorator, was ever in a state of extreme irritation as she listened to unformed, inexperienced, and highly opinionated judgments. Swami heard everyone out and weighed every opinion. At length, he chose the scheme of floor covering, wall color, woodwork, and metalwork that would best give an appearance of strength and serenity, of dignity and vitality, of light and solidity—all combined to create a living, welcoming, and uplifting space fit to house the deity and give peace to whoever entered it to meditate and pray.

Jo and Helen were not the only devotees who supplied materials. Anna Webster worked assiduously, making clay models of the bronze grilles for the entrance doors and cutting life-size patterns in heavy black paper to hang in place as samples, which groups of devotees standing across the street passed judgment upon. Kathleen Davis

Plaster cast of Swami Vivekananda's statue for
the altar of the new temple, 1959

sketched variation after variation of the symbol for *Om,* and both she
and Anna made models of the carvings that would adorn the altar itself.

At one point Swami entered Old Saint Mary's, a Catholic church on
the border of San Francisco's Chinatown, to see its floor. He was overcome by the strong, living presence of Sri Ramakrishna and Holy
Mother, but out of courtesy to the Christian devotees who were watching him, he knelt and crossed himself. The gesture was made out of

The New Temple in San Francisco

reverence as well, for he also strongly felt the living presence of Christ and the Virgin Mary. Another time, he looked at the floor of I. Magnin, San Francisco's most fashionable store of women's clothing, which smelled not of incense but of cloying perfume. Almost every day he crossed the Golden Gate Bridge to the sculptor's studio in the hills of Sausalito to supervise, frustratingly, the sculpting of the statues.

Finally, in 1959, the temple was ready to be dedicated. The days chosen were those of the celebration of the Divine Mother, which in India is an autumnal festival—in Bengal the most important celebration of the year, comparable to Christmas in the West. During those five days an elaborate worship was performed on the chancel of the new temple, requiring many ingredients, some of which had to be sent for to India. Among other items were black sesame seeds, unhusked rice, *kusha* grass, mustard seeds, unhusked wheat, oats, blades of Bermuda grass (which were grown for the purpose), and water from many

The New Temple, shortly after its dedication, 1959.
(The author is seated before the altar.)

different sources—ocean, river, well, lake, rain, dew, and so on. Rose-bushes were specially grown for the occasion. Their bloom was nipped in the bud so that all their life force would go into the production of perfectly formed, luxuriant, and glossy leaves to be offered to Sri Durga and to all the holy images on the altar. Other kinds of plants were also grown and tended so that their leaves would reach perfection in October.

All the swamis in America were invited, and almost all were able to come. Among others, there were Swami Vividishananda from Seattle,

Swami Ashokananda at the New Temple
on Sri Ramakrishna's birthday, March 1960

Swami Aseshananda from Portland, Swami Satprakashananda from St.
Louis, Swami Akhilananda from Boston, Swami Nikhilananda from
the East Side center in New York, and Swami Pavitrananda from the
West Side. Together they created a veritable crowd of *gerua*, and considering that all these swamis were disciples of Holy Mother or the direct disciples of Sri Ramakrishna, the sight was awe inspiring. At times
they were all on the chancel together, each playing some part in the
worship and chanting some scripture. Swami Satprakashananda was
asked to chant from the *Chandi* continuously throughout the ceremonies, and this he did, sitting to the left of the chancel, oblivious to all

else that was taking place. The chancel had an unmistakable air about it of *sattva* (which could in this instance be translated as "holiness"), and one appreciated the elaborate care that was taken to keep it ceremoniously clean, utterly pure. How else could Durga Herself be persuaded to set foot there—as She undoubtedly did? As had the Temple in Berkeley twenty years earlier, the Temple in San Francisco vibrated with a Presence come to stay.

Many devotees took part in the ceremonies, engaged for the most part in preparing the ingredients of worship in the flower room, from which tray after tray was carried to the chancel and placed before the altar. They also cooked in the kitchen, which was reserved for the immaculate preparation of food offerings—an abundance of dishes to be offered first to the holy images on the altar and then as *prasad* to the congregation, which numbered well over two hundred. All in all, the dedication of the New Temple was a grand affair.

And now the work—of building concrete and brick and tile, of soil changing, of growing ground cover, of planting trees, of digging wells, of preventing soil erosion, of killing weeds—was almost over. There remained the temple at Sacramento to be finished and its grounds landscaped, and Olema, of course, was an ongoing work that had no end.

Perhaps no part of the work had a real end; it could always, as though by some dark magic, come undone and need redoing. Indeed, even before the new temple was finished and sealed with a dedication, other parts of the work, to which Swami had also given his heart's blood, suddenly, like a bird in buoyant midflight, crashed into unmarked and unexpected sheets of clear glass.

PART 3

SHEETS OF CLEAR GLASS

SAN FRANCISCO, 1959–69

16

HEAVY BLOWS

On January 6, 1959, Swami Ashokananda wrote a letter to Swami Madhavananda, the general secretary of the Rama-krishna Order, in which he said at the start, "I do not think I shall be only rhetorical if I say that your two letters have been like two heavy blows on my head." Swami Madhavananda's first letter from India on December 7 had stated without preamble, "As we are soon going to separate the women's section here into an independent organization, as envisaged by Swamiji, we shall have no more convents in the U.S.A."

This seemed to say, although not clearly, that the San Francisco convent, which Swami Ashokananda had struggled for years to establish, as had the women eager to be nuns, was not to be accepted by Belur Math. Alarmed, Swami had replied by cablegram, "HAVE YOU REC-OGNIZED OUR CONVENT VERY ANXIOUS PLEASE REPLY EARLY." To this, Swami Madhavananda replied in his second letter, dated December 20, "Was it not clear from my last letter that there would be no more convents in the U.S.A.? Well, that is the fact—the one at Santa Barbara being the first and the last. And I have given you the reason why." The only reason Swami Madhavananda had given was that in India the women's Math was to be separated from Belur Math and run as an independent organization. "I am very sorry," he wrote, "that in view of our definite policy about the separation of the women's section, nothing can be done regarding your convent." "My advice to you," he added, "is to take things easy."

To Swami Ashokananda, though, the establishment of a convent in San Francisco and its recognition as a bona fide organization belonging to the Ramakrishna Order were not matters to be taken "easy." By this time, the convent, which in May of 1952 had moved to the Harrigan House, was beginning to show signs of stability and permanence. Its six members had readily given up the world in favor of the regulated, austere, and often difficult life of a nun. On his visit to San Francisco in 1956, Swami Madhavananda appeared to have given the convent and its members his blessings, implying that the Ramakrishna Order had accepted them—but now?

He wrote a thirteen-page (typed, double-spaced) letter to the general secretary regarding the necessity not only for every American center to have a convent, but for that convent to be recognized as a part of the Ramakrishna Order. The writing of this letter, which was dated February 27, 1959, had taken a good deal of Swami Ashokananda's time and energy. It had undergone five drafts, and every word of it was carefully considered so as to leave no margin for misunderstanding.

He pointed out that monasteries and convents were necessary to the Vedanta societies in America, for "the purpose of our work here is to teach aspirants how to approach God essentially through the practice of contemplation and renunciation, [and] it is through the lives of monks and nuns that renunciation can be truly demonstrated." Further, as the membership grew, he added, "a permanent and large body of dependable workers will be absolutely necessary. The most reliable workers are generally to be found among those who have renounced the world, who have no other loyalties or obligations, and who are eager to devote themselves exclusively to the cause. It is, in short, men and women monastics who will more and more have to carry the burden of the work in each center."

He went on to say that he imagined that Swami Madhavananda was not opposed to "the existence and establishment of convents in [America], as long as such convents do not seek affiliation with the [Rama-krishna] Order." "But if our convent is not to be recognized by our Math," he asked, "then what are the alternatives it must face?" He listed three alternatives, "to all of which I have been giving much thought." First, the convent could continue "as it is now, though not recognized by the Ramakrishna Order." Second, "it can wait until the independent women's order is officially established in India and then apply to it for affiliation." Third, "its members can apply for admission into the Santa Barbara convent."

Each of these alternatives Swami Ashokananda decisively knocked down as "untenable and unpractical." The first would deprive the convent members of "a blessing to which they are entitled, namely, be-longing to the holy Order of Sri Ramakrishna." Furthermore, "to have some of the activities of the Vedanta Society recognized by the Math and not others would be unhealthy for the Society and unhappy for our Order in India." "Thus," he concluded, "this first alternative does not seem at all satisfactory or judicious."

If the convent members wanted to accept the second alternative—affiliation with the convent in India—he went on, "a situation would be created here which would be extremely awkward and harmful to our work." As for the third alternative—affiliation with the Santa Bar-bara convent—this would automatically transfer the women monas-tics of each center to Santa Barbara, thus disastrously depriving each center of its best workers.

Besides, Swami Ashokananda pointed out, "in each of the three alternatives to the recognition of the convent by our Math, women are discriminated against. In order to become nuns, they must either be banished from their own center or must form a convent outside of any Order. In America such special treatment of women (who form the majority of every Vedanta center) will seem, to say the least, unnatu-ral, unreasonable, and detrimental."

Swami Ashokananda went on to remind Swami Madhavananda that the Vedanta Society of Northern California has been built up through almost sixty years, has a dignity of its own and will never brook a treatment in which its self-respect is in any way injured. To recognize one American center as being fit to have a convent [that is, the Hollywood center, to which the Santa Barbara convent was attached] and to deny the same honor to San Francisco is an aspersion upon the dignity of the San Francisco Society. . . . Societies, like individuals, have their self-respect, and if they cannot maintain it, degradation comes to them. The San Francisco Society should not be treated in such a way that this harm should befall it.

He anticipated further objections that the trustees at Belur Math might raise by pointing out the fallacies and dire consequences of them all. His long letter of February 27, 1959, to Swami Madhavananda on the subject of convents in America constitutes a treatise that could help solve any crisis today or in the future regarding the disposition of American Vedanta convents—and other crises as well.

Swami Prabhavananda also wrote at some length on the convent problem to Swami Madhavananda. It was said jokingly at Belur Math that since these two powerful swamis—Swami Ashokananda and Swami Prabhavananda—could never agree on any point, their agreement on this subject *must* have something to be said for it.

In any case, the historic correspondence between Swami Ashokananda and Swami Madhavananda swung the board of trustees in favor of Swami Ashokananda's contentions. On May 13, 1959, Swami Madhavananda wrote to Swami Ashokananda, "You will be happy to know that the following resolution was passed by the trustees on the 5th instant [May 5, 1959]: 'Resolved that Swami Ashokananda be permitted to start a Convent according to the scheme passed by the Trustees on 29.11.58.' You already have a copy of the above scheme. Please follow it. We shall be glad to hear from time to time about the development of the convent."

So that was that—except that Swami Ashokananda wrote once

again to draw the trustees' attention to the fact that they were not *permitting* a convent to be *started*, but were agreeing to *recognize* a convent that had been in existence for at least one year, if not for many years, and whose members were fully ready for *brahmacharya*, if not for *sannyas*. Probably exhausted, the trustees agreed, and they granted the status of *brahmacharya* to Miriam Kennedy, Eve Bunch, Dorothy Peters, and Marilyn Pearce. Meanwhile, eight young men in the monastery were also approved for *brahmacharya*.

During this protracted correspondence, Swami Ashokananda respectfully (though unsuccessfully) opposed other opinions and decisions of the Belur Math trustees, questioning the reasonableness of, for example, restrictions regarding age and education. He also differed with an idea current in Belur Math that American devotees used such loaded terms as "my swami" and "your swami," and that "contact of the inmates of the convent with visiting senior swamis or at least with swamis of the Advisory Board is necessary . . . to ward off the inmates' attachment to only one swami."

Swami Ashokananda replied to this at some length. A few highlights read,

> I have rarely heard the use of such terms [as "my swami" and "your swami"] in our center—in fact, I can't remember having heard these expressions for years. I do not think, therefore, that this is any problem of ours.
>
> However, it is the tradition of Vedanta that disciples should have special regard for and devotion to their teacher. In the teachings of Sri Ramakrishna, Holy Mother, and Swamiji, as well as in the Vedanta scriptures, this idea is strongly upheld, and unless you want to repudiate all these authorities, I do not see how you can prevent students of Vedanta from having a special devotion to their teacher.
>
> . . . Americans believe in experimentation and progressiveness, searching always for better and better persons and places.

Under ordinary circumstances this is not a bad trait, but in spiritual life it certainly is not helpful. And when one considers the question of workers, it is deadly. Through devotion to the teacher, the spirit of loyalty grows, and nothing should be done to undermine it. . . .

The loyalty of the disciples to their teacher should not, and does not, preclude love and respect for other swamis. In this regard, however, a great deal depends also on the swamis themselves. We swamis have to admit that we are not perfect beings, nor are the members of the monasteries and convents automatons. They have their own judgements and preferences, which cannot be ignored. Generally speaking, however, if a disciple is *properly* trained, his first loyalty will be to Sri Ramakrishna, Holy Mother, and Swamiji, and as a consequence all our centers will be objects of love and respect to him and he will feel at one with all other students of Vedanta wherever they may be.

And there the correspondence regarding the convents in America and related topics rested—for the time being.

WHILE HE WAS FIGHTING for the convent, an equally threatening problem was claiming Swami Ashokananda's attention. The National Park Service, an arm of the Department of the Interior, had announced in the summer of 1958 that it was planning to create a 53,000-acre national park along the Pacific coast. One of the most important areas that the Park Service was considering included the Vedanta Retreat at Olema, which it planned to swallow, along with several cattle ranges and homes. The new park would be available to hikers, equestrians, campers, and other recreationists, and it so happened that the Vedanta Retreat plunged "like a dagger," as one U.S. congressman would put it, into the very heart of the proposed territory—at least it seemed on a map so to plunge.

Swami Ashokananda at once went to work. Knowing that public hearings would be held in which property holders could voice their objections, he made every possible move to prepare the Vedanta Society to shake its tiny fist in the face of Uncle Sam's battalions of bureaucrats. An article was written in which the benefits of a religious retreat to the community were explained at some length. A petition was drawn up and signatures to it were obtained by everyone who knew someone whose name might have meaning. Other Vedanta societies in America were asked to gather signatures, and letters favoring the Society's cause were written by every influential person that Vedantists knew.

All this was collected into a hefty three-ring binder, 8½ by 11 inches, known as the Petition Book. Several copies of the book were put together by a number of devotees in the back office of the Old Temple the night before the first hearing, which did not take place until April 1960. Swami stayed up with the devotees, encouraging them and seeing that everything was done rightly. At last, in the early hours of the morning, the book was offered to Sri Ramakrishna at his altar in the auditorium. Later that morning it was presented to the conveners of the hearing at the College of Marin in Kentfield, a small county town.

As time went on, copies of this same book, with additional pages of signatures, were given to every sympathetic person whose voice could conceivably have an effect on the government. The primary people to reach were Secretary of the Interior Udall; the two California senators, Senator Engle and Senator Moss; the congressman from the affected district, Representative Miller; a justice of the Supreme Court; and other bigwigs in Washington, D.C. Fortunately, some of the members of the Society knew people who knew friends of these key figures, and every string that could be pulled was duly pulled. Before the bill was introduced a second time, the Vedanta Society was well armed and prepared to fight.

Fortunately, nothing came of the bill to create the National Seashore Park when it was first introduced in July of 1959, and by the time it was reintroduced in January 1961 (into both the U.S. Senate and the

House, by Senator Engle and Representative Miller, respectively) it was with an informed awareness of the Society's protests. The bill now included a leaseback agreement by which the Park Service would buy the Vedanta Retreat while giving the Society permission to continue its use for religious purposes. But the revised bill failed to placate Swami Ashokananda, since it could not guarantee that the leaseback would last for as many centuries as he envisioned for the Vedanta Retreat.

More letters were written and phone calls made to men and women who knew their way through the maze of congressional corridors. Swami Akhilananda brought the matter to the attention of the Indian embassy, and Swami Ranganathananda, who was then head of the Ramakrishna Mission in New Delhi, spoke to the foreign secretary of India, who wrote to Dr. D.N. Chatterjee asking him to contact the U.S. Senate on behalf of the Society. Swami Ranganathananda also contacted the American ambassador to India, Ambassador Ellsworth Bunker, who notified the Department of the Interior that the Indian people would take a very dim view of a takeover of the Vedanta Retreat by the U.S. government. The affair became international.

With great care, Swami Ashokananda drafted a letter to Secretary Udall and other notables in which the Society offered to give the government the first option to buy the retreat should the Society ever have reason to sell it. Another letter to Secretary Udall clearly stated the Society's intended use of the retreat for religious purposes *only,* and pointed out that the property was not necessary for the uses of the Park Service (except to retain the symmetry of its map). More copies of the Petition Book, which now contained over two thousand signatures, were assembled in the back office and posted to the Society's many new friends.

In his message to Congress on February 23, 1961 (a month after the bill had been reintroduced), President Kennedy requested legislation to create three "national seashores," including the proposed Point Reyes National Seashore along the Pacific coast. Subcommittees of the Senate and the House of Representatives at once scheduled public hearings for March 24 and 28. Mr. Clifton, then president of the Vedanta Society, was sent by Swami Ashokananda to Washington, D.C. Valiantly, he attended both hearings and presented the Society's cause. He also had appointments with the senators from California and with Mr. James K. Carr, undersecretary of the interior.

Mr. Clifton reported every day by phone to Swami Ashokananda, who was masterminding these proceedings and who was heard in San Francisco to say over the phone very decisively, "Go back and tell that fellow [Mr. Carr] that his proposal is not acceptable!" It was not easy to get appointments with senators, let alone with undersecretaries, but Mr. Clifton had no alternative but somehow to do so—and somehow he won the day.

The Society's minutes at the annual meeting in 1962 read,

> While he was in Washington, Mr. Clifton was able to work out an agreement with the Department of the Interior, whereby the Society was assured (1) that it would retain complete ownership, management and control of the Vedanta Retreat entirely independent of any control by the Department of the Interior; and (2) the Society's property would not be subject to condemnation by the Department through exercise of the power of eminent domain. The Society in turn assured the Interior Department (1) that the Vedanta Retreat would be used only for religious purposes or purposes accessory thereto, (2) that if our Society were ever obliged to part with the property, the Department would be given first option to purchase it, and (3) the Society would accept inclusion of the Retreat within the seashore boundary.

After it was approved by the Society's lawyers and its board of directors, this splendid agreement was included in the final bill to create the Point Reyes National Seashore. The bill was passed by the Senate on September 7, 1961. But the Society's anxiety and suspense would not be over for another year. The House of Representatives did not pass the bill until July 23, 1962, and President Kennedy signed it on September 13 of that year. It was only then that the Vedanta Society and its many friends breathed a sigh of relief. From being a hungry, predatory behemoth, the National Park Service had become a cradling mother, in whose arms the Vedanta Retreat was safe from any further governmental encroachment—or so the Society thought.

A year after the bill was passed, Mr. Clifton received a shocking letter from Mr. Carr to the effect that the Department of the Interior had not intended that all of the Vedanta Retreat would be included within the Point Reyes National Seashore park boundary until and unless the Vedanta Society decided to sell its property to the department. Holloway Jones (the Society's attorney throughout the battle) replied to Mr. Carr that this new interpretation by the Department of the Interior was unfounded. After several suspenseful months, the Society received a reply from Mr. Carr in which he agreed, in effect, Right you are!— an admission that greatly strengthened the Society's position vis-à-vis the government, but only after much unnecessary anxiety for all concerned, particularly for Swami Ashokananda.

And then, for reasons known best to itself, the County of Marin published what was called the West Marin Master Plan, which recommended the routing of a four-lane freeway through the Vedanta Retreat property. Letters of protest were immediately written by the Society, in reply to which the Department of the Interior informed Mr. Holloway Jones that while the department had promised not to condemn any of the Society's land, it could not make any guarantees with regard to the actions of other parties. Thereupon, the Society, left without a champion on this front, battled through most of 1965 over the incursion of a four-lane highway through its retreat. At length, in late November, after many strings had been pulled, the Department of the Interior agreed with Mr. Jones that while it could not tell another arm of government what to do, it would be much embarrassed if another agency overrode its agreement with the Society. This letter, forwarded to the Marin County officials, had a salutary effect upon them. They promptly voted, "in view of the Interior Department's letter," to route the highway so that it would "bypass the Vedanta property."

Apart from these disturbances, the tax on the Olema property was suddenly raised fivefold. But this catastrophe, too, was negotiated in favor of the Society, and for a few years thereafter peace reigned over the Vedanta Retreat. The internal battles of transforming the property from wilderness to landscaped parkland had continued unabated throughout this larger war, much as though the Park Service were making distant, though ominous, noises like the far-off thud of cannons. And then all was silent.

Into these calm waters, Swami Gambhirananda, general secretary of the Ramakrishna Order, suddenly wrote to Swami Prabhavananda on August 25, 1966, and sent a copy of his letter to Swami Ashokananda. Swami Gambhirananda's alarming letter read in part,

> The Trustees [have] raised several questions which need early consideration. . . . First—What is the status of the nunneries in U.S.A. and the nuns living there? Do the nunneries . . . form a part of the Ramakrishna Math and do the nuns also belong to the Ramakrishna Math? Possibly not. . . . Kindly give this matter your earnest thought and send me some practical suggestions for placing before the Trustees here. . . .

On receipt of this letter Swami Prabhavananda fainted and, it was said, had a heart attack. Too ill to write, he dictated a letter to Swami Ashokananda, in which he said, "Should he [Swami Gambhirananda] not have known the facts before he wrote as he did, asking questions which gave a shock to you and to me? . . . All this harassment could have been avoided! In fact, Gambhirananda's letter caused such a shock to me that it almost killed me." He asked Swami Ashokananda to write to the general secretary and ask him to explain himself. Swami Ashokananda, himself ill, took his time. Not until October of 1966 did he write to the general secretary, combining his letter with the customary Vijaya greetings.

In the meantime, Swami Prabhavananda had written his own letters to both Swami Gambhirananda and Swami Vireswarananda, then president of the Order. He had received an affectionate and reassuring reply from the latter. The trustees and he himself, Swami Vireswarananda wrote, had forgotten about the previous resolution. They "would not in any way change the decision already arrived at."

So this flare-up subsided. Through the years the matter of the convent would again and again erupt. But the resolution of May 5, 1959, was in place, and although subsequent trustees routinely tended to forget it, it would not easily go away.

Swami Ashokananda's anxiety over these threats to the very existence of the convent and the retreat did not spill over into the membership. The fact that the convent was on the edge of oblivion was unknown even to the convent members themselves. Only the non-monastic disciple to whom Swami dictated his letters and perhaps one or two others in whom he confided knew about the convent's imminent and heartbreaking peril, and they did not tell. The peril to the retreat, on the other hand, was public knowledge, but that knowledge never cast a pall of worry over the membership. While the members worked to save their retreat from the clutches of the U.S. government, they never forgot that the main purpose of such work was their growth in spiritual strength and depth. In other words, the Society's purpose stood firm and its vitality never weakened.

After these threats had passed, there were a few years of peace. In the early 1960s there were no external battles to wage, and although Swami Ashokananda's health, never good, grew noticeably worse, a sense of stability and internal growth was marked. There was also a sense of tension that did not undermine or belie the Society's stability; on the contrary, it enhanced it. It came from the almost palpable vibrations caused by 150 people trying their best to realize God. Their effort was resolute. While it was not grim, there was no complacence about it. The realization of God did not seem to anyone for any length of time to be an impossible project. Success was guaranteed—but one had to stretch, to grow, perhaps to break one's neck. Under the watchful eye of Swami Ashokananda, though, the last possibility was not likely.

Even without interviews, he knew the mind of each of his disciples. When he greeted each one after a lecture (as he always did), one glance would be enough to tell him who was on the verge of nervous collapse, who had strayed into a dream world, and who was about to make a breakthrough into a higher state of consciousness. His attention, his query "How are *you*?" with the emphasis of love on the "you," elated each disciple. Every member was embarked on an adventure of the greatest kind a human being could take. The rewards it could bring were infinite and the ultimate goal was certain. Although the way was not without danger, the guide was 100 percent dependable. He was always there, always true. And he could, and did, bestow glimpses of the goal—lightning would flash on the dark and steep paths of spiritual practice. For an eternal second one knew that every word of the seminal teachings of Vedanta are true—"Brahman is real, the world is unreal, and the individual soul is nothing but Brahman."

It was a small membership, but size was not the object; intensity of purpose was, and to that intensity each individual contributed his or her whole being. To each member, Vedanta was not just an enhancing or even a transforming *part* of life; it was the *whole* of life. It was a complete departure from a way of being and thinking, which had extended over perhaps millions of lifetimes, into a new world. One would need all one's forces (and all one's faith) to go the course. It was with full commitment that most of the members entered into Vedanta: each was totally dedicated, and their combined aspiration created an air of excitement throughout the Society.

SWAMI ASHOKANANDA SUFFERED from severe bouts of flu and bronchitis in the early sixties and came downstairs much less frequently than he had done earlier. In 1961 he was not able to give as many interviews with his students as he had done in previous years—much to his own

Swami Ashokananda seated in the back office
of the New Temple, early 1960s

regret and to theirs. Because of this, he decided to give occasional
"mass" interviews, which he called "receptions." These occasions were
held in pairs—for students whose last names began with A to J, and
then for those with names in the last half of the alphabet—in order to
accommodate the entire membership of approximately 140.

The first two-part marathon was held on October 1 and 8, 1961, immediately following the Sunday morning lectures. The initial installment was held in the entrance foyer of the New Temple; refreshments
were served to the students who sat in rows of folding chairs, while
Swami passed among them, giving each disciple five minutes of his un-
divided attention. In that brief time he would gather all that was going
on in that particular student's mind and heart. With a word or flashing

glance he would untie knots, clearing away obstructions from the student's path. He would give him or her appropriate instruction, encouragement, or reproval.

The drawback to this system was that everyone in the vicinity could hear all that was said in this extremely intimate exchange between guru and disciple. Because of this difficulty, the second installment was held in the relative privacy of the first-floor library. This arrangement, however, added another problem: Swami became exhausted while standing for hours, talking intensely as seventy or more students filed in to speak to him one after the other.

Another arrangement proved unsatisfactory when the next reception, on January 7, 1962, was moved to the small vestry—a comfortable private room with chairs, but where the disciples tended to overstay their allotted five minutes. Finally, on January 14, Swami moved back to the library, where he held interviews while sitting down. This was probably the most successfully designed of the receptions. On that occasion, I clearly remember sitting in the large room adjoining the library, from which I could see (but not hear) Swami at a large desk, speaking to the student who sat close to him. I could almost see a kind of radiance pour from him, and took it to be the radiance of *guru shakti* enveloping the disciple. It was a beautiful, almost awesome, sight.

There were two more pairs of receptions—on November 4 and 11 of 1962, and on April 8 and 15 of 1963. These were also held in the library. The pattern had at last found its best resolution for all concerned. But the first of these lasted from 1:00 p.m. until 8:25 p.m., and the second was as long as, or even longer than, the first. My journal reads,

November 4, 1962
First installment of Swami's "receptions"
Swami talked to his students one after the other—over 70 of them—from 1 o'clock until 8:25! When he finally spoke to the

last one and came out of the library, Deepti (Dorothy Peters) was there waiting for him.

Swami: What is it?

Deepti: I have some notes on Sacramento that I thought you would like to go over.

Swami did indeed want to see the notes and looked over them. Back at the Old Temple Nancy arrived, and Swami stayed downstairs to talk to her. I left in a rage.

It was not that Swami did not enjoy talking with Nancy; ordinarily, he enjoyed it very much. She was a young woman with a brilliant and strong mind, trained in philosophical thinking. At Swami's instance, she held a class on Western thought in the Old Temple library every Monday evening. Five or six of us attended. Swami liked to debate with Nancy and took a child's delight in defeating her, which he always did. He would take one side of an argument and push it through to a conclusion, and the next day he would take the other side and again come out victorious—a lesson in itself. Eventually, Nancy began to teach Vedanta, rather than logical positivism, at San Francisco State University, where she was a full professor. She was not the only devotee with brains. Among others, there were Mary Lou (Luke) Williams and Miriam King. Swami immensely enjoyed getting them in a corner in any argument. But the timing was all wrong that night after the endless reception. "Lord knows," my journal continues, "when he finally got upstairs to rest."

At the close of 1962 and the beginning of 1963, Swami Ashokananda's annual flu was the worst that had so far hit him, and he seldom came downstairs. No matter how ill he was, though, he continued to lecture every Sunday morning and sometimes on Wednesday evening, when he gave one of a series of lectures on Sri Ramakrishna and his disciples. (This series, which extended from March 30, 1960, to May 31, 1967, consisted of eighteen lectures and was concerned primarily with Sri Ramakrishna and Swami Vivekananda.)

He did not go to Lake Tahoe in 1963 until August, and although he stayed until the last of September, it was not a restful or refreshing vacation. His blood pressure was very high, and fits of intractable hiccups continued to beset him. Indeed, from this time forward, long spells of hiccups would wrack his body with increasing frequency. No old wives' remedy could give him relief; good-naturedly he held his breath, breathed into paper bags, and pressed cold keys against the back of his neck, but the hiccups continued without letup.

Again, in the winter of 1963–64, Swami had a bad case of flu, but despite it he lectured almost every Sunday. His health was so uncertain that he asked Belur Math to send another swami as a standby lecturer. Fortunately, a swami of the Order was at the time staying at the Vedanta Society of Southern California without any particular position or assignment. He was sent to the northern center to help out for one year. His name was Swami Budhananda. In November of 1964 he arrived from Hollywood and almost at once took over the Friday evening class from Swami Shraddhananda, who had been holding it since May of 1957.

Swami Budhananda was a young, tall, and (some thought) handsome swami. His lecture style was very different from that of Swami Ashokananda, as was his interpretation of Vedanta. Swami Budhananda leaned far toward the Vishishtadvaita, or qualified monistic, school—a devotional form of Vedanta, which, as Swami Vivekananda said, was a valid (although incomplete) understanding of God at a stage in the soul's progress toward oneness with the Ultimate Reality. A number of devotees among Swami Ashokananda's students welcomed Swami Budhananda's less-demanding Vedanta; indeed, they welcomed Swami Budhananda himself.

Swami Ashokananda's activity in the Vedanta Society in the mid-sixties was of an intimate, private, and internal kind; therefore let me resort to my journal to give the reader some idea of the days that passed, one after the other, with a sense of timelessness. They were not typical, because Swami Ashokananda was ill, but despite that, they had a vitality about them that I hope the pages from my journal in the next chapter will convey—at least to some extent.

I 7

THE AUTHOR'S JOURNAL

January 3, 1965

Swami said, "While I was sitting on the platform after my lecture this morning, I came to the conclusion that my days of lecturing are over. I shall have to prepare for the next phase." Swami's lecture, "Let the Dead Bury Their Dead," was not as vigorous as usual. In fact, it is the first time, even when he has been ill, that his words seemed, for him, almost halting. They did not flow with the same rapidity, fullness, and force as usual.

January 6, 1965

Swami (to me): Sri Ramakrishna has given you shelter under his feet. Whatever he lets you do, though apparently wrong, will be all right, somehow.

Same date

Swami went to see Doug [Soulé]. I drove. After he had been with Doug for a while, he asked me to go in to see him. (To take leave of him? For he cannot live much longer.) Doug is so wasted! It was a shock to see him. But it was easy to dissociate the person from that body. He held my hand with both of his with such strength! I don't think he will die for several days.

Swami (back at Old Temple): That will happen to everyone. To everyone that condition of dying will come. Yet no one thinks it will come to him. We are never prepared for it to come to ourselves or to others.

Swami went on to say how much he himself looked forward to dying and to seeing other worlds: "It will be just fascinating!"

January 7, 1965
Swami Vivekananda said, "I am persuaded that a leader is not made in one life. He has to be born for it. For the difficulty is not in organization and making plans; the test, the real test, of a leader lies in holding widely different people together along the line of their common sympathies. And this can only be done unconsciously, never by trying."

And this is one of the things Swami Ashokananda does to perfection—without trying. See the diversity of people who have grown so close to one another under him and under Vedanta!

January 9, 1965
Me (apropos of not having heard from India in regard to publishing the second edition of New Discoveries*):* Perhaps they think I am too high-handed for a devotee.
Swami (fiercely): No! Don't be a cringing devotee! Be strong in the truth! Be polite, but firm.

January 12, 1965
Me: If God bestows His grace so capriciously—without rhyme or reason (which is what makes it grace)—then does He also withdraw it without cause?
Swami: No. The grace of God is irrevocable. It is like the thunderbolt. You have seen a tree after it has been struck by lightning? It cannot be restored to its original form. The grace of God is like that. It can't be taken back.

January 14, 1965

Swami: What you have here, you will have there [after death]. What you don't have here, you won't have there. That is all there is to it.

Me: I have nothing here; that is, nothing in meditation.

Swami: You haven't reached the end of your life. Do you want to rush all the time?

Me: Yes.

Swami: No! There is an important period in spiritual life in which one digests what one has gained. It is often a slow process, but it shouldn't be hurried. One reaches a certain level, then one must assimilate the ways and thoughts pertaining to that level. They must become natural; then one can go ahead again without danger. If one rushes on, it is not good; a bad reaction will come. For the average spiritual aspirant, it is a slow process. In the meanwhile, one can build up character. That is a separate process. You can watch that you don't become selfish, that you grow in renunciation, and so on. . . . Another thing is that, as it is said, for every step the devotee takes toward God, God takes ten toward the devotee.

These things become more apparent toward the end of one's life; the effects of spiritual practice bear evident fruit. Look at Douglas! He talks and thinks about Sri Ramakrishna, Holy Mother, and Swamiji; and he cries. He used to have, it is true, some respect for Swamiji, but he never had much devotion or much use for Vedanta. Now he has. It is reassuring to the devotees; we know he will be all right [after his death].

Me: Also, if Douglas can become a devotee at the end of his life, anyone can! I can.

Swami: Yes. *(He sang in Bengali.)* "If a prostitute teaching a parrot to sing the name of God becomes illumined, then so can Mirabai."

January 16, 1965

I received a letter from Advaita Ashrama, which did not answer my crucial question: Will they print the text of the book without changes, except such changes as come from me? No reply to this. They want to make the type smaller, "without changing the layout."

January 19, 1965

I drove Swami to see Ediben—not to see Doug, for Doug is unconscious now. On the way, Swami said to me seriously, "If my health improves, I will have two years more of work, that is all. In that time, you must finish the revised edition of *New Discoveries* and your second book, and also the book in progress about Swami Vivekananda—if you want me to read them." I said I would take it seriously. And I surely must.

Same date

Swami phoned me this evening to say that Doug had died.

Sunday, January 31, 1965

Swami's lecture this morning was the first he has ever given in which his lack of energy was very apparent. He has felt so ill for the past few days! I said later that he probably should not lecture when he feels that way, but let Swami Budhananda take over, for he (Swami B.) is here for that purpose. But Swami said no, because Swami B. would resent being called upon on short notice. He takes a long time to prepare his lectures, and carries an armload of books with him to the lectern. He would not want to lecture without preparation.

"I will come up again," Swami said. "If not—if I give three or four lectures like this morning—then we'll put an announcement in next month's bulletin and I shall cable to Belur to be replaced. But it hasn't come to that yet."

On his way upstairs, he stumbled on the top step and fell.

February 1, 1965

The whole Society is deeply upset over Swami's lecture yesterday. Something was so clearly wrong. Swami Shantaswarupananda phoned Swami to say that no matter how short the notice, he would lecture in Swami's place whenever Swami wanted. But Swami won't ask him, for Swami Shantaswarupananda is himself a sick man. The doctor has been informed of all that has gone on in Swami's condition. He says he will look into the matter the next time Swami comes to see him, on his regular visit—which is not, for God's sake, until next week.

Swami (to Ediben): You women make such a fuss over nothing.

Ediben: It is not only the women!

Swami: Wait until something really bad happens, then fuss.

Ediben: Oh, Swami!

Swami does not, it seems, realize that it was really bad. He did not collapse, but his thoughts did not come across clearly, his language was halting, the words not coming. It was just not Swami—for the first time in all his long, long history of lecturing. Nancy says it seems like arteriosclerosis. And Swami has complained for so long of numbness in his brain. Very likely only a trickle of blood is getting there. That great brain, through which so many great thoughts have passed! That superb instrument for thoughts so far beyond the ordinary! Far, far, far beyond—and yet so totally human.

February 2, 1965

Swami sounded better tonight over the phone. He scolded me vigorously in his old style.

February 3, 1965

Swami lies on his couch downstairs in the back room. He cannot keep awake, but he seems more to black out than to fall asleep. Lying there flat on his back, he seems so thin, so utterly exhausted.

And there is just nothing he can eat; either it is very bad for him, such as fats, sugar, or starch, or he can't digest it, or can't abide it. Jo and Ediben urge him to eat beef or to drink beef tea. He says, "I am a Hindu; I won't eat beef and lose my caste!" We tell him he is a *sannyasin*, without any caste. But that argument is of no avail. Beef is repugnant to him.

Same date
After his lecture, Swami Shraddhananda stood in the foyer. Nobody talked to him. Then finally, I did, and a group gathered. We asked him about Sacramento. He said, in talking about it, "It will surely grow. I have faith in Swami Ashokananda. He said to me, 'Vimal, this isn't just my own personal hobby—spending thousands of dollars to build a center in Sacramento. I am convinced that Sri Ramakrishna wants it and he will draw devotees there, however slowly.'"

Sunday, February 7, 1965
I think everyone held his and her breath this morning, praying, before Swami started his lecture. And with the first sentence, everyone exhaled. Everything was all right! It was a good lecture—not one of Swami's best, but good. A real lecture, in which he was in control of his thought. We felt like rejoicing. Ediben said, "He defended his title this morning!" But talking later to a large group of devotees in the foyer, he seemed so very weak, his voice barely audible. Back in the Old Temple, he said to me, "I forgot to bring down your funny papers this morning," and then he fell asleep. He, personally, was not encouraged by his lecture. "Slowly I am breaking up. I feel I no longer know anything," he said, disheartened, before going up those long flights of stairs to the second floor.

But even when he seems so exhausted physically and mentally, that beautiful, indescribable light comes into his eyes and

face, transfiguring him. There is joy, love, strength, and knowledge—everything in that light. That is Swami.

I remember once long ago, before the dedication of the New
Temple—probably several years before—Swami was sitting in
the back office in his robe after a lecture. Many devotees were
gathered around. He sat in his corner chair with folded arms,
looking like a roaring, blazing fire—such tremendous energy
and light and power. He said to Sally Martin (now Sally Hoffman), "Be sure of it, some day I will be an old man, all energy
gone, barely able to walk. That time will come. . . ." It seemed
entirely unthinkable, unimaginable. No one for a moment believed it.

February 8, 1965
Swami is after me now with vigor for not working hard, or for
simply not working. "God has let all this material fall into your
hands, and you treat it with scant courtesy." May I work hard!
With Swami behind me, what can I not do?

February 14, 1965
Swami: If one justifies laziness by saying one is the Atman, a vast
ocean, and, therefore, one need not work—if that is Vedanta,
then Vedanta is better not taught!

Sunday, February 21, 1965
Swami gave a fine lecture, in fact, a wonderful lecture. How one
misses hearing him every week! One gets off the track. But how
wonderful that he can lecture at least every two weeks.

February 22, 1965
Today Swami looked sick, but came downstairs to go over my
corrections for the second edition of *New Discoveries* and did as
much as he could. There seemed to be a light on inside his head,

shining out through his eyes, even through his skin. I told him so, and the light shone even brighter. He laughed. "Yes. The lion will rise up and frighten you all. When the lion is low, the little animals come around and poke at him."

March 2, 1965
Swami: Upstairs, I read cowboys [Westerns] and often just sit calmly and peacefully for hours. I asked someone the other day if he felt a peaceful atmosphere in my room. He said, "Oh yes! Very much so!" (Swami was pleased and surprised that anyone would feel a peaceful atmosphere around him.)

March 5, 1965
Swami was very annoyed with me for saying that he had built the New Temple—not only because I overlooked all the other people who had worked so hard for it, but because I involved him in it.

"You don't understand," he said, "that when you involve a person in anything it is a source of torture. It causes terrible trouble for everyone. I hate that involving people in things from the bottom of my heart!"

Sunday, March 7, 1965
A wonderful lecture—powerful, strong, and full of Advaita. When Swami starts talking of the divinity of man, his whole delivery becomes powerful, things start flowing and reverberating, his very appearance changes.

March 8, 1965
Swami is starting to take a walk every day—at first, only one block. His legs have become so weak from lack of exercise that he can barely make it home.

March 13, 1965
Walked with Swami this afternoon. Returning, he sat on the couch in the front room of the Old Temple.
Swami: Never do I feel a sense of well-being. For two or three years now, I have felt only a sense of sickness. When one feels a sense of sickness in every part of the body, it is not pleasant to carry that body around, is it? . . . I feel a great resistance to work or activity of any kind. The mind wants to go within. I used to get so excited about India's problems and felt so heartbroken over them. But now I no longer get worked up over it.

Same date
Swami got very annoyed the other day about there being so much activity in the New Temple—organ practice, singing practice, clacking of typewriters. . . . "You people," he said, "will drive Sri Ramakrishna away from there. You are all forgetting the real purpose!"

March 16, 1965
Swami worries about the future of the work here. If he cannot carry on, then who will take over? For one reason or another, neither Swami Shantaswarupananda nor Swami Shraddhananda could handle it. Swami Budhananda is popular so far, but he is junior to the other swamis, and, moreover, is not at all the man for the job. He will leave in November or December. Then what? Either Swami will be able to lecture every Sunday and hold the Friday evening class and in addition give many interviews—or he will need at least one more swami here.

March 18, 1965, Annual Meeting
A lively meeting. A big controversy over whether or not the bell Swami Shraddhananda persists in ringing throughout the "Khandana" [vesper song] at the birthday worships should be

changed. Swami Shraddhananda agreed to muffle it somewhat. Also, there was a discussion of whether or not there was getting to be too much ritual.

March 24, 1965

I walked with Swami this evening. Four blocks. I told him a ghost story I had just read, and he told me a true one.

Me: I am glad I can't see ghosts.

Swami: What do you say, you can't see them?

Me: I have never seen one.

Swami: Then say that. It doesn't mean you can't or won't. If a ghost wants to make you see him, he can do it. It doesn't take any special ability on your part.

Me: I wouldn't want to see one.

Swami: If you do, take the name of the Lord. Ghosts can't stand the name of the Lord. They go away.

Me: Are they all evil?

Swami: No. There are also good ghosts.

Me: But why, then, are they earthbound?

Swami: Don't say "earthbound." Good people can be here as ghosts for a while; they would do good. How many strange things in this universe!

April 14, 1965

Swami received a letter from Florence Wenner this morning! She has sent unsigned Christmas cards the last two Christmases, postmarked "Redding, California." Swami recognized her handwriting. It was found on inquiry that she was working in a library at Redding. Not long ago Swami asked Jo to phone her. Jo did and asked Florence to write to Swami. Swami was filled with joy, like his old self, full of fun, beaming, imitating radio announcers, etc. The letter was a beautiful one, he told me. She said she had had a dream on the anniversary of her initiation, a beautiful dream in which Swami took her through a ceremony of purification. The radiance of it stayed with her for days. "That is Sri Ramakrishna's grace," Swami said. "He never lets his devotees go. He always looks after them."

Me: No matter what?

Swami: No matter what.

Later, he spoke of how heartbroken he would be when his students left—such as Florence Wenner, Janet Blodgett, Miriam King. It was an agony for days and days.

He sang in Bengali and translated: "Thou hast given me Thy vision. . . ." and "Thou hast removed all my sorrow. . . ."

"It is wonderful to hear a Bengali song [in Bengal]," he said, "coming through the clear evening sky when everything is calm and serene. It stirs you to the depths."

April 17, 1965

Walking with Swami, I had to hold him up all the way around the block. He kept falling forward, unable to control his legs.

Same date

Swami never asks for service from any of the young men in the monastery, or rarely. He said he would not suggest that an usher stand at the foot of the platform steps in the New Temple ready to support him lest he stumble. I gave Ediben the message and she has quietly arranged for it. "My head is so used to rolling," she said, "I just let it roll." "Better your head should roll," I said, "than Swami fall." "Exactly!"

Easter Sunday, April 18, 1965

Swami Chidrupananda said that Swami, dressing for the lecture, could not find things that were in plain sight. He begged him not to lecture and finally said, "I can't let you lecture when you feel like this!" Swami said, "I am still my own boss!" He told me later that he felt a great insistence from within: he *must* lecture. There was only the thought that he must do Swamiji's work and mustn't disappoint the people who had come to hear him. Swami Chidrupananda at least got Swami to agree to have Swami Budhananda on the platform with him. Swami Chidrupananda went along when I drove Swami to the New Temple. Swami could barely stand up or get in and out of the car.

Then he lectured. Somehow he lectured for about forty minutes. He looked so sick, and ideas didn't come. Then he knew he couldn't go on, and with consummate grace, as though it were all planned, he turned the lecture over to Swami Budhananda, who took over beautifully, even without preparation. Then, Swami sat for a while on the platform, almost falling asleep. I finally realized there was nothing I could do. Swami Chidrupananda was in the front row, his eyes glued to Swami. I was in the back row. I closed my eyes and prayed. Then Mrs. Sanders, next to me, nudged me. Swami was leaving the platform. Swami Chidrupananda and I went out, and we drove him home. Many people were crying.

"Well," Swami said later, when he learned how it had been, "you must admit it was very dramatic!"

Me: Yes, it certainly was dramatic. But I hope there won't be another drama like it!

Swami: I feel so sorry to have caused such disturbance and to have made everyone feel bad.

Me: Please don't lecture when you feel so sick.

Swami: But how will I know?

Me: Maybe you would listen to Swami Chidrupananda next time.

April 20, 1965

The whole Society is in the doldrums. Swami is very ill.

May 3, 1965
Swami is much better, or seems so.

May 15, 1965
Swami phoned me at 8:00 this morning to tell me that we would go to Berkeley at 10:30. He went to see Swami Shantaswarupananda, who had said he was too ill to lecture as scheduled tomorrow morning in San Francisco. Many devotees were working in the beautiful well-cared-for garden. There was an atmosphere—tangible and decidedly different from that of the street outside. I waited for Swami in the garden. Finally he and Swami Shantaswarupananda came from the Temple. Swami S. did look ill and somewhat shattered. The thought crossed my mind that he had received a severe scolding. He looked like that.

On the way home, Swami told me in bits that he had scolded Swami Shantaswarupananda a couple of weeks ago and had suspected that he was still upset by it. So he had gone to Berkeley to say nice things to him. "I spoke very affectionately to him. . . . I think it made him feel a little better. . . ."

Same date, Old Temple
Swami was looking at a picture of a crowd of baby turkeys. I told him that baby turkeys were so nervous that they died of fright at loud noises. With what compassion and sorrow he said, "Ah hah-hah"—no less compassion than he had expressed yesterday when I told him how mothers screamed at their children in grocery stores.

July 14, 1965
On my way to the Old Temple from my apartment, I stopped in the small grocery store on the corner of Union and Webster Streets. On leaving, I was rude to the Italian woman who runs the store. She ran onto the street after me and yelled, "You are

supposed to belong to a religion! You should be in hell!" Although (and perhaps because) the whole thing was my fault, I was very much shaken by it.

Swami was afraid the woman would attack me when I passed by her store on my way home. He watched from the Temple steps as I walked up the slight grade to the corner. Later he said, "If I had seen any trouble, I would have run up there as fast and as far as I could!" And his legs are so weak it is hard for him to walk. But he would have tried to run to my aid.

July 20, 1965
Swami: To have to live in a body when that body is not well is a terrible thing; better not to live in a body at all.

September 3, 1965
Swami did not get to Lake Tahoe this summer; nor did he go to Olema. He had no vacation this year, when he needed one more than ever. Either other swamis were using the vacation spots, or when he could have gotten away, swamis were visiting him.

October 6, 1965
Swami Madhavananda, president of the Ramakrishna Order, died.

October 10, 1965
Swami (during a walk): God alone knows what will happen when I start to lecture in November. I don't see how any ideas will come. As my head feels now, there is little chance of it. Yet I have decided I must try, I will take a lesson from Swami Akhilananda. He never said no to anything that was asked of him. He did not always do well, but he never refused; he always made the attempt. Now, like that, I won't say no to what is asked of me.

October 18, 1965
Swami (during another walk): When one who has renounced enters the world again, he goes down and down; he cannot stop. Never again in this life will he be able to lift himself. It is as Shankara said [*Vivekachudamani*, verse 325].

October 23, 1965
I had a conversation with Edna Zulch, in which she said: "Once when I was brand-new in Vedanta [around 1940], I went to Tahoe and was staying at King's Beach [a small town on the lake a little north of Carnelian Bay]. While I was there a car drove up, and it was Ediben, driving Swami. He had her stop the car, and they both got out and came over to me. Swami asked, 'Where are you staying?' I said, 'I'm staying in a little place around here; I have a cottage.' He said to Ediben, 'Let's go and see it.' So they came over and looked at it, and Swami asked, 'Where do you eat? How do you have your meals?' My place was just a room with a bed in it, you see. So I said, 'Well, I go to a restaurant for meals,' and he said, 'You shouldn't have to do that. Now, get some cold cereal and milk and some fruit, and you can have your breakfast here in your room.' I said, 'Well, there aren't even any dishes here.' He didn't say anything, and they went home. In about an hour he came back. He had taken a basket (Ediben told me he had done it himself) and on a layer of napkins had packed it with his dishes and his silver—he even thought of a knife for cutting fruit. He thought of everything like that. Oh my, it broke my heart. He has broken my heart more than once like that. . . . The heart of him that comes out when you need it!

"Janet Blodgett [a young disciple who later left] didn't have any pretty clothes, you know. And when she went to college, why, he had her go downtown with Jo and buy a coat (as his gift) at Magnin's. When they got back to the Temple, he had her put it on and model it for him. He had us all come in and look at the coat, and asked if we didn't think it was nice and all that. That's the kind of thing he does."

October 24, 1965
I recited my miseries over the phone to Swami, thinking he would console me. He said, "Oh, BUNK!"

October 29, 1965
Swami (standing on a street corner in the evening): When one feels the presence of God behind everything, one takes a very different view; one cannot care too much what happens or what doesn't happen. When I used to lecture in the Old Temple, I would perceive that each person was God Himself—not just that God was dwelling in each person but that each was God. I felt that I was talking directly to the Soul. There were times when the lecture came out, as it were, from the very center of my being, and my whole being participated in it. As a matter of fact, many lectures I have given in that spirit.
Me: Don't you still feel that? It seems so when you lecture.
Swami: You have to be high up, and you have to be deep. You have to speak from here *(pointing to his chest)*, and you have to look everything in the depths.
Me: Do you always see God behind everything?
Swami: No. Not now. My brain has become fossilized. Before I became sick, yes, always. I always felt and saw that. . . .
Me: It must be a comedown to have seen Brahman always and not now.
Swami (laughing): Marie Louise, I am a sick man. Everything is a comedown. Still, there is a barrier, a separation, between the sick body and myself. I still feel separate from pain, sickness, and all that. Sickness doesn't cross that barrier; it doesn't touch me really.

November 3, 1965
Swami Prabhavananda came from Carmel to see Swami; with
him came Swami Krishnananda, his attendant. All went well.
Swami was very, very tired after they left.

Swami Budhananda left in mid-November of 1965. Except that he had
admittedly tried to change the current of the Society's teaching from a
monistic torrent to a more gentle dualistic meandering, he had served
the Society conscientiously, holding the class and lecturing whenever
necessary, thereby lifting much pressure from the other swamis. He
went back to Hollywood for a time and was followed by a small group
of women devotees, who visited the center in southern California for a
week or two. Among them were members of the group that was later
to cause a good deal of trouble.

Swami's health did not improve in 1966. Nevertheless, he regularly
gave the Sunday morning lectures. On Wednesday evenings, one or
another of the assistant swamis generally lectured, but now and then
throughout 1966 and the first five months of 1967, Swami Ashokananda gave one of his series of lectures on Sri Ramakrishna and his
disciples. Often on Sunday mornings and Wednesday evenings, he
could barely make it to the car that was waiting at the door of the Old
Temple to carry him up the hill.

He felt that if he could not lecture, the only alternative would be to
resign from his post. But then who would carry on the work? This
problem worried him for many months. Sometimes he discussed it
with me over the phone. In my journal there is a transcript of such a
discussion, brought on by my asking him what made him seem so sad.
My attempts to console him irritated him very much. At one point I
reminded him of what Swami Madhavananda had said—that there was
no one who could take his place. Swami replied, "You are a stupid

baby! An exceedingly stupid baby!" He went on to say that at Belur Math the trustees would not consider it important whether his place could be filled or not.

As things turned out, the problem was not pressing, for he was regularly able to give the Sunday lectures after Swami Budhananda had left. As for the Friday evening class, Swami Shraddhananda had held it since May of 1957, taking over the *Mundaka Upanishad* in midstream from Swami Ashokananda. However, during his stay in San Francisco, Swami Budhananda conducted the class, carrying a pile of books to the lectern, and one knew he had labored hard to prepare his "sermon," as Nancy called it. (Years later, Swami Budhananda once remarked that everyone in San Francisco had appreciated his preparation of *jilipis*—a Bengali sweet that looks like a pretzel and is supersaturated with sugar—but thought nothing of his lectures and classes, over which he had labored so hard. But this was not true: there had been many devotees who much appreciated his lectures—and his *jilipis*, as well.)

Indeed, it was primarily for the benefit (or rehabilitation) of those who had been swayed by Swami Budhananda that when Swami Ashokananda began to hold the class in January of 1966 he started with the *Avadhuta Gita* of Dattatreya, one of the most extreme monistic texts of Vedanta philosophy. It was a way of righting the boat that had drifted into the warm, sun-dappled waters of dualism and had listed over. He said at the end of his introductory class,

It was not for nothing that Swami Vivekananda came to a country of the West where tradition was new, where the spirit was free, where all accumulated heritages had been transplanted in a new soil and thereby vitiated, where new life had been built up without the hindrances and obstructions of old traditions. He came to America and he put the seed, the fiery seed of his teaching, into the hearts of the American people. You will find those things will spring forth. Yes, you will see it, but you can also ac-

celerate it. You are the forerunners of this wonderful age. Therefore on you is a great responsibility.

Now, in order to become established in the consciousness of
Spirit a good philosophy is very helpful, and that is where the
study of monism comes in. It puts in terms of reason—not in
terms of emotion, but in terms of reason—the basic truth about
our Self and about the nature of the universe. That is where the
benefit comes.

Swami held the class regularly through 1966 and for the first half of
1967. On Swami Shivananda's birthday, which fell on January 6, 1967,
he spoke of his memories of the great swami at the close of the class.
During the course of this informal talk, he disclosed the circumstances
of his initiation by Swami Vivekananda, his doubts that the experience
had indeed constituted initiation, and the assurances on this point
given to him by four of the direct disciples of Sri Ramakrishna. This
was the first time that most of his disciples came to know anything
about their guru's spiritual lineage—and their own. Like many others,
Bob Utter, who, the reader may remember, was a college student in
1939 and had helped the Vedanta Society contend against the Berkeley
City Council, was galvanized. He proclaimed that in his heart he had
always known that Swami Ashokananda carried within himself the fire
and power of Swami Vivekananda. It was nothing new.

Swami, however, was not satisfied with his talk. He wanted to expand it and make it into a booklet for publication, an idea that was
strongly opposed by Ediben, who felt it would be in extremely "bad
taste" to announce so publicly the very personal facts of his initiation.
Swami paid no attention. He wanted those facts now to be known. But
it was not until June of 1967 that he started to work on his *Memories of
Swami Shivananda*.

The exertion of having, in poor health, given lectures and held
classes steadily for a year and a half took its relentless toll. On June 2 of
1967, after having held fifty-three discourses on the *Avadhuta Gita*, he

gave his last class. He had reached Chapter 3, verse 42 (the text has eight chapters). On the following Sunday he gave what turned out to be his last lecture, entitled "When the Many Become One." As I remember it, that lecture was relatively short and almost a poem in its beauty. After that, he began to work on *Swami Shivananda* in his upstairs room. I was fortunate enough to become his amanuensis.

18

THE POWER OF LIGHT

I had never before set foot above the ground floor of the Old Temple, but now in July and August of 1967, when Swami was too ill to
come downstairs and yet wanted to work, he asked me to come to his
room to take dictation for his memoirs on Swami Shivananda.

His room was fairly large, extending the full width of the narrow
temple, not counting the balcony on the north side. There were a number of full bookcases and a large desk piled with books and papers.
Now and then, when he expected a visit from a doctor, he would make
the piles tidy. There was a dresser with many holy pictures on it. His
bed, which had low wicker head- and footboards, had a low coffee
table beside it, covered with books. By his desk was the high-backed
brown leather swivel chair that he had used in his office downstairs.
When it rained, there would be pans set at strategic points around the
room to catch the persistent drops of water that had been coming
through the roof since Swami Trigunatita's time.

Another feature of the third floor that probably originated with
Swami Trigunatita was the windows set in the top quarter of the doors.
These were covered with translucent pictorial paper, resembling
stained glass. On Swami's door there was a scene of a swan floating on
a river or a lake. The other doors had scenes of landscapes, and around
them all were borders of geometric designs. The walls of Swami's

room were painted white; there were white venetian blinds at the windows and a rose-colored carpet, worn threadbare in several places. Many calendars with holy pictures, which had no doubt been sent from India, adorned the walls.

In the privacy of his own quarters, Swami dressed in much the same multilayered way that he did at Lake Tahoe when he was not well—a jersey pajama suit of chocolate brown trousers, and over these sage green socks pulled up to the knee so that the pajama legs bloused over a little, like knee breeches. The top was a yellow pullover with long sleeves. Over the pajamas was a flannel shorter-than-knee-length robe, white with pink and blue candy stripes; over this, another flannel robe of pale buff, slightly shorter; and over this, a turquoise green nylon ski vest, thickly padded with down and zippered up the front, making him look very round. On his feet he wore old, beat-up leather mules.

During the days when I was in his room, Swami spoke to me of wondrous things, which I recorded in my journal. One day he told me of his experience of Holy Mother—that she was actually the Divine Mother. My journal entries for 1967 and 1968 are given below.

July 22, 1967
Me: It is hard to get such things into one's head; I mean for me.
Swami: Yes, it is hard. But all these things will enter into your head, too.
Me: I feel that I am so remiss.
Swami: If you are to get only what you deserve, you will get little. We never get only what we deserve. They give us a *great deal* more in order to fulfill us. Whether we deserve it or not, whether we have acted properly or not, or done enough, *they* do their part. Don't worry.

I felt deeply stirred by this. Swami went on to speak of the effect the words of the great swamis had had on his life—words that had seemed almost casual at the time.

On one of the days when I was in Swami's room, Fred Zulch, who had been in the monastery and had later, with Swami's full assent, become a dentist, came to take care of his teeth. Some of the monks were in the room. Swami said, "You know, Fred, these boys have become used to me. They are no longer afraid of me. Now, can you make me some big tusks?" He put his hands on either side of his mouth and curved out his forefingers like fierce protruding tusks. "Like this?" The young men dissolved in laughter.

The work on his memoirs about Swami Shivananda is going very slowly. Sometimes he sits for an hour or more without saying anything; sometimes he tells me about his early life, and sometimes he says, "Ho Ho Ho Ha Ha Ha," almost as though singing and with no expression at all of distress. At first I thought he was playing, and then I realized it was a cry of pain. "Is it pain?" I asked. "Yes," he said. "Here, here, here—all over there is pain. No part of my body is comfortable. Ho Ha"—slowly going into a sort of song, utterly detached, and his voice so sweet.

He said, "You cannot apply monism to the body; it applies only to the Self. To some extent, it is true, monism helps the body; one can transcend pain and so on, but the body has its limits."

Once, sitting on the edge of his bed, he roared like a lion to summon up the strength to stand up.

Me: Swami, why get up?

Swami: I mustn't succumb.

And he insisted on going down to the second floor to strengthen his legs. I went ahead of him. He saluted Sri Ramakrishna from the door of the shrine and then walked down the hall greeting the monks. The next day, he again went down. This time his legs were weaker. The following day he went down again. I was not there. But I learned that he nearly fell once or twice. It is too soon for these trial excursions.

Generally, Swami sat in his leather chair, and I, with my notebook and tape recorder, sat on the floor beside him. He dictated a little of his memoirs almost every day, and on August 6 the manuscript was finished. It was typed by one of the women in the convent, and three days later a copy was mailed to Belur Math with his request that the swamis there check it for any errors in fact. The atmosphere in his room was both powerful and peaceful. One morning when I was waiting for him to have his breakfast, I closed my eyes to meditate a little. My journal reads,

August 3, 1967
At once my mind went deep—or something came from all the room and entered me. What an atmosphere in that room! I had not realized it until I closed my eyes. Later, I said to Swami, "There is a powerful atmosphere in here."
Swami: Open the window a little, and it will go.
Me: Not that kind of atmosphere!
Swami (insisting that I open the window): I want to prove something to you.

I opened the window.
Swami (a little later): Has the power gone?
Me: No.
Swami: What kind of power?
Me (struggling for words): Light power. The power of light.

August 11, 1967
I went to see Swami for a few minutes to get the manuscript of

his article for Martha [a relatively new disciple] to read. He was sitting in his chair. I saw him before he saw me. He looked so ill, and yet I have never seen him look more beautiful. How to describe it? Somehow he was so full of majesty and greatness. He was not wearing his glasses and one could see the wonderful sweep of his brow and eyes, subtle and noble contours that his glasses generally hide. Or was it illness and suffering that made him seem so extraordinarily beautiful? I don't know. Physically, he is so weak; in appearance, so great, no weakness. He said of the manuscript that has been sent to India, "They will throw it back in my face. Everyone will know they have thrown it back in Swami Ashokananda's face." I began to cry. He thought I had not yet sent the manuscript, or something like that. He said, "My mind is so confused." I cried further. "I shouldn't make you sorrowful," he said. He asked me to read aloud to him the last paragraph of the article.

The gossip is that working on the manuscript has exhausted him—and yet, it was not much work. But even that little was too, too much—talking, trying to concentrate, almost every day, sometimes all day.

August 12, 1967
Over the phone I said to Swami how beautiful he had looked yesterday.
Swami (sternly and with energy): I shall cut off your tongue!

August 17, 1967
Swami is so concerned over whether or not they will like his manuscript in India. He wants to know each day what I have heard. And it is too soon to hear anything at all.

August 21, 1967
Swami has become very sick with a kidney infection and is

bedridden. I saw him this evening. His mind was confused from sedation. I could not control my tears that rained down to no purpose. If he were well he would say, "I shall prick your eyes!" But if he were well, I wouldn't be crying.

No word yet from India. Swami Shraddhananda is taking devoted care of Swami, and Swami Chidrupananda is with him always.

August 23, 1967
Swami is going to the hospital today for tests. He was not conscious.

August 24, 1967
A letter came from Swami Apurvananda, dated August 16. Swami's manuscript and letter were received. Swami Apurvananda (who had been Swami Shivananda's attendant) liked the article. He wrote of what great love Swami Shivananda had had for Swami.

August 25, 1967
When Swami Chidrupananda signed Swami in at St. Mary's Hospital, the receptionist (a Catholic nun) was filling out the forms. When she came to filling in the space after "Employer," she looked up at Swami Chidrupananda and with a very sweet smile said, "In this case, shall we say 'God'?"

August 26, 1967
The idea that Swami Chidrupananda will read "The Guru and Disciple" at the opening of the season (September 17) has been discarded. Now the idea is that a lecture of Swami's on Sri Krishna will have to be edited for Swami Chidrupananda to read, as Swami Shantaswarupananda will not be well enough by then to open the season in San Francisco. I have begun work today on "Two Lives of Sri Krishna."

All work on the proposed book of articles about Swami Vivekananda has been dropped. But I wasn't doing well with that anyway.

I don't know how Swami is. The reports don't seem very bright or definite.

September 5, 1967
I saw Swami at the hospital. I came as he was walking down the hall with Swami Chidrupananda and the nurse. He looked so stooped and frail with his green ski vest and knitted blue pajamas. It tore the heart.

September 10, 1967
Swami seemed really much better. The report is that he can walk farther now, and without help. He is very rational, except that he thinks he is in Olema in a hospital, this wing of which has been built by Nancy and her father. It seems to me that it is perfectly all right for Swami to think this; it makes the whole business of being in a hospital more bearable for him. The illusion will clear up all in good time. I talked to him and he to me, as always. But then as I left and said how much better he looked and seemed, he said that soon he would be coming back to San Francisco. Perhaps soon he can come home to the Old Temple. But the longer this complete rest, the better.

꠰

The remainder of 1967 is missing from my journal. But I know that sometime during those three months or so, Swami came back from the hospital to the Old Temple. Despite his objections, a chair lift was fitted to the stairs from the first to the second (monastery) floor, and he consented to rise and descend upon it.

On December 5, he had a cerebral stroke that affected his left side, but not his speech. A hospital bed was moved into the downstairs back room. He could see the devotees now without climbing (or riding) up and down the stairs. He had male nurses around the clock and therapists two or three times a week. He often practiced walking with a walker in the hall—valiantly forcing himself to make his paralyzed left leg move along. Sometimes he sat in a wheelchair in the front room and received visitors.

At night, when all the usual devotees gathered around him, he would give what he called "trial lectures," practicing for when he would lecture again. We all knew he would never lecture again—but he never abandoned the idea.

Despite his disability, he continually thought about others and the work. My journal entries for January 1968 follow.

January 2, 1968, Old Temple
Swami: I am so sorry I didn't go to see your brother-in-law and sister. Now I am a cripple and can't go.

The emphasis was entirely on his being sorry that he hadn't gone earlier to see Leila and Holloway. The "cripple" part was just a statement like "Now it's raining."

_◊_

Leila had had a massive stroke at the beginning of 1966 when she and Holloway were in Mexico to celebrate the New Year. Swami carefully and persistently guided me through my anguish and grief over this.

January 6, 1968
I went this afternoon to the Old Temple. Swami was sitting in his wheelchair in the front room.

His affliction is sometimes entirely bearable to witness because it seems to have no effect upon him. He is so visibly separate from his body. At other times, when one realizes that he cannot move around at all, it seems unbearable.

He says, "Finish your book! Finish your book! Finish your book! Then I will be able to have some peace."

Underneath it all, he is so serene. One derives joy from him, comfort from him. Much correspondence is going on between here and Belur Math about their sending another assistant. Nothing is done.

January 17, 1968
Fred Zulch came to pull one of Swami's teeth. His (Swami's) blood pressure was very high tonight, the nurse said.

Same date
Swami says I must write an article on the history of Kashmir now, making it short. Alas! I was just getting my mind deep into the second *New Discoveries* book. Alas, Alas, Alas! I am terribly sorry about it! I had been thinking how very much more there was to do on the book, yet somehow seeing my way to doing it—what with Swami saying I must finish. Then the other day he said I must at once finish two articles—one on Sri Ramakrishna and one on Kashmir and Swamiji, both of them long and hard. It was as though I had been carrying my full capacity and on top of it had been dumped two truckloads of crushed rock. I felt flattened. Result: I cannot move at all. Decision: Stop book.— Oh, Alas!—Take up articles, new mental setup, new research, new everything. Alas, Alas, Alas! Now is the time, I imagine, to practice karma yoga.

19

THE ROGUES

And now another problem—or an intolerable situation—arose that would cause Swami more anxiety than anything else he had faced during his many years in America. His health had never been worse than now: diabetes, diverticulitis, dangerously high blood pressure, and chronic and painful ulcers had long plagued him, and added to these were a kidney infection, intractable hiccups, and paralysis of the left side of his body, caused by a cerebral stroke in December of 1967. I think the best way to tell of the blow that was now dealt him is to give the painful tale in Swami's own words, partly as he wrote them in letters to Bharat Maharaj and partly as he spoke them in his address at the Society's annual meeting in March of 1968.

Bharat Maharaj (Swami Abhayananda) had been a close friend of Swami's from his (Swami's) days at Mayavati. In 1968, Bharat Maharaj was (and had been for many years) the manager of Belur Math. He was also one of the trustees of the Ramakrishna Math and Mission, but otherwise he had no official position in the Order. He did not want and did not need one. He was a *kingmaker* and also a policy maker, though he very likely would have denied both these roles. He was looked upon, even by the president, as *the* senior monk and was revered both in the Order and outside it for his spirituality, his unfailing wisdom, and his indomitable strength of character.

Swami Abhayananda (Bharat Maharaj), 1974

Swami Ashokananda wrote of the difficulty that had beset him to Bharat Maharaj precisely because the latter had no official position, and also because he knew Bharat Maharaj would let the problem be known to the authorities at the right time, in the right place, and in the right way. We have only some preliminary notes of Swami's first letter to the older (by a few years) swami, in which he summarized the points he wanted to make. His full letter, which was written sometime in early January of 1968, is not available. Before this, he had written to Swami Gambhirananda, then the general secretary, telling him something of the problem. This letter, also, is unavailable.

Swami's second letter to Bharat Maharaj, dated March 9, 1968, read in part,

Dear and Revered Bharat Maharaj,

I received your kind letter in due time, but I was at that time and for some time later rather tired and have not been able to reply to it. One cause of this tiredness is a sort of rebellion amongst a small number of members of our Society. I may have written to you or Prabhu Maharaj [Swami Vireswarananda, president of the Order] or both, about checking on the Constitution and Bylaws of our Society here. It has been a long process. It started—I don't remember exactly—probably toward the end of 1966. The last changes in the Constitution and Bylaws were made at my instance in 1939 when the Berkeley Temple was established and therefore some changes had to be made in the San Francisco Constitution and Bylaws. I then used to go to the attorney. . . .

I wanted to study these things again, for the changes in 1939 were done in a hurry and I had to attend to so many other things at the same time that I always suspected that some errors might have remained in the Constitution and Bylaws. Now that I am getting old and sick, I wanted to leave everything in a good order; hence this desire for revision. It so happened that the attorney became very seriously ill in the beginning of this year; so Al had to see the assistant of this attorney and also two other prominent lawyers of the city. Of course it goes without saying that I could not see the lawyers myself, being bedridden, but Al reported everything of his conversations with the attorneys, and I would then think about those things and give my own reaction to Al. Eventually we together—that is to say, the attorneys, myself and Al—came to some final conclusion. The attorneys all affirmed that there were many legal mistakes in the Constitution and the Bylaws which required to be corrected. We lost no time in deciding which corrections had to be made. First, of course, the Constitution had to be corrected. Two items had to be corrected at once. Accordingly, the Board of Directors here was asked to hold a meeting and discuss it among themselves and give their verdict. They met in February, 1968, and composed a paper which they all signed and in which they recorded their own conclusions. I saw this, and I approved of this and signed it, as is required by the rules of the Society. The next step was to have the members of the Society sign this.

It is at that point that a handful of probably six or seven members became rebellious, and they spread all kinds of accusations against me and the President and Secretary of the Society. They went so far as to say that because of the stroke I had, I had lost my sanity and ability to think; therefore my words were to be spurned. They were so ill-behaved and defiant that the only thing I could do was to apply one of the Bylaws that has been in the Society's rules since Swami Trigunatita's time, which I [had] softened a little in 1934.

So those people are now out of the Society, and I will not be surprised if they write complaining to Belur Math, hoping that Belur Math will act to control and change our action. I hope Belur will not make this terrible mistake of interfering in the internal affairs of the Society for the sake of six or seven rebels who were good-for-nothing members. Two of them you know—that is, Sally and her husband. Whatever Sally may have been in the distant past, she has not been the same person during the last several years, and I know her husband to be a good-for-nothing man although we know that he comes from a good family in New York. He is unfit and so is Sally to be a member of the Society. Although having received initiation from the President of our Math, he is taking advantage of it, spreading himself out as a very important person. He told in the Temple one day after a meeting that I was trying to separate the Society from the Belur Math. After that, there was only one thing left for me to do: to declare him as outside the membership of the Society.

You may think that I have not done anything for the Belur Math. Probably many of our brothers think so. However, I have been very faithful to Sri Ramakrishna, Holy Mother and Swamiji and the ideals for which our Math exists, and I have done my best to serve their cause as earnestly as I have done; and thus I have reached the end of my life, and I am not being boastful when I say I do not feel I have many things to regret in my service to the Lord.

Thank you for your present letter, and I appreciate it deeply, especially what you have written about Mrs. Soulé and Al. They have been great devotees of Sri Ramakrishna and Swamiji, and they have served their cause with great earnestness and incomparable selflessness. No foreign work is possible, either in America or elsewhere, unless we have some local earnest devotees. I have always felt that Sri Ramakrishna has brought some devotees to the center in order that they may serve [his] cause here. Ediben and Al have been two of them. I am very happy to say there are many others like them here who are my strength and support. . . .

I don't know how long I shall be able to carry on work here. From my present condition of health, I don't think there is much prospect of my doing further work here, but I have not decided anything yet. Surely you will know when I shall decide what I shall do in the future. This is not an official information; therefore I shall be glad if you do not talk about it officially to anyone.

Will you please tell Gambhirananda that I have received his letter and later a cable from him. He said in the cable that he was writing a letter but I have not received any more letters from him and therefore could not write to him anything, but I hope to write to him when I hear from him again.

I hope your health is good, that everything is going on well at the Math. I cannot say that I am out of danger, but everything is being done for my comfort and cure. Apart from the personal services of some devotees, I have three employed male nurses every day, and also there come two women nurses on alternate days. They are called therapists, who give me exercises to heal my paralyzed left leg and left arm. This is called physiotherapy. I shall have to wait several months more before I come to a conclusion whether I shall be healed or not. In the meantime, I spend all day and night in a bed, sometimes rising up and sitting in a wheelchair. That is my life, but although I don't lecture or hold class or give interviews to the students, I attend to all the problems of the Society, financial and otherwise, and see that the works of the Society are carried on properly. Al has worked very hard in every respect, and I get somewhat concerned about his health, because he has become so weak. But some important work is being done now at the Retreat at Olema. . . .

Please accept my love and respectful greetings. I wonder if I shall ever see you again in this life.

Ever yours in Swamiji,
Ashokananda

P.S. It has not been easy for me to pass through this period of turmoil of some of the members here. For several days I could not sleep, and my mind would not quiet down, and the brain seemed to be in a state of whirl. For a time I was afraid I might have another stroke. The brain has not quieted down yet fully, but I think the immediate danger of a stroke is not there anymore. I am saying this to indicate that things here are not easy. I hope you at Belur do not add to this agony by wrong thinking and wrong action. We are fully able to take care of it. We are doing what has to be done. I think very soon the turmoil will be over.

IN ORDER TO BE clear about the ostensible cause of the turmoil we have to go back to the inauguration of the Berkeley center in 1939. At that time it had been necessary to change the bylaws of the San Francisco Society so that they would accommodate a branch center. The reader may remember that Swami Ashokananda was then extremely busy supervising the construction of the Berkeley Temple, along with attending to all his other duties. Thus, the new bylaws had been some-what hastily drawn up—a matter that had preyed on his mind for many years and that came to a head in 1965 or 1966 when a donor questioned the tax-exempt status of her donation. Swami asked the attorney who had drawn up the bylaws in 1939 and had given his assurance that they were legal whether they still were in accord with the laws of California. The lawyer, Morse Erskine, restudied the bylaws and said no, they were not quite correct. Swami Ashokananda was ill at that time and sent Swami Chidrupananda to consult with Mr. Erskine.

For the remainder of 1966 and the whole of 1967 the wording of the bylaws was discussed and rediscussed until at length a satisfactory so-lution was reached—a solution that gave the American board of direc-tors authority over the regulation of the Society's temporal affairs and, at the same time, retained Belur Math's spiritual association with and ultimate spiritual leadership of the Society.

On a Sunday morning in February of 1968 in the foyer of the New Temple, after a lecture by Swami Shantaswarupananda, Edith Soulé, the secretary, sat at a desk, wearing one of her large ocean-going hats, and asked each member as he or she emerged from the auditorium to sign a document that stated his or her approval of the revised by-laws. Almost all the members signed without hesitation, knowing that, although Swami Ashokananda was not present, whatever he asked of them was for the Society's good. But not everyone took this on faith.

A small group of disciples had for long silently borne a grudge against their guru and what they looked upon as an exclusive and con-niving "inner circle," said to be headed by the president and the secre-tary of the Society—Swami Chidrupananda (Al Clifton) and Edith Soulé. Actually, there was no such thing as an inner circle either in Swami Ashokananda's mind or in the minds of those who worked in the Temple or who habitually attended the evening meetings (among the last of whom were neither Swami Chidrupananda nor Ediben).

The very idea of an inner circle was abhorrent to Swami Ashokananda, and he had made it resoundingly clear again and again that those who might seem especially close to him were not in the least so. "Never think," he once said to the evening group, "that you people are particularly close to me. I have students in San Francisco and all over America who are as close, if not closer, than any of you!" Nor, as has been said earlier, was anyone excluded from those evening meetings, except by their own volition. Still, a few devotees harbored a grudge and a need for retaliation. With paranoid suspicion, they refused to sign the paper that Swami Ashokananda, through Ediben, asked them to sign. (This made no real difference legally, as it was enough that the board of directors had ratified the changes in the bylaws.)

The dissidents, as they came to be called, did not stop with mere negative action, nor did they request Swami Ashokananda to clarify the changes. Instead they composed and distributed a letter, which said in effect that Swami Ashokananda had lost his mind and was being influenced by Mrs. Soulé and Al Clifton, who were scheming together to take over the Society, divorcing it entirely from Belur Math. Copies of this incredible letter were sent to many members of the Society and to the general secretary (then Swami Gambhirananda) at Belur Math.

Like Swami Trigunatita before him, Swami Ashokananda could not condone dissension in the Society or defamation by the members of the Society of their spiritual leader. He expelled the lot of them—one man (John Hoffman, Sally's husband) and six or seven women. But lying in his hospital bed in the back office, half paralyzed, he would say with affection, "If those rogues would phone me, if they would ask for an explanation, and if they would apologize to Ediben and Mr. Clifton, I would reinstate them." Only one of them phoned. "I forgive you," Swami told her. "But I doubt very much that the others will." They did not—nor did any of the dissidents ever ask them to.

One of the tales these "rogues" spread in San Francisco was that the trustees in India were not going to send another swami to America as assistant to Swami Ashokananda. Swami Swahananda, who had actually been chosen by the trustees in India to come to San Francisco, had indeed been dragging his heels, thus giving credence to the report that no swami was ever going to come. For this reason, his procrastination was a matter of great concern to Swami Ashokananda. He wrote again to Bharat Maharaj on March 19, 1968:

Dear and Revered Bharat Maharaj,

I received your kind letter of February 9 in due time. Many things have happened since then; hence this delay in replying to it.

I should tell you that my health is still pretty bad, and I have not reached any noticeable state of cure. I spend my days in patiently lying in bed and hoping for signs of healing to appear in my sick body. As you know, my left arm and left leg are affected by the paralysis. The doctor and nurses say it will be some time—two or three months yet—before the signs of cure will begin to show, though I am able to move the arm and leg a little. I am patient, as a patient should be, but have no peace as a patient should have.

I received a cable and a letter from Swami Gambhirananda announcing that Swami Swahananda has been selected for San Francisco, but Swami Swahananda himself, it seems, is full of doubt and hesitations. That frightens me. Anyone coming here—that is to say, to a foreign field of work—with hesitation will make his work difficult for himself. . . .

Gambhirananda wrote to me that if I urge Swahananda he might come here before the end of June. I however proposed that he might come toward the end of June—that is to say, the beginning of the fourth week of June, and I wrote him a long letter giving him directions about what he should prepare in the way of clothes. . . .

Can you make Swahananda come to Belur and start for San Francisco early enough? I have sent fifteen hundred dollars to the Advaita Ashrama Manager. . . . Swahananda could draw from this fund to do his shopping. . . . I shall send through the American Express Company money for his passage on Pan American Airways, which he can take in Calcutta and arrive in San Francisco without, I think, any change on the way. . . . He has written to Chidrupananda that he wants to go to Kedar Badri [in the Himalayas] on pilgrimage before leaving for San Francisco. Also I think he wants to stop at Singapore and other places to visit on the way. It seems to be a rather ambitious program he has. . . . Kindly impress on his mind that he should curtail all these programs. It is very important that he come here before the end of June. . . . The mischievous people who have been dismissed from the Society are spreading all kinds of stories amongst the members, namely that no swami is coming here, that Belur Math is separated from the Vedanta Society, and . . . is not willing to send any swami here. Of course, the more these stories spread the more the members of the Society become affected, and already the congregation . . . has been affected. Their number is dwindling. This ill effect is due to my long illness of course, and so the coming of another swami will halt this dwindling tendency.

MEANWHILE, SWAMI ASHOKANANDA found relief in his evenings with the devotees who were gathering again in the back office of the Old Temple. The room, of course, was no longer "the back office." Swami's hospital bed occupied the east wall where the secretary's desk had once been, and the small typewriter tables were gone. Six or seven straight-backed chairs still lined the walls, but Swami's armchair was no longer in the corner. A male nurse sat in the front room waiting to be called, diverting himself with Chinese puzzles that a devotee had provided for his amusement. But there was never a sense of sickness in these downstairs rooms, never a sense that they had become a small hospital or a nursing home. They were still filled with the presence of

holiness; they were still temple rooms where one's mind felt effort-
lessly quieted and uplifted, even though the talk was as different from
what it used to be as was the furniture.

For weeks, Swami wove a tale every evening about how he was
going to take the author to India. My journal entry for January 19,
1968, reads,

> Again Swami went through a whole play, acting out his part
> and others' parts of how I will be given a reception at the Insti-
> tute of Culture in Calcutta. There will be a banquet; Swami will
> introduce me, which introduction he gives at length; then I will
> give a long speech; then everyone goes off, leaving me to find my
> way to a hotel alone. "That's the way Hindus are," he says.

With variations Swami wove the dream night after night, until even
he, I think, became bored with it. Another nightly diversion and one
that required more effort on Swami's part was his "practice lectures."
Every evening he would speak into a microphone for almost one hour,
as though giving a lecture before a congregation. Sometimes they were
good lectures; sometimes (more often, in fact) they were rambling and
without fire. Luke (Mary Lou Williams) and I recorded them all, and
have since destroyed the tapes. He did this "to make his brain work,"
he said, and to keep in practice—to which Swami Chidrupananda,
who once happened to be there, remarked censoriously, "That is just
what the doctor doesn't want him to do until he recovers from this
relapse." But Swami paid no attention.

We also had music. LPs were then the state of the art, and we had
quite a large collection of classical Indian and Western music. Swami
had noticed the hunger with which some of us listened to the Western
selections, as though starved for them, and, though they were of very
little interest to him, he had them played over and over.

One afternoon, a devotee brought to him a small television set so he
could watch the first landing on the moon. Breathlessly, we watched
the indistinct picture over his shoulder, and in the midst of it he said,

"Oh, enough of that! Turn it off!" At his bidding, the screen went black, and for all we knew, those bouncing astronauts could have dropped dead up there, or moon-people could have appeared and swallowed them. We had a lesson in detachment.

In the daytime Swami sometimes sat in the front room in his wheelchair. He wore a deep maroon Chinese jacket and talked with visitors, giving them, as always, his full attention. Sometimes when there were no visitors he would look out the window and watch the activity of the neighborhood. He once commented upon some young playboy-type men getting into their sports car in front of the Old Temple. "Something awful will happen to the young people of this country," he said; "it is bound to be. There is a saying in India that Mother Earth cannot stand the weight of such people."

Of three or four longhaired, amazingly dressed hippies who were passing by, he said approvingly, "They are breaking their bonds." (But in the Temple, neckties were *de rigueur*.) Another time, while watching two Italian women talking animatedly with one another, he said with feeling, "What a tragedy that they don't know they are the same person!"

Thus the days passed. Swami's left arm and leg got noticeably better, and he decided one day in January of 1969 to go to the New Temple and there give a real "practice lecture." My journal entry for January 22 reads,

> At the New Temple Swami climbed up the vestry stairs and chanted in a clear, strong voice at the lectern. My face was completely drenched in tears. The convent women and other devotees had gathered in the auditorium; some were also crying. He was so valiant, so (as Ediben would say) "game!" This was the second time he made that magnificent effort to walk and to climb that long flight of steep stairs.

He did it, in all, four times. The last time, he directed me to drive home by way of Steiner Street, one block west of Fillmore Street. On the corner of Steiner and Vallejo Streets stood a four-story apartment building. It extended almost one-half of the block down Steiner and was painted pink. As we passed it, Swami said, "We must buy that place." I was horrified, for it seemed an immense and not particularly attractive building. "We must have it for the convent," he said. That was the last time Swami went out, and the acquisition of the nine-unit "pink house" was the fulfillment of his last dream for the Society.

At first, Swami wanted to house both the monastery and the convent within the walls of the pink house, trying to arrange things so that the men and women would never collide with one another. But no amount of juggling with the floor plans could make this possible, and in the end the building housed the convent in three large apartments. Five other apartments accommodated five women devotees. A sixth devotee—Kathleen Davis (one of Swami's first students and among those who had hovered on the outskirts of the first trial convent)—was given a bedroom, a bathroom, and a kitchen within the convent itself, with the idea that the convent would eventually assimilate her. But the assimilation process did not take place, and much later Kathleen, now fully satisfied that her long-held desire to become a nun had from the start been misbegotten, was allotted an apartment to herself.

Swami reserved the fourth floor of the "pink house" for his own quarters. It was more of a penthouse than a full floor, but the rooms were large and could serve as bedrooms for him and for a nurse, as well as a general meeting room and library.

PRODDED BY THE "ROGUES," the authorities at Belur Math agitated themselves over the bylaws of the Vedanta Society of Northern California, and some of the trustees, including the president, wrote to Swami Ashokananda questioning his judgment. Swami Gambhirananda cabled Swami that the trustees were waiting to receive a draft of the bylaws, in order to pass on them. Swami was incensed.

"I never knew that the Trustees wanted to pass on the By-laws of the Society here," he wrote to Bharat Maharaj on April 18, 1969;

I think I made it quite clear in my past letters that the Board of Directors here is an independent body. The Directors are not supposed to be under anybody else. That is what the law here is. I would not ask the Board of Directors to submit the By-laws or anything to the Trustees of Belur Math. That would create unimaginable trouble. The Directors will first of all refuse to do that, and if any of the members of the Society learn about it, they will then accuse the Directors of acting illegally. I have sent to Belur Math the substance of the changes in the By-laws on three different occasions . . . I do not know what more you want. The Board of Directors adopted these changes on April 14. Now these By-laws will be presented to the members of the Society on Tuesday the twenty-third of April in a special general meeting. It is not necessary to have the approval of the members if the Board of Directors passes the By-laws, but since there has been a lot of discussion about these changes, I hope to be present at the meeting to explain whatever I can about the meaning and the necessity of the changes and to answer any questions that any members will want to ask. I don't know how peaceful the meeting will be. I am hoping and praying that there may be no trouble as there was during the annual general meeting, about which I no doubt wrote to you.

The annual general meeting had taken place the year before in the Old Temple on March 21, 1968, and was an event that no one who attended would soon forget. One of the "rogues" had had the job of helping to clean the auditorium; she was, in fact, the leader of the cleaning crew and had, therefore, a key to the street door. "They will try to disrupt the meeting," Swami said to an incredulous Jo. "Have the lock changed." And sure enough, on the evening of March 21, 1968, before the meeting opened, the "rogues" attempted to enter the auditorium with their key, which, of course, no longer worked.

Their only recourse was to attempt to enter the auditorium after the door had been opened to the members. Swami had also anticipated this and had asked a sturdy and devoted member of the Society to stand before the door like a *darwan*, a guardian of the Temple, admitting only members "in good standing." One of the "rogues" flew at him, pummeling him with her small fists and shouting, "Police brutality!" The *darwan* stood solidly, like a rock. The next thing the "rogues" did was to picket the Temple, marching up and down the sidewalk outside the auditorium, shouting, among other things, "Police brutality!" Indeed, there were some policemen, who had been called by Swami and who stood about, watching impassively. The same "rogue" who had attacked the *darwan* went to the office door on Webster Street and banged on it, demanding admittance. *This* act—banging on the door of Sri Ramakrishna's house—was the one thing, Swami later said, he could not forgive.

Inside, the meeting was called to order. After the secretary, treasurer, and president had read their respective reports, there was a hush; the back curtain parted where a door led into the offices, and Swami Ashokananda was wheeled out by a young monk in a dark, very dignified suit. Swami himself wore an Oxford gray clerical suit, and around his shoulders, covering the top half of his body, was a *gerua* shawl. His white hair, brushed back from his forehead, was like a crown. He was majesty itself, and on his entrance the entire assembly rose as one to its feet. It had been months since most of the members had seen their guru, and one could sense, as though they had spoken it, the reverence and love with which every person greeted him. And then, not majestically, but with a sort of gentleness and humor, he spoke:

> It behooves me to say a few words (laughter), because I hear many strange stories about me have been spread amongst you. I am glad that not any of you are responsible for such stories. One terrible story is that I have lost my head and my mind (laughter), so I have become an easy victim of the president and the secretary of the Society, and they have been trying to influence me to serve their own purposes.

With those few words, spoken clearly and with solid self-confidence, Swami Ashokananda then and there established the soundness of his mind. He went on to say that the dissidents had spread the tale that he (under the influence of Swami Chidrupananda and Mrs. Soulé) had been trying to separate the Vedanta Society from the Ramakrishna Order. The dissidents had written to the authorities at Belur Math to apprise them of this "treachery." "And of course," he said, "the swamis there have renounced the world and they are a rather innocent sort of people. It would be hard for them not to believe anything that comes to them in black and white. So they inquired what truth there was in these things. They also wrote to the two [assistant] swamis." He said that after thinking about the whole thing, he had come to the conclusion that the dissidents' plan was to gain control over the Society.

Swami then explained very clearly and concisely the reason for the change in the bylaws. He told of the long consultations with the lawyers, and he assured the membership that Swami Chidrupananda and Mrs. Soulé had never attempted to influence his decisions. "Many of you do not know," he said,

> though some of you do know, that to be a worker in this church is a very hazardous task. It requires a great deal of discipline and self-control, and self-abnegation. We [swamis] are trained that way, and those whom we find to be worthy material, we try to train accordingly. I am glad to say that Mr. Clifton has stood that training and he is true to that training. He did not try to influence me, since you require that assurance. Nor did Mrs. Soulé ever try to influence me. They brought the facts to me; and I thought about them a lot, and I came to certain conclusions. Mr. Clifton also consulted with Mr. [Allen] Singer, who is the assistant [attorney] on this case and who has been a lot of help. Only when the attorneys approved of the proposed changes were they brought about.

A part of Swami's address had his audience on the verge of both tears and laughter: he asked Swami Chidrupananda to read a letter from the doctor, which affirmed that there was "nothing wrong with Swami's brain or thinking processes." "Nothing," Swami said, "like a doctor's certificate!" In closing, he asked whether anyone would like to ask any questions—anything at all—and a voice from the audience called out, "No." "Thank you," Swami replied softly, and the meeting was adjourned.

A special general meeting was held the following month, April 1968, in which the new bylaws were spelled out in some detail and ratified by the members—for their own satisfaction, at least. That evening, nothing was heard from the "rogues." At the close of his address on that occasion, Swami said,

> I shall remind you of the thing I said to the old students of Swami Trigunatita: you cannot both [fight with the swami-in-charge and receive spiritual instruction from him]. You might say, "Well, Swami, you could be a little accommodating." No. All that would happen is that you won't get anything out of us spiritually. So my advice would be, don't try to do that. Why should you bother about the politics? Wherever there is property, there is money, there is power, and there is politics. But why do you have to worry about the politics? Suppose you did talk with the lawyers and have discussions and committees and so on. At the first opportunity we would get rid of you. Because you will only create trouble and spoil a good thing. We, the swamis, feel a responsibility about those things. And we try to discharge our responsibility in the best way we can. If we fail once, we shall try another time and another time. Look at me; you do not have to bother about the bylaws and the articles of association. If the worst happened to me, I would pass on, finished. Or if I should become very sick, I would resign from my position and let another swami come and bother about it. I did not have to do

it [change the bylaws], but conscience began to creak, so I did it, and I shall do the best I can. It may be that my best is not good enough. But what does it matter? Somebody else will do it. But you people do not have to do this dirty job. So my advice is that you follow what I said before the members in the early times. Don't bother about politics. If you say, "If we have to do things which you ask us to do, how can we just remain neutral? If you want us to do things, we should have something to say about it." By all means you should say something; fighting is a different story.

Or if you think that we just do things out of our own will, you are much mistaken. . . . Before I do anything, I ask advice of many people apart from the board of directors, who are the official advisers. So things will be taken care of. In the meantime don't get upset. You have to have some faith in your swamis. Particularly [in] the swami who is actually doing the things, you should have some faith. You must not think that he is a knave or that he is a fool. And if you say, "Well, since you ask for our help, we have to say something." To help is not to fight. To help requires a lot of sacrifice on your part. If you want to do that thing, not only will the work be well done, but you will derive a great spiritual benefit from it. Don't for a moment doubt it.

Swami then asked for questions.

Question: Is there any way by which the board can oppose the appointment of a swami? Swami answered in effect that if the swami did not have the necessary qualifications, the board could object. But he went on to say that it was very difficult to get a swami because they were in short supply and the demand in India was very great, and also all over the world the centers were asking for assistant swamis. It was not always possible for Belur Math to give swamis. "So," he said, "we have to take what we can get. Maybe in the future we will train American swamis to run the centers."

There were no other questions, and the meeting was adjourned.

20

IN PERFECT ORDER

U nfortunately, some of the Belur Math trustees had paid attention to the allegations of the "rogues" against Swami Ashokananda. They had also questioned the advisability of changing the
bylaws. On grounds of their worldly innocence, Swami had excused
the authorities at Belur Math for doubting his judgment and probity,
but the fact that they had done so had deeply wounded him. On August
2, 1968, he wrote officially to Swami Gambhirananda. His letter read in
part,

> I have not been able [to write to you earlier] mainly because
> my brain has been exceedingly tired, and every effort of the
> brain has a sort of numbing effect. This weakness of the brain
> was brought about by the letter I received a few months ago from
> the revered President Maharaj [Swami Vireswarananda].
>
> I do not think that any of you realize that I had a serious ill-
> ness in this stroke of the brain and that I have not recovered from
> it fully yet. But then why should you? Everybody is busy with
> his own affairs. You are all busy proving how wrong we are in
> changing the Articles of Association and the By-laws, and you
> are making all efforts to change them according to your wish.
> You have passed two resolutions. Such resolutions do not require

much thinking to pass. The trouble is that none of you have any real experience of the work in America. From letters received from some of you, it would seem as if by changing the By-laws, etc., I have been seeking to promote some of my own evil wishes. I want to tell you here and now that I have not any specific wish to fulfill in this regard. I have worked many, many years in this country. I came here in '31 and this is '68—that is thirty-seven years! Even before that I worked quite some time in India. I have not sought for name and fame or power, and I have not wanted these at the present time. Several years ago I prayed to Holy Mother very earnestly that she would soon let me pass on, and I have been waiting for that day. True, I still have one or two works to do—particularly to build up the Retreat, for which we bought about twenty years ago some two thousand acres of land. It is a big project and will require a lot of money, no doubt. When the opportunity will come I do not know.

However, it is not to serve any purpose of my own that I was so anxious to change the By-laws. I wanted to make them legal and therefore I made every effort to make them so. I should, however, tell you one thing further. In this country laws continually change, and the laws are differently interpreted by the judges; and another trouble is at the present time both the federal and state governments have become eager to find new incomes. They spend a lot of money for the people and therefore they have to have new taxes to have new revenue. Generally the churches are tax exempt, but the tax agents are continually checking on churches and all cases of tax exemption in order to find out if anybody is not paying taxes who can be made to pay taxes. There is always this danger, and for that reason these agents may come any time to search our account books, our other papers, and our By-laws, etc. We have, therefore, to be very cautious and be as perfect as possible. . . .

However, this is not to trouble you in any way, because we are consulting the lawyers here and we hope that we shall be able to find ways by which donations can be made wholly tax exempt. In the very beginning the problem that faced us is that a nonprofit corporation, which ours is, to be exempt from taxation should not be under the control of a foreign corporation. That is why we had to change the Articles of Association, which said that the Swami is to be appointed by the Belur Math. We made the appointment of the Swami into a joint affair of the Belur Math and the Board of Directors here.

Swami went on to explain that if the swami-in-charge could exercise veto power over the board of directors, the tax exemption of the Society could be rescinded. "So," he continued, "we had to give up this veto power. It has this benefit that we were able to carry out your wish as expressed in the resolutions which you sent us. However, I think you will agree with me that the Swami-in-Charge should have some veto power—though the Swami in Hollywood doesn't think so. Everyone decides according to his experience.

"Anyhow [he continued], considering everything, I have changed that By-law about the Swami having the veto power, and unless I get some more reassuring legal opinion, I won't revive it. . . ."

Of course, I am bedridden. Al is not well, and the other swamis cannot go to the lawyers and run from office to office and discuss things with them, nor are the young monks equal to that job. To make things worse, my condition has become definitely more serious. Of course, because of the stroke, my head has been very weak. For a time it was getting better; I was able to do brain work better, but then I received that letter from the President Maharaj. It was exceedingly shocking to me, and I had another stroke that day. The doctor told me that I have received several small strokes during the last few months. The resolutions that you sent were also a cause of shock as far as I can remember.

I am not blaming any of you. You have done what you thought best. But you tried to finish everything in a hurry, it seemed to me. There was no such hurry. . . . However, I am not getting any worse since then, and I am hoping that maybe my head will get a little better. . . . I am warned that for the next few months I should relax my brain and not exercise it much. . . . So if you don't get any letter from me quickly or any quick answer to your letters, please give me a little opportunity. I have no intention of embarrassing you in any way, but I must save my brain so that I don't have another stroke. My leg was getting better, and I was walking better, but since these little strokes this walking ability has decreased noticeably.

This was a letter Swami Ashokananda should not have had to write, nor did it do anything to change the president's or the trustees' view that it had been unnecessary to rewrite the Society's bylaws. However, the bylaws remained as Swami and the attorneys in San Francisco had thought best—and the "rogues" were not reinstated as members of the Vedanta Society.

Of this whole episode, Swami once said that Sri Ramakrishna was cleaning the Society of accumulated trash before placing a new swami in charge. Whatever the cost, this was as Swami Ashokananda wanted—everything, even the membership, was ready to be handed over in perfect order to his successor. Indeed, when the time came, the new swami was handed a membership fully trained in loyalty to Sri Ramakrishna alone. There would be no exodus of members. No one budged—a circumstance that was rare in the Vedanta movement in America during a changeover from one swami to the next.

Swami Ashokananda did not recover from the blow he had received from those whom he revered more than anyone else in this world. In the tradition he had held sacred for over fifty years and to which he had given his life, the heads of the Order represented Sri Ramakrishna and Swami Vivekananda themselves. Yet those officials had apparently given credence and sympathy to a gaggle of worthless people who wrote against him—at least, the Math authorities did not otherwise assure him. Even Bharat Maharaj was silent on this point, perhaps thinking that it was not necessary to repeat his unqualified faith in his brother monk.

Fortunately, before the trouble with the "rogues" began, Swami Dayananda had written to Swami Ashokananda on October 20, 1967, expressing his love and appreciation (see Appendix B). As the reader may remember, Swami Dayananda had been in charge of the Vedanta Society in San Francisco when, in 1931, Swami Ashokananda arrived in America. Because Swami Dayananda, now a revered trustee of the Order, had lived in the West and knew the nature and difficulty of the work there, his letter had meaning. Swami Ashokananda kept it—a sign that it was of importance to him. Despite its well-intended suggestion that Swami retire, it was no doubt of some comfort to him.

Swami still enjoyed talking in the evenings with his disciples downstairs, and he attended to the editing and publication of six of his lectures, which Nancy, Kathleen, Edna, and I had put into readable shape. We tried not to bother him too much about this, but now and then Nancy and I would enter into a prolonged and heated argument over the correct wording of a passage and could come to no conclusion about it. There was nothing for it but to consult Swami. With a few words he would solve the problem, and it would seem that his brain was as strong and clear as ever, but the doctors knew better, and as early as August 10 all of us were told not to stay at the Temple later than nine o'clock. Lying on his back, he would say very gleefully, "I will go *whoosh,*" his right arm shooting straight up at the ceiling, "to Tapaloka"—the realm of meditation and certainly of bliss.

In his last years, Swami gave initiation to two women, barely in their twenties, who were in adoring awe of him and whom he almost instantly placed in the convent. Though the fire that had once visibly blazed within him seemed now to be just flickering, it was still there, and he enveloped those whom he knew to be his own in its heat and light. Perhaps there were some young men also whom he inspired and claimed as his own.

Swami Ashokananda seated in the library
at the Old Temple, 1968

MY JOURNAL, once so full of entries, has just a few for the year 1968, and none of a personal kind for 1969. The place of the following excerpts was always the "back room" in the Old Temple, where Swami lay half-paralyzed on his bed:

February 11, 1968
Swami (speaking of lions): You people have so poor an idea of greatness. . . . When the many begins to enter into the One, then for the first time, you begin to appreciate greatness. . . . All bondages fall off, then you really perceive greatness.

June 21, 1968
Swami (to me): For all the years to come I wish you health, hap-

piness, peace, accomplishment, and devotion to Sri Ramakrishna and Swamiji.

Me: Thank you, Swami. Please say it again on Sunday (the day of my birthday).

Swami: I have said it now. Don't doubt! Can one want more? Isn't that everything?

Me: Realization?

Swami: That is included in devotion and accomplishment.

August 5, 1968
Swami Swahananda has arrived.

August 9, 1968
Swami has talked to the new swami. He *likes* him! "He is a *very nice* person, very nice!" One anxiety is over, at least.

September 18, 1968
Swami: Purification of our emotion comes when the object of our emotion is divine.

October 6, 1968
Swami tells me again and again to write my memoirs of him someday. Though tonight he said, "Oh, forget that! Rest when you finish your books. No one will care about me."

On December 1, 1969, Swami's kidney infection suddenly flared up. He was rushed to the hospital. No one was allowed to visit him except Al, Ediben, and Jo—his three crown jewels. In response to my complaints about this, Ediben said one day, "You know, dear, if I were you, I would just go." So I just went, unaware, until their drivers yelled at

me, that I had nearly sideswiped one or two cars on the way. At the
hospital, Swami lay very weak and thin. I was able to tell him that the
typing of "Second Visit" (the second *New Discoveries* book) had been
completed that day, and that the manuscript of "My Philosophy and
My Religion" (later titled "When the Many Become One," the last
pamphlet that we had edited) had been given to the printer. He smiled
to hear these bits of news. Except for the unending work at Olema, no
other work was pending. It was all done.

The next day, at ten minutes to one in the afternoon of December
13, Swami Ashokananda left his body.

THE FUNERAL WAS HELD on December 17. Swami Satprakashananda,
Swami Vividishananda, Swami Prabhavananda, and Swami Bhashya-
nanda had flown to San Francisco from their respective centers, and
each one spoke at the service. The day before, Swami's body had lain
in a large room of the mortuary. Many of the devotees who had come
there to pay their last respects to their guru later spoke of the atmosphere of peace and power that pervaded that room. Years later, Marion
Langerman asked Swami Shantaswarupananda about it. He was then
in India and replied in a letter dated November 26, 1981:

> It is hard to say anything about your experience about Swami
> Ashokananda in the funeral room where his body was kept.
> Some other devotees, too, spoke of their experience to me. Some
> felt a wonderful peace there, while others had a feeling of
> strength and power. Anyway, there was something very unusual
> there. One explanation of such phenomena is given that all of it
> is due to the presence of the departed soul. This is quite possible.
> Swami Ashokananda was a source of peace, power, joy, and
> many other great qualities. So his presence invoked these various
> feelings in different people. His love for the devotees, and the
> devotees' love for him, might have induced him to lend his pres-

ence there for a few days. That is all that we can guess. The experiences of course were real.

From the mortuary, the casket, covered with garlands of flowers, was taken to the New Temple, where it was placed at the foot of the chancel stairs in the center of the main aisle. Swami Chidrupananda read a valedictory that he had written, probably through tears, and few of the many devotees and friends who filled the auditorium heard it with dry eyes:

> We have gathered to salute and say farewell, for a time, to one who has meant more to many of us than life itself.
>
> Often before we have thought this day was near at hand, seeing the burdens of labor and illness that he carried. But he was greater even than our wondering measure of his valiant will and indomitable spirit. He himself told us, "When you find no strength left in the body, when you find no strength left in the mind, you have to stand on the strength of the Self, the Spirit."
>
> It is but natural that on this occasion we look back over the years that he was with us here and recall those bright facets of character that now glow brighter for his having gone before us to the other side:
>
> The penetrating insight that could see through and through us and meet our every spiritual need,
>
> The powerful intellect that won the respect and admiration of the great ones of both the world and the spirit,
>
> The unfailing sense of humor that could brighten the darkest hour in an instant,
>
> The profound understanding of man and all his aspirations,
>
> The impatience of faintheartedness in the spiritual seeker, when he saw so clearly the limitlessness of the soul,
>
> The unwearied patience with all our failings and short-comings,

The keen sense of beauty, whether in art or nature or human character,

The loving heart, which for our sake he tried so often to conceal by scolding and stern discipline,

The generous nature, the vast nobility of the man—how shall we pay worthy tribute to him? How shall we give expression to our love, or make fitting monument to his memory?

The monuments are already here, the way to make record of our love is in our hands, if only we have the courage to acknowledge them. I do not mean the temples and retreats that he built and dedicated to the worship of the Spirit. You and I, who call ourselves his students, are his monuments, whether we wish it or no. For we are the fruits of his untiring labor, and men will surely judge him by what we are and what we shall be as seekers after Truth.

I said that we have come to bid farewell for a time. An ancient tradition in India declares that once the teacher accepts the disciple, the teacher stands by him, life after life, to the very end—until the disciple attains to the highest spiritual goal. Swami Ashokananda believed in that tradition, and I, for one, believe that he will indeed be with us to the very end.

Let us, then, forget to grieve, in recollection of the release and the fulfillment which he now has won.

Now he belongs to the ages.

The casket was then carried down the stairs, the devotees following, and into a waiting car.

It was then that we saw the pelicans. They were flying overhead—a sight rare in San Francisco. Rarer still, they were white. They had circled all that morning over the vicinity of the old and new temples, and at the hour of the funeral service in the New Temple they had circled over that building alone, soaring and playing. As the car that bore the casket drove slowly off, they fell into a V formation and flew into the southeast, as though escorting it.

When I came out of the New Temple, someone caught my eye and pointed upward, and there they were. I had never before, nor have I since, seen pelicans flying in the city. But it really happened, and everyone who saw it felt uplifted and somehow deeply comforted.

Swami had said that he wanted his ashes immersed in the Pacific Ocean. Fortunately, a close member of the Berkeley center owned a small sailing ship, and on a clear, sunny day after the cremation, he and Swami Chidrupananda took the ashes out through the Golden Gate to the open sea. At first the container floated on the waves. "He was unsinkable to the very end," Swami Chidrupananda would later say, and when the urn finally sank, Swami Chidrupananda chanted from the Gita and threw a wreath of gardenias onto the spot where the waters had closed over it.

From the top floor of the pink house—the large apartment that Swami had been going to occupy—Ediben and I watched as the little motor-driven ship, with its single bare mast standing straight and stalwart, moved through the Golden Gate. We watched in silence until the ship disappeared, and then we stood for a while gazing at the water and the hills beyond. At last Ediben said, "He would have loved this view."

It was like saying that a released prisoner would have loved the view from a window newly cut in his old cell—if only he could have stayed. I started to protest, and then I could almost hear Swami's laughter ringing all around us, joyous and free.

NOTES AND SOURCES

Unless otherwise noted, the material cited below is preserved in the archives of the Vedanta Society of Northern California.

PART I
THE WORLD OF THE SPIRIT

1. After Swami Ashokananda's death, his maternal uncle Daikunthanath Dhar confirmed that the date of the Swami's birth was September 23, 1893 (undated memo).

2. Most of the information regarding Swami Ashokananda's family comes from a letter written by his youngest sister, Monohorini Day, to Swami Chidrupananda on October 16, 1970.

3. Aswini Kumar Datta, *Bhakti Yoga*, 2nd ed. (Bombay: Bharatiya Vidya Bhavan, 1971).

4. Ibid. The three quotations in this paragraph from *Bhakti Yoga* are on pages 102, 103, and 147, respectively.

5. *A Study of Religion* was first published by the Udbodhan Office, Calcutta, in 1908. It contains seven of Swami Vivekananda's lectures on religion: "What Is Religion?" "Reason and Religion," "The Ideal of a Universal Religion," "The Way to the Realization of a Universal Religion," "Soul, God, and Religion," "Vedic Religious Ideals," and "The Hindu Religion."

6. *The Complete Works of Swami Vivekananda,* 8 vols., birth centenary ed. (Calcutta: Advaita Ashrama, 1963), 1:337.

7. Ibid., 1:375.

8. M (Mahendranath Gupta), *Sri Sri Ramakrishna Kathamrita,* 5 vols. published sequentially (Calcutta, 1897–1932). The definitive English edition is entitled *The Gospel of Sri Ramakrishna,* translated and with an introduction by Swami Nikhilananda, foreword by Aldous Huxley (New York: Ramakrishna-Vivekananda Center, 1942).

9. Swami Vivekananda, *Jnana Yoga* (Madras: Sri Ramakrishna Math, 1908).

10. Swami Saradananda, *Sri Sri Ramakrishna Lilaprasanga,* 5 vols. (Calcutta: Udbodhan Press, 1911–1918). The definitive English edition is entitled *Sri Ramakrishna: The Great Master,* translated by Swami Jagadananda (Madras: Sri Ramakrishna Math, 1952).

11. Swami Vivekananda, *Inspired Talks* (Madras: Sri Ramakrishna Math, 1908).

12. *Complete Works of Swami Vivekananda,* 7:29.

13. Swami Ashokananda, *Memories of Swami Shivananda* (San Francisco: Vedanta Society of Northern California, 1969), 4; and from the author's journal.

14. Ibid.

15. Parimal Chandra Dhar, *Swami Ashokananda: A Biographical Study* (Assam, 1978), 3.

16. His Eastern and Western Disciples, *Life of Swami Vivekananda,* vol. 4 (Mayavati: Advaita Ashrama, 1918).

17. Flashing of knowledge occurs in a spiritual state of mind called *pratibha.* It is mentioned in Patanjali's *Yoga Sutras,* 3:34.

18. From a class held by Swami Ashokananda entitled "An Amalaka in the Hand (Hastamalaka)," April 3, 1953 (unpublished transcript).

19. Swami Ashokananda, *Swami Premananda* (San Francisco: Vedanta Society of Northern California, 1970), 32.

20. Author's interview with Atul Chandra Chaudhuri, Calcutta, December 26, 1975, tape recording.

21. Swami Ashokananda, *Swami Premananda*, 43–44.

22. Ibid., 45.

23. Ibid., 45–46.

24. Not surprisingly, similar encounters with Swami Saradananda have been told by one or two other monks of the Ramakrishna Order.

25. M, *Sri Sri Ramakrishna Kathamrita* (see note 8).

26. Some seventy-five years later one of Swami Ashokananda's disciples visited the village of Gosainagar and was paid great honor by the inhabitants, some of whom must have been the grandchildren of those the Swami had cared for.

27. Swami Ashokananda, *Swami Brahmananda* (San Francisco: Vedanta Society of Northern California, 1970), 39–44 passim.

28. *Vedanta Kesari* (Madras) (December 1997): 524.

29. M, *Gospel of Sri Ramakrishna (According to M., a Son of the Lord and Disciple)*, vol. 2 (Madras: Sri Ramakrishna Math, 1922).

30. Swami Ashokananda, *Swami Brahmananda*, 45–50 passim.

31. The entire correspondence between Swami Ashokananda and Romain Rolland later disappeared from Advaita Ashrama, Mayavati, having been, presumably, discarded by one of Swami Ashokananda's successors in a wholesale clearing of the decks.

32. Romain Rolland, *Inde* (Paris: Éditions Albin Michel, 1960). The selections from *Inde* quoted in this book were kindly translated from the French by Maryse Bader at the request of the author.

33. *Prophets of the New India* was also published in 1930 in New York by Alfred & Charles Boni.

34. Katherine Mayo, *Mother India* (New York: Harcourt Brace, 1927; republished, Delhi: Anmol Publications, 1986).

35. Dhan Gopal Mukherjee, *The Face of Silence* (New York: E.P. Dutton and Co., 1926).

36. Richard B. Gregg, *The Economics of Khaddar* (Madras: S. Ganesan, 1928).

37. Sankari Prasad Basu, *Economic and Political Ideas: Vivekananda, Gandhi, Subhas Bose* (New Delhi: Sterling Publishers, 2000), 100.

38. For a fuller discussion of Swami Nityaswarupananda's translation and commentary on the *Ashtavakra Samhita,* see Shelley Brown, M.D., *Centred in Truth: The Story of Swami Nitya-swarup-ananda,* 2 vols. (New York: Kalpa Tree Press, 2001), 1:18–22.

39. Swami Ashokananda, *Spiritual Practice* (Calcutta: Advaita Ashrama, 2000).

40. From a class on the Upanishads held by Swami Ashokananda on February 19, 1954 (unpublished transcript).

41. Swami Ashokananda, *The Influence of Indian Thought on the Thought of the West* (Mayavati: Advaita Ashrama, 1931).

42. Swami Ashokananda, *Swami Shivananda,* 15; and from the author's journal.

43. Author's interview with Brahmachari Vimukta Chaitanya, Olema, August 6, 1997, tape recording.

PART 2

A HEART POURED OUT

44. It is possible that Swami Vivekananda gave Shanti Ashrama its name, but it is more likely that Swami Turiyananda did so.

45. In 1930 Romain Rolland's book *Prophets of the New India* was published in New York by Albert & Charles Boni, as well as in Calcutta by Advaita Ashrama.

46. *Jnana Yoga,* in *Complete Works of Swami Vivekananda,* 2:57–288.

47. Edith B. Soulé's unpublished reminiscences of Swami Ashokananda in interviews conducted by Dorothy Madison and Ann Myren, tape-recorded. Most of Edith Soulé's memoirs that are given in this book are from that source.

48. Special meeting of the Vedanta Society of Northern California, April 23, 1968.

49. Interview with Thelma (Fine) Landau by Eleanor Reynolds (now Sister Eleanor Margaret of the Episcopal Community of Saint John the Baptist).

50. Edythe Allan to Ida Ansell, December 17, 1935, Vedanta Society of Southern California Archives.

51. Ibid., November 26, 1948.

52. Swami Ashokananda, *Meditation, Ecstasy, and Illumination: An Overview of Vedanta* (Calcutta: Advaita Ashrama, 1990), 61.

53. Swami Ashokananda, *Sri Ramakrishna: The Godman of India* (San Francisco: Vedanta Society of San Francisco, 1936).

54. Every night during Edith Soulé's stay one summer at Yosemite, a large bonfire would be pushed off Glacier Point, its embers showering down like a waterfall of fire to the floor of the valley far below. As the fire fell, Edith, standing at the top of the cliff, would, at the request of the Yosemite authorities, sing "Indian Love Call"—Native American Indian, that is.

55. The Soulé cabin is used today as a summer retreat for the members of the convent of the Vedanta Society of Northern California. Jo and Helen's cabin accommodates devotees, one at a time, eremitic style, throughout the summer months. The Swami's cabin is used exclusively by the swamis and their guests.

56. It should be said that the Christian Science Mother Church in Boston reprimanded its Berkeley branch for the stand it took against the Vedanta Society in 1938. In later years, the two Berkeley churches, standing back to back, lived in peace with one another.

57. Notes of Marion Langerman.

58. Author's interview with Brahmachari Vimukta Chaitanya, Vedanta Retreat, Olema, August 8, 1997, tape recording.

59. Swami Yogeshananda, *Six Lighted Windows*, 2nd ed. (Hollywood: Vedanta Press, 1997).

60. Edythe Allan to Ida Ansell, March 9, 1942. According to other sources, Swami Yatiswarananda had chicken pox.

61. Draft of a letter written by Swami Ashokananda to Swami Prabhavananda, undated.

62. Swami Ashokananda, "How to Cultivate the Love of God," a lecture given on January 20, 1957.

63. July 26, 1946 was a Friday, not a Saturday as Ediben recorded in

her diary. Immediately following the legal transactions at the San Rafael courthouse, Swami Ashokananda and a small party of his students drove to Olema for the informal dedication ceremony of the new property; this ceremony was probably the reason Swami Ashokananda wanted the transactions at the courthouse to be over by noon.

64. Swami Ashokananda slightly misquoted the Bible. According to the King James version, Christ said, "Take my yoke upon you, and learn of me. . . . And ye shall find rest unto your souls. For *my yoke is easy,* and my burden is light." (Italics added.) Matt. 11:29–30.

65. Author's interview with Brahmachari Vimukta Chaitanya, Olema, August 8, 1997, tape recording.

PART 3
SHEETS OF CLEAR GLASS

No references are cited for Part 3. The materials are taken from the author's journal or are preserved in the archives of the Vedanta Society of Northern California.

INAUGURATION OF *The Voice of India*

Swami Ashokananda's office, Hindu Temple, February 28, 1941
Present: Swami Ashokananda, Florence Wenner, Kathleen Davis, and
Edna Zulch

These notes, taken by one of the students present, record Swami Ashoka-
nanda's instructions for bringing out a magazine that would present the phi-
losophy and religion of Vedanta to the West (Archives of the Vedanta
Society of Northern California).

Swami: This is Sri Ramakrishna's birthday; therefore I thought it an
auspicious day on which to inaugurate a new venture. As you know,
we have thought of publishing a magazine. Now we shall begin to
think of it definitely.

This magazine will not be published by me or by the Vedanta Society, but by an editorial board. You three are to be that board. In the beginning, you will have to do some writing, but as time goes on, you can
find other writers.

I would not even begin by having a small magazine such as the ones
published in Hollywood and Boston. It must have fifty-nine pages. At
first it will be mimeographed, and the form will be exactly like the form
when eventually it will be printed—the same number of pages, and the
same number of words on a page. There will be no advertising. We

shall plan to publish it in this form for three years. At the end of that time, if it is successful, we shall plan to print it. We shall have to charge four dollars a year for it, and we should have four hundred subscriptions to make it pay for itself. After three years, I shall try to raise the money to publish it for a year. We shall have to be prepared to finance it without any return for ten years.

This magazine must have well-written material in it, no sloppy writing, but writing that would be acceptable to scholars. There are available a few persons who can help you. First, there is Mr. Utter. Of course, he is not only a busy man, he is a family man, and that means his time is limited. Then there is Al Clifton. He has a gift for writing, but he, too, is a busy man. In matters of grammar, you can go to Dr. Soulé. Mr. Brown is in the printing business and he can get supplies, and possibly even a mimeograph, wholesale. We can get people to type and do the mimeographing.

First, you are to think of it, meditate on it, pray to Sri Ramakrishna about it. When you have thought of it, arrange a meeting and talk it over. Then report to me. You should have enough material for three issues before you start publishing it. It will be a monthly.

Now, let me tell you something. There must be no jealousy. You will see twenty thousand things wrong with one another, but you must have no feeling about it. If you do, it will be a poison that will destroy you and everything. Work for the Lord, do it all for Him. Be prepared to work hard. And if you bring me something that has taken you days to write—a long article—it may be that I shall reject it altogether. Be prepared for this.

Student: It is what you would call "a tall order."

Swami: You have come to a *great* place. Now you must do great things. If you just meditate and go on without serving the Lord, you will make very little progress. If you struggle and work hard for Him, something great will develop within yourself.

A LETTER FROM SWAMI DAYANANDA
TO SWAMI ASHOKANANDA,

OCTOBER 20, 1967

Ramakrishna Mission Seva Pratishthan
99 Sarat Bose Road, Calcutta 26

My dear Yogesh Maharaj,

I am delighted to receive your very affectionate Vijaya greetings and best wishes, which I reciprocate. Please convey the same to Parvati, Bimal, Chidrupananda, and others.

Although I do not write to you (I am a very poor correspondent), I often think about you, and the pleasant memories of the days we spent together come back to me.

We were terribly worried when you suddenly went to the hospital. Thank God that your recovery, though slow, has been satisfactory and that you have returned to the centre much improved and are convalescing steadily. We understand that you are still confined to bed most of the time and are unable to write letters, etc. Please do not try. Let others do it for you.

Like a true karma-yogin you have worked hard for the last 35 years in San Francisco and not only conducted regular Sunday services, gave interviews, and moulded the spiritual life of your students, but also built the most beautiful temple of the Master in the whole Western world, along with a monastery, a convent, and a retreat—all planned by some of the best architects of the U.S.A. under your able guidance.

Just now I got a letter from Sister Aruna from Hammersmith Hospital, London. She writes that of all the centres she has visited in the U.S.A. she likes the San Francisco centre best, and particularly its convent. Now don't you think that the person who has been instrumental, through the grace of the Lord, in achieving all these in spite of failing health without taking a day's rest has earned a good vacation and retirement from active work? You have built up such a personality that your presence alone will inspire others. And this may give you a longer lease on life, which will ultimately benefit the Vedanta Society and everybody connected with it.

Please do not bother about replying to this letter. Just think about it and take good care of yourself. We are doing well. But the country is going through a terrible upheaval. Heaven alone knows where it will lead.

Thanking you for your kind Vijaya greetings,

Yours affectionately,

Dayananda

GLOSSARY

A guide to the English pronunciation of Sanskrit and Bengali words has been placed in parentheses after each entry using the following vowel sounds:

a sounds like *o* in *come*
ā sounds like *a* in *car*
e sounds like *e* in *prey*
i sounds like *i* in *fin*
ī sounds like *ee* in *feel*
o sounds like *o* in *note*
u sounds like *u* in *pull*
ū sounds like *oo* in *pool*
ai sounds like *ai* in *aisle*
au sounds like *ow* in *now*

Advaita (ad vai′ ta). The nondualistic philosophy of Vedanta. *See* Vedanta.

Advaita Ashrama. The ashrama and publications department of the Ramakrishna Order at Mayavati, with a branch in Calcutta. *See* Mayavati.

ananda (ā nan′ da). Bliss; the last part of the monastic name.

arati (ā′ ra ti). Worship of the Deity with waving of lights; evening vespers.

ashrama (āsh' ra ma), also ashram. A religious community, usually monastic.

Ashtavakra Samhita (ash tā' vak ra sam hit' tā). A classic treatise on Advaita (nondualistic) Vedanta.

atmajnani (āt ma gya' ni). A knower of the Atman, or the Self.

Atman (āt' man). The Self, or individual soul; also denotes the Supreme Soul, which, according to nondualistic Vedanta, is one with the individual soul.

Avadhuta Gita (a va dhu' ta gī' tā). A nondualistic treatise on Vedanta attibuted to the sage Dattatreya.

Babu (bā' bu). A well-to-do gentleman; a title equivalent to "Mister" placed after a name.

Belur Math (be' lur mat'). The monastic headquarters of the Ramakrishna Order (Ramakrishna Math and Mission), situated on the Ganges river about four miles north of Calcutta at Belur, Howrah, India.

Benares, also Banaras. *See* Varanasi.

Bhagavad Gita (bha' ga vad gī' tā), or Gita. Lit., "Song of God." A well-known Hindu scripture that forms a part of the *Mahabharata*.

bhakta (bhak' ta). A devotee of God.

bhakti (bhak' ti). Divine love; devotion to a Personal God.

bhakti yoga. The path of devotion; one of the four main yogas, or paths, leading to union with God.

brahmachari(n) (bra' ma chā' rī[n]). A celibate religious male who has taken the first monastic vows; the first stage of monastic life (fem. brahmacharini).

brahmacharya (bra' ma chār' ya). First monastic vows; the first stage of Hindu life (continence in thought, word, and deed).

Brahman (bra' man). The Absolute; the Supreme Reality of Vedanta philosophy.

Brahmananda, Swami (1863–1922) (bra' mā nan da), also known as "Maharaj." A direct monastic disciple of Sri Ramakrishna, re-

garded as his spiritual son, and the first president (after Swami
Vivekananda, the founder) of the Ramakrishna Math and Ramakrishna Mission, both of which grew into widespread organiza-
tions under his guidance.

Brahmaputra (bra' ma pu' tra). A wide and often treacherous river that
flows north to south between India and Bangladesh.

brahmin (brā' min). A Hindu of the highest caste, traditionally assigned to the priesthood.

chadar (chā' dar). Upper body cloth; shawl.

Chaitanya (1485–1533) (chai tan' ya). A Hindu saint of Bengal who
preached a form of Vaishnavism based on the worship of Sri
Krishna.

charkha (chār' kha). A spinning wheel.

Chhandogya Upanishad (chan do' gya u' pa ni' shad). One of the oldest, longest, and most important Upanishads. *See* Upanishad.

Dakshineswar (dak' shi nesh' war). The village on the Ganges about
five miles north of Calcutta with a temple complex where Sri
Ramakrishna spent most of his life.

devotee. A spiritual seeker who, generally, is devoted to the Personal
God.

Dhritarashtra (drī ta rāsh' tra). The blind king of the Kurus, whose
one hundred sons fought against their cousins the Pandavas in the
Kurushektra war, as related in the *Mahabharata*.

diksha (dīk' shā). Initiation by a guru into spiritual life.

Drona. The military teacher of the Kurus, whose story is told in the
Mahabharata.

Durga. A name of the Divine Mother.

Durga Puja (dur' gā pū' ja). The autumnal worship of the Divine
Mother.

Gauri-Ma (1857–1938). A woman disciple of Sri Ramakrishna who devoted her life to strenuous spiritual practice and to the cause of women in Bengal.

gerua (ge′ rū a). A cloth of ocher color symbolizing renunciation.

ghat (ghāt). A bathing place on a river or lake.

gopi (go′ pi). A milkmaid of Vrindaban. The gopis were companions and devotees of Sri Krishna. Their lives were examples of the most intense divine love.

Great Master, or Master. Sri Ramakrishna.

guna (gu′ na). The three qualities of Nature: sattva (wisdom), rajas (action), and tamas (inertia), discussed in the Samkhya philosophy (one of the six systems of Hindu philosophy). *See also specific gunas.*

guru shakti (gu′ ru shak′ ti) The spiritual power of the guru.

Holy Mother. The name by which Sri Ramakrishna's wife was known among his devotees; the spiritual consort of Sri Ramakrishna. *See* Sarada Devi.

Ishta (ish′ ta). The Chosen Ideal.

Ishvara (īsh′ va ra). The Personal God.

Jagaddhatri (ja′ ga dhā′ trī). A name of the Divine Mother.

Jai (jai), also Jaya. "Victory" or "Glory to."

japa (ja′ pa), also japam. Repetition of the name of God in a sacred formula. *See* mantra.

Jayrambati (jai′ rām bā′ tī). The village in West Bengal where Sri Sarada Devi was born.

jnana yoga (gya′ na yo′ ga). The path of knowledge to Divine union.

jnani (gya′ nī). One who follows the path of knowledge and discrimination to realize God; a nondualist.

Kali (kā lī). A name of the Divine Mother; the presiding deity of the Dakshineswar temple.

Kamarpukur (kā' mār pū' kur). The village in West Bengal where Sri Ramakrishna was born.

karma (kar' ma). Action; the fruits of action.

karma yoga. The path of selfless action to Divine union.

Krishna (krish' na). Divine Incarnation, widely worshiped in Hinduism and prominent in the *Mahabharata* and Bhagavad Gita.

Lakshmana (laksh' ma na). The third brother of Sri Rama. *See* Rama.

lila (lī' lā). The divine play in the phenomenal world, a special manifestation of which is the advent of an avatar.

Mahabharata (ma hā' bhā' ra ta). The famous Hindu epic poem of the fourth to fifth centuries B.C. that includes the Bhagavad Gita and comprises one hundred thousand couplets.

Maharaj (ma' hā rāj). Lit., "great king." Refers specifically to Swami Brahmananda in the historical sense but is commonly used to address any monk of the Ramakrishna Order (it can be used alone but is often preceded by the monk's familiar name prior to sannyas; for example, Yogesh Maharaj).

mahasamadhi (ma hā sa mā' dhi). Lit., "the great samadhi." Usually refers to the final absorption in the Divine of an illumined soul in which the body is given up.

mantra (man' tra), also mantram. A sacred formula repeated in japa as a spiritual practice to concentrate the mind on the Ishta.

math (mat). Monastery.

maya (mā' yā). A term of Vedanta philosophy denoting both the power of Brahman to create, preserve, and destroy the universe, and the cosmic ignorance veiling Brahman that leads man to identify with the phenomenal world.

Mayavati (mā' yā va tī). The location in the Himalayas of the Ramakrishna Order's Advaita Ashrama that Swami Vivekananda dedicated to nondualism, which includes the publishing house of the same name. *See* Advaita Ashrama.

Meru, Mount (me′ rū). A mythical mountain in the center of the earth abounding in gold and other treasures; the Olympus of India.

Mirabai (mir′ a bai) (1547–1614). The queen of Chitore and a mystic poetess renowned for her devotion to Sri Krishna.

moksha (mok′ sha), also mukti (muk′ ti). Liberation from the phenomenal world.

moong dal (mūng′ dāl). A thick soup made from moong beans.

Narendranath (na ren′ dra nāt′). The premonastic name of Swami Vivekananda.

Om (aum). The most sacred word of the Vedas; a word symbol representing both the personal aspect of God and the impersonal Absolute (Brahman).

Patanjali (pat an′ ja li). The founder of the Yoga philosophy, who is thought to have lived in the first century B.C.

pranam (pra nām′). Respectful salutation(s), usually by touching the feet or by prostrating.

Premananda, Swami (1861–1918) (pre′ mā′ nan da). A direct monastic disciple of Sri Ramakrishna and a leading figure at Belur Math in its early days, who managed the monastery while leading an unostentatious life of contemplation and service and was beloved of all for his selfless affection.

puja (pū′ ja). Ritualistic worship.

Radhakrishnan, Sir Sarvepalli (1888–1975). The president of India and president of the Ramakrishna Mission Institute of Culture, respected as one of the most remarkable philosophers and religious thinkers of modern India.

raja yoga (rā′ ja yo′ ga). The path of mind control to Divine union, as described by Patanjali in his *Yoga Sutras*.

rajas (ra′ jas). Quality of activity or restlessness. *See* guna.

Rama (rā' ma), also Ramachandra. A popular divine incarnation of
Hinduism, the king of Ayodhya, and the hero of the *Ramayana*—
one of India's great epics, said to have been composed around 500
B.C.

Ramakrishna (1836–86) (rā' ma krish' na). Hindu mystic considered to
be a divine incarnation (avatar). By his direct spiritual realization
of the Ultimate Reality following various paths, he established the
harmony of all religions and the veracity of both dualistic and
nondualistic forms of religious discipline.

Ramakrishna Math and Ramakrishna Mission. The monastic order
founded by Swami Vivekananda in 1897. "The Ramakrishna Math
and Mission represents a synthetic ideal of renunciation and service, which not only emphasizes a course of strict discipline, contemplation and study, but also a life of self-dedication at the altar of
humanity for the attainment of the highest goal of human existence" (*Sri Ramakrishna Centenary Souvenir 1836–1936* [Calcutta:
Belur Math, 1937]).

rishi (ri' shi). Ancient Hindu seer of truth to whom the words of the
Vedas were revealed; general term for a saint or illumined sage.

sadhana (sā' dha na). Spiritual practice.

sadhu (sā' dhu). Holy man; a monk.

samadhi (sa mā' dhi). Ecstatic trance; ultimate communion with God.

sannyas (san' yās). Final monastic vows; fourth stage of Hindu life (renunciation).

sannyasin (san' yā' sin), also sannyasi. Hindu monk (fem. sannyasini).

Sarada Devi (1853–1920) (sā' ra dā de vī). The wife of Sri Ramakrishna, also known as Holy Mother, felt to be an incarnation of
the Divine Mother of the Universe.

Sarada Math (sā' ra dā mat'). An order of nuns established in India in
1954 in the name of Sri Sarada Devi with monastic headquarters at
Dakshineswar, Calcutta.

Saradananda, Swami (1865–1927) (sā' ra dā' nan da). A direct monas-

tic disciple of Sri Ramakrishna and the first secretary of the Ramakrishna Math and Mission. He wrote the definitive biography of
Sri Ramakrishna, *Sri Sri Ramakrishna Lilaprasanga* (Sri Ramakrishna: The Great Master), while sitting as Holy Mother's "gate-
keeper" at the Udbodhan Office.

sattva (sat' va). Quality of wisdom or spiritual poise. *See* guna.

Shakti (shak' ti). God as Mother of the Universe; the dynamic aspect
of life; the primal energy of Brahman manifesting in the phenomenal world.

Shivananda, Swami (ca. 1850s–1934) (shi' vā' nan da), also known as
"Mahapurush Maharaj." A direct monastic disciple of Sri Rama-
krishna and the second president of the Ramakrishna Math and
Ramakrishna Mission.

Sri (shrī). A title of respect meaning "revered" or "holy" (doubly
honorific as Sri Sri), used as a prefix to address a male or female
deity or holy personality; also used commonly as the Hindu equivalent of "Mister."

sutras (sū' tras). Scriptural aphorisms; compressed teachings of Hinduism.

Swami (swā' mī). Lord, master, spiritual teacher. Title of a Hindu monk.

Swamiji (swā' mī jī). Refers specifically to Swami Vivekananda in the
historical sense; a respectful way of addressing any swami ("ji" in-
dicates respect).

Tagore, Rabindranath (1861–1941). The greatest nineteenth-century
poet and writer of Bengal, and an eminent spokesman of modern
Indian spiritual humanism.

tamas (ta' mas). Lit., "darkness." Quality of inertia, dullness, and im-
purity. *See* guna.

tapas (ta' pas). Austerity; spiritual discipline.

Udbodhan (ud' bo dhan). The Bengali journal of the Ramakrishna
Order.

Udbodhan Office. Also known as Mother's House; the house in the Baghbazar section of north Calcutta that served as a residence for Sri Sarada Devi upstairs and the publishing office for *Udbodhan* magazine downstairs.

Upanishad (u′ pa ni′ shad), plural Upanishads. Philosophical portion of the Vedas (Vedanta). These sacred Vedantic texts of the fifth or fourth century B.C. explain the identity of the individual soul (Atman) with the Universal Soul (Brahman).

Vairagya (vai′ rāg ya). Renunciation.

Varanasi. Formerly called Benares and now Kashi; a sacred city on the Ganges in Uttar Pradesh, believed to give liberation to all who die there.

Veda (ve′ da), plural Vedas. The most ancient scriptures of the Hindus, regarded as direct divine revelation and the ultimate authority of the Hindu religion.

Vedanta (ve′ dān′ ta). Lit., "end of the Veda." The best known of the six systems of Hindu philosophy, discussed mainly in the Upanishads, the Bhagavad Gita, and the Brahmasutras. Vedantic schools of thought include nondualism (Advaita), qualified nondualism (Vishishtadvaita), and dualism (Dvaita), which encompass all paths to the Ultimate Truth and all levels of spiritual aspiration.

Vedanta Centers and Societies. Regional centers of the Ramakrishna Order outside India.

Vedantist, also Vedantin. A follower of Vedanta.

Vijaya greetings (vi′ ja yā′). Festive greetings to celebrate the fourth and final day of the Durga Puja.

viveka (vi ve′ ka). Discrimination.

Vivekananda, Swami (1863–1902) (vi ve′ kā′ nan da), also known as "Swamiji." A direct monastic disciple of Sri Ramakrishna and his chief apostle, the leader of his brother monks and founder of the Ramakrishna Order. He revitalized Hinduism in India and was the first to bring the message of Vedanta to the West.

Yoga (yo′ ga). Lit., "union." Union of the individual soul and the Universal Soul; also the spiritual paths and practices by which such union is effected. The four yogic paths, bhakti, karma, raja, and jnana, suit spiritual aspirants with different needs.

yogi (yo′ gī). Ascetic following a yogic path (fem. yogini).

ILLUSTRATIONS

Unless otherwise noted, the illustrations are courtesy of the Vedanta Society of Northern California.

Frontispiece: Swami Ashokananda, early 1960s

ABOUT THE AUTHOR

Marie Louise Burke became Sister Gargi in 1974 when she took her first vows in India from the Ramakrishna Order. She was honored with the monastic name of Gargi after the renowned Vedic scholar in recognition of her brilliant accomplishments as a researcher and a writer—and later, in 1983, with the first Vivekananda Award given by the Ramakrishna Mission.

She became a prominent literary figure as the author of the monumental six-volume classic *Swami Vivekananda in the West: New Discoveries,* as well as other works. The *New Discoveries* books have long been indispensable sourcebooks in India and in Vedanta circles worldwide, and the knowledge they have given of Swami Vivekananda's personality has changed the lives of many readers. "You have become immortal, Gargi, for your colossal and pioneering work on Swamiji," wrote Bharat Maharaj, a revered senior monk of the Ramakrishna Order.

Ms. Burke met Swami Ashokananda in 1948 when he was in charge of the Vedanta Society of Northern California in San Francisco—with which she became closely associated and where she lived from 1969 until her death at the age of ninety-one in January 2004. The hardcover edition of *A Heart Poured Out,* Sister Gargi's biography of Swami Ashokananda (1893–1969), and *A Disciple's Journal,* Sister Gargi's personal story of her spiritual struggle and growth in the company of her illustrious teacher, were both published to critical acclaim in 2003.